EVERY DAY BRADFORD

A calendar of stories that shaped a city

MARTIN GREENWOOD

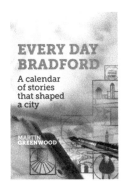

Front cover

The design uses images from panels in the Ivegate Arch, a forged and fabricated steel gateway at the Market Street entrance to Ivegate, one of Bradford's oldest streets. Erected in 1988, the Arch was commissioned by Bradford City Council. It was designed by Peter Parkinson and made by Richard Quinnell, who have both kindly given permission for the images to be used for this cover.

EVERY DAY BRADFORD
MARTIN GREENWOOD

ISBN: 978-1-8383423-1-9

Published by Kirklands Publications in conjunction with Writersworld. This book is produced entirely in the UK, is available to order from most book shops in the United Kingdom and is globally available via UK-based Internet book retailers and www.amazon.com.

www.writersworld.co.uk
WRITERSWORLD
2 Bear Close Flats
Bear Close
Woodstock
Oxfordshire
OX20 1JX
United Kingdom
✆ 01993 812500
✆ +44 1993 812500

The text pages of this book are produced via an independent certification process that ensures the trees from which the paper is produced come from well managed sources that exclude the risk of using illegally logged timber while leaving options to use post-consumer recycled paper as well.

CONTENTS

EVERY DAY BRADFORD

ACKNOWLEDGEMENTS

Bradford's rich history has been well documented since the start of the 19th century. A book such as this depends a great deal on the many people who have written about the city.

The local newspapers provide a wealth of material, especially the *Bradford Observer* (from 1834) and *Bradford Daily Telegraph* (from 1868) and since then, of course, the *Telegraph & Argus,* which for nearly 100 years has been the city's voice. The T & A helpfully published a large number of interesting stories to celebrate its 150th anniversary and its special 1999 publication *Stories of the Century*. I should not forget the *Leeds Mercury,* going back into the 18th century, and the *Yorkshire Post* as excellent alternative newspaper sources.

The earlier years of Bradford's history are well covered by its three main Victorian historians – John James, William Cudworth and William Scruton. Without their extensive research we would know little about pre-industrial and early industrial Bradford. The latter two were also founder members of the Bradford Historical and Antiquarian Society founded in 1878, which has published to the current day via its annual *The Antiquary* many fascinating pieces of research about every aspect of Bradford life.

Many other writers about Bradford have followed their path in the 20th century such as Joseph Fieldhouse, Gary Firth, Jim Greenhalf, Alan Hall, Horace Hird and George Sheeran. I am also indebted to John Dewhirst as the prime source of information about early professional sport in Bradford. In addition, there are hundreds of books about specific people, events and issues associated with the city.

A few of Bradford's places are also mines of historical information. The Industrial Museum, Brontë Parsonage Museum and Undercliffe Cemetery (the place and the website) are predictably helpful sources. Above all, the collection and the staff in Bradford's Local Studies Library proved an essential resource for which I am extremely grateful .

Finally, I need to acknowledge the help of close ones. My brother Adrian, now a German resident, has shared his excellent knowledge about our home city with a stream of regular emails, suggesting new stories, commenting on drafts and helping to unravel clashes of stories on the same calendar day. My wife Jenny has been extremely supportive and tolerant of frequent trips up north. Finally, my 12 year-old granddaughter Maisie had quite an influence on the early versions of the cover.

Without all these people this book would have not been possible.

CREDITS

The following organisations and persons have kindly granted permission for use of their material:

Bradford Library for use of quotations from various titles that it published in the past:

• From *The Chartist Risings in Bradford* by DG Wright (1987), an 1842 Chartist mass meeting (see 14 August entry) and the final 1848 Chartist uprising (see 29 May entry).

• From *Victorian Bradford*: Twelve essays edited by SG Wright and JA Jowitt (1981), the new 1851 religious census (see 30 March entry).

• From *Poverty and Progress*: *Social Conditions in early and mid-19th century Bradford* by Gary Firth (1979), Sir Isaac Holden's work commitment (see 12 October entry).

• From *Street Characters of a Victorian City: John Sowden's Bradford* by Gary Firth (1993), an 1888 John Sowden painting (see 26 May entry).

• From its Local Studies blog, the new 1915 open-air swimming pool (see 19 June entry)

• From *Rebel Tyke* by Peter Holdsworth (1994), the 1954 sale of the iconic Swan Arcade (see 29 November entry).

• From *Salt and Silver* by Jim Greenhalf (1997), the 1987 redevelopment of Salts Mill (see 27 April entry) and Jonathan Silver's 1996 charity event (see 3 March entry).

Community Care magazine for use of quotation about Lord Patel of Bradford (see 19 March entry)

Faber & Faber for use of TS Eliot quotation about the 'Bradford millionaire' (see 25 October entry)

Anne Fletcher for use of photographs about her great-great-great-uncle Joseph Hobson Jagger, the man who broke the bank at Monte Carlo (see 1 May entry)

Mountaineers' Books for use of quotation about the eccentric adventurer, Maurice Wilson (see 21 May entry)

JB Priestley Estate for use of quotations from the *Bradford Pioneer* (see 31 January entry), *Voice of Britain* radio talks about the Blitz in 1941 (see 5 June entry) and his novel *Bright Day* (see 31 October entry)

Salisbury Review for use of quotation about the Ray Honeyford affair (see 16 April entry)

Telegraph & Argus for use of quotations about the smallpox outbreak (11 January entry), Salman Rushdie book-burning (14 January entry), the cancer treatment breakthrough (23 May entry), city centre flooding (2 July entry), Kiki Dee (7 August entry), Busby's fire (30 August entry), the demise of the Bradford & Bingley (29 September entry) and the BBC TV documentary *Lost City* (26 October entry).

Telegraph & Argus (continued) Also for use of quotations about bitter newspaper rivals (see 6 May entry) from its special publication, *Read All About It: The story of Bradford's Telegraph & Argus 1868-1981*, and about World War Two bombing (see 31 August entry) from its special publication, *Stories of the Century*, 1999.

The British Academy for use of quotation from Alan Bullock's lecture (22 November 1967) about Adolf Hitler

The Guardian for use of quotation from Naseem Shah MP (see 7 May entry) and for use of quotation by Simon Jenkins about Sunbridge Wells (see 10 December entry)

The New Yorker for use of quotation about David Peace's *Red Riding Quartet* on the Yorkshire Ripper (see 5 March entry)

Waterstone's, Bradford for permission to show the grand hammer-beam roof of the old Wool Exchange, now its bookshop (see photograph on page 204 and 21 April entry)

PREFACE

A Bradford upbringing

It is now over fifty years since I left Bradford, but it still has a strong hold. Both sides of my family were Bradford born and bred, going back over three generations, as they came to the city looking for work like so many others before and since.

When I came to write a biography in 2017 about my grandfather, Percy Monkman, who lived all his life in and around the city except for four WW1 years in Northern France, I found myself digging back into the past to find out more about the city he loved and the Bradford lives of his parents and grandparents. I learnt just how little I really knew about the place where I myself had been brought up for 20 years.

Born within a stone's throw of Valley Parade in Manningham, I had no idea of the wealth of the area in the 19th century, home of Bradford millionaires in the wool business. Yet, a few streets away lived the poor in the most difficult circumstances: my great-great grandmother died of cholera at the age of 34 in a house just off Manningham Lane, leaving behind eight young children.

At Bradford Grammar School I belonged to Keeling House. The school had a Jagger Library, a Delius Music Room, a Rothenstein Art Room and a Behrens Geography Room. I sometimes went for a walk in Lister Park. The light-blue trolley-buses often stopped at Forster Square. The red West Yorkshire motor buses dropped me off in Godwin Street. I passed the Margaret McMillan College of Education on the walk from the centre to cricket at Bradford Park Avenue. In Baildon where I lived as a boy, I went up Holden Lane to Sunday School. Who were the people behind these names? Growing up, I knew very little about them, but I do now.

Expansion of Bradford

Bradford has changed greatly. Its name is derived from the Old English 'brad' and 'ford', the broad ford which referred to a crossing of the Bradford Beck at Church Bank below the site of what became Bradford Cathedral, around which a settlement grew in Saxon times.

Until 1800 it was a very small town, situated in the bowl of the surrounding hills and centred on the old Kirkgate, Westgate and Ivegate. Then with a rapidly rising population the adjoining townships of Manningham, Bowling and Horton came together in 1847 with the old Bradford to grow into the new borough with its new corporation. Another fifty years later the town became a city, having gradually acquired neighbouring townships such as Eccleshill and Idle. Then in 1974 under a comprehensive local government reorganisation it doubled in size again, now including towns such as Keighley and Ilkley.

A story for every day

Dan Snow, the TV historian, prompted the idea for this book. In 2018 he published *On This Day in History* – a story from world history for each day in the year. Why not treat the history of Bradford in the same way? It was amazingly quick to discover how much material existed about the city.

There are two practical problems in selecting from such a deep reserve of material. First, how do you decide what to leave out when there are competing stories for the same day? Sometimes, you can include two stories for the same day, sometimes you can find alternative dates for the same topic and occasionally you just have to decide which story is more important.

Second, how do you decide whether a story refers to Bradford or not, especially as the city has grown so quickly. I have considered the current boundary of Bradford as the book's focus. The city and outlying districts have always been closely interconnected. In the 19th century wealthier Bradfordians worked in the city but lived outside. For example, the great reformer WE Forster lived near Ilkley and the great entrepreneur Isaac Holden lived near Keighley.

Strong connections with Bradford

Much of the book is about people who have shaped the city in some way. Often, of course, they are born and bred in the city, but sometimes come from elsewhere. They all, however, have strong Bradford connections. Southerners like William Byles came to the city as adults and never left. The two heavyweight Labour politicians, Denis Healey and Barbara Castle, came to the West Riding as children with their parents, but educated here it is Bradford they remembered. The one just missed out on being Leader of the Opposition (who knows, Prime Minister?) and the other became the only 'freewoman' of the city. The photographer Don McCullin is a Londoner who has travelled across the world, but he has developed a strong link with Bradford. Margaret McMillan, education and social reformer, was an American living in London who was attracted to Bradford by its Socialist credentials and lived here for nine years making a big impact on early years' education before returning to London. She is certainly worth her place in Bradford's history. All these are included. Yet Timothy West, the famous actor who was born in Bradford but left after a few months, had no influence on his birthplace, and so cannot be included.

Although these editorial decisions are not always clear-cut, there is no doubting the richness and variety of material available. Much of this comes from the fascinating social history and much from the remarkable individuals who have made their mark.

The rich and the poor

Bradford has always been a city of contrasts. In the 1840s and 1850s it was the wealthiest in England outside London yet at the same time one of the unhealthiest. Grand Victorian buildings were constructed alongside endless rows of cheap back-to-back housing, many just hovels.

It has been a city of bosses and workers. The bosses have usually been self-made men, developing mills and factories. The workers have often been rebellious, involved in strikes, campaigning for the Ten Hours and Anti-Poor Law Movements, supporting Chartism and then Socialism. But the distinctions are not always black and white. Both groups have been Whig rather than Tory, radical rather than conservative, non-conformist rather than Anglican and from pacifist rather than military traditions. For example, both groups supported the case for universal suffrage throughout the 19th century.

A wealthy Victorian city for a few, it was also extremely unhealthy for the many – memorably described by Friedrich Engels as a 'stinking hole'. It was not until the early 20th century that the root causes of disease were eradicated with long-term solutions for water supply and sewage, and not until the middle of the 20th century that clean air gradually reduced smoke pollution.

The immigrants

Another major influence that adds much interest to Bradford's history has been its dependence on immigration, and that has often caused tension. The 1840s saw a mass influx of Irish immigration. By 1850 10% of the whole population were first generation Irish immigrants. Fleeing from poverty and the potato famine, they were very poor and largely Roman Catholic. Their willingness to accept very low pay caused much resentment, made worse by general anti-Catholic feeling.

Over a century later mass immigration from the Indian sub-continent, largely Pakistani and Muslim, led to similar reactions from the resident population. In this case, a clash of cultures led to conflict over the Ray Honeyford affair, the Salman Rushdie book-burning and the Manningham riots. However, as it did in the 19th century, the city is once again learning how to absorb such large inflows.

One flow of immigration had an immediately beneficial impact. In the mid to late 19th century there was a significant influx of middle-class German immigrants, often Jewish. Though small in number (just a few thousand), their arrival clearly improved the life of the city. From 1850 till the First World War most of Bradford's developments depended remarkably on their commercial expertise that contributed to the city's wealth and on their philanthropy that contributed to the city's public institutions and buildings. Now a conservation area, Little Germany symbolises today their contribution from that time.

Shadow of Leeds

One of the curious impacts on Bradford's development comes with its proximity to Leeds. Despite being the sixth largest city in Britain, it has always lived in the shadow of its even larger neighbour. For example, the canal, the railway and the motorway all came first to Leeds, followed by an extension to Bradford some 10 or 20 years later. Even today its two railway stations are both at the end of a spur from the mainline at Leeds; both are extremely modest for a city of over half a million. The two cities do at least now share an airport on a 50-50 basis, although, of course, it is sited within the boundary of Leeds. In fact, however you arrive in Bradford and however positive you feel about the city, you do not feel that you are entering a large vibrant metropolis.

Occasionally Bradford has stolen a march on Leeds as it did in 1853 when building St George's Hall as a concert venue. A London reporter coming up for the opening and impressed with what he saw declared that now Leeds should be described as Leeds near Bradford, not the other way round.

Yet despite all this Bradford was for most of the 19th century the wealthier. Writing in the Edwardian era, JB Priestley memorably claimed that, when it came to the people, Leeds might have the quantity but Bradford had the quality.

20th century decline

World War One had a devastating impact on the city as a generation of men were killed in the trenches of Northern France. No day in its history was worse than 1 July 1916 when some 1,000 Bradford Pals were lost in the Battle of the Somme. When peace returned, the days of a city built on the wealth of wool were over and gradual decline set in.

Although World War Two thankfully did not have anything like the same impact in Bradford, the city could not easily invest in new industry. In the post-war years not only did Bradford lose its mills and factories, its wool business and its wealth, but the Corporation made things worse. It appointed an engineer to oversee the modernisation of the city centre. The effect was by common consent disastrous as the heart of the fine Victorian city was ripped out to accommodate the car and new concrete office blocks. It took the best part of two generations to repair the damage with sensible, more recent improvements such as the National Science and Media Museum, City Park and the Sunbridge Wells development.

There were isolated exceptions of regeneration in the worlds of leisure (such as the redevelopment of Salts Mill as an arts centre), of film (such as the new national museum) and some areas of technology. The city is to some extent still searching for a new purpose and new ideas for regeneration.

Bradford's dark side

Bradford has been the home of notorious serial killers including the Yorkshire Ripper, the Black Panther and the Crossbow Cannibal, but how many readers know about the 16th century lord of the manor murdering his wife and young children? And then there was in 1858 the notorious case of Humbug Billy and the sweets poisoning killing some 20 people, although nobody was convicted.

At the same time Bradford was the home of four state executioners, three of them from the Pierrepoint family. The first, James Berry, and the last Pierrepoint both wrote books which surprisingly perhaps argued the case for abolishing capital punishment.

The city has been the scene of several disasters such as industrial explosions and fires that have caught the national headlines, none more so than the 1985 fire at Valley Parade. Many of these incidents resulted from neglect and lack of investment. Some were caused by the geography such as the hills down into the city centre that led to many floods and tram crashes.

Growth of sport

In the late 19th century increased leisure led to growth in sport. Lancashire had paved the way for association football, and the West Riding was seen as rugby territory. By 1903 at Valley Parade this was sorted out as Manningham FC had ditched rugby league in favour of Bradford City playing association football. By 1907 over at Park Avenue Bradford FC ditched rugby union in favour of association football but not without creating a rugby league offshoot to be called Bradford Northern (much later, Bradford Bulls) playing at Birch Lane (later, Odsal). All the while ever since 1832, amateur league cricket developed and flourished at Park Avenue, alongside later the new football team. It also became a favourite ground for many for the Yorkshire County Cricket Club.

In hindsight the pre-WW1 years were a golden age of professional team sport with Bradford teams vying with the best in rugby (union and league) and then soccer. The highlight was Bradford City winning the FA Cup in 1911 which has lived long in the memory.

Since World War One regular success has by and large eluded Bradford's professional teams, handicapped by lack of funding and poor management. The diversification of sport during the 20th century has seen some outstanding individual successes. In the past 50 years, we have seen a clutch of remarkable athletes achieving global status in their respective disciplines - Boris Rankov (rowing), Adrian Moorhouse (swimming), Richard Nerurkar (marathons) and the Brownlee brothers (triathlon) - all incidentally from Bradford Grammar School.

The city has also seen a snooker world champion in Joe Johnson and a cycling world record holder in Yvonne McGregor.

Bradford has never had a world boxing champion, but did have at least a challenger who stepped into the ring, and survived, with the great Muhammed Ali. It has never been a stronghold of motor sports or equestrian sports, except for one show jumping champion best remembered for his infamous 'V-sign' captured on TV.

Extraordinary individuals

Certainly Bradford has always attracted many extraordinary individuals in all fields of endeavour.

Although no more than a large village, pre-industrial Bradford nurtured the most celebrated botanist in the North of England, and, from the same family, an Archbishop of York having the ear of the queen and a distinguished astronomer giving his name 250 years after his death to a crater on the moon.

19th century Bradford saw many rags-to-riches stories during a period of rapid growth, although some such as Samuel Lister were less startling stories of riches-to-riches. In that century Bradford was dominated by two individuals – Lister and Titus Salt, both forceful, energetic and innovative mill-owners in Manningham and Saltaire respectively, who each employed thousands, with contrasting approaches to their workforce, and had major influence on lives of so many Bradfordians. Their 20th century counterparts in terms of influence are JB Priestley and David Hockney – men of culture and creativity who left Bradford as young men and built international reputations in their fields, but never forgot their roots.

Many others have risen to great heights from the most unpromising starts in life - the child working in a mill developing into an Oxford professor of philology, the Pakistani girl trapped in a dysfunctional family used to wife-beating becoming an MP and the bullied boy with Crohn's disease, teenage mother and father in prison becoming one of the world's best magicians.

There have been powerful academics such as Alan Bullock, expert on Hitler, and Asa Briggs, expert on Victorian cities, who both ended as masters of Oxford colleges. There have been powerful scientists of international renown, such as Bradford's Nobel Prize winner, Sir Edward Appleton, and Bingley's astronomer, Sir Fred Hoyle (one of three notable astronomers who were stars in their day). In the world of medicine, two Bradford consultants led a major breakthrough in cancer treatment, a hero of the Bradford City fire created a world-class specialist burns unit and a Bradford doctor cracked the anthrax problem – the so-called 'Bradford disease'.

Bradfordians have sometimes been at the centre of national life. WE Forster's Elementary Education Act of 1870 was one of the most significant contributions in public policy. Bishop Blunt's accidental intervention in the 1936 Abdication crisis was one of the most unexpected and JB Priestley gripped the nation with his stirring radio talks at the height of the London Blitz.

Regrettably, not so many women have been able to make such contributions - a reflection of much lower expectations and fewer opportunities. It was not until the turn of the 20th century when campaigners such as Margaret McMillan, Julia Varley (trade unionism), Florence White (pensions for women) and latterly Debbie Purdy (right-to-die) made their mark on Bradford life, then national life. And, of course, two generations before them, the three Brontë sisters were amongst the earliest great writers of English classic novels, although they had to resort to male pseudonyms to get published.

Adventurers, eccentrics and pioneers

The city has inspired adventurers. One ordinary mum soon after giving birth to triplets embarked on an amazing journey that turned her into the first woman to reach the South Pole and the North Pole. A World War One hero had a crazy idea of flying to Nepal then being the first to climb Everest, but predictably died in the attempt. It has inspired eccentrics such as the first man (almost certainly) to break the bank at Monte Carlo, the first woman to walk 1,000 miles in 1,000 hours, the fastest man to swim the Channel (a record for 17 years) and the unique hoax about the fairies at the bottom of the garden in Cottingley.

The city has seen many unusual pioneers in the UK - the first Temperance Society, the first Pullman train in operation, the oldest funicular railway, the first local authority secondary school, the only municipally owned railway, the first public showing of newsreel (as early as 1897), the first school meals service, the first trolley-bus service (also the last one to close), the first municipal hospital; in Europe the first IMAX cinema and the oldest live concert venue, and the first Professor of Peace Studies in the world. It was the home of the 'Bradford system' and the 'Bradford sling', both notable innovations in different fields. It was also the first place outside Liverpool to experience Beatlemania. One Bradford astronomer invented the 'Greenwich pips' and another coined the term 'Big Bang' theory. The 'King of Pantomime' built his reputation in Bradford. It was also the birthplace of the last state executioner in Britain and of the last man in England to be the subject of a successful public prosecution for blasphemy.

Is there another such fascinating city of its size in the whole country?

EVERY DAY BRADFORD

1 Jan 2012   David Hockney becomes the second Bradfordian to be awarded the Order of Merit.

The Order of Merit recognises distinguished service in the armed forces, science, art, literature, or the promotion of culture. Introduced in 1902 by the new King Edward VII, this honour is entirely in the Sovereign's gift and applies to all Commonwealth citizens. Only a maximum of 24 such persons at one time may hold this honour. New members are honoured only after the death of previous members. Since its inception 195 persons have held the honour, including only eight persons born in Yorkshire. Today the world-renowned artist, David Hockney, became the second Bradfordian after JB Priestley to be so awarded.

Born 45 years apart, Bradford's two most famous men of the arts shared a number of things. All other awards in our honours system are in the gift of the Prime Minister. It is believed that both Priestley and Hockney turned down knighthoods, because they disliked political nominations, but respected this award from the Queen.

Priestley's skill was the word and Hockney's skill was the visual image. Although they can be simply described as just writer or artist, their gifts were multi-faceted and their output prolific well into their 80s. Priestley came to fame as a writer of popular novels, then a playwright, but is also well remembered for his inspiring radio broadcasts during the Battle of Britain and his campaigning for nuclear disarmament. Hockney is a highly talented draughtsman and painter with a love of bright colours, but he is also a great experimenter (with camera, fax, iPad) and remembered as a creative stage set designer.

Their relationships with Bradford are also similar. Both came from modest backgrounds on opposite sides of the city – Priestley, son of a primary school headteacher in Heaton and Hockney, son of a clerk in Eccleshill. Both made their homes well away from Yorkshire (Warwickshire and California respectively), but both returned regularly for visits to their home city. In both cases it took long before their work and reputation were fully recognised by the city. It seemed as if the nation appreciated them much more than Bradford. They were growing old before the City Council recognised them as Freemen of the City.

Fortunately, the Order of Merit provides external recognition that outlasts any doubters. JB Priestley, OM, and David Hockney, OM, do themselves and Bradford proud. They did meet and, naturally, Hockney drew a memorable portrait of Priestley, pipe in hand.

2 Jan 1981   The Yorkshire Ripper is arrested to everyone's relief.

Today in the streets of Sheffield's red light district, two policemen stopped a car with false number plates. As this had become a standard check in the North of England, information was relayed to the Ripper Squad in West Yorkshire. The next day police returned to the scene and found nearby a discarded hammer and screwdriver, the Ripper's trademark weapons. He had left them behind after excusing himself for a 'pee'. After six years the police had the Yorkshire Ripper. He was arrested, he confessed and was charged.

He was Peter Sutcliffe (1946-2020), a 34-year-old lorry driver, born in Bingley and now living in a quiet residential part of Heaton, married for over seven years to a teacher. From October 1975 to November 1980 he had murdered 13 women (three in Bradford), leaving 23 children orphaned, and savagely attacked at least eight more women.

Attacks took place mainly in known red light districts (eg Bradford's Lumb Lane) and in other parts of Northern cities and towns. The man-hunt for this serial killer became the largest ever in this country, grabbing national headlines after every incident and spreading fear and anger among women.

The West Yorkshire Police investigation, led by Assistant Chief Constable George Oldfield, was heavily criticised for serious mistakes, which delayed the arrest and led to unnecessary murders and attacks. Although in the late 1970s the police lacked modern forensic tools such as computers, CCTV cameras and DNA evidence, the mistakes stemmed from human errors with catastrophic consequences.

For example, the first three murder victims were prostitutes from the red light area of Chapeltown in Leeds. Oldfield was convinced that the murderer hated prostitutes, ignoring three earlier attacks of women from different backgrounds (eg a 14-year-old schoolgirl). When he received a tape from a hoaxer with a Geordie accent, he also ignored witnesses who stated categorically that the attacker spoke with a West Yorkshire accent. The police interviewed Sutcliffe nine times without arresting him, despite coming very close to having the evidence to do so.

Sutcliffe's arrest was a major relief to all concerned, not least the police. He was brought to trial at the Old Bailey, found guilty of murder and sentenced to life imprisonment on 22 May 1981.

This was not the end of the case. Investigations, books, films, plays and TV programmes have since all examined what went wrong to allow such a tragedy to happen.

3 Jan 2016   Jonny Bairstow dedicates his maiden Test century to his father David.

It has become something of a cliché for a professional footballer to dedicate a goal, or a cricketer a century, to a loved one. In the case of Jonny Bairstow's first Test century today in Cape Town against South Africa, there can be no doubting the sincerity of the gesture and emotion in the event. In front of his mother and sister in the large crowd, he was remembering his father.

As an eight-year-old boy exactly 18 years ago (minus two days), he had heard that his father, like Jonny also a wicket-keeper batsman for England and Yorkshire from Bradford, had committed suicide. Nobody had suspected the despair that drove him to do this, eight years after he had retired. David Bairstow (1951-1998) was a 'larger than life' character and whole-hearted cricketer loved by the crowds and his team-mates, and the last person one might think would take his own life. The cricket world was truly shocked.

David Bairstow played for Yorkshire for 21 years, starting as an 18-year-old, including three years as captain at a very difficult time in Yorkshire's history, a club riven by controversy surrounding Geoffrey Boycott. He played just four games for England's Test team and 20 one-day internationals at a time when England had very good wicketkeepers, but, unlike Jonny, did not merit a place just for his batting. His county record as a wicketkeeper was second only to the legendary Jimmy Binks in terms of matches played and wicket-keeping dismissals. With 10 first-class centuries he was a more than useful batsman.

Father and son were red-haired with the same nickname of 'Bluey'. The father was primarily a wicketkeeper who could bat aggressively and win matches. For England the son both keeps wicket very competently (but does not always play as wicketkeeper) and bats very convincingly. No other England wicketkeeper, for example, has dismissed nine batsmen in one Test on two occasions. As he can justify a place for batting and keeping, he has been a regular in both the England Test and one-day teams.

Jonny's day today finished on a high, as he featured in a record partnership with Ben Stokes, which put on 399. Stokes was out for 258 just before a declaration; Bairstow ended 150 not out.

Source: *A Clear Blue Sky*, Jonny Bairstow and Duncan Hamilton (2018)

4 Jan 2016   From start-up to cash-cow, Saltaire-based Pace plc is bought out by American giant.

The huge Salts Mill which opened in 1853 finally closed in 1986. Bradford City Council took advice from consultants who recommended the Council regenerate the mill into a new industrial and leisure complex. Jonathan Silver arrived on the scene to implement the plan. Pace Micro Technology plc is an excellent case study from the late 1980s that reflects well on all parties.

It was the first significant entrepreneur to move into the new complex. Operating first from a bedroom in Clayton, co-founders David Hood, Barry Rubery and Robert Fleming had invented a low-cost, commercially available modem in 1985 and then two years later a satellite television receiver. They saw the potential of the complex. The company was soon leasing 300,000 of the 800,000 sq ft of available space. In 1985 it employed 30 people. By 1994 this had risen to 900 with a turnover of £80m, which three years later had nearly trebled to £227m.

Pace had sales and distribution centres in many parts of the developed world and manufacturing capacity in South Yorkshire and Dorset as well as four developing countries. It claimed to be the only company in the world mass-producing digital decoders for cable and satellite TV.

The booming company went public in 1996 and the owners became very wealthy men. The Salts Estate, too, shared in the new wealth with more than £0.5m income per year from the lease. Many other organisations, albeit smaller, followed the lead of Pace in renting space at Salts Mill.

Such a technology company cannot stand still. In 1998 Pace started shipping digital satellite television equipment for BSkyB. A year later it purchased the set top box division of Acorn Computers. In 2001, it outsourced the last of its manufacturing capacity at Saltaire, which became its administration and development centre. Expansion continued until 2008 when it doubled its size by acquiring the set top box division of Royal Philips Electronics. In 2012 Pace sold its one hundred-millionth digital set top box!

The culmination of all its development was the announcement in 2015 of a planned merger with the USA corporate Arris Group, a global leader in entertainment, communications and networking technology.

Today's press release confirmed the deal.

Source: *Salt & Silver: A Story of Hope*, Jim Greenhalf (1997)

5 Jan 1877   The death of Sir Titus Salt attracts record funeral procession across Bradford.

Bradford had never seen anything like it. Nor has it since.

A week ago Sir Titus Salt died aged 73.

Today the procession started at his family home of Crow's Nest, Lightcliffe. His body lay in two coffins, one of lead inside another of oak. Just after nine o'clock in the morning, four horses pulled away with the hearse, followed by five carriages with his family and close friends and escorted by 16 policemen.

As it came down into Bradford, shops were closed and most mills silent. Flags everywhere were at half-mast. The bell tolled at the brand new Town Hall, in front of which stood the new marble statue of Sir Titus, funded by the people of Bradford and unveiled three years ago. Business was suspended at the prestigious Wool Exchange.

By now the cortege had expanded to comprise 70 carriages carrying the large number of mourners. It wound its way up to Manningham Lane, past the Salts' first family home and on towards the new Saltaire model village that he had created. Three miles later, opposite the recently famous Saltaire Mill, it ended at Saltaire Congregational Church, where the funeral service started.

Some 100,000 people were estimated to have paid their respects.

Sir Titus Salt was born in 1803 just as Bradford was starting its rapid growth into the wool capital of the country. He died at the end of 1876 when Bradford was at the height of its wealth and influence. He had been the largest local employer for up to 40 years, Bradford's Chief Constable, its mayor, the President of its Chamber of Commerce and then its Liberal MP.

The next day, the *Bradford Observer* wrote:

'Titus was perhaps the greatest captain of industry in England not only because he gathered thousands under him but also because, according to the light that was in him, he tried to care for all those thousands. We do not say that he succeeded in realising all his views or that it is possible to harmonise at present all relations between capital and labour. Upright in business, admirable in his private relations he came without seeking the honour to be admittedly the best representative of the employer class in this part of the country if not the whole kingdom.'

Source: *Salt and Silver: A Story of Hope*, Jim Greenhalf (1997)

6 Jan 1895   Three days after rabies clampdown, rabid dog with damaged muzzle has to be destroyed.

When the Muzzling Order on dogs came into operation nationally on 1 January 1890, there had been 312 cases of rabies in the previous twelve months. While it remained in force, the number fell to 129 in 1890 and by 1892 to just seven. However, the enforcement of the law was relaxed with the result that 1893 saw 94 rabies cases and 1894 256 cases.

So on 3 January 1895 West Riding County Council tightened the screw by applying the Muzzling Order throughout its jurisdiction. The rule was that now no dog be at large without being effectively muzzled.

Yet today just three days later the *Bradford Daily Telegraph* reported this story from Eccleshill:

While Police Constable Crossley stationed at Eccleshill was going his rounds early on Sunday, he heard a disturbance in a hencote. Police Constable Ross came up and, removing a board on the top of the cote, perceived a dog worrying fowls. Having obtained the key of the hencote from the owner, he opened the door, when the dog flew at him, but the constable succeeded in stunning it and then killing it with a stick. The dog had a wire muzzle, but one of the side wires had torn away, and the animal had contrived to kill three hens and a cock. A veterinary surgeon, on examining the dog, pronounced it to have been suffering from rabies.

This was the first of a spate of stories over subsequent weeks. For example, just in January rabid dogs had to be destroyed on the 10th in Calverley, the 14th in Horton, the 19th in Idle and the 26th in Great Horton.

In many cases people that were bitten travelled to Paris for treatment at the new Louis Pasteur Institute, which claimed a cure for rabies. In March the *Bradford Daily Telegraph* championed the cause of a girl who had been bitten. Her father could not afford the trip, but the paper secured the funds from readers' donations. In one letter, a Harrogate doctor even believed that having a Turkish bath was the cure for anyone bitten!

In March the paper reported *'unreasoning panic'* – 458 unmuzzled or stray dogs were put down by the police, but only eight were suspected of rabies.

Incidences of rabies continued for two or three more years but by the turn of the century had almost disappeared.

Source: *Bradford Daily Telegraph* (8 January 1895)

7 Jan 1863 The failure of Thomas Appleton's first photographic venture is soon forgotten.

Neither of today's statements in the *Bradford Observer* gives an explanation, but one marks a new start for Bradford's most prominent photographer of the day.

One statement read: *'Henry Berlon (late Appleton & Co) respectfully informs his numerous friends and the public that, since the dissolution of the partnership, he continues the PHOTOGRAPHIC BUSINESS, at the top of Manor Row, on his own account and will endeavour to merit a continuance of the patronage he has hitherto enjoyed'.* In the same publication Thomas Appleton announced separately that he had bought the freehold of some land on Horton Lane and contracted to erect an establishment *'which for extent and perfection of its arrangements and appointments shall be second to none in the provinces'.*

Born in North Yorkshire, Appleton (1828 -1912) moved to Bradford as a young man to help his brother run a drapery shop. After his brother emigrated, Appleton sold up and started a photographic partnership with Henry Berlon at the top of Manor Row. The business clearly went well because by 1860 they had opened a second studio in Horton Lane. However by November 1863 the partnership was declared bankrupt, Appleton taking the Horton Lane site, his ex-partner the Manor Row site (later going bankrupt again).

From this point Appleton's new sole business seems to have steadily grown until he became the best-known photographer in Bradford. His reputation spread no doubt because he took portraits of all Bradford's most celebrated men. For example he took photographs of 17 mayors, the full set appearing in William Cudworth's *Historical Notes on the Bradford Corporation.* Appleton also took the best-known portrait of Sir Titus Salt, often copied in oils

In 1872 Appleton expanded into a substantial studio on Manningham Lane and in 1887 bought the property next door. A 1888 book on Yorkshire's industries describes the studio as *'The stately and elegant entrance is more suggestive of a public art gallery than of the business premises of a private firm, but ... the fine staircase and the large and lofty rooms ... confirm the first favourable impression. After a careful examination of the specimens of photography... Messrs Appleton Co are in every way deserving of the patronage they receive from the elite of the West Riding.'*

Appleton's entrepreneurial legacy should also include son Richard and grandson Richard who both became prominent in cinematography / X-rays and gramophones respectively.

Source: www.undercliffecemetery.co.uk/about/history/thomas-william-appleton/

8 Jan 2019   Asian girls balance cricket dream with home life in TV documentary.

The last 50 years has seen a dramatic change in Bradford's demographics with some 25% of the population now from a South Asian background, most of whom are also Muslim. This has led to major challenges in their integration into the life of the city.

Today, *Bats, balls and Bradford girls,* a charming documentary, subtly illustrated some of the tensions for Pakistani girls in their teens. Cricket is one sport that both Yorkshire people and South Asians are passionate about. The film tells the story of the only Asian all-girls team in the country from Carlton Bolling College. Last year it reached a Lords final and lost by just one ball. Now in the next season the team has started to break up with some leaving school after GCSEs.

They are preparing for an all-Yorkshire contest for girls' teams at Headingley. They go to the Test Match ground to watch Yorkshire and Pakistan practise. We see a giggling group of girls taking a selfie with a sheepish Jonny Bairstow and we see Joe Root, the hero of one of the girls, sign a bat. *'For us cricket is more than a sport'* says one, *'giving us freedom to enjoy life outside the home'.* They have absorbed enthusiasm for the game from watching live cricket on the TV. For one girl it brings back memories of a grandad, recently died, who introduced her to the game.

But all is not well. Pressures from the girls' families start to be felt. The parents have never actively supported the girls, but have been happy for the schools to organise the games. Now family expectations crowd in. One father insists on acting as chaperone to his daughter. Another daughter has to be carer for her mother tragically paralysed after a car accident on holiday back in Bangladesh.

The girls can no longer practise as regularly as they need to and regretfully the sympathetic coach has to pull the plug on the whole venture.

At one level the film with plenty of humour is just about growing up as teenagers are finding their way. At another level it reinforces different cultures, not about religion as such, but more about different family priorities and attitudes to girls. The tensions are all understated. There is no dramatic conflict or unreasonable pressure, but the girls come to accept the inevitable.

This is life in contemporary Bradford.

9 Jan 2006 John Humble of Sunderland is charged with hoaxing the police over the Yorkshire Ripper.

Some 25 years after Peter Sutcliffe had been sentenced to life for murdering 13 women in the 1970s, the final chapter in the Yorkshire Ripper story ended today.

The first murder took place in October 1975, but it was over five years before Sutcliffe was arrested. The West Yorkshire Police were heavily criticised for mistakes and delays in tracking him down. After three years of little progress, a new line of enquiry developed, convincing the police that at last they were getting nearer to the Ripper's identity

The incident in March 1978 concerned a mysterious tape and handwritten letters that were received by the police from 'Wearside Jack', a man with a North-Eastern accent, claiming to be the Ripper. The credibility of the voice on the tape was enhanced when analysis of saliva on the envelopes used for the letters showed that 'Wearside Jack' had the same blood group as the Ripper had left at crime scenes, a type shared by only 6% of the population.

Leading the investigation, Assistant Chief Constable George Oldfield used the voice and handwriting as a way of eliminating possible suspects, thereby allowing Sutcliffe who had a strong West Yorkshire accent to remain at large, despite being interviewed by police nine times.

The tape was a hoax. The local hero in finding this out was Bradford-born Stanley Ellis from Lidget Green, just three miles or so from Heaton where Sutcliffe was brought up. Ellis was an authority on English dialects and a pioneer of the forensic analysis of voice recordings. He recognised that the voice belonged to a man from a specific area in Wearside, yet witnesses who survived the Ripper's attacks were all convinced that their attacker came from West Yorkshire.

Although Ellis and a colleague advised the crime team about the tape being a hoax, the advice was kept out of the public domain until well after Sutcliffe's arrest. Eventually his colleague felt obliged to go public with an article in the *Yorkshire Post* on 3 December 1990.

John Humble, a labourer, came from Castletown on the edge of Sunderland within walking distance from where Ellis placed the linguistic origins of the Ripper hoax voice. After today's arrest arising from a cold-case review of original files, Humble finally pleaded guilty to perverting the course of justice. On March 21, 2006, he was sentenced to eight years in jail.

Source: http://www.yek.me.uk/ykrprhoaxtp.html

10 Jan 1803   Prominent Bradfordians meet to propose an Improvement Commission.

Today the first tentative step was taken towards a form of local government in Bradford.

A deepening sense of crisis from public disorder led to a group of prominent citizens meeting in the vestry office of St. Peter's Church. They agreed to fund £500, via a ten guinea subscription, for establishing a commission, backed by statute. This would discharge broad administrative, policing and regulatory powers and levy rates from Bradford's inhabitants.

This led to the Improvement Commission being created by the Improvement Act 1803 for the purpose of *'paving, lighting, watching and improving the town of Bradford and part of the hamlet of Little Horton, and for removing and preventing all nuisances therein'.* The Act named 58 commissioners, mainly those who had subscribed, who also had the right to co-opt new members, subject to a £1,000 property qualification.

The commissioners included Edmund Peckover (wool merchant), Samuel Hailstone (solicitor), Matthew Thompson (father of future mayor) and John Hardy (factory owner). It comprised four men described as gentlemen, five professional men, twelve from the worsted industry, three from the ironworks industry, two from other industries, 18 tradesmen and the rest 'unknown'. Most were described as Tory and Anglican. Over time the numbers from the worsted industry nearly trebled, but relatively few were Whig and nonconformist, even though most new to this industry were. This meant that the commissioners gradually became unrepresentative of their class.

The first meeting took place on 1 July 1803 at the Bull's Head Inn (Westgate). Initially meetings rotated between here, the Nag's Head (Kirkgate), Sun Inn (Ivegate), Fleece Inn (Bank Street) and White Lion (Kirkgate). From 1814 they met at the White Horse (Kirkgate), then from 1826 at the Court of Requests (Darley Street) and from 1831 in the Exchange Building (Piccadilly).

Most services were contracted out to private enterprise, eg street cleaning, lighting and water supply. Only policing was undertaken directly. One of the commissioner's first acts was to appoint seven night watchmen (raised in 1827 to 13), which suggests that law enforcement was a top priority.

The self-appointed Improvement Commission became increasingly ineffective and unwilling to confront growing problems of squalor, filth and disease. Eventually, the case for different governance became overwhelming. In 1847 the Commission was replaced by a new, elected municipal Corporation.

Source: *Historical Notes on the Bradford Corporation,* William Cudworth (1881)

11 Jan 1962   Outbreak of smallpox is confirmed after death of patient in St. Luke's Hospital.

Smallpox, for centuries a deadly killer across the world, was thought to have been eradicated in the UK for at least a generation. The news from Bradford indicated otherwise.

A 40-year-old abattoir worker died in St. Luke's Hospital today. A cook at Bradford Children's Hospital was also taken into isolation and later died. Both were native Bradfordians. Diagnoses of smallpox were only confirmed later. The source of the outbreak was a Pakistani child who had flown into the country on 16 December with a fever and been admitted into the Children's Hospital. It turned out that a child of the St. Luke's patient had also been recently in the Children's Hospital. Six small children there were discovered to have smallpox symptoms.

Afterwards, in a report to the House of Commons (15 February), Arthur Tiley, MP for Bradford West, hit out at the press sensationalising the story. For example, the *Daily Express* had headlined *'The Frightened City'* on 13 January. The reality was anything but. People went on with their daily business. The medical profession tackled the problem efficiently and sympathetically, quickly identifying some 900 who might just be at risk. Locals queued patiently to receive their vaccinations (over 250,000 in the end). Tiley continued:

'Our trade was injured. We have this world-famous textile export trade, and people abroad, and especially in Italy, were refusing to receive our goods because of this epidemic. Bradford is famous, too, for its mail-order businesses, but catalogues were being refused.

Our main hospitals were closed. Our shops were empty. The large stores tell me that their turnovers dropped by 50 per cent. The cafes had no business. The cinemas closed, and our famous Bradford pantomime is coming to an end a month before it should. Football came to an end—and that is not much of a tragedy for Bradford, although Honorary Members must not say that I said that.'

Quick action by Bradford's Chief Medical Officer contained the outbreak. The final count was 14 people diagnosed with smallpox, including six who died. *The Telegraph & Argus* had the last word. It reported that at least 50% of the 2,200 deaths in Bradford that winter *'had been caused by the real mass-killers of bronchitis, pleurisy and pneumonia caused by the deadly fogs and smogs which had been arriving every winter for almost 100 years'.*

Source: *Stories of the Century (Telegraph & Argus, 1999)*

12 Jan 2011   Alastair Campbell gives evidence to the Iraq Enquiry.

Today, Alastair Campbell *'defended every single word of the September Dossier'* on the threat posed by Iraq published in 2002 and arguing that *'the UK should be proud of its role in changing Iraq from what it was to what it is now becoming'*. He also revealed that Prime Minister Tony Blair had told President George W. Bush in private that the UK would support the US in military action against Iraq. The Chilcot Enquiry took evidence from all those who played a part in the Iraq War. As Prime Minister Blair's Director of Communications and Strategy, Campbell was heavily involved in putting the case for war, especially the critical and controversial dossier on Weapons of Mass Destruction.

Campbell comes from Keighley, where he was born in 1957, the son of a vet and Scottish parents. He won a place at Bradford Grammar School where he stayed just one term before the family moved to Leicester, much to his disappointment. He has stated that his West Yorkshire childhood was very happy and left him with the best of memories of Keighley. He also became a lifelong supporter of Burnley FC.

Having studied modern languages at Cambridge University, he became a junior reporter in the South-West before he moved to the *Daily Mirror* in London and then three years later to *Today* as the news editor. Alcohol abuse led to depression and absence from work, but he rebuilt his career as the political editor at the *Mirror*, then at *Today*.

When Blair was elected Leader of the Labour Party in 1994, Campbell became his press secretary and played a major role in shaping New Labour, in securing the Labour win in 1997 and in managing public relations for the Labour Government. He created a Strategic Communications Unit in Downing Street to co-ordinate all government activity. His role was high-profile and influential, being a key member of the team behind the Good Friday Agreement in Ireland and then the Iraq War.

His Government role came to an end later in 2003 when he resigned. Since then he has kept in the public eye with a range of assignments, TV appearances and books on several topics (including seven volumes of memoir).

Campbell has been a significant participant in, and commentator of, political life over 30 years. No journalist in Bradford's history has been so close to power in this country.

13 Jan 1906   Fred Jowett is elected the first Independent Labour MP in Bradford.

Election Results 1906	W Claridge (Liberal)	3,580 votes
	Sir Ernest Flower (Unionist)	4,147 votes
	FW Jowett (Labour)	4,957 votes

Today, the 13th anniversary of the founding of the Independent Labour Party (ILP), Frederick William Jowett (1864-1944) is duly elected the Member of Parliament for Bradford West.

This was a momentous event for the ILP with Jowett in a batch of 29 Labour MPs (the rest from the Labour Representation Committee founded in 1900, becoming in 1906 the Labour Party). It was also momentous for Bradford returning its first Socialist MP and for Jowett personally, who had lost by just 41 votes in 1900 to the same Unionist opponent vanquished today.

There was no doubting what shaped Jowett's socialism:

'Of her eight children, my own mother lost three – two in infancy and one at four years,, the average death-rate of children in their first year in three municipal wards was 206 in every 1,000 ... The houses in which a very large proportion, if not the majority, of the working people lived were like the one in which I was born – one room upstairs, one downstairs and a windowless cellar.'

Jowett was committed to radical change in working people's lives. He had spoken at a large protest meeting about the 1891 Manningham Mills Strike, was the first socialist councillor elected in Bradford in 1892 and an ILP founder member in 1893.

Over the next 15 years he proved that he was not just a passionate campaigner, but an effective social reformer as councillor. Fighting much opposition, he made slum clearance a reality. He was a major champion of the first municipal school meals service; his maiden speech in the House of Commons argued for its national adoption.

In Parliament Jowett established himself as a leading left-wing figure and in 1909 was elected ILP Chairman. Re-elected in both 1910 elections, he argued for a new system of government, abolishing the Cabinet system. However, the Labour leadership disagreed and he resigned as Party Chairman. Strongly anti-war, he was also at odds with national Labour policy over the war and lost his seat in 1918. He had two more spells as MP in 1922-1925 and 1929-1931.

A true pioneer, he was a man of unwavering principle and conviction, but ultimately not suited to the reality of political compromise.

Source: *Socialism Over Sixty Years: The life of Jowett of Bradford (1864-1944)*, Fenner Brockway (1946)

14 Jan 1989 1,000 Muslims celebrate the burning of Salman Rushdie's novel *The Satanic Verses*.

'The book contains distorted, unfounded, imaginary and despicable material about a Prophet of Islam and the Islamic history. The Muslim concept of God, the character and personality of the Prophet of Islam, the lifestyle of the Companions of the Prophet of Islam, the sanctity of Muslim institutions of prayers and pilgrimage, and any other areas of Muslim culture, and history have been ridiculed with the sinister motive of portraying millions of Muslims all over the world as barbarians.' Before the Rushdie Affair flared up in Bradford, the *Telegraph & Argus* had already published a letter with these words.

Salman Rushdie was born in Mumbai in 1947, the year of partition on the Indian sub-continent. He was brought up as a Muslim in a well-educated middle-class family from Kashmir. He was educated in Bombay, Rugby School and Cambridge University. He lived in London.

The Satanic Verses was his fourth novel. He was already a very well established writer, especially after his second novel, *Midnight's Children* (1981). This had won the Booker Prize in 1981 and also was deemed to be 'the best novel of all winners' on two separate occasions, marking the 25th and the 40th anniversary of the prize. Later in 2007 Salman Rushdie was to be knighted.

Today, with a large crowd behind him, a representative from the Bradford Council of Mosques took the book down to the centre of Bradford in front of the city's key public buildings around City Hall. It was a thick hardback, difficult to set on fire. He had to soak it in paraffin and nail it to a piece of wood before applying a light. Pictures of the book-burning quickly appeared across the world's media and, within the UK, it marked a new stage in deteriorating community relations with Muslims.

One month later the controversy was subsumed within a greater one when the Ayatollah Khomeini, leading cleric in the Islamic Republic of Iran, issued a fatweh against Rushdie. *The Satanic Verses* was blasphemous. Any Muslim who decided to kill the blasphemer would be a hero or, if killed in the attempt, a martyr. In fear of his life, Rushdie had to go into hiding where technically he remains.

Attempts failed in the High Court to prosecute Rushdie for blasphemy and get the book banned. The book sold 750,000 copies in five months.

Source: *The Satanic Verses: Thirty Years On*, (BBC TV, 2018)

15 Jan 1771   John Hustler's influence secures the funds for the Bradford Canal.

John Hustler (1715 -1790) was probably the most influential man in Bradford helping to develop the small market town with the changes that led to the Industrial Revolution.

Born into a Quaker family in Bolton, adjoining Bradford, he joined the family wool business as a sorter and stapler of wool. His family had been Bradford's leading wool- staplers profiting from their resale of raw wool purchased from farms and wool fairs all over England. As first chairman of the Yorkshire Worsted Committee, he became a focal point in representing wool-staplers' interests in introducing a system of inspection and supervision to prevent bad practice and fraud.

Wool-stapler, businessman and landowner, he had a finger in many pies. Today's meeting was a case in point.

Not surprisingly, Hustler had become a fervent advocate of the canal for providing the cheap and efficient network that was required for transporting goods. After the original promoter had to withdraw with a terminal illness, Hustler became heavily involved in the Leeds/Liverpool Canal that was now being constructed. He took over as prime mover, organising the committee that dealt with the Yorkshire side of the canal. He also produced a promotional leaflet and lobbied Parliament to enact the legislation.

That new canal, however, was three miles away from the centre of Bradford at its nearest point in Shipley. A spur was needed to take barges direct into the centre. He was now the obvious person to champion the need for the Bradford Canal.

So, today he brought together 14 potential subscribers at the Sun Inn, the place where important business meetings were often called in the absence of any public buildings. He secured from them the funds of £3,800 which was a very good start for the target of £6,000. Subscribers included Abraham Balme who was to work closely with him on the building of the canal in three years' time after the legislation had been passed.

One measure of his energy and influence was his simultaneous commitment to another major development for trade – the construction of the new Piece Hall that opened in 1773, the year before the canal. It is appropriate that the street Hustlergate still survives, close to that site (now the Wool Exchange) and not too far from where the old Bradford Canal started.

Source: *The Bradford Canal: The first promoters*, John Allison (1999) in *The Antiquary*

16 Jan 1893 Local paper casts doubt on inaugural meeting of Independent Labour Party.

Reflecting on a momentous weekend marking the foundation of the Independent Labour Party (ILP), today's *Bradford Daily Telegraph* did not share the celebrations. *'A good many general resolutions and few immediately practical ones'* it claimed and went on: *'The terms of Socialism and Communism ... still have an ugly sound in the ears of an Englishman...we scarcely think the working men are yet of this contention'.*

The six-month Manningham Mills Strike in 1891, which ended in humiliation for the workers, was the catalyst for the ILP, and was also the reason why it was founded in Bradford. At a major meeting towards the end of the strike, attended by an estimated 30,000 to 40,000, speakers denounced the Liberals (and Tories) who owned the mills and advocated independent Labour candidates for local elections.

As a by-product of the strike, the Bradford Labour Union was founded as a political organisation to function independently of either major party. The young Bradford socialist, Fred Jowett, was a founder member. He believed in independent political action on behalf of the workers with socialism as its goal.

Activists such as the Glaswegian Keir Hardie had become convinced of the need for a labour voice independent from radicals in the Liberal Party. Local ILPs were springing up across the country. The Bradford Labour Union soon evolved into the Bradford ILP and in 1892 Jowett was elected its first councillor. The 1892 Glasgow Trades Union Congress proposed that it should support a national ILP and that Bradford should be the venue for the first annual conference.

On 13 January at the Labour Institute (later Jowett Hall, then Civic Playhouse) in Peckover Street the two-day conference started. The ILP was formally founded with Keir Hardie its first chairman.

When the broader Labour Party was created in 1906, the ILP immediately affiliated to it, thereby enabling it to continue to hold its own conferences and devise its own policies.

After World War One its influence gradually declined. In the 1929 general election it was reduced to one MP – Fred Jowett being returned for his fifth and final time. However the ILP did not finally cease until the mid-1970s. There was still time in 1963 for the ILP to hold its annual conference once again in Bradford, 70 years after the first.

Source: *Socialism Over Sixty Years: The life of Jowett of Bradford (1864-1944)*, Fenner Brockway (1946)

17 Jan 1872 Rev WH Keeling starts 44 years as headmaster of a reformed Bradford Grammar School.

After a radical review by the newly-established Commission for Endowed Schools, a new Governing Body was announced, containing influential local businessmen such as Sir Titus Salt and Jacob Behrens. On 17 November 1872 it appointed the Reverend William Hulton Keeling (1840-1916), Headmaster of Northampton Grammar School.

Today, two months later he started work. By the time the school moved into new permanent premises in Manor Row in June 1873, it had an ethos, purpose and method that is still recognisable, including *'an ethos of academic excellence, frequent exams and tests, a staff of highly qualified masters, a wide curriculum and entrance criteria that were classless but clever, with both fee-paying and scholarship pupils'* (Moxon).

The importance of these foundations was strongly reinforced by WE Forster, Minister of Education, opening the school on 1 July 1873: *'It is pleasant to come to the place with which I am most intimately connected of all places in the kingdom and to find out that we are not considering how it is to be done but how it has been done'.*

Five years later, it had become the 13th school in the country in leaving results (ie 'A' Level equivalents). In 1883 it sent 11 students to Oxbridge. Keeling's predecessor had achieved just seven in 18 years. By 1895 it was the most successful city grammar school in the North after Manchester Grammar School with its 60% higher intake.

The Select Committee of the House of Commons reviewing success of grammar schools sent Mr JG Fitch again in 1895 to Bradford. He was the inspector that had condemned the school in the mid-1860s. This time he found: *'Bradford, which was in a lamentable condition of uselessness and decay when I saw it there, is now a very fine grammar school with 443 boys and it is doing, I believe, a very great service.'*

Keeling maintained the school's academic success until his retirement and death in 1916 after 44 years in charge. When he died, there were many tributes to a legendary headmaster. At his memorial service, the Vicar of Bradford praised his *'indomitable perseverance, power of clear decision and indefatigable energy for work'.* He went on:

'His life story is the history of Bradford Grammar School itself.'

Source: *Hoc Age - Bradford Grammar School 1818-1996*, Tony Moxon (1999)

18 Jan 1887 Opening of Manchester Road Baths at last marks a turning point.

We all now take for granted the importance of keeping clean at all times with baths and showers on demand. However, up and till the 1840s, this was not understood. Moreover, in towns like Bradford homes often lacked running water and bathrooms were certainly scarce.

Back in 1846, the Government had passed an Act To Encourage the Establishment of Public Baths and Wash-houses, giving power to any borough *'if they think fit'* to make such provision. Some places were quick off the mark. Municipal baths had already predated the act in Liverpool (1842). Others soon followed in London (through the 1840s) and Birmingham (1848).

Bradford Corporation was at best half-hearted in its response. In 1864 it adapted premises from an old waterworks company in Thornton Road, but in a few years these were inadequate. In 1883 it bought a terrace house in Great Horton and fitted it out as a ladies' Turkish bath, but it closed in 1896 losing money. The main reason for lack of progress was that councillors could not be persuaded that the ratepayer should fund what were seen as expensive facilities.

It is said that what changed minds occurred at the opening of Bowling Park in 1880 by Mayor Angus Holden. Although the press mentioned nothing at the time, the *Leeds Mercury* (24 November 1886) revealed that *'As the corporation and municipal officials wended their way to the park, they were abashed at the sight of so many of the "great unwashed" among the assembled spectators in the line of the procession... and probably on that day some members of the council were won over to the side of the advocators to district baths.'*

Today's opening of Bradford's first purpose-built baths finally showed serious intentions in municipal provision for encouraging cleanliness and better health. When new public baths (plus free library) were opened on Manchester Road midway between West Bowling and Little Horton, the municipal party was clearly proud of its commitment. All that was required now, according to Mayor Holden, was *'the patronage of the people'*. However, he continued, the baths were expensive and there might be no further investment.

In the event, by 1905 the Corporation had built new central baths (Morley Street) and five more district baths (Manningham, East Bowling, Leeds Road, Undercliffe, Low Moor).

Source: *Bradford's Municipal Baths and Wash-Houses*, Betty Longbottom (2006) in *The Antiquary*

19 Jan 1982   The Home Secretary makes a statement to the House about the Yorkshire Ripper case.

The Yorkshire Ripper case became a national political issue. On 20 November 1980 Prime Minister Margaret Thatcher wrote to Ronald Gregory, Chief Constable of West Yorkshire Police, expressing her concern that the murderer was still at large. Peter Sutcliffe's arrest on 2 January 1981 was timely in preventing further escalation.

As soon as the trial ended in May 1981, Willie Whitelaw, the Home Secretary, asked Sir Lawrence Byford CBE QPM, Chief Inspector of Constabulary, to carry out a full review of the lessons to learn from the case. The fact that it took Byford only seven months to complete this task indicated that it did not require an extensive investigation as all the evidence already existed.

Today's statement admitted major weaknesses in managing the incidents such as the complete ineffectiveness of the card index system for managing information from tens of thousands of interviews. It also admitted major errors of judgement such as the overlooking of photo-fit likenesses of Sutcliffe. The biggest error had been the over-reliance on the voice on what turned out to be a hoax tape which completely diverted resources into the blind alley of searching for a Geordie voice, and not one from West Yorkshire.

Individuals in the Ripper squad were not named, but the evidence pointed to George Oldfield, in charge of the Ripper investigation, and a few senior officers (all male) being too fixed in their thinking about who the murderer might be and his motives. Disturbingly, they ignored credible evidence from victims who survived (all women).

The final irony is that one month later the West Yorkshire Police moved George Oldfield sideways to become the Assistant Chief Constable in charge of the Western Division, based in Bradford. Bradfordians who had been so affected by the trauma of the murders committed by one of their own cannot have been much reassured to see that the one senior police officer linked so clearly to the force's heavily publicised failures was now responsible for combating crime in the city.

To everyone's relief Oldfield retired in July 1983 on grounds of ill-health after a second heart attack. He died on 5 July 1985.

Source: *The Yorkshire Ripper Case - Review of Police Investigation*, Sir Lawrence Byford (1981)

20 Jan 2006   After nearly 50 years Michael Wharton writes his last Peter Simple column.

It was the end of an era. Michael Wharton (1913-2006) signed off in his 93rd year as Peter Simple. He had been writing his column for the *Daily Telegraph* for nigh on 50 years, four columns a week for the first 20 years, then down to three and, finally, just one weekly column.

Until he found this niche, his life had been chaotic, complicated and largely unsuccessful. Born in Shipley as Michael Bernhard Nathan, the son of a German-Jewish businessman, he was educated at Bradford Grammar School and Lincoln College, Oxford. (Not until his 20s did he change his name to Wharton, his mother's maiden name).

His time at Oxford was undistinguished, to say the least. He managed to leave without a degree, having been sent down for throwing a Scotch egg at high table in hall. He chose instead to write a novel, *Sheldrake*, featuring Tibetan thought-forms in a Yorkshire mill-town. Unfortunately, to start with, he did not find a publisher. He finally did in his mid-40s after he became well-known.

For many years Wharton struggled as a jobbing journalist, mainly with pieces for Punch magazine. When World War Two came, he served in the army in India, improbably ending up as acting lieutenant-colonel. After being demobbed, he secured a job with the BBC as a scriptwriter, but he did not fit in with what he saw as its left-wing bias.

An unexpected encounter with an acquaintance gave him his break and the opportunity for making a name from his way with words and satirical humour. He was invited to contribute to the *Daily Telegraph's* Peter Simple column and within three years became its only contributor.

Wharton created a large number of satirical, fantastical figures such as *'Alderman Foodbotham, the 25-stone, crag-jawed, iron-watch-chained, grim-booted perpetual chairman of the Bradford City Tramways and Fine Arts Committee' and 'Mrs Dutt-Pauker the Hampstead Communist thinker in her fine "Marxmount" mansion'.* Through them he built satires of the many deplorable aspects of modern life such as cars and television. He was well to the right of the most right-wing politicians, abhorring anything to do with socialism. He had a strong nostalgia for the past.

As well as his novel, he also published two volumes of autobiography and several compilations of his columns.

Three days after today's last column he died – a true eccentric.

Source: Michael Wharton *(Oxford Dictionary of National Biography)*

21 Jan 1963   A man's body is dug out of the snow in the Big Freeze.

It was the longest and hardest freeze in living memory. For 76 days from 21 December 1962 to 6 March 1963 Bradford's population lived in sub-zero temperatures with just a few minor breaks, like almost the rest of Britain. Normal life came to a halt with burst pipes, power cuts, restricted public transport and no sport.

Experiencing a poor season in the old Fourth Division, Bradford City fans had been delighted with getting a home draw in the FA Cup Third Round with big-time Newcastle United in the old First Division, a replay of the famous FA Cup Final in 1911. Another 1-nil win would be a big boost. Planned for 5 January, the match was inevitably postponed with a frozen pitch.

Worse news was to come. Today, a 62-year-old man from a farm near Allerton was found dead. His body had to be dug out of a nine-foot snowdrift by four ambulance-men. Until that weekend, although everybody was grumbling about the weather, there had been no heavy snow. The weekend brought strong winds and snow clouds, creating big drifts of snow. Across the country, more than 30 people died.

Two days later news about the weather covered the whole of the front page of the *Telegraph & Argus*.

As well as loss of human life, there was a big financial cost from the Big Freeze as it came to be known. By the end of February Bradford Corporation's snow-clearing bill was reportedly £116,000 – at least four times more than normal. These huge costs excluded the bill for mending burst pipes, repairing roads and resetting pavements disrupted by burst water mains. Unemployment soared with lay-offs in the building industry and from reductions in power.

Finally, it ended and ended quickly. On 5 March, the morning temperature of 6.4C recorded at Lister Park was the highest since December 16, ten degrees warmer than the previous day. As snow and ice melted, scores of roads were inundated with water up to three feet deep in places.

The FA Cup match had been postponed a record twelve times, but finally took place on Thursday 7 March. The pitch was very muddy from the thaw. City played an 18-year-old rookie goalkeeper still at school. They lost 6-1 to Newcastle United, City's heaviest-ever home Cup defeat.

Life had returned to normal.

Source: *'Fifty years on' - Telegraph & Argus* (16 January 2013)

22 Jan 1959 The BAFTA-winning film of John Braine's *Room at the Top* is released.

Today, *Room at the Top* put Bradford and the film's Bradford-born creator, John Braine, on the map.

The film was voted Best British film of 1959 by BAFTA. Simon Signoret won both an Oscar (1960) and a BAFTA for Best Actress in a Leading Role. It also won a BAFTA for Best Adapted Screenplay (Neil Paterson) and another Oscar, plus four Oscar nominations. In addition, the film launched the directing career of Jack Clayton and the acting career of Laurence Harvey who took the leading role and also received an Oscar nomination. It also had established stars (eg Donald Wolfit, Hermione Baddeley as well as Signoret).

John Braine (1922-1986) left St. Bede's Grammar School when 16; after a number of jobs he studied at the Leeds School of Librarianship before working as a librarian in Bingley. Recovering from tuberculosis at Grassington Sanatorium gave him the opportunity to write. He gained instant success with his debut 1957 novel. *Room at the Top* caught the mood of the times. He was one of a loose group of new writers called the Angry New Men who railed against the class system and traditional middle-class values.

The book is the story of ambitious young man, Joe Lampton, from a modest background, working in a local government office in a working-class northern town. He makes a play for the daughter of a wealthy industrialist, who is also a senior local Tory politician. Thwarted in his advances on her, he turns to an older married woman. To his dismay, he then finds out that the daughter is pregnant by him and reluctantly has to marry her. One tragedy leads to another before Joe finally accomplishes his ambitions; but sadly he no longer values what he has achieved.

Both the film and the book broke new ground. They aimed for social realism and authenticity. The passionate affair with the older married woman is portrayed very explicitly for the time. Unusually, it was filmed mainly on location – in Bradford, Bingley, Halifax and Keighley, the first of at least 50 major films directly or indirectly connected with Bradford over the next 60 years.

There was also a sequel in 1965 with *Life at the Top*. Like the book, this film was quite successful without ever reaching the heights of the original story.

Source: *Stories of the Century (Telegraph & Argus, 1999)*

23 Jan 2000   Ann Daniels is a member of the first all-women team to reach the South Pole.

Until she was 30, Ann Daniels led an ordinary life in her home city of Bradford. Her father (insurance salesman) and mother (secretary) brought her up in a terrace house in Allerton with four elder brothers. She did well at comprehensive school with nine GCSEs, but her family had no expectations of her staying on for university.

She wanted to join either the police or the services, but being short-sighted ruled her out. She settled for a job in the bank. Her ambition was to get married and raise a family. Aged 21, she did marry, but having a family was not quite so straightforward. After several years of unsuccessful fertility treatment, she tried IVF just the once and was delighted that it worked. She gave birth to triplets.

She responded enthusiastically to her new life of busy mother. Then once more, her life changed forever. In August 1995 she spotted an advertisement for women to join the first all-female team to travel to the North Pole. Never before having even carried a rucksack, she applied speculatively. She was amazed to be invited to a weekend of assessment, then equally amazed to be selected from some 300 women for a second four-day SAS-style assessment. Finally, she was selected for the team, making the first relay for the North Pole. Her parents stepped in to look after the triplets.

Today, she reached the South Pole as a member of the first all-women team; two years later, she achieved the same in finally reaching the North Pole. She completed seven more trips to the North Pole. Her only setback in this extraordinary personal journey was to abandon an attempt to be the first woman to walk solo to the North Pole, because without warning the Russian authorities withdrew permission when she was well on her way.

Her headline achievements take no account of the difficulties. Extreme cold, risks of storms, frostbite, gangrene and hypothermia, dangers of breaking ice, fear of being attacked by polar bears, they all dominated her polar adventures.

At the start of her explorer life her marriage was falling apart. Two years after separating from her husband, she met a new partner with whom she had a fourth child.

Latterly she has developed her new career by using her unique experience as a polar explorer to becoming a motivational speaker.

Source: *Desert Island Discs*, 26 January 2007 (BBC website)

24 Jan 2015   Bradford City knock champions Chelsea out of the FA Cup at Stamford Bridge.

The odds were stacked high against anything other than a convincing defeat as third-tier Bradford City travelled down to Premiership Chelsea for a fourth round FA cup-tie.

Last season's champions, Chelsea had won all their 10 home Premier League matches this season and were already five points ahead of their nearest rivals. All the talk was about an unprecedented quadruple in English football - Premier League, Champions League, FA Cup and League Cup.

In 1999 Bradford City had started a two-season spell in the Premier League. After that they had been relegated three times and twice placed into administration. Since 2001, Chelsea had won the Premier League four times, the FA Cup four times, the League Cup twice, the Champions League and the Europa League.

Today's result was hailed by most commentators as the biggest FA Cup shock of all time as City came back from 2-0 down to win 4-2, sending 6,000 fans stunned and delirious on their way home to Yorkshire.

As Chelsea manager Jose Mourinho had made nine changes from the previous game, one might think his was a weakened team, However, it was still packed with experienced internationals, players such as Cech, Terry and Drogba and highly promising youngsters such as Mo Salah, the same team that had beaten Watford 3-0 away in the 3rd round.

For the first 40 minutes the game went according to expectations with Chelsea taking a 2-0 lead through Cahill and Ramires. With the game heading to a predictable 4-0 or 5-0 defeat, Jon Stead scored a spectacular goal out of the blue just before the interval, giving City fans some hope. The second half was completely unpredictable as City started to dominate. They equalised through Fil Morais in the 75th minute. Amazingly, they took the lead seven minutes later through Andy Halliday and sealed the victory in style with a last minute fourth by Mark Yeates. Manager Phil Parkinson was ecstatic; Mourinho chastened but gracious in defeat.

As the scale and manner of the victory sunk in, fans learnt that Mourinho had never conceded four goals at home in his managerial career, Chelsea had not conceded four goals to a third-tier side for 57 years and City had not scored four goals away for 16 months.

At the end of the season Chelsea won the Premier League and the League Cup; City finished seventh, just missing the Championship play-offs.

25 Jan 1850 Christian leaders agree cross-denominational approach for new Bradford Town Mission.

In March 1949 Mayor Titus Salt had received the report he had commissioned into the moral state of Bradford. Ten months later, progress was made on one of the key recommendations to set up a town mission.

The report found that *'a large proportion of our inhabitants are neither connected with any of our congregations nor are in the habit of regularly attending divine worship, but are either opposed or indifferent to the religion of Christ, and in too many cases grossly ignorant or immoral'* (*Bradford Observer,* 7 March 1849). The concept of a town mission, an idea taken from London and elsewhere, was to support a small number of town missionaries to visit the poor in their houses *'for the purpose of imparting religious instruction and consolation, and perpetually explore as messengers of truth and mercy the retreats of vice and wretchedness'.*

Today's first meeting was attended by representatives of many Christian congregations in the town who fully supported the concept. They had secured sufficient gifts and subscriptions to give the mission the go-ahead. They also confirmed the appointment of four missionaries allocated to the areas of the greatest need – around Westgate, the lower ends of Manchester Road and Wakefield Road and, finally, White Abbey where a female missionary would operate.

Although supported by many prominent citizens, Titus Salt remained the driving force and the largest subscriber for the rest of his life. As well as their religious role, the missionaries acted as social workers and advocates for education. For example, within two years the female missionary in White Abbey was providing well-attended classes for young women in reading, writing and arithmetic. Within ten years the missionaries were offering free medicines and medical consultations.

Source: *The Great Paternalist: Titus Salt and the Growth of 19th Century Bradford,* Jack Reynolds (1983)

26 Jan 2005   The President of Poland presents honour to Bradfordian Rabbi.

The Order of Merit of the Republic of Poland was created in 1974, to be awarded to persons who have rendered great service to Poland. It is granted to foreigners or Poles resident abroad. There are five classes - Grand Cross, Commander's Cross with Star, Commander's Cross, Officer's Cross and Knight's Cross. Today, Dr Walter L Rothschild received the Knight's Cross from President Kwasniewski for his work in Christian-Jewish and Jewish-Polish relations. His story is remarkable.

Born in Hanover, his father Edgar arrived in England as a schoolboy in 1939 as his family fled from Germany. His mother Esther was born in Bradford, but her parents came from Eastern Europe (father from Latvia and mother from what is now Belarus). Born in Bradford in 1954, Walter grew up in the city and was brought up in a Reform Jewish household and congregation, based at the Bradford Reform Synagogue. He attended Bradford Grammar School before reading theology at Cambridge University.

Since his early student days he has been active in Jewish organisations organising a Progressive Jewish Society and founding a new Reform Jewish community in Cambridge. In England, he trained to be a teacher, taught religious studies and then studied to be a rabbi before being ordained in 1984. Over the next 20 years he became first a rabbi in Leeds, (with responsibilities for Bradford, Hull and a new Sheffield congregation), then in Vienna, the Dutch Antilles (West Indies), Berlin and Munich, each for periods of two to four years. From 1998 to 2000 he was a liberal rabbi in Berlin, then became rabbi responsible for several congregations around Germany and for ten years was the 'State Rabbi' in Schleswig-Holstein. He now serves the liberal community in Hamburg and Polish communities in Warsaw and Gdansk on a part-time basis.

He is a prolific writer – essays, sermons, articles, Torah commentaries, speeches. He has written many short stories, some serious, some light-hearted, some scurrilous parodies. He also writes on history and biography, and publishes a quarterly magazine on his passion for the railways of the Middle East. Other activities include extensive media work, bible classes and seminars and lectures on religious issues. He is firmly on the reform, liberal side of Judaism, believing it his mission to lead young Jews to an accommodation with the 21st century and not a false replica of 18th century Central Europe.

Source: www.walterrothschild.de

27 Jan 1840   Robert Peddie fails in starting a Chartist revolution.

Under oath at York Assizes the spy gave the testimony needed to convict the Chartist revolutionary:

'Peddie said that, if they brought up half the quantity of men they said they had, he could beat the soldiers and establish the Charter in two or three days, that it could not be obtained without physical force and they would use physical force. After taking Bradford they would take all places on their way to London – after they got to London they would upset the Government. Peddie and the others said they wanted annual parliaments, universal suffrage - no qualification – vote by ballot.'

The spy was James Harrison who had infiltrated the conspirators. Their leader was Robert Peddie who was convicted to three years hard labour for riot and conspiracy for a failed insurrection in the early hours today. Aged 37, Peddie was described as a *'wild, romantic and rather unpleasant staymaker'* (ie corset-maker) from Scotland. He had arrived in Leeds earlier in January where he had first met his conspirators.

With Peddie leading about 40 armed men, they had seized a watchman in the centre of Bradford, but then ran into a group of police and special constables, lying in wait after Harrison's tip-off. The insurgents flung down their armour before being arrested. So ended in a fiasco the first of Bradford's Chartist uprisings. More were to follow in 1842 and 1848.

Chartism was a working-class movement for political reform in Britain that existed from 1838 to 1857. It took its name from the People's Charter of 1838 and was a national protest movement, with particular strongholds of support in industrial areas such as the West Riding. The strategy employed was to use the scale of support which these petitions and the accompanying mass meetings demonstrated in order to put pressure on politicians to concede manhood suffrage. Although Chartism relied on constitutional methods to secure its aims, there were some like Peddie who became involved in insurrectionary activities, notably in South Wales and in Yorkshire.

Source: *The Chartist Risings in Bradford*, DG Wright (1987)

28 Jan 2008 Car designer Afzal Kahn pays record price for prestigious F1 number plate.

Today, Bradfordian Afzal Kahn paid a record £440,625 for the vehicle registration number F1 (Formula One) from Essex County Council. F1 was the first number issued by the Essex County Register of Motors in 1904, the year when motor vehicles legally had to bear a registration plate. Kahn planned to display it on his £317,000 Mercedes SLR McLaren supercar.

Entrepreneur Kahn, who describes himself as a 'car fashion designer', owns a specialist car design company based in Canal Road.

Born in 1974, he originally wanted to be an architect but dropped out of Leeds College aged 17. Kahn had early experience in working in a factory making plastic coffins, where he quickly learned different plastic moulding techniques and also how to manage a factory. He then set up a small factory, building glass fibre components as body parts for rally shops in the UK. By the age of 19, he had 30 staff.

As trends changed, Kahn decided to move into making wheels. In 1996, he travelled to Italy with designs for a new specialist alloy wheel. The RS-R was considered to break new ground in the industry – the spokes gave the appearance of continuing all the way to the rim. He ordered 1,000, and they were all sold before he made it back to England.

Using capital from this, he established the company, Kahn Designs and added exterior styling and vehicle interior design to the product range. Then in 2002 the company diversified into production of complete vehicle upgrades. This required a move to new, purpose-built premises in 2004, which incorporated body shop and leatherworking facilities. Kahn bought some Land Rovers; when the cars were in his studio, he re-styled and re-engineered them. Kahn Designs became one of the world's most famous design houses for wheels, interiors, and customised vehicles.

He has won several awards within the car industry that recognise his innovation and entrepreneurialism.

Five years after his expensive investment he was rumoured to have turned down a multi-million bid for the same registration plate. Reportedly, he believed it would only increase in value. Five years later the *Metro* (10 April 2018) reported that he had put it on sale starting at £12m. The rising value of his F1 registration plate can perhaps be seen as a symbol of his success.

Source: *Telegraph & Argus* (28 January 2008 and 23 August 2013)

29 Jan 1962   Bradford starts the celebrations for centenary of birth of Frederick Delius.

Without a doubt the most renowned musical composer from Bradford is Frederick Delius (1862-1934). Today the city celebrated his centenary in style. Two hundred guests attended a special opening recital at the Cartwright Memorial Hall performed by international cellist (Jacqueline du Pre), close friend Eric Fenby (playing on Delius's own piano) and the Bradford Festival Choral Society.

This was just the start. A week of music from Delius followed in late March. Three days of choral and orchestral concerts were held at St. George's Hall, given by the Royal Philharmonic Orchestra conducted by Rudolf Kempe. At the Alhambra Theatre three performances by the Sadler's Wells Opera were followed by the Delius opera *A Village Romeo and Juliet*.

Born 100 years ago at Claremont, Horton Lane, Fritz (as Frederick was known growing up) had German parents. His father had moved to Bradford to work in the wool trade. The young Fritz learnt at home to play the piano and violin, and improvise. He attended Bradford Grammar School.

His father planned for him to take over his business and so he worked as a commercial traveller in England and abroad. However, his heart was not in textiles. In 1884 his father suggested a different business. So Delius went to Florida to manage an orange plantation, but he still devoted his spare time to musical study. Then, funded by his father, he studied music formally in Germany, before embarking on a full-time career as a composer in Paris. He and his wife were to live in France for the rest of their lives.

Delius befriended many writers and artists. For example, he became a close friend of Thomas Beecham who described him as *'the last great apostle in our time of romance, emotion and beauty in music'.*

In 1929 Delius was appointed Companion of Honour, and later that year Beecham mounted a magnificent six-day Delius Festival in London.

In reality Delius did not develop his reputation as a composer until well after he left the city. Unlike his counterparts in literature (JB Priestley) and painting (David Hockney), he seems to have had little connection with the city again. This may be why the city did little to celebrate the connection until making him Freeman of the City two years before this year's centenary. Better late than never!

30 Jan 2013 Magician Dynamo wins Best Entertainment Programme of the Year.

Stephen Frayne was born in Bradford in 1982 to a 16-year-old English girl and a Pakistani father, who was to be in prison for most of his childhood. He was brought up on the Delph Hill estate in Wyke, one of the UK's most deprived areas. The smallest boy in his class, he suffered from bullying at school. When 17, he was also diagnosed with Crohn's disease, a debilitating inflammatory bowel condition requiring daily medication.

Today, just 14 years after this traumatic childhood, he received a major accolade in his career. As the magician known as Dynamo, he won the Best Entertainment Programme of the Year at The Broadcast Awards 2013. The Magic Circle's President commented: *'Congratulations for entertaining audiences with awe-inspiring feats of illusion and encouraging a new generation of young people to explore the wonder of magic. The award is truly deserved'*. Later in 2013 he won TV Show of the Year at the Virgin Media Awards, seeing off stiff competition from the likes of *Doctor Who, Homeland, Sherlock, Downton Abbey* and *The Walking Dead* for a prize voted for by the public.

His grandfather introduced Frayne to magic. Developing his skills as a way of fending off bullies, he quickly gained a reputation within his local community as a unique talent with his incredible sleight of hand.

In 2004, he moved to London to make his name as a magician. Along with a small team he filmed his performances on London streets and backstage at events, where he managed to blag his way in front of the stars by impressing doormen and tour managers. He promoted his skills making extensive use of YouTube to secure a following of fans.

Appearing some years later at the New York Hilton during Houdini's centenary celebrations, Frayne performed in front of his peers, including acclaimed magician David Blaine. After one amazing display, a person in the audience shouted: *'This kid's a ****ing dynamo!'* The name stuck.

The show that made his name was *Dynamo: Magician Impossible?*, first broadcast exclusively on Watch in 2011 and quickly broke all viewing records with over 1m viewers. It continued for three more series in 2012 to 2014.

In 2016 Dynamo unveiled a blue plaque at London's Pinoli's Restaurant to celebrate the centenary of the Magic Circle founded there. The young magician from Wyke had pulled out another rabbit out of the hat.

Source: www.magiccircle.co.uk

31 Jan 1913   An 18 year-old JB Priestley appears in print for the first time.

The *Bradford Pioneer* was a weekly socialist newspaper published from 1913 to 1936 under the auspices of the Bradford Independent Labour Party, Bradford Trades Council and Workers' Municipal Federation. If it is remembered at all now, it is for two things. One is that one of its later editors was Frank Betts, father of Barbara Castle. The other is that it gave JB Priestley his first opportunity to write for the public.

Today was his first contribution. For the next ten months he put together a column of about 1,500 words called *Round the Hearth* which was a miscellany of stories, comments, opinions and aphorisms usually sparked by recent books or local events.

He received no payment but he did get free tickets for plays, concert party entertainments etc., about which he would then write.

Today's column comprised short pieces headed *Memories of a Spectator, Funding of the Independent Labour Party, Unionist Musical Evening, Socialism for East and West, London and the Provinces, Music, Games, The Use of a Chin and Bradford Arts Club*. He found a way of expressing personal views such as on this occasion: '*I have never been more bored by games and people who talk about them. Games are the refuge of people who are bored with life.*'

Within a short time the editor added to the column the statement that '*It must be distinctly understood that (this) is pre-eminently a personal feature so that the opinions expressed therein are not necessarily those of the paper itself*'.

Some of the writing, too, is distinctly that of JB Priestley. Take, for example, this piece from his first column, prompted by a London writer, extolling the virtues of London life:

'*Practically every new movement, artistic or political has originated in the despised, much-maligned provinces. As a matter of fact, it is not really London that these writers are fond of. It is, in all probability, the society of so many brilliant men and women that makes them stay in the metropolis. Of course, these brilliant men and women have also come from the provinces. The average Cockney will not bear comparison, physical or mental, with the average citizen of Manchester or Bradford.*'

A forthright opinion, robustly made... a style to which one soon became accustomed.

Source: *Bradford Pioneer* (31 January 1913)

1 Feb 1918   Yet another tram accident, this one bucks the trend.

Hilly Bradford was not the best of places for operating trams. From the first horse-drawn trams in 1882 to the end of World War One, Bradford had more tram accidents than anywhere in Britain. Out of over 30 fatal accidents involving mechanical failure, four occurred in Bradford, as trams came down the hills into the city centre.

First, on 12 September 1885, a steam tram with no passengers ran out of control down Manchester Road after leaving the Bankfoot depot. In joining the main route, it narrowly avoided a passenger-laden tramcar, gathered speed and only came to a halt when hitting a lamp-post. Two men and two horses died, but miraculously not the driver. The engine design had a weakness, the driver may have made a mistake and the steep gradient compounded the problems.

Next, an electric tramcar crashed, within weeks of being introduced with great fanfare. On 19 September 1898, it ran away on Horton Bank, before derailing. One person was killed, fourteen seriously injured. The dead man was travelling by tram for the first time in his life. The inquest focused on the brakes. The jury returned an open verdict with a recommendation that emergency brakes should be fitted on all trams.

Nine years later, another accident, on a different hill ... Around 6am on the morning of 31 July 1907 a tramcar from Undercliffe went out of control and hit a building. Two people were killed and 13 others were injured. For about 100 yards Church Bank coming down into Forster Square is a 1 in 9 gradient, the steepest stretch in Bradford. Here the accident occurred. The driver and conductor escaped with minor injuries. The cause of the accident was the front axle snapping.

Another 11 years on, today, a tramcar derailed on another hill, this time in Allerton. The driver died and 19 were injured. Initial reports indicated yet again problems coming down a hill. However, at the inquest, evidence confirmed a different story. The tramcar had been recently overhauled and this gradient had never presented problems before. The morning was dark and foggy with no light, except for the tramcar's front lamps (wartime conditions against possible air raid). The driver had lost control in the poorest visibility. The inquest recorded 'Accidental death'. (*Leeds Mercury*, 14 February)

By this time, trolley-buses were well established and they were much safer.

Source: *Bradford Daily Telegraph*

2 Feb 1963   Bradford is the first place outside Liverpool to experience Beatlemania.

Today the Beatles embarked on the first date of their debut UK tour at the Gaumont Cinema (now Odeon). It was an inauspicious start, in the middle of the Big Freeze, one of the coldest winters of all time with temperatures across Yorkshire reaching a 'high' of minus 1C. The *Telegraph & Argus* did not cover the event. The early evening performance was not even a sell-out.

The Beatles were fourth in a six-act bill, headlined by 16-year-old singer Helen Shapiro, voted Best British Female Singer for 1961 and 1962. Advertised as *The Helen Shapiro Show*, the tour coincided with the release of her single *Queen For Today*, which she hoped would revive her already flagging career. Behind her, 'Special guest star' Danny Williams and Kenny Lynch took precedence over The Beatles. Shapiro herself was quoted in *Beatlemania!*

'For this new tour I'd be accompanied by Danny Williams and Kenny Lynch ... Dave Allen would be the compere and there would also be this new group called The Beatles. He asked if I'd heard of them and of course, I had. I loved their song "Love Me Do" and I was looking forward to the tour. Dave Allen didn't have a halfpenny to his name in those days, but he was a lovely guy and very funny. I was always touring with Danny and Kenny, and so I knew them well.'

The Beatles performed four songs – 'Chains', 'Keep Your Hands Off My Baby', 'A Taste of Honey', and 'Please Please Me'.

Beatlemania had arrived.

What a contrast to their next Gaumont appearance in December, just ten months later. This time it was one of two Northern previews of *The Beatles Christmas Show* at the Astoria in London (the other being at the Liverpool Empire). Now their reputation was international.

When tickets went on sale on 1 December, thousands queued, many overnight. Leave for two thirds of Bradford City Police was cancelled. The *Telegraph & Argus* gave it the full treatment: *'The faces of many of the swaying, head-rocking girls had an expression of dervish ecstasy.... Yet wild as it all may sound, the feeling of merriment and pleasure was contagious. For the big scream was an infectious youthful endorsement of the joy of being alive.'*

Source: *Stories of the Century (Telegraph & Argus, 1999)*

3 Feb 1825   Bradford celebrates the festival for Bishop Blaise for the last time.

Blaise was an obscure Armenian bishop in a time of religious persecution. In AD 316, he was captured, imprisoned, beaten with iron combs (used to comb wool) and beheaded. A popular saint in medieval Europe, he became the patron saint of woolcombers and a legendary figure in Bradford's wool history. Every seven years there was a day of celebration. The biggest and best documented occurred today in 1825.

The day's celebrations were organised by Richard Fawcett, one of Bradford's early mill-owners at Holme Mill.

From the early hours crowds poured into Bradford. Representatives of different trades in the wool business gathered at the Bull's Head in Westgate. Their route went via Kirkgate, Ivegate, Market Street and Horton Lane to a field near Holme Mill.

Dr John Simpson, an early Bradford doctor, recorded the procession in his journal:

'A herald came first ... Then a band of music. Afterwards the Woolstaplers on horseback riding on fleeces ornamented with sashes. Then the Spinners on horseback, with sashes and slivers of wool, blue coats and white stuff waistcoats; their horses covered with white worsted nets. Next ... the Masters' Sons and Apprentices on horseback most gaily dressed in scarlet stuff coats, white waistcoats, blue pantaloons, blue sashes and most beautiful caps ... Next came the Merchants on horseback ... Next were people dressed up as King and Queen ... Jason and Medea [of the Golden Fleece myth] ... Bishop Blaise passed, followed by 'the Shepherd and Shepherdess ... Swains on horseback carrying crooks. Then came the Combmakers on horseback with combs and rams' heads with gilt horns ... Wool-sorters ... Master Dyers. There were also some 470 woolcombers.

At their destination the participants had abundant refreshments of beer and *'enormous sandwiches in their hands, shivering with the cold, bleak February wind'.*

The celebration was a complete success. Who was to know that 1825 would end so disastrously when, four months later, woolcombers went on strike, capitulating in complete failure after 23 weeks?

There has never been another celebration of St. Blaise, but he has not been completely forgotten. There is a statue in the Wool Exchange, he appeared in the 1931 Pageant in Peel Park and two pubs (long since closed) and a school (still open) were named after him.

Source: *Bradford*, Joseph Fieldhouse (1972)

4 Feb 1888   The Chamber of Commerce presents Sir Jacob Behrens with a portrait of himself.

Jacob Behrens (1806-1889) had played the pivotal role in founding the Chamber of Commerce in 1851. It commissioned his portrait from Ernest Sichel, eminent painter and Bradford-born son of fellow German Jewish family. Today it presented the painting to him and he made his last speech in public - *'a speech full of gratitude for a happy past, but full of loneliness in the death of almost all his fellow-founders, his friends and his relatives'.*

Nearly every improvement in Bradford's public life in the second half of the 19th century had the fingerprint of Jacob Behrens.

As a buyer in his father's business, he had moved from Germany to Yorkshire in 1832, recognising the value of having a permanent agency in England. He settled first in Leeds before realising that Bradford offered greater opportunity. *'He did not lose much and gained a very great deal by the move to Bradford, where "all was different, all was on the make" ... he found Bradford, when he came to it in 1838 "an overgrown village" with no social and civic organisation.'*

The Chamber of Commerce promoted trade in textiles in Germany and across the world. It also advised government on tariffs, policy and legislation affecting trade. He was its president for six years from 1869. Many of its members were immigrant German merchants who formed part of what became known as the Little Germany quarter.

He founded the Bradford Eye and Ear Hospital in 1865. He played an active part in Bradford Grammar School becoming one of the best schools in the North. In 1882, he helped set up Bradford Technical College. He was a prime mover behind the opening of St. George's Hall in 1853 and initiated the idea of the Subscription Concerts held there from 1869.

In 1882 for an immigrant and a Jew he received the ultimate accolade of a knighthood.

When he died a year after receiving his portrait, the Chamber of Commerce sent his family a memorial that included the words:

'Sir Jacob may truly be said to have been the founder of the Bradford Chamber of Commerce and for nearly forty years he has been unceasingly occupied in every good object which might serve the interests of the town and neighbourhood. He seemed to exist only to be of service to his fellow men.'

Source: *Sir Jacob Behrens* 1806-1889 (memoir)

5 Feb 1924   Sir Frank Dyson introduces the Greenwich 'pips'.

'Beep', 'beep', 'beep', 'beep', 'beep', beep' occurring on each of the five seconds leading up
to the hour and on the hour itself ... the first five pips each last a tenth of a second, while the
final pip lasts half a second. The start of the final pip indicates the moment when the hour
changes.

The pips on the hour are so familiar on the radio that you can easily believe that they have
always existed, but before today they had not. What is more is that they were created by a
man from Bradford.

Sir Frank Dyson (1868-1939) was born in fact in Leicestershire, but, when very young, moved
with his family to West Yorkshire. He won a scholarship to Bradford Grammar School and
Cambridge University, where he studied mathematics and astronomy.

After a first-class degree with very high marks, he became a fellow at Trinity College in
1891. In 1894 he was appointed Senior Assistant at Greenwich Observatory. He made an
important contribution to the International Astrographic Catalogue, a world-wide project
involving photography of specified regions of the sky, followed by measurement of the
positions of the stars recorded.

In 1905 he moved to Edinburgh when he was made Astronomer Royal for Scotland and
Regius Professor of Astronomy at the university. Five years later he came back to Greenwich,
this time as the ninth Astronomer Royal, and the only one to have held both Scottish and
UK posts.

From 1900 when he observed the phenomenon from Portugal, Dyson became very interested
in observing solar eclipses and was involved in six such expeditions. He realised that Einstein's
recently propounded theory of relativity could be subjected to an observational test at the
1919 solar eclipse. This predicted that stars seen near the eclipsed sun would appear to be
shifted in position by a small, but measurable, amount. Dyson was able to demonstrate
that the data supported Einstein's predictions. This was a major turning point in scientific
thought.

The Greenwich Observatory had always been involved in time measurement. After the
war Dyson (now knighted) was approached by John Reith of the British Broadcasting
Corporation that the Observatory should provide time signals to the public via the BBC.

Thanks to Dyson, the idea of the Greenwich Time Signal – the world standard for time –
was born.

Source: Sir Frank Dyson (*Oxford Dictionary of National Biography*)

6 Feb 1834   Bradford's first significant newspaper appears on the streets.

Bradford's first newspaper was the *Bradford Courier* and *Gazette* launched in 1825. It lasted three years. The *Bradford and Wakefield Chronicle* also started in 1825, but fared even worse, lasting just nine months. Both were set up primarily as financial ventures by a few entrepreneurs, but struggled to sell enough copies and to afford taxes on paper, printing and advertisements.

Today, Bradford's next newspaper, the *Bradford Observer*, appeared on the streets and was to become the most successful of the 19th century. It was set up primarily as a political venture as the organ of radical nonconformists, founded by a consortium of 86 shareholders, including prominent Liberals destined to become politicians, such as Robert Milligan, Titus Salt and Henry Ripley. By this time Leeds had its well established *Leeds Mercury*; why should not Bradford have its own newspaper?

Although not a shareholder, the Reverend Benjamin Godwin, a prominent anti-slavery campaigner, played a key role in discovering William Byles, who was to become the paper's printer, editor and owner. Godwin contacted an old friend at Oxford, whose wife's nephew might be just the man. In his letter to William Byles he wrote:

'A newspaper is about to be established in the hands and under the management of Dissenters ... An editor must be a man of high talent and information – of Liberal reforming principles ... who has just views of religious freedom and the alliance of Church and state ... It is important that the press should be under such guidance, especially perhaps in such a district as ours.'

William Byles did not at first glance fit the bill. From a modest Congregationalist family in Henley-on-Thames he left school at 13. He learnt his trade as a printer, and was content with his life. Although a splendid opportunity, he pointed out in his reply his lack of writing and editorial skills. However, he stressed his solid printing experience and his commitment that *'there could be no doubt he could be relied upon to reflect dissenting opinion accurately'.*

Godwin and colleagues were convinced. He moved up to Bradford and lived the rest of his life there, becoming one of its most influential residents.

The *Bradford Observer* was a regular weekly paper (usually eight pages) for over 34 years when it became a daily and started to face real competition.

Source: *Victorian Bradford: Twelve Essays,* edited by DG Wright and JA Jowitt (1981)

7 Feb 1857   Elizabeth Gaskell completes a controversial biography of her friend Charlotte Brontë.

Charlotte Brontë's *Jane Eyre* (1847) was an immediate success, but naturally her readers were curious about this new writer, known as Currer Bell. Its subtitle was *'An autobiography'*. Was it really Charlotte's story? The general public only found out when, two years after Charlotte's death, Elizabeth Gaskell (1810-1865), a well-known novelist and critic, published a comprehensive biography about her and her home in Haworth, a little-known hill village in northern England.

Today Gaskell completed the manuscript; six weeks later it was published. She had met Charlotte Brontë in 1850 and immediately struck up a strong friendship, corresponding regularly and meeting up whenever they could. Three months after Charlotte's death in 1855, her father, Patrick, invited Gaskell to write a biography, giving her access to his daughter's correspondence. Gaskell researched Charlotte's life as thoroughly as possible, including looking up old contacts from her time in 1842 as a governess in Brussels.

Over 400 pages, the biography covers Charlotte's life in full, illustrating key points in the narrative with much of Charlotte's correspondence. Its focus is not the novelist, rather the daughter, sister and friend. Readers would have found it a fascinating and credible insight into the life of this mysterious new writer. It also prompted deep interest in the whole Brontë family, and their life in Haworth, that has never waned since.

Yet this classic biography also prompted much controversy. Despite its frankness on many topics, Gaskell was accused of omitting references to Charlotte's romantic attachments to a teacher in Brussels and later her publisher in London.

It described very unflatteringly the regime of the school that Charlotte and sisters had attended at nearby Cowan Bridge. Charlotte, who based Lowood School in *Jane Eyre* on her experiences there, believed that the unhealthy conditions hastened the premature deaths of her two elder sisters. However, the family of the school founder published a rebuttal of Gaskell's description.

Finally, Nancy de Garrs from Bradford, who had looked after the Brontë children indicated in a letter to their surviving father that Gaskell had been very critical about both him and her. Patrick Brontë wrote to Gaskell to rebut the allegations. It transpired that Gaskell had listened to a Haworth woman with a grudge about the Brontës.

In 2017, *The Guardian* named *The Life of Charlotte Brontë* one of the 100 best non-fiction books of all time.

Source: *The Life of Charlotte Brontë*, Elizabeth Gaskell (1857)

8 Feb 1848   Family will illustrates how Keighley's Butterfield dynasty prospered.

The stories of Keighley's most prominent family and its most distinctive building were intertwined for some 120 years. The year 1848 marked an important step in the relationship when the Butterfields bought the property that became Cliffe Castle. Today also witnessed the signing of a will that illustrates how they could afford it.

Records go back earlier, but it really started when John Butterfield, a weaver, married in 1760. He had several children. One son married aged 15 and had three children. One, John a wool-stapler, must have done very well, because he died in 1817, aged 35 and unmarried, leaving to his brother, Isaac a stuff-maker, £25,000 (an incredible £2.25m in current money, although we do not know what he started with).

Isaac married in 1810 and had six boys and one girl, but he died in 1833 leaving his sons in charge of the growing business, now called Butterfield Brothers. They initially rented Cliffe Hall, designed as Gothic revival, before purchasing it in 1848. By the 1850s the firm had premises in Bradford, mills in Keighley, Haworth and Stanbury and investments in the USA.

The son that did best for himself was fifth-born Henry Isaac (1819-1910). He followed two brothers to develop the business in New York. Aged 35 he married in 1854 the 16-year-old Mary Roosevelt Burke, a relative of Theodore Roosevelt (later President of USA). They settled in France with homes in Paris and Nice. He still had time, however, to add towers, ballroom and conservatories to the family home, renaming it Cliffe Castle in 1878.

Their son Frederick William Louis d'Hilliers Roosevelt Theodore Butterfield (1858-1943) carried on the family business, becoming mayor of Keighley from 1916 to 1918 before being knighted in 1922. His daughter became a countess and chose to live in a bigger house in Nottinghamshire, thereby breaking the Keighley connection. Cliffe Castle was sold to Keighley Corporation who turned it in 1959 into a museum and art gallery.

And the will? This is one document surviving from 1848 belonging to Henry Isaac's uncle, John (1781-1849), old John Butterfield's youngest son. It is conventional, dividing John's fortune equally after his wife's death to their five surviving children. Yorkshire mill-owner families managed their money prudently over the generations, improving on what they inherited to pass on to their children. The Butterfield dynasty achieved this for at least six generations.

Source: www.lenbutterfield.co.uk

9 Feb 2002   Gareth Gates makes his name as runner-up on ITV's *Pop Idol*.

2001/2 was the first of many seasons of Saturday night talent shows. ITV's *Pop Idol* had reached its finals. The show was a singing competition for people aged between 16 and 26, with the winner receiving a £1 million recording contract to release their debut album. After auditions in October, a series of five untelevised heats in November and December produced eleven finalists. This gave a series of eight live shows, including a semi-final, in which candidates performed different songs each week and were eliminated one by one. Today's show left two finalists – 17-year-old Gareth Gates from Bradford and 23-year-old Will Young from Wokingham.

Gates was favourite, having come higher than Young on all the previous eight live shows, including being first in four of them. The final decision was a simple public vote. In the week leading to the final, travelling in their own personal bus, they both went on individual nationwide publicity tours, visiting radio stations and newspapers and giving performances to drum up support. In front of a viewing audience of over 13 million, Gates lost the final with 46.9% of the record 8.7 million votes cast.

Born in West Bowling in 1984, Gates was educated at nearby Dixons City Technology College. He showed singing talent from an early age as chorister at Bradford Cathedral, performing solo in front of the Queen as head chorister aged 11. He also achieved Grade 8 in piano and classical guitar.

Having shot to fame, Gates capitalised on his achievement with three immediate No 1 singles and a debut album that reached No 2, but his performance seemed to be slipping away to the extent that still only 22 years old he was the subject of a 2006 ITV documentary *Whatever Happened To Gareth Gates?*

By any account, however, his career has been very successful. Since 2007 he has been involved much more in musical theatre, participating in ITV's *Dancing on Ice*, taking the lead role in *Joseph and the Amazing Technicolor Dreamcoat,* playing Marius in the 25th anniversary tour of *Les Misérables* and appearing in several pantomimes.

His musical achievements should be seen against the stammer that Gates has had to contend with throughout his life. He qualified as a speech coach and works as a therapist to help others with speech impediments. He is a role model for others with similar difficulties.

10 Feb 1837   The Bradford Poor Law Union is formed.

The 1601 Poor Law Act placed responsibilities on the local community for providing work for the unemployed, apprenticeships for poor children and relief of the poor. The activity was funded by a local tax on land. Over the years provision had varied over the country and costs were rising steeply, particularly with the growth of industrialisation. The law was in need of reform.

The new Whig Government of 1832 set up a Royal Commission which recommended a new approach. This led to the 1834 Poor Law Amendment Act. It grouped parishes into unions under 600 locally elected Boards of Guardians. Each Board was to have its own central workhouse, where those unable to support themselves were offered accommodation and employment. The Boards were controlled by the Poor Law Commission, responsible for administering the new system nationally.

Welcomed by many as being more scientific and likely to reduce the number of paupers, it was much detested by others, especially in the North. Places like Bradford distrusted the centralisation from London. Bradfordians in the 1830s were disenchanted with lack of progress on suffrage and factory reform. New regimentation in workhouses enforcing degrading uniforms and separate blocks for men, women and children reinforced their alienation.

Today, the new Bradford Poor Law Union was formed, according to the requirements of the 1834 Act. Its operation was overseen by 32 elected Guardians, representing 20 parishes.

It inherited former township workhouses at Bradford, Idle, and five others, providing 400 places. A report of the Bradford workhouse recorded that *'the rooms were dirty, and paupers not at all comfortable. Some were residing in a low damp room, which they did not think fit for habitation'*. In 1839, Bradford was one of the 37 unions reported inadequate by the Poor Law Commissioners. A year later, only the Bradford and Idle workhouses remained.

By 1848 with population rising more steeply in the four central townships that the year before had formed the borough of Bradford, the Union was split into two – Bradford and North Bierley (covering the other townships and taking over Idle workhouse). Three years later Bradford Union opened a new workhouse at Little Horton, which much later evolved into St. Luke's Hospital.

Source: *The Battle of Bradford: Riots against the New Poor Law*, Paul Carter (2006) in *The Antiquary*

11 Feb 1861   WE Forster wins the first of a record six elections as Bradford MP.

Today, William Edward Forster (1818-1886) was returned unopposed as the Liberal Party candidate for Bradford in a by-election. He was to win a further five elections in 1865, 1868, 1874, 1880 and 1885, representing a Bradford constituency for 25 years until his death.

Although a distinguished politician for Bradford, Forster was a Southerner by birth. Brought up in a strong Quaker family in Dorset, he moved to the Bradford area in his 20s when his father insisted he went into textiles. He became a partner in a worsted business in Bradford before moving out to a mill in Burley in Wharfedale where he lived for the rest of his life.

He had always been interested in politics. He was a classical Liberal supporting radical views on almost all the issues of the day, eg electoral reform, the Ten Hours movement and Chartism. After an unsuccessful attempt in 1859 to win election in Leeds, he put his name forward as one of Bradford's two MPs to replace Sir Titus Salt, who had resigned on grounds of ill-health.

In government he held the position of Under-Secretary for the Colonies (1865-1866), played a major role on education reform and emerged in 1875 as a strong candidate to replace Gladstone as leader of the Liberal Party but deferred to a rival. He was an energetic member of the opposition front bench until 1880 when in a new Liberal Government he was appointed Chief Secretary for Ireland.

One issue on which he did not share typical Liberal thinking was the role of the established church. It is thought that he was heavily influenced by his wife's Anglican family. When he married Jane Arnold, he had to renounce his Quaker connections. His father-in-law was the Reverend Thomas Arnold, famous headmaster of Rugby School; his wife was also close to her brother Matthew Arnold, the famous poet who was perhaps less well-known as an inspector of schools with strong views on education. When he was being the politician in Bradford, Forster played down his Anglican connections, but they had a significant impact on his major political achievement – the 1870 Elementary Education Act.

No Bradford MP has won more elections or represented Bradford for a longer consecutive period. He is remembered to this day by Forster Square, its railway station and the statue that stood there for many years.

Source: William Edward Forster (*Oxford Dictionary of National Biography*)

12 Feb 1895   The Royal Photographic Society makes Henry Snowden Ward one of its first fellows.

When Percy Lund was building up his prominent business in Bradford as a photographer and printer, in 1885 he employed Henry Snowden Ward (1865-1911). Born in Bradford, Ward had been educated at Bradford Grammar School and Bradford Technical College. Together, they founded the *Practical Photographer*, a monthly periodical. Ward soon became a recognised authority on photography, but also became involved in other of Percy Lund's ventures. For example, he wrote the introduction to James Berry's autobiography about his life as a state executioner that Percy Lund published.

By the time in May 1895 when Percy Lund joined forces with Edward Humphries to become Lund Humphries, Ward had parted company. Today, earlier in the same year, he was made a fellow of the Royal Photographic Society. This may not have been quite as prestigious as it sounds as this Society, founded in 1853, had only just created the level of Fellow. Ward applied to become one and was part of the first group to be admitted. Soon firmer criteria were developed.

Doubtless, though, it helped to reinforce his growing reputation as a serious photographer. He produced many photographic guides (*eg Photographic Monthly*) and technical guides (*eg Practical Radiography* about rontgen rays).

After a two year trip to the United States in 1892, he had married an American, herself committed to photography. Now settled in London, they wrote jointly several literary books fully illustrated with photographs (*eg Shakespeare's Town and Times, The Shakespearean Guide to Stratford-on-Avon, The Real Dickens Land* and *The Canterbury Pilgrimages*).

Ward was an energetic traveller, making many lecture tours in Britain, Canada, and the United States. He was a devoted admirer of Charles Dickens, but sadly, his life came to a premature end when he fell ill in New York on a tour promoting the Dickens centenary.

Source: Henry Snowden Ward *(Oxford Dictionary of National Biography)*

12 Feb 1991   Sir Robert Jennings is appointed presiding judge of the International Court of Justice.

Today, Robert Jennings (1913-2004) achieved the pinnacle of a distinguished legal career by becoming only the third British judge to preside over the International Court of Justice since its inception in 1946. Born in Idle (his father a factory worker and mother a mill weaver), he was educated at Belle Vue High School, from where he was the first to attend Cambridge University, thence Harvard. In 1939 he became a Fellow of Jesus College, Cambridge.

13 Feb 1909   Park Avenue's redeveloped football ground attracts Bradford's only England international.

Today for the first and only time a full international soccer match was played in Bradford, at Park Avenue, with the opening game of the British Home Championship between England and Ireland. The ground itself had only a year before benefited from a major redevelopment, including new stand and pavilion. This was a feather in the cap for the high profile and controversial director, Harry Briggs, whose money funded it.

One might imagine that the game would be a major feature in the local press, but the coverage in the *Bradford Daily Telegraph* was certainly low-key, the match report being flat and dull. However, the *Leeds Mercury* gave it a much livelier and fuller treatment:

'Superior persons were disappointed with the game, and they have seen lots of Soccer Internationals they are perhaps right pronouncing from the academic standpoint. One critic says he hopes he will never see another International devoid of interest and good-class football.... For myself, I have not seen an association football match this season at which there was so much clever play; I have witnessed far more exciting struggles, but none which has brought out the finer features of the game so well.

The Irish played a keen, plucky game against a side obviously above their class, and that for three parts of the game they held up well. But they failed to stay the pace to the end, and four goals were rattled up against them in a very short space of time. The Englishmen played very scientific football, perhaps rather too scientific at times to please a crowd accustomed to more vigorous, go-ahead methods; but the exhibition was an education to those who see little better than Second League football as their staple fare.'

Overall, the match itself seems rather one-sided and disappointing with four late goals giving England a 4-nil victory. Both papers, did, however, comment on the one Bradford City player who played, half-back Evelyn Lintott. After a poor start they praised him for his strong second-half performance.

The attendance was 28,000 and receipts £800.

This was not the only time an international team played at Park Avenue. To celebrate the opening of its new floodlights on 3 October 1961, the club played a friendly against Czechoslovakia in front of 17,500, losing 3-2.

No representative international match has ever been played at Valley Parade.

Source: *Leeds Mercury* (15 February 1909)

14 Feb 1832   After a false start the Bradford Mechanics' Institute is formed.

From the early 1820s Mechanics' Institutes started to appear after pioneering work in Edinburgh (1821) and other cities. Their role was to provide a self-help educational facility for working men who had not received any formal education. A small group formed an embryo institute in Bradford in 1825 by creating a small library and a set of rules, but fell apart after much argument about religion and politics, as some feared it would be infiltrated by radical dissenters.

Today a new group restarted the Institute, followed by a first public meeting on 20 March. In order to pre-empt the earlier difficulties, the new group called it *'The Bradford Mechanics' Institute' or Society for the Acquisition of Useful Knowledge' with a clear statement that 'all subjects immediately connected with controversial theology, or party politics, shall also be wholly inadmissible'.* Its goals were threefold: to provide an extensive library, to supply instruction through public lectures and to develop classes under well-qualified teachers from different fields of learning.

The prime mover this time was Joseph Farrar (1805-1878), a hatter from Halifax who settled in Bradford and eventually became its mayor in 1863. He was supported by several distinguished nonconformists such as Reverend Benjamin Godwin (Baptist) and John Hustler (Quaker).

After its first year it had 350 members. Its longer-term success was symbolised by the buildings it occupied. At first, it used a room rented in Piccadilly, before it moved in 1840 into new premises at the edge of present-day Little Germany. In 1871 it moved again into much grander buildings in Bridge Street, opened by WE Forster, Bradford MP and Minister for Education.

It is one of few such institutes to survive to the current day, although now it is mainly a small subscription library in Kirkgate.

Source: *The Bradford Mechanics Institute*, C. Federer (1906)

14 Feb 1907   Lillian Armitage is arrested for trying to break into the Houses of Parliament.

Lillian Armitage was the secretary of the Bradford branch of the Women's Social and Political Union, set up in 1903 to campaign for women's suffrage. She was part of today's protest at the Houses of Parliament, where 57 suffragettes were arrested, including six other local activists and herself, (among whom Julia Varley and her sister from Bradford, Nell Kenney from Bingley and three others). They were all charged, found guilty and sentenced to 14 days in prison.

Source: http://madeinbradford.co.uk/celebrating-bradfords-heroines-who-fight-for-our-rights/

15 Feb 1870 — An inspector calls - Bradford Grammar School is failing its pupils.

In 1864 Parliament set up the Endowed Schools Enquiry. Its task was to report on some 3,000 endowed grammar schools. In 1865 or 1866 a Mr JG Fitch visited the school to obtain evidence. He produced a report that ended:

'Boys are sent out of Bradford to good grammar schools at a distance to obtain the precise training which this school was meant to give. And it is to be regretted that, under its present management it neither attracts pupils of this class nor is able to render any appreciable service to the much larger class which wants a liberal education and yet does not yield scholars likely to go to the university.'

He visited other schools in Yorkshire. Bradford was not alone: only three escaped major criticism. The findings of the enquiry led to the Endowed Schools Act of 1869, which set up a Commission that had powers to reorganise any school found wanting.

For over 200 years the school's Governing Body had been Anglican and Tory, but Bradford was now nonconformist and Liberal. It was prosperous, a city in all but name, which was based on the textile industry. Yet business and the new middle class were not represented. The school had become complacent and was stagnating. For example, under the current headmaster only seven boys in 18 years had gone on to university.

The school was in crisis and under the new regime Bradford became the first in England to be reorganised.

So, today Assistant Commissioner Feoran told the school's Governing Body what reforms to expect. The Minister who set up the Commission, WE Forster, a local resident working in and representing Bradford, could not be seen to be giving favours. The Governing Body itself was part of the problem. Its constitution and powers had to be overhauled.

In effect, it became a new school and the new school needed a new headmaster. Fortunately it appointed the very man that it needed – the Reverend WH Keeling.

Source: *Hoc Age - Bradford Grammar School 1818-1996*, Tony Moxon (1999)

15 Feb 1941 — Richard Eurich is appointed an official war artist to the Admiralty.

Educated at Bradford Grammar School, Richard Eurich, OBE (1903-1992) specialised in sea pictures. His most famous painting was *Withdrawal from Dunkirk* (1940), shown at the National Gallery weeks later. Today he became an official war artist.

Source: Richard Eurich (*Oxford Dictionary of National Biography*)

16 Feb 1998 Soap *Emmerdale* is about to be transferred from its old Esholt to its new Esholt location.

For many years Esholt village on the edge of Bradford has been closely associated with *Emmerdale*, the nation's third TV soap with *Coronation Street* and *Eastenders*.

Now running six episodes per week from two in 1972, *Emmerdale* covers life in a Dales village. Until 1976, Yorkshire TV filmed the village scenes in Arncliffe in Upper Wharfedale. It was an idyllic location, except that it was a long way from the Leeds studios where interior scenes were shot. In late 1975 they moved to Esholt. Set in a genuine rural location in the Aire valley, it was just six miles from Bradford and ten from Leeds. Built in sandstone, not traditional Dales limestone, Esholt was not a completely authentic Dales village, but it was close enough!

Accordingly, Esholt became the fictional Beckindale, until the fictional villagers changed it to *Emmerdale* in 1994. The village pub used to be the Commercial Inn, but in *Emmerdale* it had to be the Woolpack. Eventually, the real pub was renamed the Woolpack, because the real landlord tired of the frequent pub sign changes required for filming.

In 1995 it was announced that *Emmerdale* would be screened three times a week to compete with its two main rivals, who had already made this move. This required even more location filming in Esholt. For years the crew and cast had problems with tourists flocking to Esholt to watch filming. Tourists had to be quiet during 'takes' and not take photos. Villagers who were at home had to stay inside during shots and were always being asked to move their cars for filming.

These irritations already led to some rethinking along the lines of a purpose-built set away from Esholt. Now was their opportunity. The funds were raised to build an imitation Esholt on the Harewood House country estate, eight miles from Leeds off the Harrogate road. Here, the new set could be fenced off from visitors and the crew could film in peace. Visitors could tour the new set one day a week and could still visit Esholt as the 'real' home of *Emmerdale*.

Today is the end of an era. From tomorrow all episodes will be filmed in the new location. Only once, in 2016, has filming returned to Esholt village. The story justified the occasion. A long-standing character now with dementia had flashbacks to his earlier life that had been filmed in Esholt.

Source: www.emmerdalepastpresent.fandom.com

17 Feb 1870   WE Forster introduces his new Elementary Education Bill.

By the middle of the 19th century few children received education. William Cudworth quoted an 1843 survey that only one in ten children attended school in towns like Bradford. Unlike many radical Liberals who were 'voluntaryists', believing in self-help, WE Forster came to believe that the state should provide where society could not.

In 1866 he was appointed the Vice-President of the Council for Education with the brief to prepare a scheme of national education, effectively the Minister for Education before the job was created. His first task, though, was to see the Endowed Schools Bill through all its stages, which would improve the quality of endowed grammar schools provided for the wealthy (eg Bradford Grammar School).

Today, he introduced the new bill aimed at bringing the benefits of education to every child in England and Wales, irrespective of class or background. Forster had three objectives. First, he wanted to create a national system of compulsory education from age five to 13 funded from local rates. Second, he wanted to include religious teaching in the curriculum. Third, he wanted to extend, not destroy current provision.

Each area should take stock of existing schools and work out how many more would be needed to guarantee universal provision. Local Schools Boards should be set up to organise the additional provision.

After fierce debate the bill became law on 9 August 1870. Dissenters such as Baptists and Congregationalists (a large number in Bradford) were very disappointed, because existing church schools were to remain, and so the special status of the established church was untouched.

Not only is Forster remembered with a statue in Bradford (now near Forster Square), but he has a statue in London's Victoria Embankment Gardens with a plaque on the base:

'William Edward Forster born July 11 1818 died April 5 1886. To his wisdom and courage England owes the establishment throughout the land of a national system of elementary education.'

Source: William Edward Forster *(Oxford Dictionary of National Biography)*

17 Feb 1958   JB Priestley is involved in the formation of the Campaign for Nuclear Disarmament (CND).

Today was the launch of CND in Westminster. Committee member and Bradfordian JB Priestley spoke as he did many times at rallies in the next two years before he resigned. His *New Statesman* article in November 1956 in support of nuclear disarmament was extremely influential in the creation of CND.

18 Feb 2003   One-time 'lunatic asylum' closes at Menston.

On 8 October 1888 30 women were transferred from Sheffield to the new asylum built at Menston on the outskirts of Leeds and Bradford. Sixty-one women were to be admitted before one month later the first man was admitted – 39-year-old Charles Pett from Bradford, listed as a 'clerk or messenger'. Most had already spent many years in other asylums in the West Riding and were now being treated for palliative care.

The asylum was called the West Riding Pauper Lunatic Asylum and was commissioned by the West Riding Judges to serve the county. It was located near the two growing cities, technically just outside the current Bradford boundary, although it had always served the city's needs. By the 1920s its name was changed to Menston Mental Hospital. In 1963 it became the High Royds Psychiatric Hospital. It is no wonder that the name of Menston was dropped, as the name had become a stigma. Growing up in the 1950s a few miles away in Baildon, one occasionally heard parents threatening children with being 'sent to Menston' for being naughty. It was a place that people did not like to talk about.

Yet it had started with the best of intentions. The building was designed to be a self-contained community, including facilities such as a library, surgery, dispensary, ballroom and dairy and shops for baker and butcher. Over the next 40 years were added shops for cobbler, upholsterer and tailor.

Although well meaning, the concept of such a ghetto community had become outdated. Long before it was finally closed, one of the last such hospitals in the country, society had realised that it was no place for people with mental health difficulties to be treated.

Once admitted, inmates, as they were called, often lived out their lives in the hospital. In the early years only 30% left within the year and 15% remained until they died.

The *Yorkshire Evening Post* headlined today's closure as *'Final Days for Controversial Victorian Asylum'*. Later, the fine Victorian building was sometimes used for film shoots or TV programmes. David Dimbleby featured it, for example, in a prominent documentary series called *How We Built Britain*.

Twelve years after it closed, developers bought it and converted it into stylish apartments and homes for happier lives.

Source: *West Riding Pauper Lunatic Asylum Through Time*, Mark Davis (2013)

19 Feb 1880   Striking Bradford dyers are vindicated for their militancy.

The dyers at John Botterill's mill had been on strike for three weeks for a reduction of working hours from 60 to 54. Today, however, their actions led to a riot.

The strikers met in the morning at the Coffee Tavern, St. George's Hall. The chairman stressed the need to hold firm. A minister suggested that he should act as an intermediary to settle the dispute. The strikers agreed but later the employers refused. One went so far as to say that he would rather lose £10,000 than accede to the strikers' demands.

As they left the meeting, the strikers chanted the name of Botterill's and marched towards their premises in Garnett Street, a short distance away. When they reached the works, the doors were closed, but the mob burst them open. Stones were thrown, and the premises over-run by rioters.

Shortly after, a detachment of some 20 police constables arrived on the scene. With some difficulty they cleared the premises. The next day, the *Bradford Observer* reported: '*A general scrimmage ensued between the crowd and the police, and about fifteen of the most disorderly were taken into custody. While there yet remained in the yard several of the men who had entered previous to the arrival of the police, the doors were closed upon them, and the extraordinary efforts which many of them made to reach the open street were amusing. Some who succeeded in evading the police climbed upon the shed of the boiler-house and over the yard doors to the window sills of an adjoining house, from whence they dropped into the street.*'

Fifteen prisoners were taken to be locked up in the police cells by the Town Hall.

The next day, the case was heard at the Bradford Borough Court. Magistrates sent nine men to jail for one month, five more were fined ten shillings (plus eight shillings costs) and one was discharged.

The same day 29 Bradford employers met in the grand Victoria Hotel to pledge that they would not employ any workmen, except on the same terms, as paid before this strike started.

With the agreement of both sides, the dispute was passed to Henry Mitchell, President of the Bradford Chamber of Commerce. Five weeks after the strike started, he ruled almost entirely in favour of the employees with the 54 hour week due to start in September.

Source: *Bradford Observer*, (20 February 1880)

20 Feb 1919   German prisoners of war (POWs) are hit by Spanish 'flu.

It is said that more people died from Spanish 'flu in 1918 and 1919 than were killed in World War One. In the UK 228,000 are believed to have been 'flu victims. There is no evidence that Bradford suffered differently from other places in the UK, but, coming on the top of a devastating war for the city, it did make life difficult.

The illness was unfairly attributed to coming from Spain where early incidents were reported but only because, being neutral in the war, Spain had no censorship unlike their European neighbours. The pandemic came in three waves.

The first wave started in June 1918. The first report came with advice that *'it is very infectious, and the best advice that can be given the individual is to avoid crowd and get plenty of fresh air' (Bradford Observer)*. It was generally mild in its impact but still over 90 died.

When the 'flu returned in October, it was much more serious. The worst symptom came when lungs were starved of oxygen and the patient would turn purple, black or blue; death was inevitable. In the last week of October, there were 11 deaths, the week after 35. The Bradford Medical Officer of Health issued advice that those with symptoms should go to bed and isolate themselves and houses should be flushed with fresh air. Then came the Armistice and people flooded out into the streets to celebrate. In Bradford 125 people died the week after. By December 597 died.

The third wave started in February and lasted a few more weeks. 621 died, including 111 under-fives.

Perhaps the biggest single instance of infection occurred right at the end of the third wave. There was a camp for German POWs near Skipton. The camp hospital soon became full and today the most seriously ill men were transferred to Morton Banks Hospital in Keighley where 42 died, the majority being officers. Survivors wrote about the friendly treatment they received there from the medical officer.

Every year a memorial service was held in Morton, including many Germans. But in 1938 the *Yorkshire Post* reported that a party of 50 Germans from various parts of Yorkshire raised their hands in the Nazi salute at the close of the service (14 March). World War Two was approaching.

Source: *The Influenza Pandemic in Bradford 1918-19*, Christine Alvin (2018) in *The Antiquary*

21 Feb 1850   Finally, a design is selected for the new Bradford Union Workhouse.

When the Bradford Poor Law Union was created in 1837, it inherited seven workhouses offering 400 spaces. Within just four years only two remained. The main one was at Barkerend, founded in 1738 and rebuilt in 1790 for 74 inmates, but it no longer met the needs of a rising population.

After the 1837 riots against the new Poor Law Amendment Act, the Poor Law Guardians were half-hearted in following advice from the Poor Law Commissioners in London to build a new central workhouse in line with the new legal requirements. Until the Bradford Union was split into two in 1848, the Guardians kept putting off the work, but agreed finally in January 1850 to the construction of a new workhouse in Little Horton to accommodate some 400 inmates.

The next question was the design and the architect. The choice came down to two. As so often in Bradford, it was premier local architects, Lockwood and Mawson, then just establishing their reputation, and one other. In this case the competitor was Atkinsons of York who had recently designed three workhouses in North Yorkshire. The criteria were suitability for all types of pauper, within budget and future extension.

A committee was set up to examine the designs. As so often in Bradford, it was Lockwood and Mawson who won. However, it was not plain sailing as the committee had not made a formal recommendation. Today, the weekly *Bradford Observer* gave a 'blow by blow' account of the debate when the full board met the previous Friday with just about every point made reported. Arguing over mainly procedural points, in the end they plumped for Lockwood and Mawson on all three criteria.

The debate was not yet over. The Poor Law Board in London intervened to suggest several improvements. Many were thought to be too generous. For example, one suggested a covered shed under which children could play in wet weather – one Guardian pointed out that his own children had no such option. Most suggestions were rejected.

Construction work began in August 1850, and the first inmates were transferred from the old Barkerend workhouse on 29 September 1851. Lockwood and Mawson were engaged by the North Bierley Union, created by the 1848 split, to build a workhouse at Clayton, which opened in 1858.

Source: *The Place of the Pauper*, Charlotte Jane Newman, PhD University of York (2010)

22 Feb 2009   Screenwriter Simon Beaufoy wins an Oscar for *Slumdog Millionaire*.

The compere who tonight introduced the five nominations for best adapted screenplay at the 2009 Oscars quoted Charlotte Brontë: *'The writer who possesses the creative gift owns something of which he is not always master'.*

It is highly unlikely that she (the compere) knew that the winner came from the same neck of the woods as the great 19th century writer, and Keighley-born Simon Beaufoy was too modest to make the connection in his acceptance speech. Nevertheless, the story of how Beaufoy researched his adaptation of *Slumdog Millionaire* captures something about Brontë's quotation. He insisted on visiting the slums of Mumbai where most of the film is set. He spent time talking to the people who lived on the streets, especially the children, to understand how they lived, what mattered to them and the words that they used. The experience shaped the story lines for the film, which is about a slum kid winning the Indian version of *Who Wants to Be a Millionaire?* The novel on which the film was based did not have a structure suitable for a film, but the visit to the slums gave him one. He also understood the importance of Bollywood-style song and dance routines as a result of watching films in a huge Mumbai cinema – this, too, has a major influence on the film.

Born in 1966, Beaufoy was educated at Skipton Grammar School and Sedbergh School before reading English at St. Peter's College, Oxford and also graduating from Arts University, Bournemouth. His first major success as a scriptwriter was in 1997 with *The Full Monty,* a comedy that tells the story, set in Sheffield, of six unemployed men who decide to form a male striptease act. The idea came from a chance visit to the city when it was in the middle of a recession. A major critical and commercial success, it won a BAFTA for Best Film and four Oscar nominations including Best Original Screenplay. The British Film Institute ranked it the 25th best British film of the 20th century. Beaufoy also created a stage version 15 years later.

Over his script-writing career, Beaufoy has created scripts for at least twelve major feature films and three TV series which cover a wide range of topics. The journey that he has followed in developing his creative gift for writing illustrates neatly Charlotte Brontë's point.

Source: *The Guardian* (12 December 2008)

23 Feb 1956 Albert Pierrepoint resigns as last state executioner.

Today, the country's last state executioner and the most well-known, Albert Pierrepoint (1905-1992), confirmed his resignation after an argument with the Prison Commissioners over non-payment for a case where there had been a last-minute reprieval. He claimed for expenses that he had incurred, but they refused to pay, because the agreed terms were payment by execution only. There were rumours, which he completely denied, that his resignation was related to the recent highly controversial hanging of Ruth Ellis, the last woman to be hanged.

From 1884 the Home Office maintained a list of executioners and assistants to be made available when Under-Sheriffs had to organise an execution in their county. Until capital punishment was abolished in 1965, the list had seventeen names. Four of them were strongly connected with Bradford, including three from the Pierrepoint family. Born in Clayton, Albert was influenced by both his father Henry and uncle Thomas in wanting to be an executioner.

Aged twenty-seven, he became an assistant executioner and three months later carried out his first hanging. By the time he resigned, he had executed between 435 and 600 people, including 201 in Hameln, Germany just after World War Two, convicted of war crimes.

From 1941 when he became a lead executioner, he was responsible for hanging several controversial murderers. They included William Joyce (the Nazi propagandist 'Lord Haw-Haw') and three who were all highly unsafe convictions that undermined the case for capital punishment – Ruth Ellis, Derek Bentley for his part in a policeman's murder and Timothy Evans for his wife's murder at 10 Rillington Place, home of John Christie who later admitted to killing seven women.

Like Bradfordian James Berry before him, Pierrepoint wrote an autobiography which criticised capital punishment:

'Hanging is said to be a deterrent. I cannot agree. There have been murders since the beginning of time, and we shall go on looking for deterrents until the end of time ... It is I who have faced them last, young lads and girls, working men, grandmothers. I have been amazed to see the courage with which they take that walk into the unknown ... All the men and women whom I have faced at that final moment convince me that in what I have done I have not prevented a single murder'.

Source: *Executioner Pierrepoint: An Autobiography*, Albert Pierrepoint (1997)

24 Feb 2013 Bradford City reach a Wembley cup final for the first time.

The anticipation for today's match was intense. It was League Two Bradford City's first appearance in a Wembley cup final and the first-ever Wembley cup final appearance by a fourth-tier club.

City's League Cup campaign had built steadily through the autumn from several unpromising positions. In the first round an extra-time winner against League One team Notts County took City through to a second round match at Championship Watford. Here an injury-time winner led to a home tie against League Two Burton Town. Losing 2-nil until they scored two in the last ten minutes, City won again with an extra-time goal.

From now on City faced Premier League opposition. First up was away to Wigan Athletic. City fought hard for a 0-0 draw but after a goalless extra time won on penalties 4-2. Now it was a home tie against the mighty Arsenal. On a bitterly cold night a packed Valley Parade saw City go into a first-half lead to be pulled back three minutes from time with an Arsenal equaliser. No further goals in extra time meant another penalty shootout, which City won 3-2.

City faced Aston Villa home and away in the semi-final. Another packed home crowd saw City go into a 2-nil lead after 77 minutes. Villa scored a valuable away goal but with three minutes to go City scored what turned out to be an even more valuable third goal. Two weeks later at a snowy Villa Park, City lost their overall lead as Villa scored first, but in a rare second-half attack City equalised from a corner. Although Villa scored again just before the end, City prevailed with a 4-3 score over the two games.

Wembley opponents were Swansea City promoted to the Premier League in 2010-11. With a reputation as an attractive footballing side, they too were new to Wembley cup finals. After City's exploits getting to Wembley, it was not unreasonable to dream of a unique victory.

But everything that could go wrong did. The game was a complete disappointment, creating a record that City did not want of suffering the heaviest League Cup final defeat. They were outplayed, being easily beaten 5-0. Moreover, their goalkeeper was sent off after 60 minutes.

City's only consolation was to return to Wembley in May and win the League Two play-off final 3-0, gaining promotion to League One.

25 Feb 1871   Lilycroft Mill is destroyed by fire.

There was trouble at t'mill ...

A life's work destroyed in a few hours, it would have destroyed most people, but Samuel Cunliffe Lister (1815 -1906) had the resources and the character to turn disaster into an opportunity.

(Funded by his wealthy father for his brother and himself, Lilycroft Mill on the corner of Lilycroft Road and Heaton Road had opened in 1839.)

At 11pm tonight flames were seen coming out of a window in the mill. It was Saturday evening with very few people about, but the alarm was raised at nearby Manningham Police station where they had a small and totally inadequate fire-engine. A messenger also went down to the central police station in Bradford, but a chapter of problems meant that the much larger engine was far too late on the scene, by which time the warehouse roof had crashed down. As the fire started to die down and the hundreds of people who had gathered were drifting away, the damage had become extensive and sadly two men had died.

Lister arrived to survey the damage the next morning. Not everything was lost – some valuable technical drawings remained. The cost of the damage was £70,000 and he was insured for £40,000. He had invested greatly in the mill, but he seemed to have little hesitation in building a new and much larger replacement. Aged 55 years, he retained the energy and motivation to undertake this huge challenge.

He had already achieved a large fortune by mechanising woolcombing. He was to achieve another.

Within two and a half years his new Manningham Mill (Lister's Mill) opened with the tallest chimney in the city (Lister's Pride) which still marks the skyline. His new fortune was built on silk and velvet. He sold Manningham Hall and estate at well below market rate to the Corporation on condition it became Lister Park for the public. He bought a great estate in Swinton, North Yorkshire. He was ennobled as Lord Masham. He financed the new Cartwright Hall Art Gallery. In between he took on his workers who went on strike and completely defeated them. The 1891 Manningham Mills Strike did not make him popular and became a significant factor in the rise of the Labour Party. He died one of the wealthiest men in England.

Source: *Lilycroft Mill 1837-1874: The first Manningham Mill*, Derek Barker (2014) in *The Antiquary*

26 Feb 1969   Vic Feather is elected General Secretary of the Trades Union Congress.

The parents of Vic Feather (1908-1976) christened him Victor Grayson Hardie Feather. Victor Grayson MP was a firebrand Socialist who had recently won a sensational by-election. The legendary Keir Hardie was a founder of the Labour Party. Feather seemed destined for the career he chose and for today's election to the top job in trade unionism. He was steeped in the labour movement.

Born in Idle where his family lived in some poverty in a 'one-up, one-down' back-to-back, he nevertheless did well at Hanson Grammar School. However with his father dying young, he had to start work at age 14, filling flour bags at the local Cooperative Society's grocery shops.

He joined the Shopworkers' Union. A year later he was elected shop steward, and at age 21 chairman of his branch committee. He became an avid reader about socialism, learned the skills of public meetings and wrote regularly for the socialist weekly, the *Bradford Pioneer*.

Feather worked 37 years for the Trades Union Congress, becoming assistant general secretary in 1960. Nine years later he was elected today to General Secretary. Although he only held this for four years, they were momentous times.

Industrial relations were the major domestic political issue for both the Labour Government (1966 to 1970) and the following Conservative Government (1970 to 1974). Feather was at the heart of that debate. Under his leadership the unions rose to be a powerful force in British politics, giving them an influence never since achieved. He became a familiar national figure in the media.

He helped deflect Labour leader Harold Wilson from major reform of trade union practices after Barbara Castle had introduced a controversial White Paper *In Place of Strife*. When Conservative leader Ted Heath took over and did introduce legislation with his Industrial Relations Act, he forced major concessions.

Feather was plain-speaking, pragmatic, warm and passionate, respected by his opponents and with a reputation of being a fixer and highly competent negotiator. Unlike some trade union leaders of the day, he was fervently anti-communist.

Six months after he resigned, he was made a peer - Baron Feather of the City of Bradford.

Two years later, however, he died, just as the Callaghan Government was struggling more than ever in controlling the unions, making the Thatcher revolution possible if not inevitable. The days of highly influential General Secretaries were over.

Source: *Victor Feather*, Eric Silver (1973)

27 Feb 1838   England's first Temperance Hall is consecrated in Bradford.

Alcohol was all-pervasive in early 19th century England as the number of outlets increased. For example, the Beer Act (1830) caused an explosion in the number of beer-houses and reduced the control of local magistrates over them.

The first temperance societies appeared in the USA in the 1820s followed by societies in Ireland and Scotland. A Bradfordian on business in Glasgow attended a meeting there, signed the pledge and returned to set up the first English society in Bradford in February 1830.

The first public meeting took place on 14 June 1830 in the Exchange Buildings, Piccadilly. Committee members included some of Bradford's worthiest citizens. Thereafter, Bradford was at the forefront of the temperance movement for the rest of the century, including being the venue for four annual conferences.

By 1837 the Bradford Temperance Society had 1,145 members and regular weekday meetings as well as Sunday meetings. Accommodation was becoming a problem. Generally, the recognised social meeting place was the inn or public house, scarcely appropriate here. The Society agreed to build its own Temperance Hall. A Hall in London, and one in Stockport, were also proposed, but they fell through, leaving Bradford as the pioneer.

The foundation stone for a Temperance Hall on Chapel Street was laid on 13 March 1837 with quite a ceremony. Today, the Bishop of Ripon (Bradford's diocese at the time) consecrated the new Hall with a number of other ministers speaking. One thousand sat down for tea to celebrate. Within a year members increased to 2,500 with 100 'reformed drunkards'.

Being the first, the design for Bradford's temperance hall provided the model for the first wave of such places, designed in a classical style that echoed many nonconformist chapels, not surprising as many members of the Bradford Society were prominent nonconformists. It provided a large assembly room, educational facilities, a library and facilities for making tea for large numbers.

In 1839 a new rule-book for the Society established a total abstinence pledge: *'I promise to abstain from all intoxicating Drinks; such as Rum, Brandy, Gin, Whiskey, Ale, Beer, Porter, Wine, Cider and Spirit Cordials, except for Medicinal and Sacramental purposes: and to discountenance their Causes and Practice of Intemperance.'*

Within 50 years the Temperance Hall was no more – the building was taken over by the new Independent Labour Party.

Source: *Historical Survey of the Bradford Temperance Society 1830-1897*, Lecture by George Field (19 December 1897)

28 Feb 1645   The House of Commons confirms new officers for Sir Thomas Fairfax's New Model Army.

Today marked an intriguing moment in the Civil War that led directly to King Charles I being deposed by Oliver Cromwell as Lord Protector of the British Isles.

The New Model Army was conceived in 1644 by Parliamentarians dissatisfied with the conduct of the Civil War. Although they had greater financial resources and manpower than the Royalists, most of their forces were raised by local associations of counties, and could rarely be used far from their homes. The army's leaders were suspected of seeking peace with the king. Parliamentarians wanted a more committed, flexible and professional force.

At the centre of this political infighting was Sir Thomas Fairfax, deemed to be a radical who wanted the king removed and supported Oliver Cromwell. The faction of moderates who wanted just to curb the king's power failed to prevent Parliament's decision in January that Fairfax be appointed as commander-in-chief of the New Model Army. The argument was re-run with today's nomination of his officers and again the radicals prevailed. The Commons resisted an attempt by the Lords to purge some radicals from the list. As a result, the radicals predominated under the Fairfax leadership. In June 1645 his New Model Army went on to win the crucial Battle of Naseby and the die was cast for the king's demise.

Fairfax (1610-1671) was born into a long-established family at Denton Hall three miles north-east of Ilkley and just beyond today's Bradford boundary. For five years he had become the most influential soldier fighting the Parliamentarian cause in the north of England. In particular, he had led Parliamentarian Bradford, especially in fighting Royalist Leeds – the first example, perhaps, of their local rivalry.

Fairfax had led his Bradford soldiers to a victory over Royalists at the first Siege of Bradford in December 1642 and next month took them to defeat the Royalist garrison at Leeds. In June, he was still in charge when the Royalists came back at the Battle of Adwalton Moor. Here, his men lost the battle, a temporary setback that in fact triggered a more lasting Parliamentarian victory.

Fairfax, however, did not support Charles I's execution or Cromwell's invasion of Scotland. Eventually, he played an important role in the restoration of King Charles II in 1660.

For some, the New Model Army is better known as a celebrated Bradford punk group created in 1980 and still going strong.

Source: www.robert-temple.com/papers/Offprint-OfficerList.pdf

29 Feb 1824   The Prophet John Wroe attempts to walk on water.

The Prophet John Wroe announced that today, Leap Year Day, he would walk across the River Aire at Apperley Bridge without getting wet. Reportedly, some 30,000 people watched him attempt this. In the words of William Scruton, one of Bradford's most reputable Victorian historians:

'The result may be imagined. The river Aire persisted in flowing its usual course, refusing to be divided, and, when the poor prophet launched his frail and trembling frame upon its waters, they proved as treacherous as ever, and John got a ducking. Nor was he the only one who made a hole in the water that day, but fortunately no one was drowned, and the prophet himself came worst off, as, in addition to his ducking, he was well bespattered by the spectators and with difficulty escaped a worse fate.'

We do not know if the 41-year-old John Wroe thought 29 February to be an auspicious date for such a challenge, the more so because it also fell on a Sunday, but we do know that he was driven by a vision revealed by God.

In 1782 John Wroe was born in East Bowling, Bradford into the family of a worsted manufacturer and farmer. He tried his hand at both his father's businesses, but in his thirties, with a family of seven of his own, fell seriously ill with a fever. He gradually recovered, but started having visions. A message from God told him to stop his worldly life and preach God's word.

He visited many countries in Europe in doing this before he founded in 1822 the Christian Israelite Church, which became established in Ashton-under-Lyne near Manchester. This church still exists now, but only in Australia. Its website refers to its founder as 'a native of Yorkshire' and continues: *'We believe God chose him to use as an instrument through which to shed further light on Scripture regarding His promises to Abraham, and about the ultimate destiny of the descendants of the twelve tribes of Israel, namely - Immortality in its broadest sense, and the establishment of God's Kingdom on earth.'*

The website makes no mention of the occasion on Leap Year Day in 1824 when God did not come to his call.

Source: *Round About Bradford*, William Scruton (1876)

1 Mar 2018   Anne Dyer is consecrated as the first woman bishop of the Scottish Episcopal Church.

Born in Bradford in 1957 and educated at Bradford Girls' Grammar School, Anne Dyer took a first degree in natural sciences (chemistry) at Oxford University and a job at Unilever as a systems analyst.

In her late 20s she trained in theology and in 1987 became one of the first women to be ordained in the Church of England. She served as a minister for 18 years in the diocese of Rochester, becoming an adviser in women's ministry. She completed a Master's degree in theology at London University and in 2004 was announced as the next Warden of Cranmer Hall, Durham, an evangelical Anglican theological college attached to Durham University.

In 2011 she moved to the Scottish Episcopal Church as Rector at Haddington in East Lothian. She chaired a review of ministerial training in that Church, which led to the establishment of the Scottish Episcopal Institute, now the Church's theological college.

In November 2017 amidst some controversy she was elected the Bishop of Aberdeen and Orkney and today she was consecrated. Four years earlier Dyer had signed an open letter to the bishops of the Scottish Episcopal Church to express support of same-sex marriage. The appointment process itself was not straightforward. Unusually she was not elected by the diocese itself, but appointed by the College of Bishops after the diocese failed to choose its own bishop. Two senior members of the clergy in the diocese resigned in protest.

In an interview just before her consecration she stressed her ability to rise above these controversies and make a success of the role:

'I am experienced in training people for a diversity of roles and I am confident the Church has a role to play in every community, town and village, as well as nationally. Everything I do is shaped and informed by my life experience as a woman ... I am a daughter, a sister, a wife and a mother. I have been very well educated at a girls' school and a women's college at Oxford University and I see this as being a privilege.

As a bishop, I will have things to say about the experience of women, especially relating to poverty, human safety and harassment.'

Source: *The Press and Journal* (26 February 2018)

2 Mar 1900   The *Bradford Daily Telegraph* has a big news day from the Relief of Ladysmith.

One month after the start of the Second Boer War in 1899, British troops were soon trapped in the town of Ladysmith by a much larger force of Boer soldiers. The siege lasted 118 days until 28 February 1900 when a relief force defeated the Boers.

The news broke in Britain on 1 March. Within hours the *Bradford Daily Telegraph* put out a special war edition and today it reflected at length the previous day's celebrations in London and the provinces. It had separate pieces from Leeds, Wakefield, Halifax, Lancaster, Morecambe ('Bradford-by-the-sea'!), Manchester, 'fervent' (sic) Liverpool, Birmingham, Edinburgh, Dublin and Brighton, but in prime place from Bradford itself, including:

BRADFORD REJOICES   *Many Flags and More Glad Faces*

"TELEGRAPH" FIRST TO THE GOOD NEWS.

'The news of the relief of Ladysmith, spread abroad by the special war edition of the "Bradford Daily Telegraph" published at 10.15, created immense enthusiasm. Never in our thirty odd years of history has there been such a run on news, and edition after edition was rapidly swallowed up. The local organ of Tory unveracity has published the statement that it issued the news in advance of us, but the public who were about at the time will at once refute that false and impudent claim.

The news was received at the Bradford Postal Telegraph Office soon after ten o'clock, and occasioned the greatest pleasure. It is not often the decorum of the office is disturbed, but on this occasion the staff gave vent to their feelings by cheering and singing "God Save the Queen", all work being suspended for a time. Similar demonstrations took place simultaneously at the Central Telegraph Offices in London and Liverpool.

During the morning flags were hoisted on public buildings, and the Town Hall held aloft both the Royal Standard and the Union Jack. The political clubs also showed the national colours, and flags floated from scores of other buildings in the city.'

Note: the *'organ of Tory unveracity'* is the *Bradford Daily Argus*, the *Bradford Daily Telegraph's* bitter rival.

The Boer War did leave an unexpected legacy in Bradford. As in many football grounds, at Valley Parade the steep terracing for standing spectators behind one of the goals became known as 'the Kop' after the hill of Spion Kop near Ladysmith that had been captured from the Boers in January.

Source: *Bradford Daily Telegraph* (2 March 1900)

3 Mar 1996   Jonathan Silver organises cancer charity event as a 'thank-you', (but finally succumbs).

The transformation of Salt's Mill since 1987 was going well. Jonathan Silver was working on new ideas to continue the regeneration. Having become interested in Lowry's paintings, he had been seriously considering converting the top floor of the mill into a Lowry Gallery. He was mulling this over in September 1995 when the unthinkable happened. Just 45 years old, he was diagnosed with pancreatic cancer.

The world changed immediately. He was booked into a London clinic for the removal of the tumour. Naturally everyone around him was extremely shocked and concerned.

To their relief the operation was a success and soon Silver was back at work. Before going into hospital, he contacted the comedienne Victoria Wood to perform a charity concert in support of Bradford's Cancer Support Centre. Today, a Sunday, was the date agreed. Silver put 250 tickets on sale at £100 each. Within five days they were sold.

In the meantime, having returned from California, David Hockney had started a new wave of landscape painting from his new home in Bridlington. On the night of the concert ten of these paintings were on full display. Silver also used the event as the opportunity to open Salts Diner by the side of the 1853 Gallery. It was to become a highly successful restaurant, very much part of the new experience of the rejuvenated Salt's Mill.

The charity evening was not the only highlight of 1996 that allowed people to forget Silver's illness. In October Prince Charles visited the mill. One reason was to hold a seminar for the Prince's Regeneration Through Heritage Initiative that championed the conservation of fine old buildings – exactly what had happened at Salt's Mill. The Prince was thoroughly impressed.

As two years previously, September brought very bad news, again without any warning. This time it was the worst news. The cancer had returned. Silver had died suddenly at home. That morning the documents had been signed, recommending him for a knighthood.

His partner at Dean Clough, Sir Ernest Hall, spoke for everyone about Silver: *'He was the most loveable, original and creative person. His extraordinary energy and indomitable spirit were a spur and an inspiration to everyone who knew him and make a world with him unimaginable.'*

Jonathan Silver's legacy is Salt's Mill as many thousands of visitors experience it each year. His spirit permeates the whole complex.

Source: *Salt & Silver: A Story of Hope*, Jim Greenhalf (1997)

4 Mar 1890   The Prince of Wales rewards Bradfordian at opening of Forth Railway Bridge.

Today, at the completion of one of Britain's most challenging railway engineering projects, the Prince of Wales (later King Edward V11) honoured one of Bradford's most influential public servants. Matthew Thompson (1820-1891) was the chairman of both the Midland Railway and the Forth Bridge Railway Company.

At the celebratory luncheon several hundred guests, who included Prince George (later King George V) and Monsieur Eiffel whose tower had been completed in the previous year, saw the Prince of Wales turn to his host, saying *'From now onwards your chairman will be known as Sir Matthew William Thompson, Baronet of Park Gate, Guiseley in the County of York'*

Born in Manningham into a prosperous family, Thompson had benefited from education at Giggleswick School and Cambridge University where he gained a degree in law. He was called to the Bar and practised for ten years before returning to Bradford to manage the family brewery business.

He also became heavily involved in municipal affairs. After four years as a councillor, then alderman, he was rapidly promoted to be mayor in 1862. He was extremely energetic and forceful. For example, he was responsible for the town's celebrations for the marriage of the Prince of Wales.

Thompson was persuaded to stand for Parliament, was elected in 1867 but did not find the life attractive for a man of energy and stood down within a year.

Having resigned earlier as a councillor, he stood again and was swiftly and unanimously invited to be mayor again in 1871. Unusually he remained mayor for a second year, which culminated with the opening of the new Town Hall in 1873.

From 1865 he was a director of the Midland Railway Company and was influential in the building of Bradford's new Midland railway station and hotel linked with it. The company was enlarging its business, in particular to exploit the lucrative traffic with Scotland. He had overseen the completion of the Leeds to Carlisle railway line in 1876, which required at its peak the labour of 7,000 men.

Eventually Thompson became the company's chairman, responsible for the formidable project of building a railway over the River Forth. It took three years to start and another seven to complete. The new bridge was over one and a half miles long.

Today's honour seemed a fair reward for Thompson's energy and organisational skill.

Source: *Bradford Remembrancer*, Horace Hird (1972)

5 Mar 2009   *Red Riding* three-parter starts on TV, inspired by the saga of the Yorkshire Ripper.

'In 1977, I was a lonely ten-year-old boy who was obsessed with Sherlock Holmes, who wanted to be a detective, who converted a garden shed into a private eye's office, who scoured the streets for apple thieves and missing pets, searching for crimes. In 1977, I was a lonely ten-year-old boy who found the Yorkshire Ripper.

In the early hours of June 26, 1977, I was five miles away and sound asleep in my safe little bed when sixteen-year-old Jayne MacDonald was subjected to repeated violent blows about her head with a blunt instrument in a playground in Leeds, a hundred yards from her own bed.

The next morning, I had my first case. I began to snip out articles and photographs from the Daily Mirror, articles and photographs about the murder of Jayne MacDonald and the four other women who had died before her: Wilma McCann, Emily Jackson, Irene Richardson, and Patricia Atkinson. On the front of a scrapbook, I pasted a headline: "THE YORKSHIRE RIPPER".'

The writer is David Peace in *The New Yorker* (10 June 2013). Born in Dewsbury (1967) and educated in Batley, he burst on to the literary scene at the turn of the millennium, writing contemporary fiction based on current stories often with a strong Northern atmosphere.

His first major work was the *Red Riding Quartet* about the Yorkshire Ripper case that had gripped his imagination in the late 1970s, as for five long years the Ripper eluded the biggest police manhunt that had ever been mounted. The books deal with police corruption, stimulated by the many documented blunders that allowed Bradfordian Peter Sutcliffe to continue his appalling murders around West Yorkshire.

The quartet of novels was then adapted into a three-parter TV serial launched today with a star-studded cast on Channel 4 and then turned into a five-hour long marathon for the cinema.

5 Mar 1920   Workhouse inmate Mary Brannan dies aged 106.

Today, Mary Brannan, an inmate of Bowling Park workhouse, died at the age of 106. From Leeds, she had been in the care of the Bradford Guardians for 17 years, but was transferred to this workhouse just two weeks earlier. She attributed her longevity to *'a bit o' good baccy'*. An early riser even after reaching the age of 100, she had often been seen in the grounds at 5am enjoying a smoke before breakfast.

Source: www.workhouses.org.uk/Bradford/

6 Mar 1929   Albert Whitehouse scores a record seven goals in one match for Bradford City.

The first decade in the life of Bradford City AFC before World War One now seems to be its golden age. For 75 years after the war the club was in the doldrums doing little to excite its loyal fan base. At the end of the 1927/28 season there had been a real threat of liquidation only averted by generous donations from directors and fans, a not infrequent occurrence in the club's history.

The next season broke the mould when they were promoted to the old Second Division having scored a record 128 goals, still the club's highest-ever in one season.

The leading goal scorer was Albert Whitehouse who only joined the club from Liverpool in February and played just 15 matches. He managed 24 goals, a club record that was to last for another 31 years. The stand-out game for him was today's home match against Tranmere Rovers which City won 8-nil with Whitehouse scoring seven goals, another club record that still stands. A Wednesday afternoon crowd of 9,412 came to the game. Only once before, 40 years ago in its first season had the Football League witnessed such scoring and only twice has it ever been exceeded.

Three days later again at home, he scored another four in an 8-nil thrashing against Barrow and two weeks after that in their next home match a hat-trick in a 5-nil win against Wrexham. 14 goals out of 21 scored in three consecutive home games. Those were the days!

Yet in 1929/30 in their first season back in Division Two he only made 15 appearances, scoring a mere six times and in his final season at Valley Parade just eight appearances with no goals. After this he was transferred to Tranmere Rovers for whom he played one season before retiring on medical advice.

Source: *Bradford City Miscellany*, David Markham (2010)

7 Mar 1850   A council committee reports on the moral condition of Bradford.

Elected the second mayor in 1848, Titus Salt quickly set up a committee to report into the *'best means of improving the town's moral and religious condition'*. Today, the committee reported its findings to a special meeting of up to 40 aldermen.

It identified four lines of enquiry. The first theme was to *'ascertain the number and state of beerhouses and brothels, and by what legal or moral measures the iniquity and vice associated with them might be most successfully diminished or restrained'*. It found more than 150 beerhouses, almost none *'decent and orderly'*. Many were *'haunts of the vilest characters'* - brothels in all but name. The committee proposed some practical measures (eg fines for owners of such places).

The second theme concerned public grounds, music hall and closing hours of shops. Public grounds were unanimously supported for the purpose of recreation and exercise; some funds should be set aside – Peel Park became the first such amenity in 1853.

Similarly, a music hall was needed – 1853 also saw the opening of St. George's Hall. Finally, shops should close at 10pm on Saturdays, not midnight, and on other weekdays at 8pm (summer) or 7pm (winter). Many shops had already changed their hours, but the committee regretted that some back-tracking had been observed.

Third, education provision and availability of suitable periodicals were examined. As many children were uneducated, yet few of the existing schools were full, perhaps the town needed a different type of provision. Relatively little seems to have been investigated about this large problem, considering the greater depth of analysis about 'periodical literature', heavily criticised for being *'flimsy, uninstructive, licentious and semi-infidel'*. The committee praised the Mechanics' Institute (set up in 1832) which should be extended. Also, the wants of young women should not be ignored – *'on their moral and intellectual culture the permanent elevation of the other sex will greatly depend'*.

Finally, a sub-committee examined the feasibility of a town mission, or other directly religious movement, to improve the welfare of inhabitants. Many people were indifferent to religion and too often *'grossly ignorant and immoral'*. The answer was not more churches, but ways of bringing ministers closer to those people. The committee recommended two or three town missionaries to visit the poor in their houses. A cross-denominational approach was needed.

The meeting agreed the committee's recommendations.

Source: *Bradford Observer* (7 March 1850)

8 Mar 1973   Adam Curle is appointed world's first Professor of Peace Studies at Bradford's university.

The creation of the world's first department of peace studies is usually mentioned as one of the University of Bradford's key achievements, which came to fruition today with the appointment of its first professor. It brought together the university's original vision with the man who embodied its values.

It was not an accident that such a venture came to Bradford. There had been several prominent Quakers in Bradford's history and a firm strand of pacifism in the 20th century. An early champion was George Murphy. Appointed Chair in Finance at the university's Management Centre, he wanted to raise funds to establish the study of peace and conflict resolution in British universities and found willing support locally for a Chair of Peace Studies, including the Pro Vice Chancellor, a Quaker. In 1971 the Quaker Peace Studies Trust was set up by the Quakers' Society of Friends to oversee a public appeal for funds. It found influential sponsors, including the Chancellor Harold Wilson, Bradford's man of letters, JB Priestley, and major international names such as Joan Baez (American singer and champion of civil rights) and U Thant (Secretary-General of the United Nations). Funds were raised within ten weeks of the March 1972 launch.

The key appointment was the first Professor and today the university found its champion. Adam Curle (1916-2006) had an impressive CV. Educated at Charterhouse, he studied anthropology at New College, Oxford. He served in the war; after, he worked at the Tavistock Institute of Human Relations, helping to resettle British prisoners of war. After two spells in academia (Oxford, then Exeter), he travelled widely in Asia and the Middle East. In 1959 he was Professor of Education at the University of Ghana, becoming a Quaker, and then worked as Director of the Harvard Centre for Studies in Education and Development. He was a mediator during the Nigerian civil war (1967-70) and the 1971 Indo-Pakistan war. His pacifism was influenced by his mother who hated war, losing three of her brothers in World War One.

In his 1974 inaugural lecture at Bradford, *The Scope and Dilemmas of Peace Studies*, he defined what education for peace should entail. He retired in 1978 but continued to work as a peacemaker across the world. He was awarded the Gandhi peace prize in 2000 in recognition of his long commitment to peace work.

Source: Obituary, *The Guardian* (4 October 2006)

9 Mar 1694   Edmund Halley urges mathematician Abraham Sharp to apply for prestigious job.

'... being deservedly numbered amongst the most skilful mathematicians of his time, cultivated a lasting friendship with men most distinguished by a similar renown, especially with Flamsteed and the most illustrious Newton ...'

Memorial tablet, Bradford Cathedral

Today was probably the critical date in the life of Abraham Sharp (1653-1742). He received a letter from Edmund Halley (of Halley's Comet fame), the most eminent astronomer of the day, suggesting he should apply for the mathematical chair at Christ's Hospital in London – *'You may in my opinion stand as fair for it as you are deserving it, if it deserve you'.* A more ambitious man than Sharp would have grasped this opportunity. Some 15 years later, the Bradfordian confessed to another eminent friend, John Flamsteed, that *'I had no inclination for so laborious a confinement, being better pleased with an easier though less advantageous employment'.*

March 1694 was a pivotal time in Sharp's life for another reason. His notebook recorded that he came back to Bradford after living in York, Liverpool, London and Portsmouth. It never stated why he came back. He was never to leave Bradford again, until his death 48 years later.

Born into one of Bradford's most well-established families and living at Horton Hall, Sharp attended Bradford Grammar School where he developed a love of mathematics. When he was 16 years old, his father apprenticed him to a textile dealer in York, but that life was not for him.

It is not certain how he met John Flamsteed in London, who became the first Astronomer-Royal in 1675, but he started to work for him as an assistant, made himself indispensable and got to know other astronomers.

Reclusive by nature and obsessed with astronomy, Sharp maintained a close collaboration with a small number of distinguished, like-minded London-based friends, even when he returned to his home town.

He made a major contribution to astronomy. For example, he designed a new instrument, the Mural Arc, that enabled Flamsteed to measure the stars. This enabled him also to compile the three-volume *Historia Coelestis Britannica,* the first catalogue of the stars, a task that Sharp took over on Flamsteed's death to publish six years later in 1725.

One posthumous recognition came with the naming of a lunar crater as Sharp's crater – a place for Bradford on the moon some 250 years after Sharp's death.

Source: *Life and Correspondence of Abraham Sharp,* William Cudworth (1889)

10 Mar 1801 The first national census provides Bradford's population baseline.

With hindsight the first national census taken today and repeated every ten years occurred at the ideal moment for Bradford historians. It just about coincided with the start of phenomenal growth over the next 100 years that turned Bradford into one of the largest cities in Britain.

Until now there were no reliable records of the size and makeup of the population. The census provided a baseline of measurement that helped to plot future growth.

The 1801 census, however, was not in fact the first in Bradford. On 2 December 1780 a private census was undertaken as part of a legal case. Three prominent men, John Hardy, John Hustler and Samuel Lister commissioned this survey.

This shows that Bradford was already growing. The four townships were all growing faster than the average nationally, especially in Bowling and Horton that were starting to see the impact of late 18th century growth in ironworks. Across the townships the population had increased by more than one third in two decades.

Township	1780	1801	Growth
Bradford	4,506	6,393	42%
Bowling	1,119	2,055	84%
Horton	1,964	3,439	75%
Manningham	936	1,357	45%
Bradford borough	**8,525**	**13,244**	**36%**

Table 1 Growth in four townships (1780 to 1801)

Township	1801	1851	Growth
Bradford	6,393	52,493	721%
Bowling	2,055	13,538	559%
Horton	3,439	28,143	718%
Manningham	1,357	9,604	608%
Bradford borough	**13,244**	**103,778**	**684%**

Table 2 Growth in Bradford borough (1801 to 1851)

Here we can see the tremendous rapid growth over the first 50 years of the 19th century – nearly sevenfold across the parts of what became the borough of Bradford in 1847. Nationally, growth was 130%.

In contrast the growth in the nine townships bordering the borough was much less marked at under double on average in the 50 years. Most were absorbed into the new city by the end of the 19th century.

Township	1801	1851	Growth
Allerton	809	2,041	152%
Bierley	3,820	11,710	207%
Clayton	2,040	5,052	148%
Eccleshill	1,351	3,720	175%
Haworth	3,164	6,348	101%
Heaton	951	1,637	72%
Shipley	1,008	3,272	225%
Thornton	2,474	8,051	225%
Wilsden	913	3,454	278%
Outside Bradford	**16,530**	**45,285**	**174%**

Table 3 Growth outside Bradford borough (1801 to 1851)

Source: *Bradford and the Industrial Revolution*, Gary Firth (1990)

11 Mar 1893　William Gay of Undercliffe is laid to rest in the cemetery he designed.

Today was his funeral. William Gay (1814 -1893) was the 19th century version of Capability Brown in cemetery design. His name appears everywhere in the designs of prominent cemeteries in the North of England. Most of his life he lived in Undercliffe, where the cemetery is generally considered one of the most striking examples of Victorian funerary design.

Born in Ross-on-Wye, he moved to Leicester where in 1849 he was clerk of works at the new Welford Road Cemetery. While at Leicester, William was approached by the Bradford Cemetery Company to become its first registrar and manager. He moved to Bradford to design and lay out Undercliffe Cemetery that opened in 1854. The main feature of the elevated site was the great terrace running right through the cemetery, giving panoramic views over the town and hills beyond.

His advice was frequently valued by Bradford Corporation. For example, when they needed a new municipal cemetery in 1857, he assisted them in selecting Scholemoor from four proposals, because his surveys showed that it was both cheaper and more suitable for drainage than the alternatives.

In 1855 he won a competition to design the grounds of Toxteth Park Cemetery in Liverpool, opening the following year. In 1863, he again won a competition for the new Philips Park Cemetery in Manchester, which opened in 1866. In 1867 Gay laid out Belfast City cemetery in the form of a bell (possibly reflecting the 'Bel' in Belfast) and it opened in 1869.

Back in the Bradford area in 1871 he won contracts for broader landscaping work in Manningham Park (later Lister Park) and then for Saltaire Park (later Roberts Park). In 1873 he managed contracts for work at Brighouse Cemetery and Pudsey Cemetery. In 1874 he landscaped Lawnswood Cemetery in Leeds. Again in Bradford, in 1876 he designed the layout of Horton Park.

All the while he was managing Undercliffe Cemetery with regular improvements and extensions.

Gay's own headstone is very simple – *William Gay, his Wife and Son* – no dates, no names for wife and son and no mention of what he did. For the man who designed the cemetery and was held in the highest respect, one assumes he could have had the pick of the site, yet the grave is modestly sited away from the grand designs of the main terrace.

Source: www.undercliffecemetery.co.uk

12 Mar 1956 The *Yorkshire Observer* reports a surprise visitor to Bradford.

At the height of his fame Charlie Chaplin (1889-1977) was probably the best-known face in the world, and certainly the greatest comedian. Although his fame rests on the silent movie, he had already gained a reputation as a live performer before he hit the silver screen. He would have been the unlikeliest person to catch alone walking into a hotel, and certainly one in England, where he had not lived for many years.

It was, then, a great surprise that he was spotted on Saturday 10 March 1956 entering Bradford's Victoria Hotel, looking for somewhere quiet for a meal. Even more unlikely was that it was a journalist who spotted him, so ensuring a scoop for today's (Monday) paper. Actually, the hotel was full of journalists that evening as the Bradford Union of Journalists had organised a dinner dance. After a quick double-check that this was indeed Charlie Chaplin, the journalist gathered within minutes a group of photographers to capture the story.

When asked why he was in Bradford, Chaplin replied: *I've been to Switzerland to see my wife and my children, and I have some time to spare before I start to make my new film in England, so I thought I'd just come up here to look around.* It was a kind of sentimental pilgrimage and Bradford had changed greatly, he commented. He finished off by autographing and drawing on the back of a £5 note of his own for charity.

Chaplin had been to Bradford before.

At the back of the Alexandra Hotel was built the Empire Music Hall, which opened on 30 January 1899 with capacity for 2,000 customers. It was here, at the Bradford Empire, that a teenager called Charlie Chaplin first appeared on stage with his music hall act in 1906. He came back in 1909 and 1910, making in all three live appearances in Bradford.

On the last two occasions he was part of 'Fred Karno's Army'. Karno was an impresario of the British music hall and a comedian of slapstick. In order to avoid stage censorship, he developed a form of sketch comedy without dialogue, at which of course Chaplin soon became a past master.

As it was all the way to Bradford that Chaplin returned 50 years later, his early experiences in the city must have held good and strong memories for him.

Subject: *Yorkshire Observer* (12 March 1956)

13 Mar 1886   *Bradford Weekly Telegraph* runs a feature about the Polish Saltaire.

Today for the first time the story was told of one of the most enterprising ventures in the history of the city's wool business. An English-Polish partnership in the 1880s created a factory and village like Saltaire situated in the suburbs of Warsaw.

The partners comprised Edward Briggs and his younger brother John, and Ernst Posselt, a German working in Bradford. They envisaged a business that used their collective knowledge and experience to build a visionary foreign enterprise in Russian Poland, based on the Saltaire model of a village for the mill's employees. (Note: being part of the Russian Empire, Poland was not at that time an independent country.)

Their plan was to escape from fierce domestic competition and exploit the huge market for worsted yarn and cloth in the Russian Empire. Born in Heidelberg, Posselt, a naturalised Briton and long-term resident of Shipley, ran an international network of merchant and manufacturing firms from his office in Little Germany.

In December 1882 they wrote to the British consul in Warsaw indicating their intention to build a factory in Russian Poland. By the end of January he and his partners bought a 75-acre estate of undeveloped land at Marki outside Warsaw. They recruited 100 Polish girls and in June sent them for two weeks to Saltaire to learn how to run the factory.

The full story of this impressive venture is told by Sarah Dietz, whose late husband was the great-grandson of a Bradford manager who went to work at Marki. Her 2015 book is entitled *British entrepreneurship in Poland: a case study of Bradford Mills at Marki near Warsaw, 1883-1939.*

Source: *Bradford Weekly Telegraph* (13 March 1886)

13 Mar 1714   Sir Walter Calverley of Esholt purchases Dixon Mill at Shipley, the first of five fulling mills.

In the early 18th century Sir Walter Calverley of Esholt embarked on a series of purchases on the River Aire – Dixon Mill, Hirst Mill (both Shipley), Buck Mill (Idle) and Calverley Mill and Ross Mill (both Rodley). The first was Dixon Mill purchased today from the Dixon family of yeomen, owners for five generations since its construction in 1635. Water mills were essential to support the process of fulling, ie the cleansing of cloth (particularly wool). It is believed that Calverley wanted to encourage his tenants in the domestic woollen trade, then beginning to expand.

Source: *The Water Mills of Shipley*, Bill Hampshire (2000)

14 Mar 1908   A marble bust of its benefactor is unveiled at the first-ever Carnegie library.

When the great American philanthropist Andrew Carnegie (1835-1919) met Sir Swire Smith (1842-1918), prosperous local mill-owner from Keighley, for the first time on a trans-Atlantic crossing in 1892, the result 16 years later was the country's first Carnegie free library. It turned out that both men were passionate advocates of free libraries for the young.

When Carnegie was 13, his family emigrated from Scotland to the USA. The son of a handloom weaver, he received little formal education. Carnegie rose to become one of the wealthiest businessmen in America through investments in the railroad system and then in the steel industry. Aged 65, he sold his huge business in 1901 and devoted the rest of his life to philanthropy.

Born in Keighley, Smith became apprentice to a local worsted manufacturer and ended up as senior partner in a company making worsted machinery. In the meanwhile he developed an interest in technical education through the Keighley Mechanics' Institute. Believing that Britain was falling behind its international competitors, he travelled widely in Europe and the USA to develop his understanding and expertise, published many pamphlets and articles and was appointed representative on the Royal Commission on Technical Education (1881-1884). He was knighted in 1898.

When the two met, Carnegie and Smith had plenty of interests in common. Smith (a bachelor) invited Carnegie and his wife to visit him in Keighley where they met Smith's friend, Sir Isaac Holden. Also a Scot, Holden had, like Carnegie, become immensely wealthy through hard work and self-help. Smith and Holden made return visits to Carnegie in his Scottish properties. Singing the praises of local students doing well at the Institute, Smith lamented the need for a public library in the town to support them. Carnegie promised £10,000 to create such a library on condition that Keighley would invoke the Public Libraries Act (1850), which it did. The story goes that it also depended on Smith beating him at golf the next day, which he did. Carnegie was granted the Freedom of the Borough. In 1904 the new building was opened – the first of over 650 Carnegie libraries in the UK.

Today, Smith unveiled a marble bust of Carnegie that he had donated to the library in gratitude for Carnegie's generosity.

Source: *Keighley's Carnegie Public Library*, Gina Birdsall and Angela Speight (2018) in *The Antiquary*

15 Mar 1935   Inventor Percy Shaw starts making 'catseyes'.

Percy Shaw (1890-1976) had tried many jobs in factories and workshops, working for others and by himself. He always liked solving problems with the tasks that he took on. He dabbled with cars and was early to own one.

He lived all his life in Boothstown on the Bradford side of Halifax. But what made his name was what he discovered on travelling back out of Queensbury one night from his regular haunt at the Old Dolphin pub at Clayton Heights, near Bradford some four miles from home.

Queensbury is over 1,000 feet above sea level. Anyone driving towards Halifax at night from this pub has to take care in going downhill from Queensbury. In the early years of motoring, drivers might not have very good lighting at night. In built-up areas they used tramlines for reflecting back from their headlights. In 1934 the tram route from Halifax to Queensbury closed. Soon there were no tramlines that the driver could use for reflections. Shaw realised that night-time drivers needed a new source of help.

One very foggy night on descending the twisty road from Queensbury, he noticed a sharp reflection in his headlights, which caused him to stop the car. He realised that the reflection came from a cat's eyes. Moreover, he was traveling down the wrong side of the road and, had he continued, would have driven over the edge. It was a moment of inspiration.

He applied all his spare time to cracking this problem. After many trials and failures he finally took out patents on his invention. Today, a new company called Reflecting Roadstuds Ltd was created with Percy Shaw as managing director.

His life changed forever. He had a new obsession and made his fortune.

At the start he found it difficult to persuade the authorities to invest in his invention. However, the black-out during World War Two led to wide-scale adoption across the country's roads. By the 1950s he established manufacturing independence with a foundry to produce the cast iron base, a rubber processing plant to create the rubber insert and a glass manipulation plant to produce the glass reflector.

The 1960s saw the company expand its market overseas. In 1965 Shaw received an OBE for services to export. He had national exposure from a TV interview by the celebrated Alan Whicker, which revealed a reclusive lifestyle.

His is an amazing story.

Source: www.percyshawcatseyes.com

16 Mar 1848   The *Bradford Observer* reports a mass workers'
meeting at Peep Green.

'Throughout Europe, the enslaved people are casting off the tyranny of ages. Men of Yorkshire, you are now suffering in connexion with your countrymen, from the oppression of an aristocratic government. You are called upon to attend a Camp Meeting, on Sunday next, March 12th, 1848, on Peep Green to consider in what manner justice can be done to all.
— Attend in countless numbers, and make known your demands.
— The meeting to commence at twelve o'clock at noon.'

So started today's report in the weekly *Bradford Observer* about the previous Sunday's mass meeting. The venue at Hartshead Moor on high ground just outside Bradford and within good reach of the other main industrial West Yorkshire towns of Halifax, Huddersfield, Leeds and Wakefield was a favourite for such mass meetings, being also outside their jurisdiction.

During the morning many were seen walking towards Peep Green: *'The greater proportion of these pedestrians were cleanly-attired and well-dressed; but there were others, who, though they had evidently taxed their efforts, on that day, to appear decent, exhibited in their pallid countenances and their scanty and common clothing, signs of their sore and poverty-stricken condition: there were doubtless many of this class who felt indeed — and well they might — that they had wrongs to be redressed, redress them who would, or how they would.'*

Some 5,000 people had gathered when, after an opening hymn, the Chairman reminded them of the great Chartist principles of universal suffrage, vote by ballot, payment of Members of Parliament, and equal electoral districts. *'He asked whether the men of Yorkshire would submit to the tyranny and oppression which had been practised upon them for ages.'* (*'No, no',* they replied).

George White, the prominent Chartist campaigner, proposed the first resolution: *'That this meeting views with great concern the distressed condition of the great body of the people of this country, and is of opinion that it arises from the unjust system of government which at present exists.'* This was passed, as was the second: *'No measure short of the People's Charter will permanently remedy the condition of the people, and they would call upon all lovers of freedom to unite together, to make one loud demand upon government to cause such document to be enacted as the law of the land'.*

This became an important step in the Chartist revolt of 1848.

Source: *Bradford Observer* (16 March 1848)

17 Mar 1852   On St. Patrick's Day, the bishop lays the foundation stone for new Roman Catholic church.

The 1840s saw a steep rise in Irish immigration to the extent that over 10% of the 100,000 population were Irish, the largest such community in Yorkshire. Most came from rural Mayo and Sligo, were Roman Catholics and could not read or write English. One-third were woolcombers, much higher than in other groups; they were also the lowest paid workers. The Irish congregated in crowded, unhealthy slums in tightly-knit communities near the city centre. Their presence was much resented by the rest of the population.

Bradford was a nonconformist town and only had one Roman Catholic church, St Mary's, built in 1825 near the Anglican parish church of St. Peter's. To support the Irish influx, the town needed a new Catholic church.

The need had been long identified by the Catholic Church but it took time to raise the funds and find an appropriate plot. This was not easy because anti-Catholic prejudice made it difficult to buy land for such a purpose. In the end a Catholic layman had to act as middle-man buying the land in 1850 before revealing the purpose and selling it on in 1851 to the Church. The original sellers, Mary and Elizabeth Rawson, were said to be angry on finding this out.

The site was just off the top of Westgate, opposite Lumb Lane, near an area known as Black Abbey. Today in 1852, St. Patrick's Day was to be the date for laying the foundation stone of the church to be called St. Patrick's.

This was the occasion of a large ceremony. First, High Mass was celebrated by a large congregation at St. Mary's Church from where most walked quietly to the site of the new church. This was not a grand procession as the Church was sensitive to the hostility of the local population. Nonetheless, a large crowd gathered to watch the laying of the foundation stone.

Bishop Briggs of Beverley, the most senior Roman Catholic in Yorkshire, led the ceremony. Addressing the crowd, he reminded them that their Catholic ancestors had built St. Peter's parish church, where Mass had been said. He regretted the subsequent differences of creed and the recent ridicule and scorn of the local Catholics.

The bishop returned on 12 July 1853 to consecrate the completed church.

Source: *The Records and Reminiscences of St. Patrick's Church,* John Earnshaw (1902)

18 Mar 1914   The impresario's wife, Mrs Annie Laidler, opens the Alhambra Theatre.

Today at 2pm in front of a small group of friends and colleagues, Mrs Annie Laidler, the first wife of Francis Laidler, the owner, opened the new Alhambra Theatre. One hour later a more important group of guests, including the Lord Mayor, came for an afternoon tea to inspect the city's new facility, described as Yorkshire's Premier Theatre of Varieties.

In the 21st century the Alhambra is Bradford's only full-time professional theatre, but, back in 1912 when he decided to build it, Laidler faced competition from the Empire Music Hall (Great Horton Road), the Palace Theatre (Manchester Road), the Theatre Royal (Manningham Lane), and from his own Prince's Theatre across the road, not to mention the growing number of cinemas offering an evening's entertainment. However, he had spotted the opportunity for a new theatre offering a more comfortable night out in relative luxury with velvet seats and plush carpets.

The design was deliberately exotic, in Moorish style with a distinctive dome supported by Corinthian pillars, illuminated at night. It could seat 1,800 spectators, including four private boxes and tip-up seats. All seats could be reserved in advance - an innovation for the time. Situated in a commanding position in the heart of the city, it looked and became the city's premier place for entertainment.

For the rest of his life Laidler lived for the theatre and the theatre was the Alhambra, although he owned others (The Prince's Theatre, the Leeds Theatre Royal and the Keighley Hippodrome) and produced pantomimes in many other cities. He even lived nearby, not in his home but in a suite rented at the Victoria Hotel, convenient no doubt for frequent rail trips down south.

In the last 40 years of his life almost every famous variety artiste of his era trod the boards at the Alhambra – Billy Cotton, Norman Evans, Gracie Fields, George Formby (father and son), Grock the clown, Tommy Handley, Will Hay, Henry Hall and his band, an ageing Laurel and Hardy, Jessie Matthews, Ivor Novello, George Robey, a young Ernie Wise and many, many more.

A year after his death on 13 October 1956, one impresario, Val Parnell, unveiled a memorial plaque for another in the foyer of the Alhambra:

'A tribute to the King of Pantomime, Francis Laidler, a philanthropist who loved to make children happy.'

Source: *Domes of Delight: The History of the Bradford Alhambra*, Peter Holdsworth (1989)

19 Mar 2018   Lord Patel is appointed Chair of Social Work England.

Today, Lord Patel of Bradford was appointed by the Secretary of State for Education and the Secretary of State for Health and Social Care as the first Chair of Social Work England, the regulator for all child, family and adult social workers in England. He had an impressive background for this role.

Born 1960, Kamlesh Kumar Patel arrived in the UK from Kenya as a baby and did not attend school until he was seven and then spent one year in an immigrant centre. A late developer in reading and writing, he was educated at Belle Vue Boys' Grammar School and Huddersfield Polytechnic where he attained a specialist qualification in social work. He worked in inner-city areas for Bradford Social Services. He then established a number of third sector agencies working with those misusing drugs and those with mental health problems, later moving to academia working with a number of universities.

Honoured with an OBE in 1999, he entered the House of Lords in 2006 as an independent peer and was later appointed Minister in the Government Whips' Office in the House of Lords. Lord Patel has held a number of high-profile public appointments on national boards, including the Home Office's Advisory Council for the Misuse of Drugs and the Care Quality Commission. He has been Chairman of the Mental Health Act Commission and Bradford Teaching Hospitals NHS Foundation.

He is national director for the Department of Health's National Black and Minority Ethnic Mental Health Programme Trust. Finally, in 2016, a life-long cricket fan, he was appointed Senior Independent Director of the England & Wales Cricket Board, the first British Asian to hold such a position.

One month after his appointment to Social Work England he wrote in the professionals' magazine for social workers: *'Those early experiences never left me. After a myriad of jobs in the private and public sector I eventually became a social worker. My role enabled me to use my experiences, my understanding and my commitment to social justice to help and support others who were vulnerable and at risk.*

As a social work practitioner, a manager, an academic and a parliamentarian I have always been committed to ensuring that the needs of those who are most vulnerable in our society are understood and can be met effectively, based on the best evidence of what works.'

Source: www.communitycare.co.uk

20 Mar 1906   Antiquarian William Cudworth dies, leaving a valued legacy about Bradford.

The grand old man of Bradford historical research died today after a short illness. Nobody knew more about Victorian Bradford and wrote more about it than William Cudworth (1830-1906).

Was it nearly 14 years ago when the great and the good of Bradford showed that they held him in the highest respect? They held several celebrations of his 50 years' connection with the *Bradford Observer*.

It began when the Mayor presented him with a purse containing £150 (then, no mean sum) and a gold watch that had been donated from a subscription testimonial set up to honour him for his services to local history.

It ended when the *Bradford Observer* held a dinner for him at the Alexandra Hotel, chaired by editor William Byles, whom Cudworth had assisted for around 40 of those years. He was presented with a gold watch guard and pendant, (to go with his gold watch), a handsome table ornament and a substantial cheque. A colleague spoke of Cudworth's qualities of industry, thoroughness and patience in research and singleness of purpose, which had led to his success as a journalist and local historian.

Bradford-born, he received only a basic education before being apprenticed, barely in his teens, in 1842 to William Byles, the proprietor of the *Bradford Observer*. Cudworth worked as a compositor in the print room for many years until Byles started to give him journalist duties, which allowed him to witness public affairs and meet those involved.

Having always been a great collector of newspaper cuttings, he started to pay weekly visits to the villages around Bradford. From this he published *Round about Bradford* (1876), which contained comprehensive information about the town's people and places. He was later to publish three similar '*Round About...*' books on the townships of Horton, on Bolton and Bowling and a third on Manningham, Heaton and Allerton.

His second book, *Historical Notes on the Bradford Corporation* (1881) contained invaluable information about Bradford, both before and after incorporation, including portraits of all the town's mayors and other municipal officials.

Other books included *Yorkshire Dialect Sketches* (1884), *Musical Reminiscences of Bradford* (1885), *Worstedopolis* (1888), which was a history of Bradford's main industry, and the main biography of Bradford astronomer, Abraham Sharp (1889).

He was also a founder member and president of the Bradford Historical and Antiquarian Society.

We are all in his debt.

Source: www.undercliffecemetery.co.uk/about/history/william-cudworth/

21 Mar 1851   Lockwood and Mawson secure their big break in becoming Bradford's premier architects.

Today, the sub-committee, set up by the Corporation, finally decided that out of 24 designs the one submitted by Lockwood and Mawson was the winner. The competition concerned the design of St. George's Hall, the new concert hall that came to be used also for large events and public meetings.

At the start of a phase of new building, the architects now fully justified their recent move to Bradford. Henry Lockwood (1811-1878) from Doncaster had trained in London and practised in Hull for some 16 years. In 1850 he entered a partnership with the 21-year-old William Mawson (1828-1889) from Leeds; they opened an office in Bradford. Lockwood had recognised the opportunity of a town rapidly expanding.

Designing St. George's Hall was a prestigious project. Before it was built, the new partnership won an even larger commission – the building of the new Saltaire Mill and soon afterwards the new Saltaire village for the workers. This was no public competition, but clearly Titus Salt was convinced by the work of these two architects who had just secured such a major public project. When Salt ran out of family names for streets in Saltaire village, he named a Lockwood Street and Mawson Street.

Lockwood and Mawson won many important contracts and their names pop up time and again in any description of buildings designed over the next 25 years – Bradford Union Workhouse (1852), Saltaire Congregational Church (1859), Lumb Lane Mills (1861), Eye and Ear Hospital (1861), Horton Lane Congregational Chapel (1863), Wool Exchange (1867), Great Northern (later Victoria) Hotel (1867), Saltaire School (1867), Saltaire Institute (1871), Town Hall (1873), Sion Baptist Church (1873), Feversham Street Board School (1873), Kirkgate Market (1878) and the Bradford Liberal Club (1878), not to mention several warehouses in Little Germany and private houses for wealthy industrialists.

Their work changed the landscape of Bradford.

Source: *Salt & Silver: A Story of Hope*, Jim Greenhalf (1997)

21 Mar 1904   Eastbrook Hall opens.

Today, this Methodist chapel just by Little Germany was opened. Known as 'the Methodist cathedral of the north', it had a fine, galleried hall which saw large and fervent gatherings. It replaced an earlier Methodist chapel built in 1825. Previously, it had been the site of a private town house from 1797 owned by Edmund Peckover, wool merchant, that was surrounded by a park with a large lake.

Now it is a Grade II listed building, divided into flats.

22 Mar 1866 Henry Ripley issues the first tender for construction of Ripleyville.

WORKING MEN'S DWELLINGS

To Excavators, Masons, Joiners, Plumbers, Plasterers, Slaters, and Painters. TO BE LET. The several Works required in the Erection of Fifty One DWELLINGHOUSES, in the township of Bowling, in three blocks. Contract A, 18 houses, contract B, 19 houses, contract C, 1 house.

Today's advertisement in the *Bradford Observer* marked the first step in a new housing development called Ripleyville. Henry Ripley (1813-1882) was a prominent Bradford businessman, owner of the Bowling Dyeworks which had a near local monopoly in dyeing, and also owner of several mills. Like some other industrialists Ripley came to realise that factories would be more profitable if the workforce were housed in more comfortable dwellings than the hovels (usually back-to-back houses) that most of them were forced to inhabit in Bradford.

In recent years there had been a significant debate about back-to-backs. In 1860 the Corporation had passed a bye-law banning them, because they were unfit for habitation; builders fought back on the grounds that they could not build 'through' houses at an affordable price for working-class people. In 1866 the Corporation revised the bye-law to allow the building of back-to-backs *'provided they met stringent requirements for space, ventilation, water supply and sanitary provision'.*

Frustrated by the situation and perhaps encouraged by Sir Titus Salt's commitment to the Saltaire model village (1853) and by his school friend Edward Akroyd who had built Akroydon near Halifax (1859), Ripley issued a prospectus in November 1865 for the construction of 300 working-men's dwellings on his own land, comprising 'through' houses with rear yards, front gardens and internal WC. This was Ripleyville in the Broomfield area of West Bowling. Unlike Saltaire, inhabitants of the dwellings did not have to be employed by Ripley.

By 1871 200 houses had been built (a few included shops), also a school and schoolmaster's house, within a site bounded by three railway lines between East and West Bowling and to the north of Bowling Dyeworks. Next year the Church of England built St. Bartholomew's Church on land donated by Ripley. In 1881 ten almshouses were added.

History has not been kind. In 2001 Saltaire became a UNESCO World Heritage Site, a living testament to its founder. Some 30 years before, Ripleyville had been demolished with now barely a trace beyond the almshouses. Ripley is scarcely remembered.

Source: *When was Ripleyville built?*, RL (Bob) Walker (2008)

23 Mar 1827   Businessmen in Bradford meet to discuss a new bank for the town.

Rapid industrial growth needed a stable banking system. Banks in the 1820s were far from stable in Northern towns. For example, in Huddersfield five banks out of six came to grief. Banks were privately owned, not regulated and could freely issue their own notes. Money could be easily withdrawn at times of crisis. 1825 was a bad year for Bradford business with the Great Bradford Strike and stagnation of trade.

Towards the end of 1825, one prominent bank in the town collapsed and another, known as Bradford Old Bank, only survived after personal guarantees from local businessmen.

Copying what already worked in Scotland, new legislation created the joint stock banking system. This combined features of a general partnership, in which owners of a company split profits and liabilities, and a publicly-traded company which issues stock that shareholders are able to buy.

Today, a well-advertised meeting took place for *'inhabitants of Bradford and its vicinity at the Court House, Darley Street'*, presided over by Ellis Cunliffe Lister, one of the city's most prominent businessmen and father of Samuel Cunliffe Lister. The Bradford Banking Company was floated, one of the first such in England. Firm regulations about governance were established.

The new bank soon became successful, trusted and stable. The key person was Samuel Laycock (1786-1867), the new Treasurer and Secretary. Born in Wakefield, he moved to Bradford to manage the bank that later collapsed, but he secured the confidence of the five directors of the new bank, who were all members of well-established local businesses.

In gratitude for Laycock's contribution the directors proposed in 1844 a subscription for his portrait and a 'piece of plate' carrying the inscriptions of 147 subscribers, presented at a dinner in his honour. Laycock became the first Treasurer of the new Bradford Corporation in 1847, a decision no doubt influenced by Robert Milligan, its first mayor, who by now was also chairman of the Bradford Banking Company.

The bank itself in 1910 became part of the London City & Midland Bank which eventually became the Midland Bank in 1969. The new manager found Laycock's original plate hidden in the bank vaults. On 23 March 1971, just 144 years to the day after the first Darley Street meeting, the Midland presented the plate to Bradford Corporation, now on display at City Hall.

Source: *Bradford Remembrancer*, Horace Hird (1972)

24 Mar 2012   City Park becomes the new focal point of the city centre.

Today was an important day in the redevelopment of the city centre just as the opening of St. George's Hall had been, nearly 150 years previously. Then, a concert hall might not have been the top of the list of many people's priorities, any more than a new public space boasting over 100 fountains was today. Now nobody would question the value of St. George's Hall. Nearly a decade later, it is too early to judge the long-term value of City Park, but the signs are promising and remain so.

City Park is a six-acre public space right in the heart of the city. Situated against the backdrop of City Hall, it complements well the Victorian municipal building. It provides a link between the Victorian city centre of Bradford, the National Science and Media Museum, the Alhambra Theatre and the university, up a road to the west. If and when the derelict Odeon cinema by the side of the Alhambra is brought back to life, then the picture will be complete.

It contains the largest man-made water feature in any UK city, comprising fountains, fog machines, geysers and a 4,000 square metre mirror pool with laser lighting. The three tallest fountains can produce a jet 30 metres high, making it Britain's highest fountain. Camera-controlled lasers may play tricks with visitors after dark, as they capture them with loops of light in their stroll around an area as big as three full-sized football pitches. Other features include children's fountains throwing balls of water at one another and 'walking on water', which is a narrow causeway across the flooded area.

Originally conceived in 2003, it failed to secure funding from the National Lottery, but eventually work commenced in 2009. Controversially, it cost £24.4 million. However, the City Council estimated that City Park could generate £80 million per annum for the city's economy. It has made possible many events which could not otherwise have been held such as the 2013 Bollywood-style production of *Carmen*.

Later in 2012, the Academy of Urbanism awarded City Park with the title of Best Place in the UK and Ireland.

25 Mar 2015   Wishing to become a 'normal 22-year-old', megastar Zayn Malik quits One Direction.

'After five incredible years Zayn Malik has decided to leave One Direction. Niall, Harry, Liam and Louis will continue as a four-piece and look forward to the forthcoming concerts of their world tour and recording their fifth album, due to be released later this year.

Zayn says: "My life with One Direction has been more than I could ever have imagined. But, after five years, I feel like it is now the right time for me to leave the band. I'd like to apologise to the fans if I've let anyone down, but I have to do what feels right in my heart. I am leaving because I want to be a normal 22-year-old who is able to relax and have some private time out of the spotlight. I know I have four friends for life in Louis, Liam, Harry and Niall. I know they will continue to be the best band in the world."

One Direction say: "We're really sad to see Zayn go, but we totally respect his decision and send him all our love for the future. The past five years have been beyond amazing, we've gone through so much together, so we will always be friends ... "'

Can any Bradfordian have ever issued a more surprising resignation statement? In the world of pop music, can there have been a split so seemingly free of rancour or personality clashes?

Born in East Bowling in 1993 into a working class family, his father a British Pakistani and his mother mixed British/Irish, Zayn Malik had shot to celebrity status in his late teens after appearing in the ITV talent show *X Factor*. In 2010 he was put with four others to compete as a boy band, finishing third. They completed an *X Factor Live* tour of the UK. The programme's Simon Cowell gave them a £2m record contract and they hit the USA No 1 spot with their first four albums – a record. They also completed three world tours and were on the fourth when the news broke today.

Despite the stardom, Malik remains proud of his roots. In a 2017 *Vogue* interview, he said: *'I am from Bradford... a place with a long history of survival, an essential beat in the heart of what makes Britain great.'*

Source: *Sydney Morning Herald* (26 March 2015)

26 Mar 1972   Bradford's last trolley-bus completes its journey.

A Bradford trolley-bus in its familiar light-blue livery and with a special sign at the front saying 'SPECIAL - BRADFORD'S LAST TROLLEYBUS' set off from the city centre bound for Thornton on its last journey. It also marked the end of a 61-year-old association with this 20th century form of transport. With crowds watching, when the bus finally pulled into its garage, the Lord Mayor officially switched off the power, signalling the end of the city's trolley-buses.

As it was the first place in the UK to start operating trolley-buses and today was the last to close them down, Bradford can claim to be the country's home of the trolley-bus. Just before this date it had the distinction of being the longest surviving trolley-bus system in the world, although soon after this record was handed over to Shanghai.

The distinctive trolley-buses were a familiar sight moving silently up and down the hills of Bradford, in and out of the city centre. Not only were they quiet, but they were clean and could accelerate well on Bradford's hills.

They, however, had drawbacks. If there was a power cut, they all ground to a halt. As they were not able to overtake, they sometimes ran in convoys with the front ones packed and those at the rear almost empty. Occasionally the trolleys, which carried the wire from the overhead cables to the bus's motor, came off the wires on corners and roundabouts. In such cases the conductor had to dismount, pull a long pole with a hook on it from beneath the rear of the bus and use it to put the trolleys back into position.

In 1971 the diamond jubilee of the city's trolley-bus service was celebrated with enthusiasts from all over the country coming to admire what was the last remaining service. It had become a transport showpiece. Yet a year later the Corporation decided to switch to motor buses. It seemed as if the city should follow every other place in discarding the trolley-buses.

But they were popular and many regretted the decision.

Source: *Stories of the Century (Telegraph & Argus*, 1999)

27 Mar 1977 Integrated public transport at last becomes a reality at Bradford Interchange.

Since the railway arrived in 1846, public transport in Bradford always felt disjointed. The city had two mainline stations, each being a terminus less than a mile apart and each with services on different lines to Leeds. The West Yorkshire Road Car Company had a small bus station in Chester Street about 15 minutes' walk away from both train stations, its red buses largely providing out-of-city services. Dotted around the city centre were several termini for the light-blue trolley-bus and motor bus services catering largely for more local services around the city.

Local government reorganisation in 1974 created the possibility for better integrated services with the new Passenger Transport Executive for the whole of West Yorkshire.

Today saw the first step towards greater integration. A new bus and coach station called Bradford Interchange was built alongside the old Bradford Exchange railway station so that far more passengers could transfer from bus to train and vice versa. A large car park was also provided.

Six years later, the train station was renamed Bradford Interchange to link buses and trains in a covered environment. Even now Foster Square railway station remains separate, although a shuttle bus provides a link on a three-mile loop around the city.

27 Mar 1963 The 'Beeching axe' proposes closure of 13 railway stations around Bradford.

Today was a momentous day in the history of British railways. The controversial Dr Richard Beeching announced swingeing cutbacks with the closure of 2,363 stations (55% of total) and 5,000 miles (30% of total), especially in rural areas. In the Bradford area he proposed 13 stations for closure – Addingham, Apperley Bridge, Ben Rhydding, Burley in Wharfedale, Frizinghall, Guiseley, Ilkley, Laisterdyke, Low Moor, Manningham, Menston, Saltaire, Steeton & Silsden.

In the event, as a result of strong local pressure, the Bradford to Ilkley service was saved, including the stations of Guiseley, Menston, Burley in Wharfedale and Ben Rhydding (Note: Baildon on the same line had closed in 1953 but reopened in 1973.). Over the years since Beeching, Saltaire was reopened in 1984, Frizinghall in 1987 (after one teacher's campaign at nearby Bradford Grammar School), Steeton & Silsden in 1990, Apperley Bridge in 2015, and Low Moor in 2017. This left Addingham (lost as part of the Ilkley to Skipton line closure) and inner-city Laisterdyke and Manningham as the only three stations lost for ever as a result of the 'Beeching axe'.

Source: www.urbantransportgroup.org

28 Mar 1949   Sir Fred Hoyle coins the term 'Big Bang' in a radio talk.

In the early 1950s Fred Hoyle (1915-2001) was the world's leading astrophysicist. He was most famously involved in the debate about the origins of the universe, framed by two opposing theories – 'big bang' or 'steady-state'. He was a strong advocate of the 'steady-state' theory that the universe had always existed, and will exist for ever; as old galaxies die, they are replaced by new ones, created spontaneously in space. He contemptuously dismissed the 'big bang' theory, even coining the phrase in today's talk on BBC Radio Three: *'These theories were based on the hypothesis that all the matter in the universe was created in one big bang at a particular time in the remote past'.*

Hoyle came from the village of Gilstead, on the edge of the moors above Bingley, his father a cloth merchant and mother a piano teacher. He was educated at Bingley Grammar School, becoming its most famous pupil. He showed an early interest in astronomy and progressed to Cambridge University to read mathematics.

After a war break working in radar at the Admiralty, he returned to Cambridge as lecturer in mathematics, but focused mainly on research into the structure and evolution of the stars. This took him into the thinking behind the 'steady-state' theory. He was very aggrieved much later in 1983 to miss out on a Nobel Prize, which went instead to his American collaborator, when they explained how all the materials found on earth and elsewhere have been formed inside stars. Many of Hoyle's colleagues, too, were mystified that he had not been included.

In 1958 he became professor of astronomy at Cambridge and founded its Institute of Theoretical Astronomy, being director from 1967 to 1972. He resigned from Cambridge amidst arguments about funding, but collected many honours, including presidency of the Royal Astronomical Society (1971-1973), a knighthood (1972) and the royal medal at the Royal Society (1974) where he had been made fellow in 1957.

Alongside his research in astronomy, he wrote over 20 books about science fiction, many co-authored with his son, including his most famous *The Black Cloud* (1957) and *A for Andromeda* (1962) made into a TV series.

Although the 'steady-state' theory had been discredited by the time of his death, Hoyle was a very influential and highly respected astronomer.

Source: Sir Fred Hoyle (*Oxford Dictionary of National Biography*)

29 Mar 1881   Bradford's Reform Synagogue is consecrated.

On Bowland Street, off Manningham Lane, stands Bradford's Reform Synagogue. In the late 19th century this was a prosperous area, close to Victorian villas and private roads created for wealthy industrialists, their families and servants. Today the synagogue was consecrated, but why had this taken so long?

For around 100 years Bradford contained a small Jewish community of around 300 that was distinctive and influential. Most were Germans, merchants and philanthropic, all exemplified by Sir Jacob Behrens, who settled in 1838 and became a major contributor to commercial and civic life.

Bradford was turning into a prosperous town and German Jews had mercantile skills that it lacked. When they came to Bradford, they were middle-class, well-educated and committed to making it a better place from educational, social and cultural perspectives.

It was not a community, however, that was strong on Judaism. The *Jewish Chronicle* captured this in 1865: *'Merchant and professional families who had abandoned Judaism or were very lax, religious life was almost totally corroded, circumcision was rare. Christian marriage and burial common and they do not wish to pass for Jews, although every child in Bradford knows them to be Jews'* (11 August). When that year the Chief Rabbi visited Bradford in his provincial tour, only six persons came to meet him.

Although Bradford had already in 1864 seen its first Jewish Mayor, Charles Semon, it was not until 1872 when a Reform (rather than Orthodox) congregation was established. The next year Dr. Joseph Strauss from Stuttgart was appointed rabbi and later a Jewish Association (the congregation's first name) formed. From 1874 Sabbath services were held in the Masonic Chapel, Salem Street and later in the Unitarian Chapel, Town Hall Square. Other institutions followed – a local branch of the Anglo-Jewish Association, a religious school and a Jewish burial ground at Scholemoor Cemetery.

Finally in 1880, Jacob Unna, the oldest member of the congregation, laid the foundation stone for a synagogue. The *Jewish Chronicle*'s report of today's consecration was critical, its correspondent objecting to the lack of decorum, the use of a Christian choir, and too much English in the service.

Another 100 years later, Bowland Street had now become a poor deprived area, surrounded by largely Muslim residents, but the synagogue remained open for a much smaller and far less influential Jewish community.

Source: *Provincial Jewry in Victorian Britain*, Jewish Communities and Records (1975)

30 Mar 1851 New census finds Bradford the most militant non-conformist town in England.

For the first and only time today's census contained a separate survey on religious worship, completed by ministers of religion. The results showed:

In 1800 there had been six places of worship in Bradford – one Anglican church and five nonconformist chapels. The census showed that there was an increase of 12 conformist churches (including one Roman Catholic) and 36 nonconformist places of worship.

The attendances for conformist religions comprised 32% against 68%. The high percentage of nonconformist attendances in Victorian Bradford was

Denomination	Places of worship	No. of attendants	% of attendants
Conformists			
Anglicans	12	10,155	23%
Roman Catholics	1	4,028	9%
Nonconformists			
Wesleyan Methodists	12	9,785	22%
Other Methodists	12	6,852	15%
Baptists	5	5,082	11%
Congregationalists	6	5,803	13%
Other nonconformists	6	2,600	6%
Total	**54**	**44,305**	

no surprise, being reflected in the high number of nonconformist places of worship and the much higher profile of nonconformist ministers and public figures.

It was thought at the time that Methodists were politically quiescent, but other nonconformists could be considered militant. By this method Bradford had the highest percentage of militant nonconformists in the 65 largest towns of England.

Perhaps more surprising is the high percentage who did not participate in any religion – 57% of the official population of 103,778. This figure is common in all urban areas. The official census report writer commented: '*Even in the least unfavourable aspect of the figures ... it must be apparent that a sadly formidable portion of the English people are habitual neglectors of the public ordinances of religion.*'

Jonathan Glyde, minister at Horton Lane Congregational Chapel and the most respected Bradford clergyman of his day, had commented the year before the census: '*A large proportion of our inhabitants are neither connected with any of our congregations nor in the habit of regularly attending worship, but are either opposed or indifferent to the religion of Christ, and in too many cases grossly ignorant and immoral.*'

Source: *Victorian Bradford: Twelve essays* edited by SG Wright and JA Jowitt (1981)

----

30 Mar 1936 The boy Ernie Wise makes his first stage appearance.

A stage-struck, 10-year-old Ernie Wiseman from Leeds performed today in the sixth annual Nignog Review at the Bradford Alhambra. '*Like an old-timer, with such droll airs that the audience roared with laughter. In his tiny bowler hat and check suit he made a wonderful hit*' wrote the *Telegraph & Argus*.

31 Mar 1884   State executioner James Berry carries out his first hangings.

With three members of the family being hangmen in the 20th century, the name of Pierrepoint is generally associated with Bradford. However, the first hangman from the city lived in Bradford a generation earlier. Today, James Berry (1852-1913) executed the double hanging of Robert Vickers and William Innes in Edinburgh.

Born in nearby Heckmondwyke, Berry moved to Bradford. Aged 22, he married and started his first job as a policeman with the Bradford Police Force, serving eight years. As this did not earn him enough to support a growing family, he applied for the post of executioner after the death of William Marwood in 1883, but, despite being shortlisted. was unsuccessful. The successful man, one Bartholomew Binns, however, did not last long after two controversial executions and Berry took over within a year.

In eight years as a public executioner, he hung 131 people including five women. He admitted that he only did the job for the money - £10 per hanging or £5 if the condemned man or woman got a last-minute reprieve. This averaged out £350 per year – a good income for the time. He did make an important contribution to the technology of hanging via his refinement of the long drop method, which diminished the mental and physical suffering and became standard practice until the abolition of capital punishment in 1969.

There were some difficult hangings. For example, in the case of John Babbacombe Lee - *The Man They Couldn't Hang* - the trap door repeatedly failed to open. His sentence was eventually commuted. At another hanging later that year, the prisoner, Robert Goodale, was given too long a drop that the rope decapitated him, the only recorded instance of this happening in Britain. He also hung William Bury, a man who was suspected by some of being Jack the Ripper.

Berry was haunted by his experiences, especially when he hanged those he believed to be innocent. He was converted to Christianity. In 1894 Berry became an Evangelist preacher and a strong campaigner against capital punishment for the rest of his life.

He was the first executioner to write a book about his life.

Source: *My Experiences as an Executioner*, James Berry (1892)

LEFT: Bradford had never seen the like of Sir Titus Salt who dominated its life long after his death in 1876 (story on 5 Jan).
Credit: Richard Wilson Photography

BELOW: One of the finest memorials in Undercliffe Cemetery is a fitting tribute to German-born Jacob Behrens, one of Bradford's finest Victorians (story on 4 Feb).
Credit: Richard Wilson Photography

ABOVE: WE Forster, Bradford's most prominent politician of the 19th century, is best remembered by the square and station that bears his name (story on 11 Feb).
Credit: Richard Wilson Photography

RIGHT: The building of the huge new Saltaire Mill not only made Sir Titus Salt's reputation, but also that of Bradford's premier architect Lockwood & Mawson (story on 21 Feb).
Credit: Richard Wilson Photography

ABOVE: When his mill burnt down, Samuel Cunliffe Lister built a new fortune with his new mill and gave Lister Park to the city (story on 25 Feb).
Credit: Richard Wilson Photography

LEFT: Sir Titus Salt looks on in the rejuvenated Salts Mill arts and shopping complex, created by Jonathan Silver (story on 3 Mar).
Courtesy: Salts Mill

ABOVE: The Alhambra, Bradford's famous theatre, was opened just before World War One (story on 18 Mar).
Credit: Richard Wilson Photography

RIGHT: City Park transformed views of City Hall in 2012, one of several city centre improvements since the disastrous 1960s and 1970s (story on 24 Mar).
Courtesy: Bradford City Council
@ Dean Smith, Camera Crew

1 Apr 1974   Bradford Corporation expands into the City of Bradford Metropolitan District Council.

Overnight Bradford quadrupled its area and doubled its size, population and budget. Waking up today to the news, Bradfordians must have rubbed their eyes in disbelief before realising it was April Fools' Day. But they were wrong, it was true.

The most comprehensive local government reorganisation ever had taken place across the country, getting rid of a patchwork of local councils that had 'grown like topsy' over the years. The new blueprint comprised a two-tier structure of counties and districts. Bradford was one of 36 new metropolitan districts in six new metropolitan counties across England.

In the case of Bradford and surrounding areas, out went the borough of Keighley, the urban districts of Baildon, Bingley, Cullingworth, Denholme, Ilkley, Shipley and Silsden, part of Queensbury & Shelf urban district and part of Skipton rural district. Bradford Corporation also disappeared to be replaced by the City of Bradford Metropolitan District Council, which now took over all these neighbouring councils that had been abolished. People living in these areas (eg Keighley, Ilkley) would from now on pay their rates to the new City of Bradford Council. Bradford would, for example, become the custodian of Ilkley Moor, Shipley Glen, the Brontë Country and Saltaire. The new council was to have 93 councillors.

The old West Riding County Council also disappeared to be replaced, with largely the same boundaries, by West Yorkshire Metropolitan County Council, which now covered the five new metropolitan districts of Bradford, Calderdale (based around Halifax), Kirklees (based around Huddersfield), Leeds and Wakefield. The new metropolitan counties took over certain functions (eg strategic planning, fire service, transportation, trading standards). As part of this radical change, Bradford lost its police service, which became part of West Yorkshire Constabulary; it also lost its public transport function, which became part of the West Yorkshire Passenger Transport Executive (WYPTE).

There was no public pressure in support of the new structure, which had been the outcome of several reviews from 1966 with a focus on administrative efficiency. None of the old councils being abolished supported the new expanded Bradford.

The public were much confused over the new structure. Within 12 years the unloved metropolitan counties were abolished, their functions carved up and absorbed by the metropolitan districts. However, the West Yorkshire Constabulary and WYPTE both survived, and have done so to the current day.

1 Apr 1930   Clayton merges with the County Borough of Bradford.

2 Apr 1983   Boris Rankov makes his record-breaking sixth win in the Boat Race.

Today Boris Rankov broke a Boat Race record and at the same time inadvertently ensured that it would now be very difficult to even emulate. He had rowed for the Oxford University crew five times from 1978 to 1982 (once as undergraduate and four times as graduate). This was to be the sixth time, a record for any Boat Race oarsman.

However, he almost had to pull out two weeks before the race. Cambridge had threatened a boycott, because they claimed that 28-year-old Rankov was ineligible; he was now a paid Fellow, and not a student. Oxford denied this, maintaining his eligibility because he was carrying out research for his doctorate. He had been at Oxford since September 1973, graduated in 1978 and became a Fellow of St. Hugh's in 1981. After a meeting between the two sides, Cambridge withdrew their protest and agreed that Rankov could participate on condition of a rule change. Under 'Rankov's rule', no oarsman can compete in the race more than four times as an undergraduate or four times as a graduate,

Would Cambridge have objected if Rankov had not each time been on the winning side? In this sixth race he was in the winning boat again, by a comfortable margin of four and a half lengths. Much later he commented: *'Heaven knows what it must feel like being the losing captain. I can only imagine. Unbelievably awful, given what you go through. So much effort getting into the crew and then six months of your life sacrificed. The victory stays with you. I imagine the defeat does, too.' (Daily Telegraph,* 27 March 2009).

The biggest margin was eight lengths in 1981 and the smallest in 1980 just a canvas. The most unexpected victory was the first when the Cambridge crew sank. Later he umpired the Boat Race four times (2003, 2005, 2009, 2015).

Born in Bradford, Rankov was educated at Bradford Grammar School where he studied classics, learnt to row and left for Corpus Christi College, Oxford. With an MA and DPhil, he was bound for an academic career after rowing. He became professor of Roman history at Royal Holloway, University of London with research interests, inter alia, in ancient shipping. In 1987 this made him the ideal person for rowing master of the *Olympias,* the reconstructed trireme (170 oars over three levels) and most important ancient Greek warship.

3 Apr 1822   The Bradford Gas Light Company is empowered by an Act of Parliament.

The Commissioners who were set up to improve life in Bradford after the 1803 Improvement Act had responsibility for lighting. For the first 20 years little of any substance happened. Bradford streets remained dark after dusk, especially in the long winter nights, unless there happened to be a full moon.

Early steps to buy lamps and lamp-brackets had been taken. Lamplighters were appointed first to position the brackets, fit the lamps, and then supply for each a wick and some oil. However, the work did not go well. The lamplighters were disgruntled because they had to pay for breakages, which easily occurred on cold days. In the end the Commissioners decided to enter an agreement with a contractor, but again the experience was not satisfactory, as contractors had to be replaced for one reason or another.

New technology by the way of gas-lighting came to the rescue. From 1817 it had helped to light up the streets of London and a few other cities. In 1820 the Bradford Gas Light Company was formed with share capital of £15,000, but it required an Act of Parliament so that it could light the streets. Today that Act was passed so that it could *'construct works and supply the town of Bradford and the townships of Manningham, Horton and Bowling'*.

The first gas was supplied on 17 September 1823 for lighting; it was many years before it could be used for power or heating.

The supply of gas led to a new type of supplier/consumer relationship as the supplier now had new rights, eg to dig up streets to lay pipes, gain access to premises and check on usage. This led to some friction. It was, nevertheless, a popular innovation and led to pressure to designate more public highways, which then could be lit. Lighting also deterred people from dumping household rubbish in the streets.

Some 48 years later Bradford Corporation obtained another Act of Parliament for the compulsory purchase of the company. Ownership was transferred from the private to the public sector on 11 July 1871.

Source: *Bradford in History,* **Horace Hird** (1968)

4 Apr 1850   The inspector is shocked by the sanitation at Haworth.

During the 1840s an official government inspector described Bradford as one of the unhealthiest towns in England. Doubtless his comments were based on observations of the dirty slums in the town centre where many mills had sprung up in the town's rapid expansion. Had he ventured to the small village of Haworth on the edge of the district, he might have been even more shocked.

The clergy had a wider role in communities than just pastoral care; it extended to social welfare and sanitation. In Haworth, the Reverend Patrick Brontë was passionate in championing the need for better living conditions. He had, for example, chaired meetings about the controversial Poor Law Amendment Act in 1834.

He was only too well aware of the poor sanitary conditions in Haworth and surrounding area. His two eldest daughters had died young, both probably from consumption. In 1842 his curate died of cholera. Generally, there was a high mortality rate with average life expectancy as low as 25 years.

The lack of fresh water in Haworth was a major concern. In an effort to improve sanitation, Brontë prepared a petition, sent on 28 August 1848 to the General Board of Health in London, Having had no reply, he sent a second petition two months later.

Today, at last, saw some action. *'A preliminary enquiry into the sewerage, drainage and supply of water and the sanitary condition of the inhabitants of the hamlet of Haworth'* started. It was carried out by Benjamin Babbage, described as a 'superintending inspector'.

He was shocked by what he found. There were 69 toilets for 2,500 people - 24 houses shared one toilet and seven had no access to any toilet. The whole village had just 11 taps; two were out of order. One tap was within two metres of a large cesspit in the middle of Main Street. There were no drains, and human and animal effluent ran down the sides of the steep street. The village drinking water was polluted by rotting flesh from the overcrowded graveyard by the church at the top of the village. Finally, 42% of children born in Haworth died before the age of six.

As a result of the Babbage Report, and Patrick Brontë's persistence, Haworth gained a reservoir, a cleaner water supply and more toilets, which led to a transformation for the village that saved many lives.

Source: http://haworth-village.org.uk

5 Apr 1884   Bradford FC win the prestigious rugby union Yorkshire Challenge Cup for the only time.

From the 1870s, Bradford's most popular spectator sport became rugby union. Its most established club was Bradford FC, especially after the opening in 1880 of its new ground at Park Avenue near the new Horton Park (later, the home of the soccer club Bradford Park Avenue). This was also a new home for cricket with the summer game played on the other side of the main stand.

In 1880 a new club Manningham FC was then formed that quickly rose to rival Bradford FC with a new home at Valley Parade in 1886 (later, the home of the soccer club Bradford City).

Bradford FC had started playing rugby in 1866/67. As it prepared for the new stadium, it became desperate for playing success. The coveted Yorkshire Challenge Cup was the competition to win, especially as its new rivals across the city had already performed better.

Today at last in the seventh year of the competition Bradford FC reached the final against Hull, the match to be played at the ground of Leeds St Johns FC. Some 6,000 people travelled from Bradford, mainly by special excursion trains. A crowd of around 15,000 waited in much anticipation before the 3.30pm kick-off.

Bradford started as favourites, having had a much better season than Hull. The game went to form with a convincing win for Bradford, who scored one goal, four tries and one touchdown against Hull's one try and three touchdowns (Note: today's points scoring system was not introduced until the end of the decade).

Unexpected heroes of the day were managers in the telegraph offices in Leeds and Bradford. They ensured the regular transmission of scores, as thousands more gathered outside the telegraph office in Bradford to catch news of the game. The final result arrived three and a half minutes after the end of the match.

The crowd of *'several thousand strong'*, accompanied by the Great Horton Brass Band, gathered at the Midland Station to greet their heroes on the 7.17pm train and to carry them shoulder-high down Market Street and Kirkgate for a celebration feast at the Talbot Hotel. Decked in black, red and amber, the crowd cheered their heroes.

Bradford was not to see such a celebration of sporting triumph until that day in 1911 when Bradford City won the soccer FA Cup.

Source: *Room at the Top*, John Dewhirst (2016)

6 Apr 1896   The Riley Brothers put on the first provincial cinema performance at the People's Palace.

The advertisement for tonight's entertainment promised a new and exciting experience.

People's Palace, Bradford

Enormous Attraction for the Easter Holidays at enormous expense of

THE ORIGINAL CINEMATOGRAPHE

The greatest of all inventions

The rage of all London at present

See the Animated Pictures depicting every movement as in real life

Supported by a splendid Company of Star Artistes

The *Bradford Observer* promoted this special week-long attraction by explaining: '*The visit of the Cinématographe to Bradford (Peoples' Palace) will give the curious an opportunity of becoming acquainted with one of the most remarkable and suggestive of all scientific toys that have been provided for a generation which has almost ceased to believe in any scientific impossibility. ... A series of photographs of a scene depicting moving figures are presented to the eye in such rapid succession that the movements seem lifelike and natural.*'

The *Bradford Daily Telegraph* reported the next day a '*long and lively entertainment*', worth all the admission money: 'A *number of scenes – a barber's shop, a dentist's operating-room, a smithy, a regimental band in evolutions, etc, were thrown to the screen, and in the most vivid and realistic fashion the life-size figures went through various actions in the most life-like manner. A contortionist's performance and a couple of skirt-dancing views were depicted with life-like faithfulness.*'

The Bradford men behind the venture were the Riley Brothers, Herbert and Willie. Their father had bought them in their late teens a magic lantern, which fired their imaginations. They started by giving photograph shows for charities. The father formed a lantern-slide business in 1884, which the sons took over. It grew rapidly. Herbert emigrated to the USA to set up an American branch.

In 1895, inspired by a visit to Paris, Willie acquired the rights to the Kineoptoscope projector. Riley Brothers distributed the machine and started to make short films.

Willie continued in the emerging film business until 1914 when the business folded. Fortunately, he had already started writing novels and moved into a new career as a highly popular and prolific writer of middlebrow fiction.

The People's Palace at the bottom of Manchester Road became the Palace Theatre. Eventually it was demolished. Appropriately, where the cinema was born in Bradford, the land was bought for the new National Museum of Photography, Film & Television opening in 1983.

Source: https://www.victorian-cinema.net/riley

7 Apr 1847   Isaac Holden loses first wife to tuberculosis at critical stage of his working life.

When in old age and great wealth, living in some luxury at his Victorian pile of Oakworth House, Sir Isaac Holden looked back at his life, he might well have thought back to the crossroads he reached in his early forties both professionally and personally.

Having spent 16 years working his way up in a small mill at Cullingworth, Holden planned better things and approached Samuel Cunliffe Lister with ideas for mechanising woolcombing. Eight years younger, but already a much wealthier man, Lister, too, shared the same motivation. They soon developed a new partnership for a new square motion woolcombing machine. They agreed to set up a joint enterprise in France, then considered good for textile investments, where Holden would manage the factory and Lister would provide capital and machinery.

The partnership was initially very successful and Holden soon became rich. However, the two men had conflicting objectives. This led to a major split when they disagreed over the ownership of the patent for the square motion machine. This became an argument that was carried out in public via letters to newspapers and flared up from time to time for the rest of their lives.

The 1840s was also a difficult time in Holden's personal life. He had fallen in love with Marian Love when she was 16 years old. Five years later in 1831, after a clandestine courtship they married. Now today his beloved wife died of tuberculosis, leaving him with four young children.

At the time he was building his new business in France with Lister, he undertook to find a new wife. It was no easy task. From his Cullingworth days he identified Sarah Sugden, a deceased mill-owner's daughter. They were both Wesleyan Methodists who attended Eastbrook Chapel. He had to build a relationship with her almost entirely by correspondence from France. She seemed reluctant. He had to persuade her over several months with protracted negotiations about the terms.

Eventually they married in April 1850. Sarah did not like Catholic France very much and tried to persuade her husband to move back. Eventually they returned to Bradford in 1860. Still retaining a highly profitable stake in France, he opened another very profitable woolcombing factory at Alston Works. He became one of the city's wealthiest and most influential men.

His second wife died in 1890, seven years before him. They had no children.

Source: *Holden's Ghosts*, Tony Holden (2015)

8 Apr 1968   Brave air stewardess Barbara Harrison dies in runway drama of burning plane.

Today Barbara Harrison set off for Heathrow Airport to join the cabin crew on Flight 712, bound for Sydney, Australia. Born in Bradford, she went to a local primary school before her family moved to Scarborough when she was around eleven.   An air stewardess for almost two years, this would be her last flight and soon she would be known as one of the bravest women in the history of aviation disaster.

Shortly after take-off, the plane had to make an emergency landing on the runway after one engine had caught fire. Barbara's job was to help the steward open the emergency rear chute and help passengers off. However, the chute became twisted and the steward was stranded in sorting it out. Left alone, she assisted many to leave, but the flames intensified and she tried desperately to help the last passenger, who was elderly and disabled. Both died in the smoke and flames.

One year later, Barbara was awarded the George Cross, the first woman to ever receive it in peacetime and one of only four women ever to receive it.

8 Apr 1919   The tram girls step down.

Passing of the tram girls – An appreciation

'Today was the leave-taking of the dainty conductresses who in war-time emergency "punched our tickets" on the Bradford Tramways. How sorry we shall be to see the last of you we cannot fully express. You have been a war-time wonder. Munition girls, land girls, WAACs (girls of the Womens' Army Auxiliary Corps).. and all the great host of patriotic girls who slipped into the breach when the boys went away. All have their paeans of praise, but you seemed to be in danger of passing without recognition and unhonoured.

It must not be.

You achieved the impossible. At least, everybody told us when you went on the cars that it was "no woman's job" and that you would be under the doctor most of the time.'

Bradford Daily Telegraph

The war was now over. The economy went into a downward spiral. Jobs became difficult for returning soldiers ... Life returned to normal.

9 Apr 1890   The Barbarians Rugby Club is conceived in Leuchters' Restaurant.

It is not now an important sport here, but Bradford was once a major centre for rugby union. Before the advance of the Northern Rugby Union (rugby league) in the 1890s, Bradford FC was one of the country's leading union clubs. Its fixture list included prominent sides such as Blackheath, Newport and Oxford and Cambridge Universities. In the ten years up to 1895 it regularly provided two English internationals.

One of the long-term consequences of its influence was that Bradford was the place where the famous touring side, the Barbarians, was conceived. On their travels the 'Baa-Baas' play famous club sides and sometimes international teams. Membership is by invitation. Traditionally they play an Easter tour in Wales, which includes matches in Cardiff, Swansea, Newport and Penarth.

The famous Leuchters' restaurant in the city centre was an important hub for social gatherings, especially linked to sporting teams. On the corner of Darley Street and next to Kirkgate Market with its famous fish and fresh oysters, it was the place where Bradford FC committee men and others connected with the sport met.

At the time Bradford FC was the most active touring club in England and often attracted fixtures by clubs on tour. In April 1890 a team from Cambridge University touring Yorkshire clubs was based at the Alexandra Hotel in Bradford. Today, in the early hours after a team dinner at Leuchters following a game at Huddersfield, the idea behind the Barbarians emerged. The new club should be cosmopolitan, bringing together players from different clubs to play a few matches each year of adventurous, attacking rugby, and with the aim of spreading good-fellowship amongst rugby players.

The 'Baa-Baas' have played four times in Bradford. Their first tour in December 1890 included a match against Bradford FC (the winner is disputed). Returning a year later, they lost 14-nil, a record defeat over the next decade. In a sign of the sport's decline in the city it was not until 1965 when they came back to celebrate a centenary of rugby at Bradford RUFC and again in 1990 against Bradford & Bingley RUFC at Bingley, winning both convincingly.

What were once thriving places to meet, both Leuchters and the Alexandra Hotel have long since been demolished.

Source: *Room at the Top*, John Dewhirst (2016)

10 Apr 1848   Local Chartist meetings give strong support to National Convention in London.

Revolution was in the air. Across Europe mass protests were taking place – for different reasons in different countries. In Britain the Chartist movement was coming to a head. Today (Tuesday) in London a massive Chartist Convention was taking place.

'Fellow Men, the grievances of us (the Working Classes) are deep and our demands just. We and our families are pining in misery, want and starvation! We demand a fair day's wages for a fair day's work! We are the slaves of capital – we demand protection to our labour. We are political serfs – we demand to be free. We, therefore, invite all well-disposed to join in our peaceful procession'... ran one advertisement.

The venue was Kennington Common. Trains from all parts of the country brought demonstrators in their thousands. Press estimates varied from 15,000 to 50,000. Chartists returning to Bradford later claimed that the *'lying press'* got it wrong – *'300,000 people assembled together in one living, moving mass'.*

On the same day at noon, in line with the recommendations of the National Chartist Committee, a large local meeting was held in Bradford city centre at Peckover's Walk. It had started with a procession, waving Chartist tricolour flags (red, white and red with the words *'Humanity, Liberty, Equality'),* and with a hymn. The purpose of the local meeting was to stand formally by the National Convention. Here they did so with gusto and passion. Simultaneous meetings across the country would reinforce the unity of the movement.

Sadly, the National Convention was in the process of disintegration. The Government had made it clear that a procession would be illegal. Feargus O'Connor, MP and Chartist leader, had over-ruled some of his colleagues by going ahead, but on the morning changed tack by cancelling the procession and just presenting the petition, which the police allowed. All the bridges across the Thames were blocked by the police, the protesters were uncertain and heavy rain intervened. The gathering came to a dismal end.

Four days later (Saturday) another local meeting was held at Peckover's Walk. The attendance was *'meagre',* the mood downbeat and the weather dismal. The speakers were, however, defiant.

Further meetings on Sunday (Bradford Moor) and Monday evening (Peckover Walk) stiffened the Chartist resolve locally, but the bubble nationally had burst. Local protests were to remain for a few more weeks. The revolution was fizzling out.

Source: *Bradford Observer,* (13 and 20 April 1848)

11 Apr 1962   1960s Bradford is now described as *'a new ... city, designed for a multi-level style of living'.*

He probably became the most unpopular figure in Bradford public life in the 20th century – the man responsible for the wrecking of the city centre and many of its old buildings. But it all started with such optimism for post-war rebuilding and the official plan sounded so straightforward.

First period – 1960 to 1964

'The development of a portion of the Central Ring Road - Forster Square to Leeds Road thence to Manchester Road and Thornton Road and a road from Leeds Road to Bridge Street – are expected to be under construction or completed.

It is proposed to add to the existing shopping areas an area of land within the Central Ring Road.... It is intended that multi-storey buildings should be constructed on the area stated above for shopping and commercial purposes.

The development of the Central Ring Road involves the removal of warehouses....'

Development Plan for the City and County Borough of Bradford, approved by the Minister of Housing and Local Government, (21 December 1959)

The press reports of the initial phase were very positive, like today's piece in the *Daily Mail*. Bradford was now at the forefront of city regeneration and its architect was commended by his profession. The profession, though, was not architecture but engineering. The architect was engineer Stanley Wardley (1901-1965).

Appointed in 1946 by the City Council as City Engineer, Stanley Wardley was thought to have the most relevant qualifications in leading the city's post-war planning. His plan first produced in 1953 focused on city centre shopping and business offices supported by an inner ring road with underpasses. Wardley became an expert in planning for mass 'motorisation' of the city. *The Times* observed later that the new city centre was *'unashamedly the work of a great city engineer rather than a great architect'.*

Iconic Victorian buildings like Swan Arcade were pulled down and replaced by concrete and glass. Most Bradfordians watched in horror at the destruction of the city centre and its replacement by something that lacked any character.

Wardley was not to see the fruits of his vision for Bradford. While still working, he died suddenly in 1965. He did not see the full implementation. Nor was he to discover that the dream had failed. By the turn of the century the new 1960s buildings were being demolished so that the city might do better.

Source: Stanley Wardley (*Oxford Dictionary of National Biography*)

12 Apr 1839 A Bradford Philosophical Society finally gets off the ground.

There had been earlier attempts to found a Philosophical Society where the leaders of Bradford life could gather to hear talks on learned subjects.

The most recent attempt had been made in 1823 by Samuel Hailstone, a solicitor who lived at Horton Hall and also collected rare botanical plants. The Bradford Literary and Philosophical Society was to be funded by a £50 subscription, 42 persons subscribing. This would help to fund a meeting place and library. The scheme, however, was discouraged by the Vicar of Bradford who preached a sermon *'in which he enlarged upon the irreligious tendency of a philosophising spirit, several of the subscribers took fright and withdrew their subscriptions and thus a society so conspicuously formed was broken up'* (John James, *The History and Topography of Bradford*).

Today, 16 years later, a more successful venture was announced. This time it was the new Vicar of Bradford, Rev William Scoresby who was one of its leading lights. The founder was William Sharp, surgeon of the fledgling Bradford Infirmary on Darley Street, who had delivered that winter a series of scientific lectures. They must have been well-received because, when he suggested a new society to promote such talks, several prominent townsmen met to agree the arrangements. A first year programme emerged.

Most unusually for a vicar of his time, Scoresby had a strong scientific background. He spoke *'On the influence and advantages of Scientific Institutions'* and about *'Astronomy, or the Arithmetic of the Planetary System'*. Sharp spoke about *'The Formation of Local Museums'*. Other locals spoke on Grecian and Roman architecture, the construction of carriages and phrenology. Outside speakers were engaged for short courses on English vocal harmony, the poets of England and acoustics. The rules forbade any discussion of politics or religion!

The future looked bright, but Sharp, then Scoresby (elected President in 1842) left Bradford. There is no record of activity after 1843.

In 1864 a further attempt was made to resurrect the society. Leeds had a thriving philosophical society; why not Bradford? Led by Mayor Charles Semon, the revival was aimed at a much broader audience and offered not just high-class lectures, but a museum, library and reading room. It employed a paid secretary and curator. This time it lasted for the rest of the century.

Source: *Pen and Pencil Pictures of Old Bradford*, William Scruton (1890)

13 Apr 1904   Lord Masham opens the Cartwright Memorial Hall in Lister Park.

After revisiting in 1898 his old boyhood home of Manningham Hall in Lister Park, Samuel Cunliffe Lister (now Lord Masham) requested a meeting with the Lord Mayor. Shocked at seeing the building in a dilapidated state, he suggested a new building dedicated to Dr Edmund Cartwright (1743-1823). Although Cartwright had no direct connection with Bradford, he was the inventor of the first woolcombing machine, the basis of Bradford's 19th century prosperity, and he had been an inspiration to Lister. The invention had not earned Cartwright his fortune, but it had for Lister.

Lister later offered a gift of £40,000 to fund the new building. The Corporation agreed to make it a new art gallery and natural history museum with reception rooms for municipal functions. Unusually for Bradford, the contract was awarded to a London firm of architects, rather than a local firm.

The foundation stone was laid by Lister, now 85 years old, on 24 May 1900, but the construction was beset by problems. A violent rainstorm in July highlighted problems with the foundations, which added cost and delay, and then several strikes caused further delays of up to a year. By now Lister was nervous that he might not live to see his gift to Bradford come to fruition. After official openings had been twice delayed, finally the day arrived.

Today Lister led the procession in heavy rain from the city centre into the park, past his own statue, lavishly decorated for the day, and performed the opening ceremony. The building was grand and baroque, in stone and marble. The broad staircase led to a splendid statue of Cartwright, seated in academic gown, which won a Royal Academy award.

Lister was then entertained to lunch with 200 guests at the Great Northern Victoria Hotel. Cartwright's great-great-grandson toasted Lister, who in reply spoke about the nature of inventions. Prophetically, he commented: *'I have a very strong impression that the East will overcome the West in the coming years and that instead of our clothing the East, they will want to clothe us'* (Laughter!).

Three weeks later Lister Park was the venue of a much grander occasion – a royal visit to open the six-month Bradford Exhibition. Never can the city have felt so good about itself.

Source: *Cartwright Memorial Hall and the Great Bradford Exhibition of 1904,* Anne Bishop (1989) in *The Antiquary*

14 Apr 1841   Future Bradford MP Edward Miall launches *The Nonconformist.*

Edward Miall (1809-1881) lived mostly in and around London, but circumstances brought him to Bradford at a critical point in his life and during a turbulent period in Bradford's politics.

Like his elder brother who was a Congregational minister in Bradford, Miall was ordained as a minister, but he also became both a journalist and politician. As a Dissenter he was a strong advocate for disestablishing the Church of England. Today, Miall produced the first edition of *The Nonconformist* that became the national newspaper supporting disestablishment. He also published substantial books on the topic and set up the British Anti-State Church Association.

His campaigning led naturally to him wanting to become an MP so that he could change the law, but that did not turn out to be easy.

In 1852 he was elected to represent Rochdale, which according to the 1851 Census had come closest to Bradford in terms of its militant nonconformism. In 1856 he proposed a motion to consider the state of the Irish Church with the view to its disestablishment, but he lost by a large margin. As a result the next year he lost his seat.

When a by-election came up in Bradford in 1861, he considered standing, but withdrew in the face of opposition by many moderate Liberals. He also failed to get the nomination in the 1865 General Election. Another by-election, however, in 1867 gave him another opportunity. This time he was nominated but failed to get the seat by 400 votes.

In the 1868 General Election he was squeezed out of the second seat (two MPs for each constituency) in a vigorous contest by what were seen to be sharp practices by his opponent Henry Ripley. A court case ruled the election illegal and three months later it was rerun. This time Miall won. The victory after twelve years outside Parliament by the veteran campaigner was greeted enthusiastically by advocates of disestablishment.

Forster's Elementary Education Bill (1870) unfortunately meant Miall had to oppose Gladstone's new Government, because he refused to support its proposal to fund Anglican schools. He was rebuked. When it came to his own motion to disestablish the Church of England, it was heavily defeated on two separate occasions. He resigned in 1874 at the end of the Parliament.

Miall admitted defeat. The issue never returned as a serious political proposition.

Source: Edward Miall (*Oxford Dictionary of National Biography*)

15 Apr 2015 Thirty years on, victim of Bradford City fire raises legitimate concerns.

Any regular Bradford City supporter watching games from the old wooden main stand would have said, in hindsight, that the 1985 Valley Parade fire disaster was bound to happen. Years of accumulated rubbish under the wooden seats would easily go up in flames from dropped cigarettes.

The official Popplewell Inquiry fully supported this view. There was no dissenting voice until today, 30 years later when a new book was published. The author was Martin Fletcher who as a 12-year-old had lost his father, brother, uncle and grandfather in the fire. No fan had suffered worse losses. He had spent much of his adult spare time in researching the fire and found disturbing discrepancies, which challenged the official account.

For example, why did the Home Office Fire Research Unit show how difficult it was for dropped cigarettes to start fires in such a stand? Did people know that the then chairman, Stafford Heginbotham, had seen business premises burnt to the ground on eight occasions over 20 years?

Fletcher could not provide proof of an alternative explanation, but the circumstantial evidence raised reasonable doubts. However, despite some sympathy for his case there was strong opposition from the Heginbotham children (father died in 1995) and no stomach from the club or anybody else to instigate a fresh inquiry.

Fletcher's questions will now almost certainly never be investigated.

Source: *The Story of the Bradford Fire*, Martin Fletcher (2015)

15 Apr 1907 The 'great betrayal' splits Bradford FC.

Park Avenue had been the home for rugby union from 1880, then from 1895 rugby league. Now 12 years later change was in the air again. In 1903 the city's first professional football team, Bradford City, had burst on the scene, replacing its predecessor rugby league team, Manningham FC.

Harry Briggs, the man with the money and influence at Park Avenue, was known to favour a similar switch, but how might he persuade others? The 1895 changes had been deeply unpopular.

An extraordinary meeting of voting members was called today to discuss options. Briggs excused himself on grounds of illness, but he made the case by letter for conversion to soccer. Unexpectedly, members voted to return to rugby union. This led to a fierce argument in the press. A week later Briggs had the decision reversed on a technicality. Bradford FC were set on football, after all.

Source: *Life at the Top*, John Dewhirst (2016)

16 Apr 1985 The House of Commons debates the Honeyford affair.

Marcus Fox, MP, was lucky enough to win the ballot for tonight's half-hour adjournment debate in the House of Commons. He chose the Honeyford affair as his topic. (Adjournment debates are slotted into gaps in the House's normal business but have no motion to end them.)

Ray Honeyford (1934-2012) was the headmaster of Drummond Road Middle School, Manningham. He had written an article in the right-wing monthly *Salisbury Review,* which only had a small readership. It was picked up by the *Yorkshire Post* who reprinted it to a much larger regional readership, including local officers for Bradford City Council who decided it infringed its race relations policies.

Honeyford's point was that multi-culturalism (ie commitment to the presence of distinct cultural or ethnic groups within a society) was not working for children of Pakistani origin – 92% of his children came from the sub-continent. For example, he wrote: *'It is no more than common sense that, if a school contains a disproportionate number of children for whom English is a second language (true of all Asian children, even those born here), or children from homes where educational ambition and the values to support it are conspicuously absent, (ie the vast majority of West Indian homes, a disproportionate number of which are fatherless), then academic standards are bound to suffer.'* He also doubted whether his children were best served by common practices such as withdrawing children from school for months at a time in order to go 'home' to Pakistan, on the grounds that this was appropriate to the children's native culture.

Honeyford was suspended, reinstated and finally persuaded to take early retirement with an attractive financial package. He never taught again.

Fox was Conservative MP in neighbouring Shipley, where few, if any, of Honeyford's parents lived. He used his opportunity to defend Honeyford who, he claimed, was supported by all staff, most governors and many parents for exercising a democratic right to free speech in a professional matter affecting his job.

Max Madden, Labour MP for Bradford West, where almost all parents did live, was not allowed to speak, according to the rules of adjournment debates.

The issues, however, rumbled on and arguably played a role in the riots of 1995 and 2001, and in the reports produced about them that noted poor educational attainment in inner-city schools.

Source: *Education and Race - an Alternative View*, Ray Honeyford (*Salisbury Review*, January 1984)

17 Apr 1822 Luddites destroy new machinery at Shipley mill.

'On Wednesday last one of those scenes which have so frequently disgraced our operative manufacturers took place at Shipley near Bradford. Some gentlemen of Bradford had lately taken a room at a worsted mill of Mr Joshua Taylor at Shipley for the purpose of trying the experiment of weaving worsted by steam. The weavers of Shipley and some neighbouring villages, having learnt the intentions of the worsted manufacturers of employing steam looms assembled on Wednesday morning at Mr Taylor's mill and having obtained possession of the loom, broke it in pieces, and destroyed the warp on the loom. The constable of the township was obliged to consult his own safety by flight. The rioters, having effected their purpose, then dispersed.'

So ran the report in the *Leeds Mercury* on 20 April 1822.

The Luddites were a secret organisation of English textile workers in the early 19th century who aimed to destroy machinery as a form of protest against the loss of their jobs and livelihoods. They were not seen as politically motivated. They were said to be named after a Ned Ludd, an apprentice who allegedly smashed new machines in 1779, but he was completely fictional. Punishments were harsh as Parliament in 1812 made 'machine-breaking' a capital offence.

The movement started in Nottingham around 1811 and soon spread to the West Riding and Lancashire. This was the first incident reported in the Bradford area.

Not many other local incidents were reported, but John James, the local historian, refers to a much more serious incident on 1 May 1826 when a meeting of some 250 unemployed workers assembled at Fairweather Green. At around 5pm they proceeded to a mill owned by a Mr Horsfall with several power looms and started to attack the machinery. They moved on to Bradford Moor where they recruited another 200 before returning for a second attack between 8 and 9pm. The police read the Riot Act, the mob separated but returned two days later for further attacks. They were thwarted by some security measures that had meanwhile been implemented. Gunfire was returned. Two were killed and several wounded. A couple of rioters were sent for imprisonment at York Castle.

Source: *Village to Mill Town: Shipley and its society 1600-1870*, George Sheeran (1984)

18 Apr 1825   The Bradford Dispensary is officially opened.

At the start of 1825, with a population of over 26,000 and rapidly growing in extremely unhealthy conditions, Bradford had no hospital, the nearest being in York (from 1740), Leeds (from 1767), and Sheffield (from 1797). Local medical provision came in the form of three physicians and three surgeons operating from their private premises.

The problems arose not just from unhealthy living conditions such as lack of sanitation. One doctor, John Simpson, recorded in his journal: *'Within the last few months four people have been killed at the different mills by the same kind of machinery. On Saturday night last, a young man was accidentally shot and today a manufacturer has taken a quantity of poison ... also a man has had his skull fractured with an iron crow by one of his companions.'*

Something had to be done. At a public meeting on 3 November 1824 it was agreed that a dispensary be established, initially in temporary accommodation. Dispensaries were places that people could attend to receive medical help, but they had no beds, hence were relatively cheap. Patients either visited them or received home visits.

Today, five months later, Bradford had at last its first dispensary in High Street, opening its doors to around 10 patients attending a surgery held by Dr Simpson and a surgeon.

At the end of the first quarter Simpson provided a report to the local newspaper with a profile of diseases and treatments. Some 505 people were treated, of whom 15 died, 16 were 'relieved', the rest 'cured'. Over 19% complaints were described as 'digestive' and 11% as 'pulmonary'. The annual cost per patient was 4 shillings. The first year also saw the need for a waiting list for admission and a shortfall against expenditure of income from subscriptions and donations.

Within a year 2,465 people received treatment. In-patient accommodation was needed. Two beds were quickly provided and a four-bed unit was offered within a year for people requiring operations. In 1827 a new permanent dispensary was opened in Darley Street at a cost of £3,500 after extensive fund-raising.

The demand for beds increased. By 1833 the Dispensary had 12 beds. In 1835 it was officially described as Bradford Dispensary/Infirmary.

Source: *Bradford Charity and the Public Purse: A History of Bradford Hospitals from 1780*, Gary Firth (2000)

19 Apr 1891   Strikers win a propaganda victory to no avail over management at Manningham Mills.

On 9 December 1890 Samuel Cunliffe Lister, Bradford's biggest employer, posted a notice outlining 25% pay reductions for weavers, pickers, spoolers and winders affecting 1,100 workers (20% of his workforce), triggered by a tariff placed on imported velvet by the USA. His workers, he claimed, should accept more realistic wages. The virtual monopoly in velvet was now over. The cuts would apply from Christmas Eve; if the workers revolted, he would lock them out.

Lister refused to negotiate, despite in the previous year making a profit of £138,000 (£27m at current prices) and paying a 10% dividend to shareholders. The workers went on strike. Unions and others clubbed together to provide a strike fund, but it was a hard winter with snow till mid-March. The *Bradford Daily Telegraph* had regular updates, though past Easter nothing much had changed to give hope of a settlement.

They say that information is the first weapon of war. On 11 April the paper ran a piece from an unnamed source that Manningham Mills had bought a mill at Attleborough, near Nuneaton, with capacity for up to 2,000 workers and a large plot of land for immediate extension. The piece ended darkly: *'The opening of the mill ... gives cause for serious consideration for the strikers. I am afraid many of those who are now out on strike will never find work again in Manningham Mills.'*

Today (Sunday) two worker representatives visited Attleborough to see for themselves. They communicated their findings immediately to Lister's: *'The mill is only a small one ... The rumour that 120 women and girls and from sixty to eighty men are employed is a complete fabrication as the whole place is not big enough ... Whilst the rumours that a bigger one to be built behind may be correct, as yet the land is covered with trees ... The mill is not yet empty of machinery and the sale only takes place next Thursday. The Manningham strikers need not fear the Attleborough venture hurting them in their struggle.'* (21 April 1891)

A propaganda victory for the strikers quickly became irrelevant. By the end of April the whole strike had collapsed. Workers accepted the reduced pay.

In less than two years, the bitterness from the strike led directly to the formation of the new Independent Labour Party, appropriately in Bradford.

Source: *Little Germany: A History of Bradford's Germans*, Susan Duxbury-Neumann (2015)

20 Apr 1964   Brown Muff & Co celebrates 150 years of trading.

There seems to be no record of the precise date in 1815 when Mrs Elizabeth Brown opened a one-room draper's shop in Market Street, selling 'underclothing, fustian goods and corduroy' using a legacy from her late husband. However, the directors of Brown Muff chose today as the date to celebrate 150 years' trading.

In 1834 her son Henry took over the running of the shop and married Betsy Muff, daughter of a timber merchant. On his mother's death in 1845 he took his brother-in-law, Thomas Muff, into partnership. Two years later, as they expanded, they bought the shop next door. By 1850 the shop was styled 'linen and wool drapers, tailors and hosiers, portmanteau, trunk and travelling bag makers'.

Over the next hundred years the shop gradually grew in range and size, becoming Bradford's premier store – 'the Harrods of the North' as it became known.

The staff newsletter for April showed that the day was celebrated with a visit by the Lord Mayor and Lady Mayoress. The directors also commissioned a 20-page brochure about the Brown Muff story and a fine painting of the store by Percy Monkman, a celebrated Bradford artist (see picture at end of June).

The 1960s were to be the high point of their trading as they expanded into premises in Bingley and Skipton. The 1970s saw major changes that led to a takeover by Rackhams, owned by the House of Fraser. On 27 February 1978 the store's name changed to Rackhams. The name of Brown Muff disappeared for ever. The week before, Debenhams (previously Busby's) up on Manningham Lane, owners of the city's second biggest department store, had also closed. Rackhams continued till 1995 before it too closed.

It was the end of an era. Now the fine old building in its prominent position still stands largely empty, except for a coffee bar, small building society and betting shop on the ground floor.

Source: *The Bromuff Story*, Brown Muff (1964)

21 Apr 1864   John Ruskin's talk criticises designs for proposed Wool Exchange.

John Ruskin (1819-1900) was the most influential art critic and thinker in Victorian England. He had already given one lecture at the Mechanics' Institute in Bradford – his inaugural talk on 1 March 1859 for the Institute's new School of Design. The *Bradford Observer* called it a *'beautiful and suggestive discourse'* from a *'master of refined philosophical analysis and of gorgeous poetic eloquence'*. He had been scathingly critical of the relentless advance of industrialisation, the *'Goddess of Getting On': Mills, then, more mills, is that all?'*

Now he had been invited back to Bradford and to the Institute. This time the brief was his opinion of the designs for the prestigious new Wool Exchange. The final decision had not yet been made from those submitted. Seven hundred members of Bradford's establishment waited in eager anticipation.

We do not know the motives of those who invited him, but it seems most unlikely that they expected his opening remarks:

'In a word, then, I do not care about this Exchange, — because you don't; and because you know perfectly well I cannot make you. Look at the essential circumstances of the case, which you, as business men, know perfectly well, though perhaps you think I forget them. You are going to spend £30,000, which to you, collectively, is nothing; the buying a new coat is, as to the cost of it, a much more important matter of consideration to me than building a new Exchange is to you. But you think you may as well have the right thing for your money. You know there are a great many odd styles of architecture about; you don't want to do anything ridiculous; you hear of me, among others, as a respectable architectural man-milliner: and you send for me, that I may tell you the leading fashion; and what is, in our shops, for the moment, the newest and sweetest thing in pinnacles.'

Ruskin's criticisms were that the designs were arbitrary, not reflecting any prevalent taste. There was no coherence to the thinking of those commissioning the design.

Within a month the Exchange directors met and, after much debate, chose the Venetian Gothic design offered by leading local architects Lockwood and Mawson who won most of Bradford's important building design competitions from 1850 to 1880. They had played safe.

Source: *Bradford Observer* (3 March 1859 and 28 April 1864)

22 Apr 1898 Bradford Corporation belatedly honours Sir Henry Mitchell as its first freeman.

The Honorary Freedom of Boroughs Act 1885 allowed the municipal boroughs created in 1847 to honour as freemen *persons of distinction and any persons who have rendered eminent services to the borough*. Prominent cities such as Birmingham (1888), Leeds (1886), Liverpool (1886) and Manchester (1888) had within a year or two already honoured their first freemen, but it took 13 years before Bradford decided to honour one of its own. When it did do so, it was overdue and almost too late.

Certainly the man's achievements that led to the honour were well known by the start of the 1890s when his reputation had already extended well beyond Bradford. For example, *Vanity Fair* published his portrait by a famous watercolorist on 5 July 1890.

Sir Henry Mitchell (1824-1898) was seriously unwell when today Bradford Corporation held a special meeting to support the recommendation that he should be made its first freeman. Many councillors gave fulsome tribute to Sir Henry's commercial leadership, philanthropy and steadfast support of the city.

In particular, the Mayor asserted: *'The resolution, he was sure, would have their hearty and cordial support. It was the first time in the history of Bradford that a citizen had been placed in this important and unique position. He was sorry to say that circumstances did not permit of much time being lost'*. A small deputation, including the Mayor and the Town Clerk, agreed to visit him later that afternoon at his Manningham home, having checked that he would be well enough to see them.

Notwithstanding the hurried circumstances, Sir Henry Mitchell was a worthy recipient of the honour bestowed upon him. Not only had he been the main champion of Bradford Technical College that opened in 1882, he had been at the forefront of city life for many years. He had been President of the Bradford Chamber of Commerce for six years, he had been for many years a Governor of Bradford Grammar School during its resurgence under the headmastership of Rev WH Keeling and he had been Mayor of the city.

Five days later Sir Henry Mitchell died, followed after three days by a funeral attended by thousands.

Source: *Bradford Daily Telegraph* (23 April 1898)

23 Apr 1702   On St. George's Day Bradford's Archbishop of York preaches at the Queen's coronation.

John Sharp (1645-1714) was the first Bradfordian to become a national figure. As Archbishop of York he developed a close relationship with Queen Anne that led her to ask him to preach today at her coronation rather than the Archbishop of Canterbury.

Born in Ivegate into a well-established Bradford family, John Sharp was educated at Bradford Grammar School and then for seven years at Christ's College, Cambridge. His father, a tradesman, was a Puritan and his mother a Royalist. This gave the family some protection during the Civil War and after.

In 1667 he was ordained deacon and priest in Westminster. He entered into service tutoring the sons of a prominent MP who eventually became the Lord Chancellor. Sharp was appointed the rector of St. Giles-in-the-Fields where he developed into a well-respected preacher often in front of influential congregations. In 1681 he also became Dean of Norwich, and then in 1689 the Dean of Canterbury. His connections in the Anglican Church led him to be appointed the Archbishop of York on 5 July 1691.

Back in Yorkshire, Sharp travelled widely across the see of York that covered the whole of the North of England, including Nottinghamshire. Travel was often difficult with roads bad in winter. He also had to spend many weeks each year in London.

All the while, the country lived through turbulent times with each new monarch. In 1686, when chaplain to the Catholic James II, he was suspended for ten months on a charge of having made some reflections on the king, and in 1688 was cited for refusing to read the *Declaration of Indulgence,* seen as a device for promoting Catholicism. When William III and Mary became joint monarchs, he became popular with Queen Mary and her sister Anne who became Queen in 1702.

He became Queen Anne's Lord High Almoner and confidential adviser in matters of church and state, completely eclipsing the Archbishop of Canterbury, whose Low Church views were not popular with her. He gave her support in introducing the 'Queen Anne's Bounty' that supported the poorer clergy. She valued his integrity and kindliness and he was her confidant until his death.

To this day, Sharp remains the most prominent Anglican to have come from Bradford.

Source: *Bradford Remembrancer,* Horace Hird (1972)

24 Apr 1847   The Privy Council grants a charter for Bradford to become a borough.

The 1840s were dark days for Bradford. Growing fast, it was not coping. During the decade the population of the four townships increased by 50% to nearly 67,000. No regulations existed for sewage, drainage or house-building, and very little medical or educational provision, except for the wealthy. The Board of Commissioners had some nominal responsibility for Bradford township, but no remit in Bowling, Manningham and most of Horton, where there was no form of local government. Its 58 members were self-elected and most hardly ever participated.

The case for elected governance ('incorporation') seemed overwhelming. Many were strongly in favour, but many were not, fearing the costs and offering other solutions. It was a continuous debate in the decade, especially in the columns of the only paper, the *Bradford Observer,* who were ardently in favour.

One petition to the Privy Council was rejected in 1845. The protagonists returned in November 1846. This time, 10,833 were in favour of incorporation out of the 12,187 who signed.

Today, the Privy Council, with Queen Victoria present, approved incorporation for the new borough of Bradford, comprising the townships of Bowling, Bradford, Horton and Manningham.

The new Municipal Corporation consisted of a mayor, 14 aldermen and 42 councillors. To qualify as an alderman or councillor, you had to be owner of property of £1,000, or a rating of £30 per annum, and be a resident (not a parson) within seven miles of the borough, and occupy a house, warehouse, counting-house or shop within the borough.

Assets were transferred on 29 December. The home of the new body was Station House in Swaine Street until the Town Hall was opened in 1873.

The Corporation's first officials comprised one head of police, three inspectors, six sergeants and 61 policemen; a town clerk, assistant clerk and accountant; a meat inspector, a nuisance inspector and nine others. These few officials had an enormous task of monitoring, enforcing and reporting on bye-laws passed by elected councillors of a borough growing rapidly beyond 100.000 inhabitants. Between 1852 and 1854, the Corporation approved 4,311 house plans, 138 warehouse and mill plans, the building of 246 streets, 15 churches and chapels and the supply of 202 privies serving 608 houses.

By any account, this was an extremely low-cost administration, but at least it was a start.

Source: *Historical Notes on the Bradford Corporation,* William Cudworth (1881)

25 Apr 1896   Manningham FC are the first champions of the breakaway Northern Rugby Union (NRU).

'A great deal of feeling was now displayed by the partisans of the respective teams and, as the game was rapidly drawing to a close, excitement was at fever heat. A huge rush of the Parade forwards got the ball to the home territory, and Brown, getting hold, dropped a goal, the ball striking the post and bounding over. This performance was received with tremendous cheering.'

What a way to end a dramatic match and a dramatic season!

In the last match of rugby league's inaugural season, Manningham FC became champions in this most exciting fashion. Thousands of rugby fans had travelled by train, coach and char-a-banc to Leeds to watch their team win at Hunslet to secure the championship. The game was tense, still with no score, when in the closing minutes winger Jack Brown had his 'Jonny Wilkinson' moment to secure a 4-nil victory.

The team returned in triumph by road to the city centre, then toured Manningham before arriving at the Belle Vue Hotel where they stood on the balcony giving speeches to the cheering thousands. The hero was full-back George Lorimer who had scored a third of the team's points in the 42 match season (33 Manningham victories).

The season had started almost as dramatically. Over the summer there had been much controversy amongst rugby clubs in Yorkshire and Lancashire about breaking away from the English Rugby Union. The issues were complex but payment to players was one central question. Finally, on 29 August 1895 at a famous meeting 22 northern clubs agreed to break away. The NRU was born, and with it rugby league. Nine days later they played the first round of matches.

Seven years afterwards in an equally dramatic close season Manningham FC stopped playing rugby league to be replaced by Bradford City AFC playing soccer in the Football League.

Source: *Bradford Daily Telegraph* (27 April 1896)

25 Apr 1964   Jim Fryatt of Park Avenue scores fastest-ever goal in English professional football.

Today Jim Fryatt, Bradford Park Avenue's centre forward, scored what remains the fastest-ever goal in English professional football. His first touch was to kick off to a colleague who passed forward to the right winger who centred for Fryatt to head home. Four touches, four seconds!

No film evidence survives, but referee Bob Simons was adamant that, stopwatch still in hand, he had timed the goal accurately.

26 Apr 1911   Bradford City beat Newcastle United in a replay to win the FA Cup for the only time.

Newcastle United were one of the top dogs in English football. They had been First Division champions three times between 1905 and 1909 and losing FA Cup finalists in 1905, 1906 and 1908, finally winning in 1910. As current FA Cup holders, they had now reached the Cup Final again. They were the favourites.

Their opponents were new boys. Bradford City, a football club for eight years, had never won a trophy. On the way to the final they had beaten New Brompton (away), Norwich City (Southern League), Grimsby Town and Burnley (all at Valley Parade), and finally Blackburn Rovers 3-0 in the semi-final at Sheffield United.

Today was, in fact, a replay at Manchester's new Old Trafford stadium. The previous Saturday the two teams had met at Crystal Palace in front of 70,000 and drawn 0-0 – one of the dullest finals on record with Newcastle the better team, according to the *Bradford Weekly Telegraph*.

The Lancashire & Yorkshire Railway organised five special trains from Bradford Exchange, calling at Bowling Junction, Low Moor, then trams from Manchester Victoria to the ground. The Great Northern Railway ran an excursion direct to Old Trafford, setting off from Thornton via Queensbury, Clayton, Great Horton, Bradford Exchange and Dudley Hill, but not stopping at Horton Park, opposite Bradford Park Avenue's ground. The Midland ran a train to Manchester from Bradford Midland, via Manningham, Shipley and Keighley. It was the biggest game yet to be staged in Manchester.

Gates were closed 40 minutes before the 3pm kick-off with some 30,000 locked out. This time the game was much better. City took the lead after 20 minutes with Jimmy Speirs, captain, heading into the net after the Newcastle goalkeeper had failed to punch clear and that was enough to win the game.

Thousands of City fans invaded the pitch at the end as Speirs led his team to receive the FA Cup. This was a new cup designed by Fattorinis of Bradford after the previous cup was stolen on display from a Birmingham shop.

On returning home to Bradford Exchange at 9pm the team were greeted by cheering crowds, estimated to be 100,000, nearly one third of the city's population, before they struggled to reach the Midland Hotel for a celebration dinner.

Amazingly, the next day City had a league fixture to complete at home to Middlesbrough, winning 1-0.

Source: *Glorious 1911*, David Pendleton (2010)

27 Apr 1987   Consultants advise council to redevelop Salts Mill as new industrial and leisure complex.

After Sir Titus Salt died in 1873, his business had a chequered history.

Twenty years later it was bankrupt. Only one of his five sons, all extremely well provided-for, remained in the business. The market had changed. The workforce was cut from 4,000 to 3,000 after a syndicate of four businessmen took over in June 1893. When the remaining three retired, James Roberts became sole owner in 1899. At the end of World War One he sold out to a new syndicate.

Business prospered in the inter-war years with mohair and alpaca now in demand for new products such as car upholstery. In 1958 Illingworth Morris plc acquired Salt's Mill, but the textile industry was in slow decline, shrinking in 20 years to less than one third. Salt's Mill closed finally in 1986. No longer useful for large-scale manufacturing, the building gradually became derelict.

Today the *Telegraph & Argus* published a story about a consultant's report commissioned by Bradford City Council. It set out how the mill could be redeveloped into a new complex at a cost of £14.5m. Before the council had time to consider the report, entrepreneur Jonathan Silver had already made his offer. It is highly unlikely that Silver's costs were anywhere as close to that figure. The writer Jim Greenhalf, close to him at the time, suggests that less than £1m was paid.

Months after the purchase in June, further information came to light from council meetings discussing Silver's planned change of use for the site. Now the feasibility study showed conclusively that Illingworth Morris believed that any income from renting out space would fall £80,000 short of running costs. This explains why they wanted to sell.

Later the report included this: *'Above all we recognise that Salts Mill and the adjoining greenfield site could provide a unique and exciting opportunity for Bradford to lead the way in urban regeneration by securing major reuse of this historically important complex .., Salts Mill as a major tourist attraction and with new commercial and cultural uses will stimulate the economy of the area in terms of wealth creation and most importantly up to 1,200 new jobs.'*

This summary anticipates more or less exactly what Silver did achieve. Remarkably, Silver would effect a lasting transformation in the asset of Salt's Mill for a fraction of the consultant's cost.

Source: *Salt & Silver: A Story of Hope*, Jim Greenhalf (1997)

28 Apr 1884   Manningham FC agrees a new claret and amber strip for the new 1884/85 season.

Today the AGM of Manningham FC, then playing rugby union, took a seemingly mundane decision about the colour of its new strip. It was to have a long-term impact on what we now might call the brand of professional sport in Bradford. The club had previously played in a black strip with red and black stockings. It now agreed to play in claret and amber hoops from the start of next season. On 20 September it turned out in the new strip at its Carlisle Road ground, giving what the *Bradford Daily Telegraph* called *'a decidedly better tone to the team's general appearance'*.

Outside the city, claret and amber are distinctive because they are so rarely used. In the city nearly all professional teams have worn these colours.

In England Bradford City is the only professional football club with these colours. In Scotland only Motherwell FC plays in them, a choice thought to be influenced by Bradford City. In Europe AS Roma and Galatarasay (Turkey) sport these colours. Elsewhere they are worn exceptionally by Washington Redskins (American football) and Brisbane Broncos (rugby league).

Yet within the city claret and amber have been the dominant colours. When Manningham FC (then rugby league) became Bradford City AFC, the colours were retained, probably to avoid upsetting further rugby fans who lost out to soccer.

Before 1884 red, amber and black were the colours of Bradford Cricket Club, formed in 1836. It amalgamated with Bradford Football & Athletic Club, formed in 1863, when they moved to the new Park Avenue ground in 1880. They, then, became the original colours of Bradford FC. These were retained when from 1907 the club split into Bradford (Park Avenue) AFC, Bradford Northern (later Bradford Bulls) and, soon after, Bradford Rugby Union (FC). Park Avenue did change to green and white twice (1911 to 1924, then 1958 to 1967). Other sports organisations in Bradford have adopted red, amber and black.

The original colours from 1836 are thought to have been influenced by the original Bradford Volunteers of the Napoleonic era. About today's decision, the influence again was the military, who were much in people's minds after the 1884 Siege of Khartoum. The same colours were used by the West Yorkshire Regiment based at the nearby Belle Vue Barracks, often used by the club for meetings and changing facilities.

Source: *A History of Bradford AFC in Objects*, John Dewhirst (2014)

29 Apr 1771   An Act of Parliament approves the Bradford Link from the Leeds/ Liverpool Canal

Today an Act of Parliament was passed that was to have a critical impact on the industry developing in and around Bradford for at least the next 50 years. The Act enabled the construction of the short Bradford Canal. It allowed the *'making of a navigable Cut or Canal from the Town of Bradford in the County of York, through several Townships, Parishes or Hamlets of Bradford of Bradford, Bolton and Idle ... to join and communicate with the ... Canal Navigation from Leeds to Liverpool at Windhill.'*

Twenty-eight subscribers were empowered to raise among themselves £6,000 before the works could start. John Hustler and Abraham Balme who had been instrumental in promoting the Leeds/Liverpool Canal also played a leading role with the Bradford Canal. Hustler raised the money, Balme as treasurer of the canal company controlled the expenditure and both bought the land.

Starting from Hoppy Bridge just under what is now the Cathedral, the canal was to follow the only valley route out of Bradford for three miles to link up at Windhill, near Shipley with the yet-to-be-opened Leeds/Liverpool Canal. It dropped 86 feet through ten locks before reaching the larger canal. The locks were the same dimension as those on that canal. The water was 5 feet deep.

We do not know exactly when the canal opened, but records imply that it was open by March 1774. There exists a note in Balme's diary that on 7 September he spent time loading up coal. He traded 25 loads of coal down the canal and sold it three days later. The fact that one horse could pull 50 to 60 tons by canal reduced the price of coal by half. Barges could now move coal up to Skipton and bring limestone back to Bradford to be processed into lime for building mortar. The extension of the Leeds/Liverpool to Leeds in 1777 opened up routes to Hull, London and the Continent.

The canal flourished until problems started to present in the early 19th century. Water had to be taken from the heavily polluted Bradford Beck near the source of the canal, polluting the canal which came to be called *River Stink*. With the new competition from trains, the canal never really recovered, although it managed to keep going until 1922.

Source: *The Bradford Canal: A Brief History*, John Allison (2005) in *The Antiquary*

30 Apr 2020   Centenarian Captain Tom brightens the
coronavirus gloom.

With the depression that descended from the 2020 Covid-19 pandemic, the country desperately needed some good news story to brighten people's lives. One hundred years old today, Captain Thomas Moore (1920-2021) certainly provided it.

It all started as a family joke in early April. If the old Army officer, born and bred in Keighley, walked around his garden with the help of a walking frame, 100 laps over ten days, ten laps a day, each lap 25 metres, then could he raise £1,000 for the NHS? His '100th birthday walk' started on 6 April. He gave a TV interview. Things snowballed. By 10 April he had raised the money, but he kept going and the money kept rolling in. By 14 April, he reached £2m, by 16 April £8m, by 18 April £23m and by today £30m.

He received congratulations from all quarters. Prince William called him *'a one-man fundraising machine'*. Tom teamed up with singer Michael Ball to sing together *'You'll Never Walk Alone'* live on television; the record from it unbelievably made Tom the oldest person to become top of the UK singles chart.

Tom came from Keighley. The son of a builder, he was educated at Keighley Grammar School. When World War Two broke out, he enlisted in the army and then in 1941 was commissioned as an officer. He saw active service in India, Burma and Sumatra. Now in the public eye, his home town embraced him, giving him the Freedom of Keighley.

When people saw him on screen, dressed in his blazer and medals, they saw a sprightly 99-year-old, speaking gratefully about recent treatment by the NHS and optimistically about the future. Most of those who died from the coronavirus were the elderly. Many over-70s had to be 'shielded'. Yet here was a war veteran, nearing his 100th birthday, who rose above all that and sent a message of hope to the nation.

Today was the climax of his story. He received over 125,000 birthday cards with a special birthday postmark, was made honorary colonel by the army, heard tributes from the Prime Minister and ex-cricketer Michael Vaughan (Tom loves cricket), watched a special three-times flypast by a Spitfire and Hurricane – it was on all the front pages.

What a month! What a story! And in July he was knighted!

Sadly, he died in February 2021 of the illness that led to his fame. .

1 May 1884   A commemorative key is presented to the man who broke the bank at Monte Carlo.

As I walk along the Bois de Boulogne
With an independent air,
You can hear the girls declare
"He must be a Millionaire."

You can hear them sigh and wish to die,
You can see them wink the other eye
At the man who broke the bank at
Monte Carlo.

This was a very popular song of its day (1890s). The man in question was long thought to be fraudster Charles Wells in the early 1890s. In fact, the bank was broken ten years earlier by a Bradford man. His name was Joseph Hobson Jagger (1830-1892). He was almost certainly the first to do this.

He was born into a weavers' family in a working-class, nonconformist community near Shelf. An unlikely candidate for this unlikely achievement, he was in deep financial difficulties, in danger of the dreaded debtors' prison and needing to support his young family.

In desperation he developed the idea of winning at roulette in Monte Carlo, then receiving much publicity. Familiar with managing machinery, he sensed that roulette wheels must have some slight bias to some numbers. He stayed in Monte Carlo for up to four years. Analysing winning numbers, he found that his hunch was valid. He applied his new knowledge and returned with a fortune of around £7.5 million (current prices).

Overnight, Jagger's life was transformed, but he did not exploit his fame. He invested his money in over 30 properties near his home in Little Horton, which he gave to family members. Some lived very comfortable lives as a result.

Only in 2018 has the full story been published after painstaking research by a family descendant, historian Anne Fletcher. The key to unlocking the true story came with a real key in stainless steel. Who designed it is not known, but it might well be Bradford jewellers Fattorinis who had a strong reputation for work of this kind. It has this inscription.

Presented to: JH Jagger Esq
By his friends and admirers
On the occasion of his great and unprecedented
Success in the ROULETTE
Which he achieved over the BANK at MONTE CARLO
Extending over a period of FOUR YEARS,
Having thus accomplished what the whole world had
Failed to do for more than a century.
Monte-Carlo 1st May 1884

Source: *From the Mill to Monte Carlo*, Anne Fletcher (2018)

1 May 1882   Bradford is extended to include Allerton, Bolton, Heaton, Thornbury and Tyersal.

2 May 1924   Newspaper reports Bardic Chair for Bradfordian poet at Eisteddfod.

Eisteddfods are associated with Wales. Occasionally, these music and literature festivals take place elsewhere. Today, the *Western Times* reported that a Bradford woman took the Bardic Chair for the poem *The Forsaken Princess* at the Southern Counties Eisteddfod in Torquay.

Information about Alberta Vickridge (1890-1963) is scant. From what we do know, her life is intriguing. She lived all her life in the Frizinghall house where she was born. Her father was a prosperous wool importer. With her two younger sisters she was educated at home and then at Bradford Girls' Grammar School. Inspired by both her governess and headmistress, Alberta became immersed in literature, especially poetry.

Admired by the likes of JB Priestley, she managed to eke out an existence as a poet and reviewer. She published about ten collections of poetry and to her credit published a long-running quarterly about poetry. Ten years on, the *Yorkshire Post* (29 June 1937) commented:

'With the summer number of that unique Yorkshire quarterly "The Jongleur", Alberta Vickridge completes her ten years as editor. She also completes her ten years as compositor, printer and bookbinder – in fact, the whole staff. For this journal is a single-handed effort produced in the attic workshop of Miss Vickridge's home at Frizinghall. I don't know of any other woman in the country who has carried out a similar idea over such a long period. The idea of the magazine, when it was first started in 1927, was to encourage a Romantic movement in modern poetry, and, though it has been slightly modified with the passing of the years, the main idea is still the same.'

The Jongleur lasted another 27 years.

Source: https://alberta-vickridge.info/

2 May 1981   The pink *Yorkshire Sports* prints its final edition.

Today Bradford sports fans lost an iconic newspaper. Ever since 1900, from around 5.30pm every Saturday, they could buy on the streets of Bradford and beyond a special *Telegraph & Argus* sports edition on pink newsprint. Before the days of the internet and the mobile phone, the "Pink'n" was the quickest way of finding out results and match reports of soccer, rugby league and cricket. The inside pages provided features about Bradford City, Bradford Park Avenue and Bradford Northern and in the summer about Yorkshire CCC. Justifying its title, the paper also covered neighbouring Leeds United, Halifax Town, Huddersfield Town, rugby league clubs and the supporting amateur leagues in the West Riding.

3 May 1974   Bradford Park Avenue goes into liquidation.

For 52 seasons Bradford had two professional football clubs mainly operating in the third and fourth divisions. For most of that time one or both had struggled financially, rarely having any funds to invest in either the team or the ground. Today that struggle came to an end with Avenue the one going under.

Liquidation with debts of £57,652 was on the cards ever since Avenue suffered the ignominy of being voted out of the Football League in 1970. At that time relegation from the fourth division did not depend, as it now does precisely on results, but on being voted back into the Football League by one's peers if you finished in the bottom four of that division. Usually the bottom four were voted back, but on 30 May 1970 for only the third time since the end of World War Two a new team (Cambridge United) was voted in. As Avenue had already had to seek re-election in their previous three seasons, the writing was on the wall.

After 1970 Avenue survived three years in the Northern Premier League, then had to sell its ground and in its final season shared Valley Parade with disastrous results on the field.

Ever since Avenue joined the Football League in 1907, there had been a running debate in Bradford's football circles whether the city could support two clubs. Other large cities did, but generally at least one was successful (eg Nottingham, Sheffield). In Bradford's case the two had competed in the same division for half the 52 seasons, and for 20 seasons from 1950 they both played in the bottom two divisions.

City only enjoyed First Division status for 11 seasons and Park Avenue for three seasons, both around World War One. Since then each had enjoyed just two promotions in 40 years. Although City did win the FA Cup in 1911, neither club achieved much in the Cup. Park Avenue had one famous victory against Arsenal in 1947/48 and City a good run in 1959/60 beating Everton and drawing against champions Burnley.

Although its performance on the field was marginally better, we should not forget that in January 1967 City nearly folded. Its chairman Stafford Heginbotham made an emotional plea to a packed St. George's Hall about City's dire financial straits. The situation was retrieved, but no such help was forthcoming for its rivals seven years later.

4 May 1904 The Prince and Princess of Wales open the Bradford Exhibition in Lister Park.

Today was a high point in the life of Edwardian Bradford. It was the first royal visit since Bradford became a city in 1897 as part of Queen Victoria's Diamond Jubilee. The occasion was the opening of the special Bradford Exhibition in Lister Park. Three weeks earlier the new Cartwright Memorial Hall art gallery in the centre of the park had been opened by Lord Masham (previously Samuel Cunliffe Lister). To mark the occasion of the six-month Exhibition the Prince and Princess of Wales (future King George V and Queen Mary) were invited to open it.

Having stayed over at Harewood House, the royal party arrived by train at Bradford Midland. With mills, factories and offices closed for the day, many thousands thronged the streets as the royal procession travelled in perfect weather up Darley Street, into Manningham Lane and thence to the park.

Now it housed not just Cartwright Hall, but two large and impressive temporary structures – a specially built pavilion and a concert hall – and an unusual but highly popular feature of a Somali village peopled by natives. There was also a Crystal Maze and lake used for a naval spectacle.

After the formal opening, speeches and a tour, the celebrations moved to the unveiling of Queen Victoria's statue in Morley Street outside the Alhambra Theatre. Earlier, the Prince of Wales had asked *'Where is a statue of Queen Victoria more appropriate than in Bradford, for is it not essentially a city of the Victorian age?'*

The local paper was fulsome in its praise: *'It was a remarkable demonstration of affection for the Royal House from an industrial community which has never been in the habit of concealing its political opinions. We have Liberals and Tories, Labour men and Socialists, but strange to say one can scarcely find a Republican pure and simple. We hear sounds of political discontent, but the Throne is held by the great bulk of the people as something sacred from assault.'*

The Standard (London-based) proclaimed it *'a complete success'*, as did *The Times*. While praising the day's arrangements, the *Manchester Guardian* commented that *'A Yorkshire crowd is a little undemonstrative ... and the Royal visitors did not arouse any extravagant enthusiasm'*.

For six months the Exhibition was a tremendous success with over 2.5 million visitors and a profit of £15,000 (approx. £3m currently).

Source: *Bradford Daily Telegraph* (4 and 5 May 1904)

5 May 1954   World record crowd attends Rugby League Challenge Cup Final replay at Odsal Stadium.

When Bradford Corporation made Odsal Stadium available for Bradford Northern, it was considered to have much potential. Previously a disused quarry, it was turned into an amphitheatre by the dumping of household waste. Opened in 1934, it became the biggest stadium outside Wembley, although initially it had only 1,500 seats.

Tonight it had its largest-ever crowd of 102,569. For only the second time in its history the Rugby League Challenge Cup Final had been drawn. Halifax and Warrington had to replay. Odsal was the obvious choice for the midweek fixture.

At the time it was the highest attendance for any rugby league match in the world. It is still the highest for any rugby game (union or league) in the Northern hemisphere, the highest for any midweek fixture in Britain, the second highest for any match (rugby or soccer) in England and nearly treble the size of any Bradford sporting event.

The crowd stretched local systems to the limit. Payment was mainly by cash at 36 turnstiles. Gates were open from five o'clock and fans were entering as late as half-time. Extra police, buses and gatemen were brought in from Leeds. Some 8,200 vehicles arrived, including 1,239 coaches. Twenty special trains came in from Halifax and Lancashire to Low Moor Station.

There was no evidence of misbehaviour, but local reports indicated the crush. Some climbed to the old stand roof and refused to budge until the end. The huge banking was crammed with spectators, and ambulance units attended many fainting cases.

For the record Halifax beat Warrington 8-4 in another tight match.

Afterwards, there was some talk of Odsal replacing Wembley as the regular cup final venue, but nothing came of it. A night out in Bradford perhaps did not have the appeal of a weekend celebrating in Soho.

Source: *Yorkshire Post* (6 May 1954)

5 May 1986   150-1 outsider Joe Johnson beats favorite to become world snooker champion.

Already three times world champion yet five years younger, Steve Davis was expected to overwhelm the outsider Joe Johnson at the Crucible Theatre, Sheffield. From Bradford Moor, Johnson had never won a tournament in seven years as a professional. It turned out to be a gripping match which he won 18-12 in one of the sport's greatest-ever surprises.

Proud not to be a one-day wonder, Johnson faced Davis again in the following year's final. Normal service resumed with Davis winning 18-14.

6 May 1908   Bitter rivalry between Bradford's two main newspapers breaks out in fisticuffs.

Ever since the *Bradford Daily Argus* appeared on the scene in 1892, the city's two daily newspapers were bitter rivals. An unsigned note left from today's flare-up gives an indication:

'Scene in the Town Hall this morning. Fleming of the Bradford Daily Telegraph and Illingworth of the Bradford Argus entertaining a crowd of people near the Lord Mayor's Parlour with brawling and abuse of each other. Another victory for a Telegraph blackguard. One would expect a Sunday School Superintendant to have men of respectability and clean mouths about him.'

From the beginning the *Argus* had taken the fight to the *Telegraph* by luring away the *Telegraph*'s editor for its launch. The *Telegraph* was an orthodox Liberal newspaper supportive of the working classes. Some prominent Conservatives, including Lord Masham (formerly Samuel Lister) saw an opportunity for a Conservative newspaper. They persuaded Jasper Patterson to be its first editor.

Patterson, 20 years old at the time, had been one of a small team that Thomas Shields, the *Telegraph*'s founder, had brought with him from South Shields (sic) in 1868 and taken over from him when he died in 1887. Shields even left Patterson some money in his will. Having dedicated himself for half a lifetime to the *Telegraph,* Patterson was tempted away to become the general manager for his new rivals. He hesitated, but in the end accepted the challenge. He was to remain in that position for the next 30 years.

In the meantime, ownership of the *Telegraph* changed. The Shields family retained possession of the title until 1898 when it was bought by the newly formed Bradford & District Newspaper Company Ltd, whose chairman was James Hill, later Sir James Hill, self-made wool magnate, later Lord Mayor and Liberal MP for Bradford Central.

Further consolidation was in the air. Alongside these changes, Bradford's oldest newspaper, the *Bradford Observer,* became the *Yorkshire Daily Observer* in 1901 and then in 1909 the *Yorkshire Observer* when it was bought by Sir James Hill. In 1916 the *Telegraph* moved into the *Yorkshire Observer* offices in Piccadilly.

The *Telegraph* and the *Argus* were still rivals. There was more consolidation to come.

Source: *Read All About It: The story of Bradford's Telegraph & Argus 1868-1981* (1981)

7 May 2015   After years of poverty, abuse and family turmoil, Naseem Shah is elected Bradford MP.

The achievements of most politicians start when they are elected to Parliament. In the case of 42-year-old Bradford-born Naseem ('Naz') Shah, the achievement was just to win the election after a traumatic upbringing. Bradford had only ever had one other female MP and that was 60 years earlier. Naz Shah's story is remarkable.

Today she won Bradford West with 11,420 more votes than the controversial George Galloway (Respect Party). The election was stormy and divisive. Immediately after Shah's victory Galloway accused her of lying about her life. She replied with an open letter which tells that story:

'I was only six when my father abandoned my mother with two young children and pregnant with a third when he eloped with the neighbour's 16-year-old daughter. I remember being thrown into the back of a taxi with black bin liners full of our belongings and packed off from the family home on Hartman Place ... We never really saw the end of black bin liners over the next few years as we moved from squalor to squalor, 14 times in less than two years, from back-to-back houses where the toilet was outside to rat-infested damp houses where we lived and slept in just one room'.

Then her mother met somebody else whom she thought would save her children from an insecure future. It was another abusive relationship. Her family sent her to Pakistan at the age of 12 to avoid the risk of abuse. With her younger sister growing up and also perhaps at risk, her mother had several failed suicide attempts, following years of anti-depressants. *'Feeling desperate and destitute... she snapped. She killed the man who abused her'.*

Just 15 years old, Shah had been subjected in Pakistan to her own forced marriage to her first cousin. Now back in Bradford she had to find work with low-paid jobs, bring up her two younger siblings and make regular prison visits to her mother. Aged 18, she returned to college after leaving her husband *'who used his fists to communicate'.*

With three children of her own, she worked as a disability rights advocate and a Samaritans volunteer, and chaired a mental health charity, before entering politics.

In July 2018, she was appointed Shadow Minister of State for Women and Equalities. Can any MP have had more relevant personal experience for such a role?

Source: *The Guardian* (9 March 2015)

8 May 2009   Prime Minister Gordon Brown unveils a memorial to PC Sharon Beshenivsky.

On 18 November 2005 38-year-old PC 6410 Sharon Beshenivsky became the seventh policewoman to die in the call of duty and the second to be shot. All Bradfordians and members of the police community were shocked at her tragic and cruel death and paid tribute to her bravery.

With her female colleague she was responding to reports of a robbery at a travel agent in Morley Street just above the location of the Alhambra Theatre. They confronted three men who had just robbed the travel agent of some £5,000. Both policewomen were shot at point blank range. Her colleague survived, but PC Sharon Beshenivsky did not. It was her youngest daughter's birthday.

A mother with three children and two step-children, Beshenivsky had been serving as a police officer with West Yorkshire Police for just nine months, which meant that she was classed as a probationer under the supervision of an experienced colleague. She had previously been a police community support officer.

Two of the three men were soon arrested, charged and convicted. The third fled to Somalia but was convicted after extradition in 2007. They were all found guilty of murder and given life sentences with a 35-year tariff. Others who had acted as lookouts or get-away drivers were also arrested and convicted of manslaughter and other offences.

Today the Prime Minister Gordon Brown unveiled a memorial in Morley Street by the travel agent's office. He praised PC Beshinivsky's dedication, professionalism and courage. Three years later the memorial was moved to Norfolk Gardens across the road from the travel agency to be joined by two more memorials. One was a male police sergeant who had died on duty in Bradford in 1981 and the other was the last Chief Constable of Bradford from 1957 to 1973 before the creation of West Yorkshire Police.

The tragedy occurred during the Bradford District Peace Festival. Children had been creating images of peace, using wicker and tissue paper. At the close of the Festival, these images were crafted together by a local artist into an eight-foot high peace sculpture, taken down to the Morley Street site of the shooting. The police have since retained this in their Nelson Street headquarters.

In January 2020, nearly 15 years after the shooting the alleged ring-leader in Pakistan was arrested with a view to extradition.

Source: www.bbc.co.uk/news/uk-england-leeds-38026550

9 May 1999   Club legend Stuart McCall leads Bradford City into the Premier League.

Five consecutive defeats at the end of the 1921/22 season had sent Bradford City crashing out of top-tier professional football. Would they ever return? Supporters had become accustomed to mediocrity and lack of investment. Yet today after 77 years in lower leagues, mainly the old Division Three and Four, they did return in triumph to the top tier, now the Premier League in existence for just seven years.

What a game it was to clinch promotion on the last afternoon of the season!

Sunderland had already been promoted. The other automatic promotion place would be either Bradford City or Ipswich Town. Should City win their final match away at Wolverhampton Wanderers, they would be promoted whatever result Ipswich playing at home might achieve. Wolves themselves were in with a chance of a play-off place.

The game started badly with Wolves taking a one goal lead after 12 minutes. Fans heard that Ipswich, too, had taken the lead. Peter Beagrie equalised after 25 minutes, but Ipswich soon went into a 3-0 lead. Now City had to win. Five minutes before half-time Lee Mills scored and City were in the frame. On the hour mark Robbie Blake scored a third. Even better they were awarded a penalty with 12 minutes to go, but Beagrie missed and Wolves pulled a goal back immediately.

Ahead 3-2, City had to hold on. One final defining moment was a free-kick conceded just outside the penalty area. The shot looked goal-bound but miraculously hit the post and bounced clear (a moment that gave the name to the highly respected City fans website *Width of a Post*).

After a most exciting game, City did secure promotion. Celebrations on the field and outside the stadium, and back in Bradford, continued a long time.

It was a triumph for chairman Geoffrey Richmond who, when he took over in 1994, to general disbelief had promised promotion to the Premier League within five years. It was a triumph for young rookie manager Paul Jewell who, supported by the chairman, put together a winning team.

Above all, it was a triumph for skipper Stuart McCall, by acclaim City's best-ever player, returning 12 years after the 1987/88 side had just missed top-tier promotion. He had played with distinction for Everton, Rangers and Scotland and, now as City's Player of the Season, took his team to the heights of the Premier League.

Source: www.widthofapost.com

10 May 1848   A 31-year-old woolcomber dies of starvation.

As Bradford expanded, working class poverty increased. Woolcombers suffered more than any from overcrowded housing, very low wages and insanitary living conditions. Their grievances had led to the unsuccessful Great Bradford Strike of 1825.

Twenty years on, George White, the prominent Chartist, led a survey that concluded:

'Our dwellings are improperly constructed and totally inadequate for the uses to which they are now subjected, and, as will be seen from the report, our streets are filthy and in a most neglected condition, contagious and noxious vapours are hourly accumulating around us; even the common decencies of life appear to be disregarded.'

To give an example, in one street a family of eight lived and worked in a cellar, 15ft 6" by 13ft 7" and 6ft 3". When it rained, it often flooded up to 20 inches. Five children slept in one bed; a man, his wife and his mother in another.

Three years later, nothing had changed despite various public meetings held to protest and effect change.

Today in the early hours a man in one such dwelling died of starvation. The next day the inquest was held. As reported in the *Bradford Observer* (18 May 1848), the inquest convened at the Fox and Hounds Inn, Wapping. The coroner took a jury to the dead man's home in that area, which was largely a ghetto of Irish immigrants (this report mentioned nothing about the man's background). The body still lay there. Some examined it, *'noting that the finger nails were black— a sign that the man had died in a fit'* (a popular misconception).

They interviewed his wife. She testified: *'My husband has been ill for some time, and for two or three times a week, pains have come suddenly upon him... (he) had been eating nothing... it has been want that has brought it on.'*

The coroner did not show much sympathy. It was not material to say that this family had insufficient food to live on. The man was very thin but had not lost any flesh. After half an hour's deliberation, the jury returned a qualified verdict to the effect that the *'deceased suddenly died in a fit,'* but it *'considered that the deceased had suffered great privation from want of the ordinary supply of proper food'.*

Source: *The Great Paternalist: Titus Salt and the Growth of 19th Century Bradford*, Jack Reynolds (1983)

11 May 1985   Fifty-six fans die at Bradford City fire disaster.

For 75 years from the end of World War One, promotion only came once in a generation to long-suffering Bradford City fans (1929, 1969). So it was natural that today, having already won promotion from Division Three, they came to Valley Parade in good spirits for the last home match of the season against Lincoln City.

The celebratory mood, however, turned to one of horror and despair in just four minutes towards the end of the first half when the old wooden main stand became engulfed in flames. These moments were captured on TV and later endlessly replayed as the city and football fans everywhere watched in disbelief.

Fifty-six fans died and some 265 more were seriously injured. Trapped in the stand with the gates at the back closed and initially unaware of the scale of the fire, supporters became desperate to escape the inferno and spilled out over high walls on to the pitch, many with great difficulty. The match was quickly abandoned. It was the worst civilian disaster in the history of Bradford and, at the time, the worst football disaster in England (only exceeded later by the 1989 Hillsborough disaster).

There were many heroes on the day and afterwards. The city was generally congratulated on the way in which it dealt with the tragedy. Little blame was attached to the club which was about to pull down the old stand on the Monday after the game. Unlike Hillsborough little controversy was stirred over the causes of the disaster. It was assumed that a discarded cigarette had ignited the rubbish under the wooden stands. Fans perhaps realised that many football stadia at the time might have suffered such a tragedy. The Popplewell Enquiry, completed within weeks, confirmed such assumptions and recommended no new wooden stands.

Many feared for the future of the club as it started the new season in Division Two playing home matches at Odsal, Leeds United and Huddersfield Town before returning to Valley Parade in December 1986. The ground was gradually rebuilt, thanks to support from the Football League. At the end of 1986-87 they just missed out on promotion to the old Division One. In 1999 they eventually reached the promised land of the new Premier League, then seven years in existence.

The phoenix had arisen from the ashes.

Source: *Four Minutes to Hell: The Story of the Bradford City Fire*, Paul Firth (2005)

12 May 1922   The formation of a Jowett owners' car club is advertised.

'Owners of Jowett Cars in the neighbourhood of Bradford are asked to meet at Manningham Gates (main entrance) tomorrow Saturday 13 May from 2.15 – 2.30. It is proposed to have a short run to Boroughbridge and after tea, to hold a meeting to inaugurate a club restricted to owners of Jowett Cars'— so ran an advertisement in today's *Bradford Daily Telegraph*. The club runs to the current day, now claiming to be the *'the oldest one-make car club'* Its existence nearly 60 years after Jowett Cars stopped manufacturing is a testament to the affection with which they are still held.

Bradford built its reputation as the wool city in the 19th century. The massive car industry that developed in the 20th century became concentrated in a few places well away from Bradford. It is easy to forget that, having to adapt to new technologies, Bradford once fostered a thriving motor manufacturing capability. Jowett Cars emerged as the most significant such business.

Sons of an engineer from Girlington, the Jowett brothers (Ben 1877-1963 and William 1880-1955) created the Jowett Manufacturing Company Ltd in 1901 by making bicycles in Manningham. Three years later they began their first motor car after a move to premises near Valley Parade. It took to the road in February 1906 with the registration AK 494 (AK being Bradford's registration letters up to 1922)

The brothers started making cars in limited batch production from 1910 but, when war broke out, they had to turn to armaments. In 1919 they bought premises in Idle and formed Jowett Cars Ltd. Production increased rapidly from 100 to over 3,400 in 1927. With a focus on quality, cars continued to be made there until 1953 when the company went out of business.

The two most well-known and loved models were from the post-war period. The Jowett Javelin, launched in 1947, was a compact, streamlined car with seats for six and popular with keen motorists – 23,000 were produced. The Jowett Jupiter, launched in 1950 as a sports car, won its class three years in a row in the Le Mans 24-hour Grand Prix.

Jowett Cars never compromised by disappearing into mass production cars. This no doubt explains their iconic status and why they still support an owners' club.

Source: *Early Motoring Days in Bradford, 1896-1939*, David Croft (2009) in *The Antiquary*

13 May 1920   William Rothenstein is offered the post of Principal of the Royal College of Arts.

'Being an indifferent scholar, I thoroughly disliked my school-days. The Bradford Grammar School was a dreary building inside and out. We assembled in a hall of stained pitch-pine, its single decoration a framed wooden tablet on which were inscribed the names of holders of university scholarships. To see my name amongst these was an honour I knew would never be mine' (Memoir, *Men and Memories*).

Like David Hockney some 60 years later, Sir William Rothenstein (1872 -1945) failed academically at Bradford Grammar School, was only interested in an art career and succeeded. Unlike Hockney's working class background, Rothenstein came from a prosperous German-Jewish family. Like several others who were second generation emigres such as Frederick Delius and Humbert Wolfe, he made his way not in the family business, but in the world of the arts.

Rothenstein left school aged 16 to study first at the Slade School of Art in London and then at the Academie Julian in Paris. Here he developed his talent for drawing portraits and also came to know artists on their way to fame such as Sickert, Whistler and Degas.

For the rest of his life he developed a reputation for both his artistic talent and his friendships. He returned to England where he was commissioned to produce *Oxford Characters*, the first of several volumes of portraits of the famous. Such work also enabled him to extend his network of friends.

Overcoming some bias against his German name at the outbreak of World War One, he ended up an official war artist. After the war and a short spell as adviser to the Royal College of Art on its teaching methods and ethos, he was today offered the position of Principal so that he might implement his ideas for greater flexibility in art training. He became a more conservative artist than many of his friends, but encouraged many big names such as Henry Moore.

After some years of ill-health, during which he was also knighted for services to art, he again became an official war artist in World War Two. Unable to travel much, he completed portraits of airmen at RAF bases.

From unpromising school days Rothenstein developed into one of Britain's most influential artists and art administrators of the 20th century. Unusually, he was also an official war artist in both world wars.

Source: William Rothenstein (*Oxford Dictionary of National Biography*)

14 May 1841   Rev William Scoresby wins a hollow victory on church rates.

Most prominent clergymen in 19th century Bradford were nonconformists, such as Jonathan Glyde (Congregationalist) and Benjamin Godwin (Baptist). The one Anglican who can be added to this list is Reverend William Scoresby (1789-1857), Vicar of St. Peter's Church and head of the whole parish. He was only in Bradford for seven years from 1839 to 1846, but he was the most energetic and controversial vicar in the century. He also had the most colourful background for such a traditional role, coming to it as an Arctic scientist.

His father was captain of a whaling ship. As a ten-year-old, Scoresby made his first voyage to the Arctic. From 1803 to 1823 he sailed each summer to the Greenland whale fishery. When 21, he became captain himself on one voyage. Stimulated by studies at Edinburgh University, he became passionately interested in scientific research related to such voyages (eg navigation, astronomy), frequently lecturing on this even during his hectic life in Bradford.

He had also developed deep religious convictions and in 1822 decided to enter the church. He studied at Queens College, Cambridge over a ten-year period, taking positions of deacon at Bridlington and chaplain at Liverpool and Exeter. In 1838 he was offered the position of Vicar of Bradford.

Here he identified several problems about his new role. They included the inadequacy of church accommodation, the shortage of clergy, the neglect of education and the general lack of discipline in the parish. He ran into difficulties, explained by an autocratic management style, no doubt acquired during his youthful sailing experiences.

Although he did achieve much, he had the habit of alienating people. For example, he established four day schools after realising that the parish church did not educate any children. However, his argument against over-worked children in mills lost him the support of influential mill-owners.

The issue that caused the greatest problem was the levying of church rates to support the parish, which nonconformists still had to pay. He inherited a history of recent conflict, losing an important poll within his first year, which led to large numbers uniting against him.

Today, two years later he managed to force through the approval of a new rate, despite much vociferous opposition. However, many people refused to pay, including Titus Salt. Eventually, in a test case the High Court deemed the rate illegal.

Source: William Scoresby (*Oxford Dictionary of National Biography*)

15 May 1869   A statue of Richard Oastler, the 'Factory King', is unveiled.

Today's unveiling outside Bradford Midland station marked the end of one of the most remarkable 19th century campaigns. It started in 1830 with a famous meeting with John Wood, factory owner, had its triumph with the passing of the Factory Act, 1847 and ended when the statue of the leading campaigner was finally unveiled. Richard Oastler was that hero.

Shortly after his death in 1861, a deputation of workers called upon his friends to erect a suitable monument. They agreed to raise the funds, but it was not clear where the statue should be. Oastler came from Leeds, had lived in Huddersfield and had strong links to Bradford where the campaign had started. Those who funded the statue could vote. The results were: Bradford 1,472, Leeds 109, Huddersfield 88, Halifax 5 – an 88% victory for Bradford.

Six years later, the statue was ready. It was Whit Saturday, church bells rang out, all places of business were closed. Up to 100,000 people thronged the streets to watch the procession go from Peel Park down into the city centre. Lord Shaftesbury, politician and reformer who had fought for the abolition of slavery, unveiled the statue. Speeches were also made by Bradford's two MPs, WE Forster and Edward Miall.

Oastler was later moved to Rawson Square and a statue to Forster erected in Forster Square. Years later each was moved yet again, some 250 yards away.

Source: *Leeds Intelligencer* (7 March 1863 and 17 May 1869)

15 May 1875   A statue of Samuel Cunliffe Lister is unveiled in Lister Park.

Only five people (all men!) who achieved much in Bradford were fortunate enough to have their achievements recognised with a statue – Sir Titus Salt (three), Richard Oastler, WE Forster, JB Priestley and Samuel Lister. Today, six years to the day after Oastler, and just a few months after Salt had been so honoured in Lister Park, it was Lister's turn. If Salt deserved three, then Lister, his contemporary and fellow wool magnate, certainly deserved one. He received the honour in his park that he had recently sold to the Corporation at well below market rate for use by the public.

WE Forster MP was the man to unveil the statue. Within an hour the *Bradford Daily Telegraph* had a special commemorative edition ready. It gave tribute to this *'man of rare mechanical genius and of extraordinary perseverance and devotion'*.

16 May 1985   Roger Suddards completes the terms of reference for the Bradford City Disaster Appeal.

Gordon Moore was considered one of the ablest and most respected chief executives of the City of Bradford Metropolitan District Council. He had been in charge in difficult times - high unemployment, the city in economic decline and in dire need of investment and latterly the impact of the Honeyford affair that hit headlines when a local headmaster went public with his concerns over multi-culturalism. But on the evening of 11 May 1985 he had a new and totally unexpected challenge - the aftermath of the Bradford City fire disaster.

Hundreds were injured and some had died. Captured live on TV, it dominated the national news. Everyone was in shock. Later the city was generally praised for its response. This was in no small measure down to Moore and his team. When it came to handling the disaster appeal, he knew the man to turn to.

That critical person was Roger Suddards known as Mr Bradford for his many roles in city life. A solicitor with expertise in planning law, one of 11 English Heritage Commissioners, a governor and later chairman of Bradford Grammar School, later a President of the University of Bradford and an active participant at the Civic Playhouse, he was just the right person to appoint as chairman of the trustees of the Appeal Fund already set up to compensate victims.

Suddards immediately contacted for advice a QC with knowledge of disaster appeals and the administrators of the equivalent funds for the disasters of Aberfan (1966) and Penlee Lifeboats (1981). By the end of today, he had completed the fund's terms of reference for presenting tomorrow to the press.

Transparency, fairness and efficiency were the marks of the whole process. The distribution of over £4.25m (£12.5m at current prices) to over 400 people was completed in just 10 months with barely a complaint or adverse press comment.

Finally, Moore, Suddards and colleagues put together a short booklet documenting the lessons they had learnt to be shared by others in the future who might have to face such a challenge with no notice.

Suddards received a CBE for his contribution and went on to advise Margaret Thatcher's Government about later disasters (eg *Herald of Free Enterprise* ferry 1987, *Marchioness* Thames pleasure steamer 1989).

Source: *Out of the Valley: Bradford MDC's Response to the Bradford City Fire Disaster 1985-1986*, Gordon Moore and Roger Suddards (1986)

17 May 2001 Bradford-educated optometry professor receives Asian Women of Achievement Award.

According to its website, the Asian Women of Achievement Awards, founded in 1999, reward *'the phenomenal Asian women across the UK and across industries, who are making a valuable and important contribution to British life'.*

Two years later, four Asian female high-flyers from Bradford were shortlisted for the national awards, more than from any other place except London. They comprised (in alphabetical order of surname):

- Asama Javed, an assistant solicitor from Girlington, was honoured for her work with women and families fleeing domestic violence.
- Adeeba Malik from Allerton was Deputy Chief Executive for Bradford-based QED (Quest for Economic Development) and member of the board at Yorkshire Forward regeneration agency.
- Dr Shahina Pardhan was the UK's first female professor of optometry who graduated at the University of Bradford.
- Dr Geetha Upadhyaya was co-founder of Bradford-based South Asian arts organisation Kala Sangram.

Today, Cherie Booth, QC presented the award in London to the winner, Dr Shahina Pardhan. She came to Yorkshire as an 18-year-old from Tanzania with her family. She studied optometry at the University of Bradford. In 1984 she graduated with first-class honours and progressed through research scholarships and a doctorate to become in 1994 the university's only Asian female lecturer. In 2001 she was appointed professor of optometry at what is now Anglia Ruskin University. In the UK this made her the first woman to be appointed Professor of Optometry and first Asian woman to become professor of any discipline.

Some years later at an event for optometrists she recounted that, on her first day as lecturer at the University of Bradford, she *'couldn't go into the staff common room because secretaries weren't allowed ... It has been hard work and it has been frustrating at times. Occasionally, I felt that I had to be better to be an equal'.* (*Optometry Today*, 19 December 2017)

Since 2001, two of the others shortlisted have gone on to receive honours. Adeeba Malik was awarded an MBE in 2004 for her services to ethnic minorities and businesses and a CBE in 2015 for her services to interfaith and community cohesion. Dr. Geetha Upadhyaya was awarded an OBE in 2016 for her dedication to South Asian Arts in the UK.

These role models connected with Bradford give hope that the low glass ceiling for Asian women in the UK can be broken.

Source: *Telegraph & Argus* (5 May 2001)

18 May 1895   The Shipley Glen Tramway starts to operate.

'I had always been interested in the idea of running a little railway. I travelled all over the country to examine those which had been successfully established. It was on the little railway at Aberystwyth (the Aberystwyth Cliff Railway that was not actually opened until 1896) *that my plans were based... "Whatever do you want to put a tramway up there for?" asked the late Sir James Roberts* (successor to Sir Titus Salt at Saltaire Mill). *I told them there were seven reasons: "I am building it for the old and the young, for the lame and the lazy, for the weak and the strong, and lastly for myself"... When I retired in April 1919, I had carried over 7,500,000 passengers without a single accident. I am very proud of this record, and I attributed it to the fact that I always observed safety-first principles.'*

These were the words of Baildon entrepreneur, Sam Wilson, in an interview with the *Telegraph & Argus* on his 80th birthday.

By the late 19th century Shipley Glen was well established as a local beauty spot with fresh air and open space, which brought relief at weekends to the working classes of smoky Bradford five miles away.

Today was the biggest day in the Glen's history as a new funicular railway was opened to the public, improving significantly access to the moors and the Glen's other attractions, especially for those who could not walk up the steep footpath through the woods.

To build the railway, Wilson had fought off some local opposition to the scar down the side of the valley defacing the glen and to the unsightly black fencing posts separating the footpath and the tramway.

The tramway was built in a straight line, some 440 yards in length at a gradient of one in nine with a 20-inch gauge. There were two open-air cars, each accommodating 12 passengers on six seats. It runs from the bottom of Glen Wood to an upper terminus in the woods near Prod Lane. Here a footpath turns right towards Baildon and straight on to the Glen itself and its various attractions.

Over 125 years since its start, the Shipley Glen Tramway retains its popularity, with over 27,000 passengers in 2018 and is one of the oldest funicular railways in the country.

Source: *Shipley Glen: The History and Development of a Victorian Playground*, Alan Cattell (2018)

19 May 1770   The first Leeds & Liverpool Canal Act is passed.

Industrial growth in the mid-18th century created a demand for cheap and convenient transport. New turnpike roads with toll-booths improved things, but the cost of water transport was still around one-eighth of the cost of road transport.

Yorkshire wool merchants wanted to buy better wool from East Anglia. The Aire and Calder Navigation at the start of the 18th century strengthened the links, but in places was too shallow and did not extend beyond Leeds. It was also important for exports to have access through the growing port of Liverpool to the British colonies in the Americas. More locally, new industry in Lancashire and Yorkshire depended on cheap coal. A boom in construction in the West Riding also depended on limestone from the Dales used for making lime for mortar. A canal linking Leeds with Liverpool, the east coast with the west, would meet all these needs.

Bradford was badly located for transport to either coast and strongly in support of such a canal. Although not the original prime mover, one Bradfordian became critical to the cause. John Stanhope, colliery owner, was the originator, chairing the first meetings of potential subscribers in July 1766 and January 1767 at the Sun Inn in Bradford. John Hustler was appointed in charge of the Yorkshire Canal Committee. Like his father, he was Bradford's leading wool-stapler, trading in the resale of raw wool purchased from farms and wool fairs all over England.

When, however, Stanhope became terminally ill in 1769, Hustler took over responsibility for the entire project, including publicity, fund raising and liaising with existing landowners over the proposed route. He also produced a pamphlet – *A Summary View of the Proposed Canal from Leeds to Liverpool in 1770.* This helped in the successful bid to legislate. Today royal assent was given to the first Leeds & Liverpool Canal Act.

A critical new stage in the north's transport network was about to start. Although the canal would pass by Bradford over three and a half miles away, the town had a major influence in its development. It was no surprise that the headquarters for the new Leeds /Liverpool Canal Company were located in Bradford until 1850.

Source: *Bradford and the Industrial Revolution*, Gary Firth (1990)

19 May 1212   King John II grants Bingley a market.

Source: *Bingley and Surrounds: Forgotten Moments from History*, Alan Cattell (2011)

20 May 1895   Photographer Lund partners with bookseller Humphries to form publisher Lund Humphries.

Today a new publishing company was formed that became successful locally, then nationally in the 20th century, but we have no record of why or how the two partners met before signing the contract. Exact contemporaries, they offered complementary expertise and drive, but their backgrounds were quite different.

Photographer Percy Lund (1864-1943) was born into a hard-working Bradford family. His father (Joseph) and uncle (Charles) were both entrepreneurial and public-spirited, being pioneers in the building society movement and involved in local political and business affairs. Percy was educated at the Yorkshire College in Leeds, training to be a printer. He was also very interested in photography and natural history. Aged 19, he published *The Practical Naturalist*. A few years later he published *The Practical Photographer*. In between he was involved in other publishing ventures (eg *The Ilkley Free Press* for two years, *The Photographer's World*, *Lund's Directory of Photographers* and an autobiography by James Berry, the state executioner). Percy Lund & Co was doing well, employing some 50 to 60 people.

Bookseller Edward Humphries (1864-1948) was born in Wiltshire. He was brought up by his mother after his father's early death. Although two sisters came to Bradford to attend a private school run by his aunt, his mother moved to Norfolk where Edward became a bookseller and stationer from the age of 16.

Advising his nephew, Charles Lund suggested that he invite Humphries as a director to the company. Humphries accepted and today the contract was signed and the first formal meeting held.

Within a year the company became Lund Humphries & Co with Humphries gradually becoming the driving force and eventually its chairman. Their first national success was *The Penrose Annual* which became the bible for designers, printers and publishers. They acquired a London office and expanded into related areas such as graphic design and offset litho printing. They published a wide range of magazines, booklets, picture postcards, specialising later into the publication of fine art books and high-quality catalogues (eg Sothebys).

To protect its future in a competitive market, the company was sold in 1979 to Tangent Industries, but after a management buy-out in 1986 and some immediate success it lost its biggest contract and folded in 1994.

Source: *Lund Humphries: Bradford's Premier Printer*, Graham Hall (2010) in *The Antiquary*

21 May 1933   Adventurer Maurice Wilson sets off on bizarre solo attempt on Mount Everest.

'I believe that if a man has sufficient faith he can accomplish anything. I haven't gone mad and I haven't got religious mania. But I've got a theory to prove and I intend to prove it. I'll show the world what faith can do! I'll perform some task so hard and so exacting that it could only be carried out by someone with divine help' — Maurice Wilson told his two closest friends when he announced his ambition to climb Mount Everest.

Born into a middle class family from Little Horton, Wilson (1898-1934) would doubtless have moved into the family wool business, had the outbreak of war not intervened. Joining up on his 18th birthday, he rose quickly through the ranks. At the Battle of Passchendaele he bravely countered a German breakthrough, earning the Military Cross for *'conspicuous gallantry and devotion to duty'.* However, a few months later his left arm was badly injured. Later he would often suffer disabling physical pain.

The war scarred him emotionally. He could not settle and tried many different jobs. He was twice married and divorced. He emigrated to New Zealand and returned with his new Everest ambition.

Without taking even one flying lesson, Wilson bought a Gypsy Moth, which he named *Ever-Wrest.* His plan was deliberately to crash it on Everest and stroll to the top. He was refused permission to fly to India. But he remained undeterred.

After two months of intensive flying lessons, Wilson set off today from an aerodrome in Edgware, seen off by his two friends and a few others. Amazingly, after several mishaps, he arrived in India two weeks later.

The authorities impounded his plane that he was forced to sell. He travelled overland to Darjeeling where he found three sherpas to accompany him. As again he had no permission to proceed, he started the next stage on 21 March, disguised as a Tibetan monk. He was poorly equipped and had no experience of the terrain.

At last on 12 April they saw Everest. At 16,500 feet he was still optimistic. Preferring to continue alone, he left his sherpas behind. Whether now he still believed or was resigned to failure, we will never know.

Fifteen months later, another expedition found a desiccated corpse. Wilson had died of starvation or exposure at around 22,750 feet, over 7,000 feet short of the summit.

Source: *Strange and Dangerous Dreams,* Geoff Powter (2006)

22 May 1936   The Hindenburg makes mysterious flight over Keighley.

Tonight just before 8pm the strange-looking Hindenburg airship with its easily recognisable swastikas flew over Keighley. A parcel was dropped. On their way to a scouts' meeting, two Boy Scouts picked up the parcel. They opened it. The parcel contained a bunch of carnations, a small silver cross and a letter. They read the letter:

'To the finder of this letter

Please deposit these flowers and the cross on the grave of my dear brother, Lieutenant Franz Schulte, 1 Garde Rgt zu Fuss, Prisoner of War in Skipton Cemetery in Keighley near Leeds. Many thanks for your kindness.

Pater P Schulte, the 'first flying priest', Aachen, Luftringstr 62, Germany

PS Please accept the stamps and the pictures as a small souvenir from me. God bless you! I said the first Holy Mass on the Hindenburg, 9 May 1936.'

As requested, the boys placed the carnations on the grave, which was then visited by hundreds of people over the next few days. As it flew back over Heaton, Manningham, Frizinghall and Bradford Moor, the airship was watched by thousands in amazement, oblivious to the drama over Keighley.

Lieutenant Franz Schulte had been one of 42 prisoners of war who died of the Spanish 'flu at Morton Banks Hospital and was buried in the nearby cemetery. As a member of the German Army Flying Corps, he reportedly dropped more bombs on London than any other pilot in World War One (*Keighley News,* 22 March 1919) before being shot down in 1917.

His brother, Father John Paul Schulte, who dropped the parcel from the Hindenburg, was bound for work in the Arctic to teach local Inuit tribes the basics of Catholicism. He became known as the *'The Flying Priest'* as he was the first priest to hold a mass in the air.

The giant Hindenburg, 808 feet long and 135 feet in diameter, was returning to Frankfurt on one of its scheduled passenger flights from the USA, when it changed direction over Yorkshire and descended a significant level in altitude over Keighley. It was the only known time when it flew so low over Britain.

Some 30 years later a Granada TV programme showed a re-enactment of the two boys (now in middle age) placing the items on the grave and later meeting Father Schulte.

Source: *Leeds Mercury* (23 May 1936)

23 May 1959 BMJ reports new treatment for breast cancer by Bradford's two cancer specialists.

'A new method of treating breast cancer by combining endocrine theory with the administration of an antimitotic agent has been tried at Bradford Royal Infirmary' ... so began the article about the *'new attack on breast cancer'* described in today's leading article in the *British Medical Journal*.

Or, as the *Telegraph & Argus* put it in an exclusive two days before:

'There's a security clamp on information but the world will know tomorrow.
BRADFORD CANCER DISCOVERY
Backroom researchers at Infirmary hit on a new wonder treatment.'

The heroes making the headlines were Professor Robert Turner (pathologist) and George Whyte-Watson (surgeon). Born in Northern Ireland, Robert Turner (1923-1990) was appointed Consultant Pathologist at the Bradford Royal Infirmary (BRI) in 1956. George Whyte-Watson (1908-1974) came to the BRI as Senior Consultant Surgeon in 1946 after several years at St. Luke's Hospital.

In their spare time they discovered a new treatment for breast cancer which was at first applied to patients at advanced stages, but then came to be used in chemotherapy as primary treatment at earlier stages. Before then chemotherapy had only been used to treat leukaemia. Until this discovery the only treatment for breast cancer had been surgery or radio-therapy.

The University of Bradford set up a special Clinical Oncology Unit and made Professor Turner its first director. A War on Cancer fund was also set up to fund the new unit by voluntary donations.

Sadly and ironically, Professor Turner discovered in the 1980s he too had cancer.

Their research into chemotherapy gave the BRI a worldwide reputation for cancer treatment and changed the management of the disease forever. Their legacy are the large numbers of women alive today from a disease that up to the 1960s would have led to premature deaths. Bradford Cathedral has a memorial to them both.

Source: *Bradford's Own*, Derek AJ Lister (2004)

23 May 1993 Richard Nerurkar wins his first Marathon.

Born in 1964, Richard Nerurkar was an all-round sportsman at Bradford Grammar School, but outside school he specialised in cross-country running. He then became a regular marathon runner in the 1990s, representing Great Britain six times. His high moments came in 1993 winning his first two marathons, one today being the Hamburg Marathon. Later in October, he won the World Marathon Cup in San Sebastian. His personal best time was 2 hours, 8 minutes, 36 seconds in the 1997 London Marathon.

24 May 1976   Richard Dunn fights Muhammad Ali for the heavyweight championship of the world.

'Muhammad Ali, I think yer a square, I'm gonna retire you to a rocking chair.
At 34, you ain't so young, yer gonna get whupped, by Richard Dunn.'

Brave words from Richard Dunn, but they counted for nothing. It felt like a mismatch at the time and it was. However, Dunn was the only man from Bradford to step into a ring for a world championship crown, one of only three from the UK to fight the great Muhammad Ali, and the only Yorkshireman.

It was an unlikely contest from the beginning. Ali came from a strong tradition of black American boxing. He started in his early teens and by age 18 won an Olympic gold medal. He is generally considered the best-ever world heavyweight champion, at the time the first to gain the crown on three occasions, a role model for all black sportsmen, BBC Sports Personality of the 20th century, recipient of the Presidential Medal of Freedom and a hero to billions on the planet.

Dunn, born in Halifax in 1945, lived in Bradford growing up, where there was no tradition of boxing. He did not start boxing until his late teens and only turned professional when he was 24, whilst continuing to work as a scaffolder. His peak came relatively late, winning the British and Commonwealth heavyweight titles when he was 30. He gained the European title in April 1976. Seven weeks later, a relative unknown, he was in the ring at the Olympic Hall in Munich facing Muhammad Ali.

It was no contest. Ali floored Dunn five times in five rounds before the referee stepped in to stop further damage. Dunn was the last opponent that Ali knocked down in his boxing career. He has recalled many times that being knocked down by Ali was the highlight of his life.

In October 1976 Dunn faced Joe Bugner, the best-known British boxer of the decade, who had survived 15 rounds against Ali (and lost) nearly a year before the Ali-Dunn fight. Bugner knocked him out in the first round and Dunn lost his three titles.

In honour of his boxing achievements Bradford City Council opened the Richard Dunn Sports Centre opposite Odsal Stadium in 1978. Nearly 40 years later it was closed, the Council announcing the intention to name a new road on the site after Dunn.

Source: *Stories of the Century, Telegraph & Argus* (1999)

25 May 1920   Emmott Robinson snatches victory from the jaws of defeat in Park Avenue Roses match.

The inter-war years formed Yorkshire county cricket's golden era. Between 1919 and 1939 they won the championship 12 times; rivals Lancashire came next with five titles. This turned the two Bank Holiday Roses encounters into virtual cup finals. Every three years the home Roses match came to Park Avenue. In seven such games Yorkshire won five times with one draw and one defeat. No victory was more dramatic than today's unexpected win.

It was also the making of Emmott Robinson (1883-1969). More than any other Yorkshireman the Keighley-born all-rounder epitomised dour competitive Roses cricket.

After two modest first innings scores, Yorkshire gained a 43-run lead, but they collapsed the second time to 144 with Robinson at No 7 top-scoring with 37 not out. On this last afternoon Lancashire required just 52 for victory with six wickets left, but in helpful bowling conditions Robinson became unplayable, taking 9 for 36. Yorkshire won by 22 runs. This was his personal best, also the best-ever by a Yorkshire bowler at Park Avenue.

Before the war he had played league cricket as a professional. Filling a gap left by war casualties, he made his first team debut in 1919 aged 35. He was a useful middle-order batsman, a more than useful swing bowler and a fine fieldsman. Unlike most Yorkshire colleagues, he never played for England, nor came close to being picked. However, his commitment and experience were highly valued by the team for the next 12 years, especially by legendary Wilfred Rhodes, the senior professional and unofficial captain.

What made him a cult hero was the writing of Neville Cardus, generally considered cricket's greatest writer. Cardus had just started his own career with the *Manchester Guardian*. Despite being a Mancunian, he developed a soft spot for Robinson.

It started with today's fine performance. Cardus blamed the Lancashire batsmen and claimed that Robinson had not bowled particularly well. A few weeks later, Robinson bumped into Cardus and complained to him, saying: *'Ah suppose if ah'd tekken all ten wickets ah'd have convinced thi'.*

Embarrassed, Cardus accepted he had been unfair. For the rest of Robinson's career they became firm friends. At every opportunity Cardus brought out his *'rich character – 'one of the most unselfconsciously humorous men ever to put on flannels'*. Robinson became one of Yorkshire's greatest cricket characters.

Source: *The Great Romantic: Cricket and the Golden Age of Neville Cardus*, Duncan Hamilton (2019)

26 May 1888   John Sowden paints a street-hawker as part of his series of characters of Bradford streets.

In the 1880s John Sowden (1838-1926) embarked on a series of portraits of familiar characters in Bradford streets. He had previously painted some 250 portraits of prominent men, so-called 'worthies' of Bradford. Now he turned his attention to society's unfortunates – hawkers, beggars, the homeless. He described this group as *'people who by their oddities and eccentric behaviour attain to some measure of local fame. They present to the investigator of the workings of the human mind much interesting material and there is a picturesque element about their vagaries of action and dress that has always appealed to the artist.'*

He invited these characters into his studio and his classes, paying them for their time. He kept notes in his diary about the conversations he had with them so that we now have some brief information about these characters' lives that support the portraits.

Today he painted 77-year-old John Ross, better known as Cheap John, for the cheapness of the brooms and brushes that he hawked around the town for over 35 years. He had worked as a stone quarrier but was hospitalised for two years in Bradford Workhouse after a huge stone fell on his head, taking out an eye and breaking his hip.

The combination of portraits of such street characters with the most eminent people of Bradford makes Sowden's work a unique and memorable record of late Victorian Bradford.

Sowden himself had become a Bradford character. Starting as a joiner, his father had got involved in small-scale property development. Articled to an architect, Sowden developed an interest in art, joining art classes at the Bradford Mechanics' Institute. A prize pupil, in 1859 he was then offered a job as art master at the Institute. Later he was appointed head of art, a post which he held until 1901.

Source: *Street Characters of a Victorian City: John Sowden's Bradford*, Gary Firth (1993)

27 May 1907   Bradford City members meet to resolve a proposed merger with Bradford Park Avenue.

On many occasions after World War One one or both of Bradford's two professional football teams struggled financially, prompting voices questioning the wisdom of having two teams. Surely, one team sharing resources, especially a ground, would have a much better chance of success?

The only time when the proposition was put to a vote occurred today one month after Bradford FC, (as it was then known) had decided controversially to switch code from rugby league (the Northern Rugby Union, as it was then known) to association football. This decision was known locally as the 'great betrayal'. One direct consequence was that Bradford FC made a proposal to merge with rivals Bradford City. An indirect consequence was that the strong rugby faction had already agreed in principle to form a break-away rugby league club called Bradford Northern (ie playing in the Northern Rugby Union), a club that confusingly was always to be based on the south side of the city.

Much of the debate centred on which ground to use – City's undeveloped Valley Parade with no promise of investment or Avenue's promise of a new modern stadium. The key issue for most City supporters, however, was how much could they trust the dictatorial and controversial Harry Briggs who had the power across the city. He was wealthy, whereas the City directors were merely well-off.

Today's all-important meeting took place at the Westgate New Hall. With the venue packed to capacity, Bradford City members voted by 1,031 to 487 against the proposal. This decision led directly to the creation of Bradford (Park Avenue) AFC, generally shortened to Bradford PA. The city now had two professional teams.

The new club applied immediately to the Football League. With Bradford City being one of the best supported clubs in the Second Division and on the verge of promotion to the First, the Football League rejected the application. Park Avenue applied to the Southern League and were accepted. It also announced the building of a new state-of-the-art stadium ready to use by the end of 1907.

Avenue applied successfully a year later to the Football League. The next season City gained promotion to the First Division, won the FA Cup in 1911, while Avenue secured promotion in 1913-14. Times were good.

Sadly, after World War One everything went downhill for both clubs.

Source: *Life at the Top*, John Dewhirst (2016)

28 May 1849 Anne Brontë dies aged 29 within sight of a favorite sea-view.

It had been a difficult time in Haworth for the Brontë family. Branwell had died unexpectedly in the previous September. Just before Christmas Emily, too, had died, having developed tuberculosis, which was probably brought on by poor sanitary conditions. Now Anne, the youngest Brontë, (1820 -1849) became seriously ill with similar symptoms to her sister.

After an early disastrous experience as a governess when 19 years old, captured in her first novel *Agnes Grey*, Anne obtained a second post as governess to the four children of a clergyman at Thorp Green Hall, near York. Here she worked more successfully for five years from 1840 to 1845. Her second novel, *The Tenant of Wildfell Hall*, inspired by that experience, was published in June 1848. This was an instant success; within six weeks it was sold out and a second edition came out in August.

During these five years she accompanied the family on their annual five-week holiday to Scarborough. She came to love the place and the sea-views. Wildfell Hall was set just four miles from the sea. One scene is accompanied by this description:

'The increasing height and boldness of the hills had for some time intercepted the prospect; but, on gaining the summit of a step acclivity, and looking downward, an opening lay before us – and the blue sea burst upon our sight! – a deep violet blue – not deadly calm, but covered with glinting breakers – diminutive white specks twinkling on its bosom, and scarcely to be distinguished, by the keenest vision, from the little sea-mews that sported above, their white wings glittering in the sunshine: only one or two vessels were visible, and those were far away.'

When the doctor diagnosed the illness, her only surviving sister Charlotte agreed to take Anne away from unhealthy Haworth for some sea air and Scarborough was the obvious choice for Anne. They took lodgings near the cliff tops. For three days Anne insisted on walking on the sands. After watching a glorious sunset, she died quietly today.

The funeral was held in Scarborough and Anne was buried next to St. Mary's Church. She was the only Brontë not to be buried at Haworth. Charlotte had not wanted her father to suffer yet another funeral for one of his children.

Source: Brontë Parsonage Museum

29 May 1848   The military put an end to the Chartist uprising in Bradford.

After the 1842 Chartist strikes and marches things quietened down in Bradford, partly because the economy improved and partly because the leaders were not sure what to do next.

However, the economic depression of 1847 changed the mood. Mills in Bradford by the end of the year were working on average just two days per week; around 5,500 were on poor relief. Chartism was on the move again. In April Bradford's first mayor Robert Milligan reported to the Home Secretary *'an unsettled state of feeling amongst large numbers of the unemployed workpeople'* and swore in over 1,500 special constables.

A third national petition presenting the Charter with at least 1.9m signatures was rejected by Parliament on 10 April. In Bradford mass meetings took place with talk of violence, evidence of manufacture of arms and drilling of men in preparation for conflict. During May magistrates reported nightly meetings and military drilling.

Things were coming to a head. On Saturday 27 May three extra companies of infantry were drafted into Bradford. On Sunday a large Chartist meeting took place on Pudding Hill near Wilsden. Magistrates feared a general rising. They resolved to take the initiative and sent in the police to the Chartist stronghold in Adelaide Street off Manchester Road. It was the police's first major challenge since being formed on 1 April.

A large crowd soon gathered and stormed into the police (70 plus some special constables) and, armed with stones and clubs, chased them back to the Court House. The mob chanted in support of a famous victory as the police were forced to retreat. Now it was the turn of the soldiers. Despite spirited resistance, the military took control and the police made 19 arrests. A curfew closed all public-houses.

This was the battle of Adelaide Street.

Mass meetings continued sporadically over the summer but peace gradually returned. Chartism never came back to Bradford.

Source: *The Chartist Risings in Bradford*, DG Wright (1987)

29 May 1918   The first-ever reigning monarch visits Bradford.

On a three-day whistle-stop tour of the West Riding King George V and Queen Mary today carried out a morale-raising wartime visit. Arriving at Bradford Midland (9.52am), they visited four factories, caught the train (1.30pm) to Shipley (lunch provided), visited Salts Mill, and finally a Keighley factory before departing by train (5 pm).

Source: *Shipley Times & Express* (31 May 1918)

30 May 1830   Rev Benjamin Godwin is invited to make a book of his successful anti-slavery lectures.

One of the most prominent nonconformist ministers in 19th century Bradford was the Reverend Benjamin Godwin (1785 -1871). On his 70th birthday he left an unusual legacy to his only son in the form of 55 detailed letters that he had written over his lifetime. Each letter comprises around 2,500 words and together they form a most valuable autobiography.

Born in Bath, his father a 70-year-old Baptist Minister, Godwin led a chequered life after school, working as a cobbler and running away to sea before finding his mission as a Baptist. He found a part-time position in Gloucestershire. Then, realising he wanted to be a full-time Baptist minister, he obtained a position for a probationary year in Cornwall. He was ordained as a minister in Dartmouth, moved to Great Missenden before being offered in 1822 a job as a classics teacher at Bradford's Horton Lane Academy teaching future ministers.

In 1824 he was recruited to head up the new Sion Church in the town. He was an immediate success in the Baptist community, but he became well-known more widely for his campaigning on a number of topical issues. From his letters we learn that he was proudest of his contribution to the Anti-Slavery Campaign, which culminated in the 1833 Abolition of Slavery Act.

From around 1829 he researched the issue thoroughly and participated actively in Bradford's Anti-Slavery Committee. In March 1830 he gave in Bradford four impressive lectures on different aspects of slavery. A powerful public speaker, he was invited to repeat them in York and Scarborough. Today, he was approached on behalf of the national campaign by Zachary Macaulay, who edited the *Anti-Slavery Reporter,* to put the lectures together as a book so that they could spread much more widely what Godwin had learned.

Source: *An Autobiography of the Reverend Benjamin Godwin* (1855)

30 May 1970   Baildon climber Ian Clough is killed in the Himalayas.

Today, Baildon-born Ian Clough (1937–1970) was killed on an expedition led by Sir Chris Bonington to climb the south face of the Annapurna. Bonington described him as *'the most modest man I ever had the good luck to climb with ... the kindest and most selfless partner I ever had'.* .

In his memory the Ian Clough Hall was opened for a library in 1971 in Baildon.

31 May 1950   Jim Laker takes 8 wickets for 2 runs at Park Avenue.

Today, at twenty-past one, off-spinner Jim Laker took a one-handed catch off his own bowling to complete a sensational session of play, what JM Kilburn, the renowned *Yorkshire Post* cricket reporter, called '*one of the most astonishing bowling performances in the history of cricket*'.

14 overs, 12 maidens, 8 wickets for just 2 runs.

It certainly was the most astonishing individual performance in first-class cricket ever seen at Bradford Park Avenue. It was also a bonus that the hero was a man born and bred in Bradford, though he was to play almost all his county cricket for Surrey.

The occasion was a three-day Test Trial for England versus The Rest before the season's Test series against the West Indies. A packed crowd of 14,000 watched the game.

It had rained overnight. At the time pitches were uncovered and The Rest batted first on a drying wicket. When Laker came on to bowl, despite discomfort from his split spinning finger, he bowled nevertheless with immaculate skill and perfect direction. He took two wickets in his first over and his control never weakened. At no point was he even hit off the square; one of his two runs conceded came from an edged shot.

By the end of the day, England had also been bowled out but had at least scored 229. The great Len Hutton top-scored with 89: Laker was left not out for six. The Rest batted again and by stumps were 27 for two wickets, one falling to Laker. The next day the match was soon over before lunch with England winning by an innings and 89 runs.

All but one of the eleven playing for The Rest were to play for England in the next few years, including two prominent batsmen who were to become English captains – Peter May and David Sheppard. Laker himself at this stage had played for England for just eight Tests, being in and out of the side over the past three years.

It was not until 1956 that Laker was firmly established. All cricket fans will remember his unique record of taking 19 wickets against Australia at Old Trafford – an amazing feat unlikely to be ever equalled. That year Laker became the only Bradfordian ever to win the BBC Sports Personality of the Year.

Source: *Yorkshire Post* (1 June 1950)

1 Jun 1972   *The Times* obituary for theatre director Esme Church omits her important Bradford years.

There is a strong case for suggesting that, after JB Priestley, Esme Church (1893-1972) was the most influential person in serious theatre in Bradford. When she arrived at the Civic Playhouse in May 1943, she was a substantial national figure in British theatre. Indeed, her later appointment as its director surprised many, who saw it as a retrograde career move. Trained at the Guildhall School (now RADA), she had been a talented actress, working with the likes of Tyrone Guthrie, and then a talented coach as Head of the School of Acting at the Old Vic.

When she died, *The Times* today gave a fulsome obituary that covered well her early years and at the end of her career some final stage appearances at the RSC in Stratford. Presumably written by a London-based critic, the obituary only refers briefly to her time in Bradford when she was at the height of her powers. The Bradford theatre-going public would have been astounded!

Initially, she was brought in as a producer of two plays, each running for 10 days in the Playhouse's second summer festival. Her first production was George Farquhar's *The Beaux Strategem*. It was hailed a tremendous success. Although her reputation lay in nurturing young talent, she clearly brought the best out of everybody. For example, reviewers highlighted Percy Monkman, a Civic stalwart for over 20 years: *'Percy kept the party going by his clever performance as the squire's amusing servant and won scores of laughs in this part, which fitted him like a glove.' (Telegraph & Argus)*

The two productions immediately convinced the theatre management to make her an honorary vice-president; a year later she became their first professional director. She was very energetic and 'hands-on', producing herself several plays each year. Her selection was broad – classics and 'world premieres', tragedy and comedy, English and foreign. Bradford has never been better served for very good productions of some 15 plays each year.

In 1945 she also opened the Northern School of Drama, using the theatre's facilities. Here she developed local talent that grew into national reputations for the rest of the 20th century – the golden generation of Tony Richardson, David Giles, Bill Gaskill, Robert Stephens, Edward Petherbridge, Bernard Hepton and Billie Whitelaw.

Source: *The Times* (1 June 1972)

1 Jun 1874   The first Pullman train in Britain leaves Bradford

2 Jun 1978   17- year-old Ellery Hanley signs for Bradford Northern to become Great Britain's greatest.

Today's signing of Ellery Hanley must have represented one of the best pieces of business that Bradford Northern, or later Bradford Bulls, ever made in recruiting players.

Leeds-born, 17-years-old, of Jamaican descent, he had not yet made his professional debut, which came six months later. After he retired, he was voted in 2007 as the greatest British rugby league player of all time. In his 19-year career he played 525 matches and scored 416 tries.

Hanley stayed with Bradford Northern until 1985, playing 126 times and scoring 89 tries. He was a very versatile player, appearing most often as a stand-off or loose forward after starting out as a centre or wing. In a remarkable 1984-85 campaign, he scored 55 tries, becoming the first non-winger to exceed the 50-try barrier in more than 70 years.

When he left for Wigan, Bradford Northern received £85,000 which later increased to £150,000. He helped the club win the Challenge Cup three years in a row and in 1987 the World Cup Challenge. After three years of success he signed for an Australian club for a then record fee of £350,000. At the start of the 1991-92 season he returned to England, this time as player and coach for Leeds for £250,000 on a three year contract.

He played 36 times for Great Britain, the first ten as a Bradford Northern player, scoring 20 tries. In 1988, he was appointed captain. In the 1988 Ashes series, he led his side to victory over Australia for the first time in 10 seasons, scoring eight tries.

No Bradford Northern player has ever enjoyed such success in his career.

2 Jun 1952   For the only time in its long history the Bradford Walk ends in a dead heat.

It was the 'longest-running' (sic) amateur race walking event in the world – a gruelling route with enthusiastic public support. The Bradford Walk took place every year on Whit Monday from 1903 to 2011, including through two world wars. Its route and distance varied, but was almost always at least 32 miles.

Today, uniquely, it was a dead heat between 48-year-old Harold Whitlock, six-time winner and 1936 Olympic champion, and 31-year-old first-time winner Bradfordian Charlie Colman. They shared a new record time of four hours, 51 minutes and 43.4 seconds.

Source: *The Bradford Walk*, Yorkshire Race Walking Club (2003)

3 Jun 1930   Margaret McMillan is awarded the Companion of Honour.

In 1917 King George V introduced the Companion of Honour for outstanding achievements, initially limited to 50 members. Today Margaret McMillan became only the fourth woman to receive the honour out of 56 appointed to date. Her achievements came from her national reputation as a highly influential innovator in education, built on nine action-packed years in Bradford from 1893 to 1902. Rarely has anyone had such an impact on city life over a relatively short time.

American-born, she was educated in Inverness and German finishing schools. Initially she became a governess. Living a bourgeois life in rural England, she developed a strong interest in the underdog and in Socialist thinking.

McMillan realised that the place to be was Bradford. She had been invited to speak here in 1892 in the new Labour Church. Her contribution must have been persuasive. Fred Jowett and other Socialists urged her to settle in Bradford. Soon after, the new Independent Labour Party was founded in the city.

A charismatic speaker on many subjects, she captured the hearts of audiences. Very soon she was urged to stand for the Bradford School Board, which became the platform for many innovations she later introduced. Although lacking experience as an administrator, she quickly grasped the importance of the early years. Elementary education had been established in Bradford since the 1870 Elementary Education Act, but no thought had been given to how children really learnt. She realised that many were held back because they came to school hungry and unwashed.

She campaigned for school baths; three schools introduced them. She promoted the need for medical inspection of children; Bradford became the first authority in England to carry this out. She tackled the 'half-time' problem, children who each day worked in factories and attended school. She fought long and hard for school meals; after she left Bradford, it became the first place in England to provide them. She advocated open-air schools to improve ventilation. She secured a wage increase for school caretakers. Whenever possible, she communicated directly with parents about her reforms.

When School Boards were abolished in 1902, she left Bradford for Deptford where she continued her good works in education, publishing several books about her experience.

Nine months after today's announcement Margaret McMillan died. Her name in Bradford lived on with the Margaret McMillan College of Education opening in 1952.

Source: *Margaret McMillan: Prophet and Pioneer*, Albert Mansbridge (1932)

4 Jun 1917   Thomas Maufe's bravery in action earns him a Victoria Cross.

Brown Muff's, Bradford's premier department store, prospered in Victorian times, and so did the family. They moved to live in middle-class Ilkley. The descendants of Thomas Muff who had taken over the family business from his brother-in-law, Henry Brown, decided in 1909 to change their name by deed poll from Muff to Maufe, because they were *desirous of reverting to the old form of our surname'.* This action inspired the local satirical ditty:

> *'In Bradford 'tis good enoof*
> *To be known as Mrs Muff*
> *But in Ilkley by the river Wharfe*
> *'Tis better to be known as Mrs Maufe!'*

Whatever the motivation, the new name continued to be used with distinction. Five members of the family were decorated for military service. The most distinguished award was the Victoria Cross earned by the 19-year-old Thomas Maufe (1898-1942). His father Frederic was a master linen draper, and later chairman of the family business.

Known in the family as 'Squash', Maufe joined up after leaving school. He trained with the Royal Military Academy and was commissioned in May 1916. Just 17 days after his older brother's death at the Battle of the Somme, he travelled to France.

Today, Second Lieutenant Maufe showed gallantry in action, which led to the Victoria Cross. The citation read:

'On 4 June 1917 at Feuchy, France, Second Lieutenant Maufe, on his own initiative and under intense artillery fire, repaired, unaided, the telephone wire between the forward and rear positions, thereby enabling his battery to open fire on the enemy. He also saved what could have been a disastrous occurrence by extinguishing a fire in an advanced ammunition dump caused by a heavy explosion, regardless of the risk he ran from the effects of gas shells in the dump.'

He received his medal from King George V at Buckingham Palace on 29 August 1917 and was also presented with a silver casket by the town of Ilkley in recognition of his bravery. His military career was meteoric; he became one of the youngest to hold the rank of major by the end of the war.

When war broke out again in 1939, Maufe wanted to serve again, However, now being diabetic, he settled for the Home Guard. Ironically, the war hero now aged 43 was killed in March 1942 during a training exercise with a misfiring trench mortar on the moors near Ilkley.

Source: www.godsowncounty.co.uk/yorkshire-history/brown-muffs-vc/

5 Jun 1940   JB Priestley gives the first of his famous *Voice of Britain* radio talks about the Blitz.

By the time of World War Two, Bradford-born JB Priestley was already a very well-known character by virtue of his writing. He was about to become a national celebrity and hero. Tonight (Wednesday) he demonstrated his skill at communication over the radio in the country's hour of need.

At the start of June 1940, Britain was in danger of invasion after the fall of France. The British army had to be evacuated from Dunkirk and a call was issued for boats of all types to make the rescue. With his words in tonight's first of 20 evening broadcasts during that summer and autumn, Priestley helped turn humiliating defeat into heroic victory. In so doing he raised morale and helped shape the national story about Dunkirk and the Battle of Britain – opposing the dark forces of Nazism, Britain winning against all the odds.

In this talk he described with affection the kind of boats that were used to cross the channel, in particular the paddle-steamer, the *Gracie Fields,* which he had often used from his Isle of Wight home. The talk is a masterpiece of well-crafted prose delivered in Priestley's warm and humorous Yorkshire voice drawing the listener in. His informal style is a perfect complement with Churchill's stirring speeches, each a consummate master of communication. It mattered not that their background and political beliefs were so far apart.

The talks (after the first, on Sunday evenings) achieved astonishing popularity. It was estimated that one third of the population listened to each Sunday evening's broadcast. Monday newspapers reprinted extracts and published many letters during the week.

In his final postscript, Priestley said goodbye to his listeners and gave his reasons for ending the series. First, he did not want listeners to tire of his voice and, second, the situation and mood of the country had changed. Thousands of listeners wrote to him and the BBC in shock and disappointment, and he did return in January 1941 for a second series.

In his 1962 memoir *Margin Released,* he wrote: *'To this day middle-aged or elderly men shake my hand and tell me what a ten-minute talk about ducks on a pond or a pie in a shop window meant to them, as if I had given them King Lear or the Eroica.'*

Source: *Priestley's Finest Hour* (blog), Alison Cullingworth (2010)

6 Jun 1997   Barbara Castle becomes the only 'freewoman' of the City.

Today, after 25 such awards to men of Bradford, the 86-year-old Barbara Castle (nee Betts, 1910-2002) became the first woman to be honoured by the city. Given her fiery personality and a life dominating left-wing politics, devoted to taking men on equal terms, it was appropriate that she should be the one to break this glass ceiling.

Born in Chesterfield, Castle came to Bradford, aged 12, when her father's job as a tax inspector moved the family. With her elder sister she was educated at the fee-paying Bradford Girls' Grammar School, surprisingly in view of their parents' egalitarian beliefs. Both parents were Labour Party activists. Growing up in Bradford with its history of radical socialism was the right place for the daughter.

She won a place at Oxford University, but was more interested in practical politics than academic study. However, as a woman she could not progress beyond Treasurer of the University Labour Party.

After much trial and error in developing a career, she decided to stand for Parliament. At 34 she became the youngest female MP, being part of the post-war 1945 intake. Some 34 years later still MP for Blackburn, she became at the time the longest-serving female MP.

She acted as private parliamentary secretary for two ministers, including the young Harold Wilson. However with Labour in opposition from 1951 and the moderate Gaitskell replacing Attlee as Leader in 1955, she lost influence in the 1950s Labour Party until Wilson became leader after Gaitskell died in 1963.

She was a prominent member of Wilson's cabinet (1964-1970). After a successful year in International Development, she was promoted to Transport Minister. Here, a non-driver, she brought in three lasting road safety reforms – the breathalyser, the 70mph speed limit and the fitting of seat belts in all new cars. Later as Secretary of State for Employment and Productivity, she fought a doomed battle for trade union reform with her 1969 White Paper *In Place of Strife*. Three years older, Vic Feather from her early Bradford days was her TUC tormentor.

In Wilson's 1974-1976 Government she was brought back as Health Minister, but became mired in an ideological battle over NHS pay beds. The incoming James Callaghan sacked her in 1976 and her effective political career ended. She continued in the House of Lords as Baroness Castle of Blackburn.

Source: Barbara Castle (*Oxford Dictionary of National Biography*)

7 Jun 1832   Bradford is to be represented in Parliament at last.

Today the Representation of the People Act 1832 was passed. More popularly known as the Great Reform Act, it finally implemented major changes in electoral reform for the House of Commons. The Act stated that it would *'take effectual measures for correcting divers abuses that have long prevailed in the choice of members'*; yet it had taken many years of parliamentary debate to achieve the changes.

For the people of Bradford they could finally be represented. Up till 1832, a town that is estimated by William Cudworth to have had a population of just over 43,000 was not directly represented at Westminster. Those who could do so voted in the large county constituency of Yorkshire. Now Bradford would be one of 22 large towns to be enfranchised for the first time and in fact was given two MPs.

Although this was a big step forward in representation, by modern standards it was well short of universal suffrage. Only male householders living in properties worth at least £10 a year could vote. In practice, 927 such voters who could vote for two candidates participated in the first election that took place between 8 December 1832 and the end of the year (the concept of a single day for elections came later.).

At the new Parliament on the 29 January 1833 Bradford was represented by two Liberals - Ellis Cunliffe Lister with 650 votes and John Hardy with 471. A third candidate, also Liberal, George Banks with 402 votes was unsuccessful. So began a 19th century tradition of returning Liberal MPs with only a couple of Conservative MPs breaking the mould.

Lister came from an ancient, wealthy mill-owning family of Addingham. He was a prominent magistrate, operating from his public house, Lister's Arms (later Spotted House) in Manningham. 'Justice Lister' was also the father of Samuel Cunliffe Lister, the industrialist who became one of the most influential men in Bradford in the rest of the 19th century. He remained MP until 1841.

John Hardy, a barrister by background, was the main owner of the Low Moor Ironworks. He was also returned in the 1835 election. but this time as Conservative until 1837 and then again from 1841 to 1847.

Both these first two MPs came from a background of industry, as did many of their later counterparts in the Victorian era.

8 Jun 2009   Bradford becomes the first UNESCO City of Film.

Today's award was a surprise to many. One might have imagined that places such as Los Angeles, Venice or Cannes with a global film profile might have been the first UNESCO City of Film, but the award came to Bradford.

This permanent title bestows international recognition on Bradford as a world centre for film because of its national museum, its rich film heritage, its movie locations and its many celebrations of the moving image through film festivals.

From the 1890s when pioneers showed one of the first-ever films in a cinema at the People's Palace and the next year brought back the first newsreel of an outside event for same day public showing in Bradford (Queen Victoria's Diamond Jubilee procession in London) to the 1980s when it opened the first IMAX cinema in Europe, the city has been at the forefront of the technology of film.

Making full use of ideal locations for filming, it has also seen many distinguished films based in Bradford and the surrounding area: Undercliffe Cemetery (*Billy Liar*), Keighley & Worth Valley Railway (*Railway Children*), Alhambra (*The Dresser*), Brontë Country (*Wuthering Heights*). It has also seen much local talent flourish such as Tony Richardson (direction), Billie Whitelaw and Bernard Hepton (acting), Simon Beaufoy (scriptwriting) and Steve Abbott (production).

The award reflects past achievements but also enables future developments. For instance it has enabled Bradford to team up with Qingdao, City of Film in China, in a bilateral partnership. This has prompted collaboration in producing a modernised version of *Jane Eyre,* almost as popular in China as in the UK.

Source: www.bradfordcity-of-film.com

8 Jun 1853   The UK spiritualist movement starts in Keighley.

The Spiritualist movement was very popular in Victorian England. Originating in New York State in the 1840s, it is founded on the belief that the spirits of the dead exist and have both the ability and the inclination to communicate with the living. The UK movement started in Keighley in 1853 when David Richmond of the Shakers Movement brought news of spiritual phenomena to David Weatherhead of Keighley. Today they gave one of three lectures held at the Working Men's Hall in Keighley.

This led to the foundation of Keighley's Heber Street Spiritualists' Society, which became the mother church of British spiritualism. In 2003 it celebrated 150 years and still operates from its Heber Street home.

Source: *Telegraph & Argus* (5 June 2003)

9 Jun 2013   The BBC commissions Bollywood-style spectacular of *Carmen* in City Park.

When City Park was conceived, it must have been for events like today's – a multicultural extravaganza on a warm summer's evening, a fusion of East and West, of modern Bollywood dance with classic European opera, a cast of hundreds with thousands more looking on and millions more watching on TV.

BBC Three commissioned one of the most colourful and dramatic live events ever seen in Bradford to celebrate the centenary of Indian film.

The venue made the event – wide, open public spaces in the middle of the city with a backdrop of the Victorian City Hall and 20th century theatre (early) and film museum (late), all illuminated by over 100 spectacular fountains and a unique mirror pool. A large temporary stage was erected in front of City Hall. As well as the songs and dances, it had a (fake) elephant and a real Bollywood star.

The event was *Bollywood Carmen Live,* a twist on Bizet's classic opera. The plot was a modern version of the famous dramatic Spanish story of love, betrayal and intrigue, but all the storylines, songs and dance routines had a Bollywood angle. Spanish arias were replaced by the music of Adele and Bizet's bullfighter was played by Bollywood star Abhay Deol.

In this version, Carmen, played by an actress from *East Enders,* is a young waitress from Bradford who dreams of making it big in Mumbai. She seems amazingly to be achieving her ambition when a major Hindi film actor rolls into town as part of a Bollywood roadshow. Things do not work out as planned.

To play this male lead, the production imported a genuine A-list celebrity, Abhay Deol, from one of Bollywood's great film-making dynasties. He led a number of TV stars from big current shows such as *Strictly Come Dancing.* To complement the professionals, the production included hundreds of local community members as extras in spectacular dance numbers.

The live audience numbered 3,000 lucky people whose names were allocated by a random draw. To round off quite a summer, the whole performance was repeated on the big screen in City Park on Saturday 7 September.

Source: *The Guardian* (5 June 2013)

10 Jun 1987   Jonathan Silver buys Salts Mill.

It turned out to be one of the most sensational transformations from Bradford's industrial past into a modern future. Salts Mill, the symbol of Victorian entrepreneurialism, had become a new hub for arts, tourism, retail and technology, fit for the 21st century. It put Bradford and Saltaire on the map again.

The creative genius behind the transformation was Jonathan Silver (1949-1997). The critical moment occurred today when Silver signed the contract to buy Salts Mill from Illingworth Morris plc, owner of the business since 1958. The business itself had been sold, but the physical asset remained. Closed since February 1986, the derelict mill had seen better days. The owner had offered it to Bradford City Council, but they were not interested. There was even talk of demolition.

Silver had other ideas. With hindsight his life had prepared him for the opportunity.

Born of Jewish parents in Manningham, Silver attended Bradford Grammar School which he much disliked and where he encountered anti-semitism. He showed his entrepreneurial flair in school lunch breaks, popping into Bradford to buy and sell bric-a-brac. He also met for the first time David Hockney, an old boy of the school. Having been given a project for the school magazine, he contacted Hockney, met him in his father's Wimpy Bar and persuaded him to design the front cover.

After Leeds University, where he studied art history and textiles, he began a clothing firm. Before he became 30, he owned 13 menswear shops around the north. He then opened a shop in Manchester for art and furniture, later selling his clothes shops. The partner in the new venture was textile manufacturer Ernest Hall, much more experienced in the business.

Silver and Hall bought Dean Clough, an old carpet factory in Halifax. There Silver acquired experience that later became helpful in Saltaire in making full use of an old building by renting space to new companies. He sold out to Hall, thereby giving Silver's young family the chance and the money to travel for three years.

Now within weeks of their return, Silver phoned the chief executive of Illingworth Morris, made his offer that was accepted, and contacted his old friend Hockney for the loan of some paintings. Almost immediately Silver turned down an offer for the mill that would have made him £1m profit!

Today the idea was born.

Source: *Salt & Silver: A Story of Hope*, Jim Greenhalf (1997)

11 Jun 1906 Woman balloonist dies in tragic accident at Haworth gala.

The witness at the inquest explained:

'He saw the balloon at a quarter to eight, on Monday night as it passed over the back of his house. He saw no one sitting until the thing "exploded". It opened out and the deceased came down head first. She fell like a cart-wheel turning over once or twice. She and the parachute had parted company ... He thought she was just alive when he got to her, he raised her up and said "My good woman if you can speak, do". There was no answer, though her eyes were wide open.'

The verdict was death by misadventure.

Miss Lily Cove was a happy-go-lucky young woman from London with an unusual occupation. She was a daredevil parachutist who travelled the country with her manager Captain Frederick Bidmead, performing at fetes and galas. He was an experienced stunt balloonist and she had made 21 ascents and six descents by parachute without any accident.

They had agreed to appear at Haworth Gala Day on Saturday 9 June. The balloon was filled with gas from the local gasworks. However, with some 6,000 spectators watching, it failed to rise into the air in six or seven attempts. They thought the reason was the heavy atmosphere and the poor quality of the gas.

They agreed to come back again today. It turned out to be a warm summer evening, ideal for the event. This time the balloon was successfully inflated. Miss Cove stepped on to the launch platform, took her seat and fastened herself to a trapeze hanging under the balloon.

She waved to the crowd as the balloon drifted towards Stanbury. At 700 feet, her parachute opened. She descended till about 100 feet, when, approaching a reservoir, she inexplicably detached herself from her safety harness and plunged to the ground head first into a field by the reservoir.

There was no evidence to justify a suicide. Bidmead could only suggest that, as a non-swimmer, she took fright of the water and believed she could land safely on the ground.

This is the sad and strange story behind the arresting tombstone in Haworth Cemetery that visitors might stumble across:

In LOVING MEMORY of ELIZABETH MARY (Miss LILY COVE, PARACHUTIST), DAUGHTER of THOMAS CHARLES COVE of LONDON who DIED JUNE 11th 1906 AGED 21 YEARS

Source: *Bingley and Surrounds: Forgotten Moments from History*, Alan Cattell (2011)

12 Jun 1605   The notorious murders by Walter Calverley, lord of the manor, become public knowledge.

On 23 April 1605, Walter Calverley of Calverley killed his two young sons and attempted the life of his wife and a third child. His gruesome deed and execution provoked great contemporary interest. The public's desire for an account was quickly gratified by publishers in London. Today, one such (Nathaniel Butter) published a prose tract with this title page, containing two stories, the first being this notorious case:

'*The most unnaturall and bloodie murthers, The one by Maister Cauverlie, a Yorkshire Gentleman practised upon his wife and committed upon his two children, the three and twentie Aprill, 1605. The other...*'

Lord of the manor, Calverley lived at Calverley Hall on the outskirts of Bradford and inherited land at Fagley and Eccleshill amongst many other places. In 1599 he married Philippa Brooke of a well-connected family. (Her uncle was Sir Robert Cecil, adviser to both Elizabeth I and James I.) They soon had three young sons. In a drunken frenzy he brutally murdered the two eldest boys and seriously wounded his wife. On his way to kill the youngest, who was with a nanny, he was arrested.

Calverley had been in serious debt, ever since his marriage and had been selling land and property. A year after he married, he was imprisoned for debt. His father had died young, age 39, a fervent Catholic and of unsound mind, and had also been imprisoned for making seditious speeches and was heavily in debt. His son seemed equally unstable. The reason and trigger for the murders are not clear, but debt, instability and pressure from a powerful family perhaps all played a part.

After refusing to enter a plea at his trial in York (reasons unknown), on 6 August he was pressed to death, a particularly cruel form of execution as heavy stones were gradually placed on a board over his naked body until he suffocated.

Calverley's story was twice dramatized. The second time (1608) a play called *A Yorkshire Tragedy* was published in the name of William Shakespeare, who was almost certainly not the author. It is generally now believed to be his contemporary Thomas Middleton.

Calverley's widow remarried. This time she bore three daughters. She died in 1613.

Source: *Heroes, Villains and Victims of Bradford*, Stephen Wade (2008)

13 Jun 1887   Joseph Wright is approached to compile the first *English Dialect Dictionary.*

Professor Joseph Wright (1855-1930) used to say to his Oxford friends that *'I've been an Idle man all my life and shall remain an Idle man till I die'.* Those hearing the words for the first time might have been mystified, for he had a prodigious capacity for hard work and a passionate commitment to his subject. Wright came from Idle on the outskirts of Bradford. His Oxford home was named after Thackley, his birthplace, in the township of Idle. He enjoyed an amazing life in moving from one Thackley to the other.

Born into a poor family that lived for a while in the workhouse at Clayton, he started part-time work just six years old as a 'donkey-boy' and then as a 'bobbin doffer' at Salt's Mill. Although he had some very basic part-time schooling at Saltaire, he did not learn to read properly until his mid-teens.

Increasingly fascinated with languages, he started evening classes at the Mechanics' Institute – a round trip of six miles to walk – learning French, German and Latin, as well as maths and shorthand. When 18, he even started teaching and charging colleagues two pence a week.

Now a woolcomber, as a 21-year-old he had saved enough to undertake a term's study at Heidelberg University, returning later to study for a doctorate in philosophy. In 1888 he took up a teaching post in German at Oxford University. Here he soon became a lecturer in German philology and a few years later professor.

His academic reputation was based mainly on being the first editor of the *English Dialect Dictionary.* Today, already a contributor, he was approached by its founder to take over this huge task started in 1872. After nine years' more research, the publication over six volumes took him another nine (1896 to 1905). The dictionary contained 100,000 words and half a million quotations.

As JRR Tolkien's philology tutor, Wright became his close friend after World War One. He was an important influence in the life of Tolkien, who was to invent his own medieval language of Elvish for his classic *Lord of the Rings.* In the 2018 film *Tolkien* Wright, played by Sir Derek Jacobi in a cameo role, reveals how important that influence was.

Wright had indeed made a long journey from Idle donkey-boy to renowned Oxford professor.

Source: *The Life of Joseph Wright,* Mrs EM Wright (1932)

14 Jun 1849   The *Bradford Observer* reports another outbreak of cholera.

Bradford had a cholera epidemic in 1832. This can have been no surprise given a powerful report in 1843 from the Health of Towns Commission: *'Of Bradford I am obliged to pronounce it the most filthy town I visited'*. Central Bradford in the 1840s is described as having *'courts, yards and dingy alleys with overflowing privies, open cesspits, pig styes and slaughterhouses and effluent-laden watercourses'*.

Today, Bradford's only newspaper reported an outbreak in some Northern towns *'In Bradford we have several cases, and four of these have already terminated fatally'*. The paper then commented: *'The conditions of transmission and infection are an impure atmosphere, and depraved physical health. The best antidotes are cleanliness, temperance, cheerfulness. As surely as magnet attracts steel, so certainly will filth and dirt develop cholera. Hard drinkers will fall the easiest prey. Incessant dread may predispose the body to take it. Let all offensive dunghills, dirt heaps, stagnant, muddy pools and decomposing matter of every description be forthwith removed. Let every house be made as comfortable as it can: comfort is at mortal enmity with cholera. Good sanitary arrangements universally applied and effectually carried out will soon drive away this oriental pestilence from England, as the plague has been driven away.'*

We know now that it is poor sanitation and lack of clean water that creates the environment for cholera to flourish, but here we read that temperance, cheerfulness and comfort also keep cholera at bay.

By the time this strain of cholera disappeared completely, 420 people had died, mainly in poor working-class districts. There was little sense of a real emergency and some blame was attached to the victims. For example, the report of the first victim emphasised that *'he was a man of intemperate habits who had been drunk the night before he fell ill'*.

Titus Salt, then mayor of Bradford, made a speech on the lessons of this tragedy: *'The cholera most forcibly teaches us our mutual connection. Nothing shows more powerfully the duty of every man to look after the needs of others. Cholera is God's voice to his people.'*

Further epidemics broke out in 1853, 1854 and 1856.

It was not until the mid-1880s before the true cause of cholera became widely known.

Source: *The Great Paternalist: Titus Salt and the Growth of 19th Century Bradford*, Jack Reynolds (1983)

15 Jun 1872   Bradford's first public library opens its doors.

Today was a very low key affair. With no opening ceremony, the new library just started lending books. In fact, Bradford was slow in getting round to offer such a facility. The Public Libraries Act 1850 had given local boroughs the power to establish free public libraries, but the Mechanics Institute had provided a popular library since 1832.

James Hanson, owner of the radical weekly *Bradford Review,* had used its columns to argue for a public library but, until the mayor called a public meeting on 15 March 1871, nothing happened. Even at that meeting, six months after the passing of Forster's Education Act, there was some opposition, but most believed a library was just a completion of that Act. The proposal passed and things happened quickly.

Premises were rented in Tyrrel Street. On 11 October the first librarian, Charles Virgo, was appointed. The long-term success of the library service was very much down to Virgo and his successor. The library also started with a huge piece of good fortune. A prominent citizen had died, leaving behind a collection of 13,000 books that his executors sold to the Corporation.

Selected from 183 applicants, Virgo aged 26 was innovative. He devised a method of card charging for issuing books, which was described for several generations as the 'Bradford system'. Each lender received a linen pocket, bearing his name and address, and each book a card, containing details arranged so that, when the card was placed in the pocket, the book number projected from a cut-away corner. The two would be filed together while the book was on loan.

Virgo saw the library service expand with branches in evenings at six of the new board schools. Growth soon led to the need for new premises. In January 1878 it moved into new premises in Darley Street, where it remained for nearly 90 years.

In 1884 Virgo resigned to become a museum curator in Manchester. He was replaced by Butler Wood (1854-1934), who had been one of the first employees back in 1872. He, too, introduced many innovations – Sunday opening, library for Braille books, children's libraries, travelling libraries, students' room, commercial library. His love of literature led to him establishing a Brontë Museum in Haworth and founding the Brontë Society. He retired in 1925 after 50 years' service as a librarian.

Source: *Bradford City Libraries 1872-1972,* AFH Newell (1972)

16 Jun 1983 The National Museum of Photography, Film and Television (NMPFT) opens.

The early 1980s were difficult years for Bradford. Major job losses and economic decline forced the City Council to look hard for new opportunities. Its chief executive Gordon Moore was the man for such a challenge. One of his legacies was a new national museum for the arts. Today, renowned photographer Lord Snowden opened the NMPFT as part of the National Science Museum.

Setting out to explore the art and science of the image, it immediately grabbed attention by offering Europe's first-ever IMAX cinema and the country's largest cinema screen. IMAX is a proprietary system developed in the early 1970s in North America, which presents high-resolution films shown in theatres with very large screens (seven storeys high) and steep seating, offering an immersive experience with high quality sound.

Central government policy from the 1970s indicated that museums should be located around the provinces rather than London. The success of York's National Railway Museum illustrated what might be possible.

The City Council identified a suitable empty site – Wardley House, named after the engineer who controversially destroyed much of the city centre in the 1960s. However the site was appropriate for a much better reason. Here in 1896 Bradford had shown its first-ever cinema performance at the People's Palace. By renovating an existing building, the City Council kept costs down to £1.8m, largely funded by EU and other grants.

Naturally such a project deserved appropriate celebrations. Four hundred guests were treated by Harry Ramsdens at Guiseley to fish-and-chip dinners and champagne.

16 Jun 1999 The NMPFT receives a major refit.

On the same day that it opened 16 years ago, the museum was formally re-opened by actor Pierce Brosnan after a £16m refit that added 25% more space. The building now had a new glass frontage, curved like a piece of cine-film, which complemented beautifully the domes of the Alhambra and old Odeon standing adjacent to the museum.

In 2007, it became the National Media Museum, reflecting a remit to include new media such as videogames and the internet.

Ten years later, it rebranded once more, this time as the National Science and Media Museum. Its focus changed to the 'science of light and sound technologies'. This covered up a controversial decision to take back to London the Royal Photographic Society's world-renowned collection located in Bradford since 2003.

Source: *Telegraph & Argus* (26 June 2009)

17 Jun 2017   AA Dhand launches his first Asian detective thriller set in Bradford.

AA Dhand hit the ground running at today's launch in the iconic Gothic building of the old Wool Exchange, now Bradford's Waterstones. *Streets of Darkness* immediately grabbed the headlines.

His police inspector hero Harry Virdee is a Sikh who has married a Muslim girl. In doing this they have both cut themselves off irretrievably from their respective families. The main racial tension is between immigrant cultures, rather than between white British and Asian. Imminent race riots offer the threat in the plot: in reality, they are a cover for a quite different threat and a different story.

Raised in Bradford, Dhand started work by helping out at the family's convenience store. After qualifying as a pharmacist, he started his own business and began writing. The city's history and diversity have already inspired three 'crime noir' detective thrillers in three years.

Dhand certainly knows his Bradford. It is not enough to refer to a visit to a well-established Italian restaurant in the city centre. It has to be Mamma Mia's in Upper Piccadilly. He rarely misses opportunities for a historical reference. For example, if his hero is in the Midland Hotel, then he remembers that every Prime Minister up to Harold Wilson has stayed there. The context for the crime, the drugs and the fights is precisely and obsessively Bradford.

17 Jun 1995   Yvonne McGregor breaks the classic cycling world record.

From Wibsey, Yvonne McGregor came late to cycling. She did not ride a bike until she was 17. She was 29 before she competed as a cyclist, coming third in the British triathlon championship in 1990. Then cycling did take over.

In 1993 she broke fellow Yorkshirewoman Beryl Burton's 20-year-old British one-mile time-trial record. The next year she scored her first major success when she won the points race at the 1994 Commonwealth Games in Victoria, Canada.

Today in Manchester she achieved her career highlight in setting an hour record for women at 47.411 km.

In 1996 she broke Burton's 25-mile time-trial record, but just missed out on a medal at the 1996 Summer Olympics. Four years later in Sydney she achieved bronze in the same event and won the pursuit at the 2000 Track Cycling World Championships in Manchester.

Her final achievement was in 2002 to set a European and sea-level hour record of 43.689 km, which remained the British record until 2015.

18 Jun 1753   Mob runs riot in destroying turnpikes around Bradford.

Until the 18th century transport links between towns were provided by ancient ridge ways and pack horse routes. With the gradual increase in trade thereafter these routes became seriously inadequate.

From 1727 the first Turnpike Trusts were set up by Acts of Parliament to improve the state of existing roads. The improvements would be funded by charging tolls at strategic points. Tolls were resented by local communities that had used existing routes freely for centuries.

After the Leeds – Halifax stretch was extended to Wibsey, today there was a riot: *'A mob arose from several parts, but chiefly from Yeadon and Otley and the adjacent places, and pulled down a turnpike at Bradford Moor end, and afterwards attempted to destroy Bradford turnpike; the same day they destroyed one at Apperley Bridge.'*

(Four days later) *'They assembled again, and were joined by many hundreds of people, from most parts of Bradford parish, when they tore down a turnpike at Tyersal Moor end and burnt it and the house together; the same day they burnt one at Newall Hall and Wibsey turnpike house, and Bradford turnpike shared the same fate.'*

Source: *Bradford and the Industrial Revolution*, Gary Firth (1990)

18 Jun 1815   War hero Christopher Ingham from Keighley wins his medal at the Battle of Waterloo.

One gravestone at Keighley's Utley Cemetery has an intriguing inscription:

'In memory of the late Christopher Ingham, landlord of the Reservoir Tavern, Keighley, who died September 9th, 1866, in the 80th year of his age. He was one of the heroes of the Peninsular War. For having served in the 95th regiment of Foot, for which he received the silver medal and 9 clasps for the engagements at Toulouse, Orthes, Pyrenees, Vittoria, Salamanca, Badajoz, Ciudad, Rodrigo, Fuentea, D'Oner and Busaco. He also received the medal for Waterloo.'

Christopher Ingham survived ten battles against Napoleon's forces in Spain, France and Belgium between 1807 and 1815. This included the Spanish Peninsula War and today's Battle of Waterloo, for which he won several medals.

His outstanding military record over nearly a decade makes him the earliest known military hero in the Bradford and district area – the record scarcely bettered by anyone in the 200 years since.

We know little else about Ingham, except that after the war he settled in Keighley and took over as landlord of the Reservoir Tavern.

19 Jun 1915   The Lord Mayor opens open-air swimming pool in Lister Park.

Today, the City Council opened a new amenity in its premier park by Manningham Lane. With thousands of Bradford men away at the trenches of Northern France, one imagines that the people who came to watch were mainly women and children.

However, the programme gave a full description of this modern swimming pool in words not likely to capture the imagination. For example,

'The Bath is surrounded by a close-boarded fence, seven feet high, fixed on the top of an embankment which has been formed from the material excavated for the pond; trees are planted on the slopes of the embankment and around the Bath and next to the inner side of the fencing flower beds and shrubs have also been planted.

The Swimming Pond is 150 feet long by 60 feet wide and will hold 286,000 gallons or 1,300 tons of water. The depth is 3ft.4ins. at the shallow end and 6ft.10ins. at the deep end.

Settling tanks have been formed at the west end of the Bath for the purpose of intercepting the solid matter in the water from the stream by which the pond will be supplied, and the outlet of the pond will discharge into the stream.

Spittoons are arranged around the pond.'

During the 1930s the pool lost its popularity, as it did not meet the standards of hygiene that swimmers demanded. The City Council agreed a programme of modernisation to ensure water purity and consistent heat and, for spectators, shelter and spacious cafe with glass-fronted lounges. The new look lido was officially opened in May 1939, four months before the outbreak of the next war.

So, by a quirk of planning, the pool saw its best days in the two world wars.

A generation later, the lido suffered from financial cutbacks. From 1973 opening hours were reduced. In 1983 it was closed when the cost of repairs became too high. The amenity was finally demolished in 1991.

As a result of local government reorganisation in 1974, the council became responsible for another open-air lido in much more salubrious surroundings by the side of the River Wharfe in Ilkley. Built in 1935, this is one of Yorkshire's last open-air swimming pools, with central fountain, slide and an Art Deco café. It features in lists of top ten lidos in the country.

Source: https://bradfordlocalstudies.wordpress.com/2015/07/23/lister-park-lido/

20 Jun 1825   The strikers in the Great Bradford Strike strike back.

'The Non-Signers of Bradford and Its Neighbourhood

Fellow non-signers,

Those hot-headed Fellows, the Inhabitants of the SUN, seem to think, because they have more Light and Heat, that they have more Sense and Wisdom, also, than we poor Mortals of the lower Regions.

It has lately also been driven into their empty Noddles, that they have a Right to rule or govern us, who are only the poor and simple Inhabitants of Earth.

On account of our independent Spirit, we did not so easily submit to this, as they the Inhabitants of the SUN had at first imagined. They have, therefore, solicited their Brethren, who live in neighbouring STARS, to come to their Assistance and help them in putting down the Upstarts of the Earth.

Not being able, with the Assistance of their zealous Brethren of the Stars, together with the King of that scorching COMET nightly seen at BOWLING, to curb by Force our independent Spirit, they have now Recourse to Stratagem.

They mean to assail us separately with a Request to sign. To sign what? ... Cannot you think or guess? Yes. We think we are to sign away our independence. We think we are to sign away our children's Bread. We think we are to sign away our Labour at any price which these Inhabitants of the higher Regions may be pleased to give. This we certainly shall do if we sign against the UNION.

Committee-Room, Roebuck Inn, Bradford, June 20th, 1825'

Note: The SUN also refers to the Sun Inn (bottom of Ivegate) where the strikers' opponents met, fitting the sarcastic, 'tongue-in-cheek' tone of the poster.

This was the first part of a poster produced today by the newly formed Combers and Weavers Union in response to pressure placed on its members by mill-owners, following the union's declaration of a strike earlier in June. The poster asked strikers not to sign a petition stating that that they disagreed with the union's action.

The issues were low pay for long hours and recognition of the union. The strikers relied on voluntary contributions from neighbouring towns and villages, and sometimes further afield. The strike went on for 23 weeks, before the strikers were forced to abandon their action, at the same wages and hours that had brought them to strike in the first place.

Source: *Bradford Woolcombers' Strike 1825* (Poster, West Yorkshire Metropolitan Archive Service)

21 Jun 1869   Titus Salt Junior commissions a new country mansion at Milner Field.

Today, the *Bradford Observer* carried an advertisement for builders about the letting of works for the erection of a property near Saltaire.

In a woodland clearing at Shipley Glen, overlooking the Aire valley, where the family's wool empire was based, Sir Titus Salt had bought a property in 1869. The land was known as Milner Field. He had the property demolished immediately and transferred the land to his youngest son, Titus Junior.

With his wife Catherine Crossley, daughter of the Halifax carpet manufacturing dynasty, Titus Junior had grand plans. By 1873 they had a magnificent Gothic edifice with two towers, a courtyard enclosed with an imposing arch, an 81ft domed glasshouse with intricate mosaic flooring, an orangery, croquet lawn, manicured grounds and boating lake.

Everything was set for the mansion to become the centre of lavish entertainment for Yorkshire's famous. For some years this was indeed the case. It was graced by two royal visits. First, the Prince and Princess of Wales visited when they opened the Bradford Technical College in 1882. Then, five years later Queen Victoria's youngest daughter, Princess Beatrice, visited for the opening of the Royal Jubilee Exhibition.

Yet in less than 60 years the mansion was abandoned.

It all started with Titus Junior's sudden and untimely death in the summer of 1887. At the time the Saltaire Mill business was struggling with foreign competition. His widow was forced to sell the business to a syndicate of four businessmen, including James Roberts who soon became its managing director and the new owner of Milner Field.

Three of his four sons all died between 1898 and 1912. The surviving son was badly injured in World War One. Worse, a nurse whom he had met in hospital and married died in the global influenza pandemic, while pregnant. The owner's two daughters each had complicated and difficult personal lives.

Milner Field was starting to attract an unfortunate reputation. It became hard to sell or let.

In 1923 one owner moved in, but lost his wife to illness within weeks. Two years later, he died of blood poisoning after cutting his foot. The final owner took up residence but his wife aged 43 died of pneumonia within a year. Three years later he, too, died unexpectedly.

After 1930 the mansion was never again occupied and gradually became a roofless ruin. It was eventually demolished sometime in the 1950s.

22 Jun 1897   Richard Appleton shows country's first-ever same-day newsreel for a Bradford audience.

It was a bold initiative and everything went to plan.

The *Bradford Daily Argus* put up the money for today's publicity stunt in its circulation war with bitter rival, the *Bradford Daily Telegraph*. Richard Appleton (1857-1946) accepted the challenge, travelled down to London in the morning, filmed Queen Victoria's Diamond Jubilee procession and brought back a newsreel for an open-air public screening in Bradford in the evening, repeated the rest of the week. This had never been done before in Britain. At the final showing in Forster Square an estimated 10,000 spectators are reported to have seen the newsreel.

Son of Thomas Appleton, a prominent Bradford photographer, Appleton took over his father's business in the 1890s and soon became interested in the developing art of cinematography. He had already produced his own 'magic lantern' for showing slides before creating in 1896 the cieroscope. This device combined the three functions of camera, printer, and projector. At the Mechanics' Institute in December that year, he had demonstrated how the new device presented what were called 'living pictures'. He also started to hire out his services for filming events.

When Appleton reached London, he placed his new film camera in a position where the state procession leaving St Paul's could be photographed. As soon as the event was recorded, he returned to St Pancras Station. Here, the Midland Railway had equipped a special coach as a dark-room, called the *Bradford Daily Argus Photo Laboratory*. On the way back to Bradford's Midland Station, laboratory technicians worked hard to develop thousands of animated negatives. It was not easy to dry out the images, but the job was done by the time they arrived. The finished job was projected onto sheets hanging from the *Bradford Daily Argus* building.

The newspaper had the last word: *'To effect this ambitious scheme, 19th century photography, as represented by the noted Bradford firm of R J Appleton and Co, was summoned to the journalistic enterprise, and this combination of progressive forces achieved a veritable triumph of scientific research'.* The only disappointment is that the film itself was lost. Appleton himself did not pursue his early interest in film-making, being diverted into the related field of X-rays. He did, however, leave his mark on the history of film-making in this country.

Source: *Movie Makers And Picture Palaces: A Century of Cinema in Bradford 1896-1996*, GJ Mellor (1997)

23 Jun 1882   Bradford's first-ever official royal visitors open the Bradford Technical School.

Sir Henry Mitchell (1824-1898) was one of Bradford's finest ambassadors and public servants.

Born in Esholt, he moved into his father's wool business where from age 14 he was taught practically every branch of worsted manufacture. Three years later he became a buyer at William Fison and Co. Ltd. Soon he was made a partner and travelled extensively, especially in the USA. He became a leading authority on the worsted trade – for example, he was appointed English juror for silk and woollen fabrics for the Philadelphia Centennial Exhibition (1876).

A councillor, magistrate and mayor, he was also heavily involved in many of Bradford's institutions – Grammar School, Mechanics' Institute and Chamber of Commerce. Without doubt his biggest single achievement was the foundation of the Bradford Technical School and today it was crowned by Bradford's first-ever official royal visit for its opening.

Mitchell's travels showed him the need for appropriate education to sustain Bradford's pre-eminent position in the wool industry. Britain was falling behind its European counterparts. Only the Mechanics' Institute filled the gap that was developing in providing educational support outside the workplace for those already in the industry. Mitchell himself had been fortunate in learning about the industry in a systematic way from his father.

The Prince (later, King Edward VII) and Princess of Wales had stayed overnight as guests of Titus Salt Junior at Milner Field and had travelled in a procession from Saltaire through Lister Park, down Manningham Lane into Bradford, greeted by cheering crowds that grew larger and noisier as it reached the destination of the new School building in Great Horton Road. All Bradford's industrial leaders were present, including Lord Masham, Isaac Holden, Alfred Illingworth, Sir Henry Ripley.

In the after-lunch speeches WE Forster, who had personally invited the Prince of Wales, toasted Mitchell: *'We owe him more than to any other man the formation and the success of this college. I do not mean to say that we should not have had a Technical College without him; but most certainly should not had it so soon. His Royal Highness has paid us a great compliment to-day. He tells us that we stand in the van in this movement in England. It is true, but England does not stand in the van as compared with countries. It was beginning to suffer very much from being behindhand in the race.'*

Source: *Bradford Observer* (24 June 1882)

24 Jun 1911 Bradford leads the way with Leeds in using trolley-buses.

Today, Bradford's first trolley-bus service started operation between Laisterdyke and Dudley Hill along Sticker Lane. It linked the tram services that ran out of the city on Leeds Road and Wakefield Road.

In fact, the formal opening had taken place four days earlier at the same time as a new service in Leeds. Both cities had taken the lead in developing a trolley-bus service, being the first in Great Britain to do so. Members of the Corporation and invited guests were conveyed by special tramcar to Laisterdyke. The Chairman of the Tramways Committee gave a brief speech before the party travelled by trolley-bus to Dudley Hill, and thence by tram to Leeds. Here they joined up with their Leeds counterparts for a celebratory luncheon. Although three other corporations had visited European cities to see new trolley-bus services in action earlier than the two West Yorkshire cities did in 1909, it was Bradford and Leeds that were quicker off the mark in implementing their service.

The new trolley-bus was an electric bus that drew its electricity from overhead wires using spring-loaded trolley-plates. Two wires and poles were required to complete the electrical circuit, unlike a tram which used the track as part of the electrical path and so needed only one wire and a pole. Locally, the trolley-bus was called the 'trackless' to differentiate it from the tram. Overall, it was a quiet, clean and efficient service. Nowadays we would also say ecologically friendly.

As well as pioneering a trolley-bus service, between 1920 and 1922 the Corporation built the first two double-deck trolley-buses in Britain, used initially on the Bolton to Bankfoot service. They were known locally as 'flying cottage loaves' because of their shape.

Although trolley-buses worked well, the Corporation decided to phase them in gradually and retain the tram system, which did not finally disappear until 1950. Nevertheless, 17 routes were adopted, including three in the post-war period, reaching out to all parts of the city boundary.

Overall, Bradford developed an extensive trolley-bus service. In contrast, Leeds hardly got going, operating just three routes, and did not last more than 17 years. When Bradford closed its last trolley-bus route in 1972, its service had lasted longer than all 49 other places in Britain that had one.

Source: *Leeds Mercury* (21 June 1911)

25 Jun 1904   Samuel Lister has the last word in his long-standing argument with Sir Isaac Holden.

Samuel Cunliffe Lister and Sir Isaac Holden were probably the two wealthiest of Bradford's wool millionaires. Holden died in 1897. Seven years later his one-time business partner Lister (now Lord Masham) published a booklet, providing his version of the 'Holden controversy' that had been a public argument between the two men for much of their working lives. The trigger for this latest intervention was a reference to *'this very disagreeable affair'* in a recent publication linked to the 1904 Bradford Exhibition that had greatly irked Lister.

The booklet was introduced by today's covering letter from Lister to Bradford's mayor and opens with strong words: *'Upon looking back at the history of the late Sir Isaac Holden it is, it appears to me, impossible to come to any other conclusion but that he was insane on the question of invention, and there is no difficulty in proving it, but IF SANE there are no words strong enough in the English language with which to condemn him'.*

The origins of the disagreement lay in the invention in the 1840s of what was called the square motion wool comb, which became a commercially viable wool comb, hitherto an innovation that had so far eluded inventors. The invention lay at the heart of the immense wealth of both men. Later Holden claimed he invented the principle behind the new device, but Lister claimed he had the patent. The controversy flared up on more than one occasion since they parted ways some ten years later. For example, they had carried out a public argument with detailed letters in the 1870s to the *Bradford Observer*. Much later Lister had been particularly angered by the publication of James Burnley's *The History of Wool and Woolcombing* (1889), extolling Holden's inventive genius, a book that Lister claimed was financed by Holden.

Here in this booklet Lister demolished Holden's reputation as an inventor. He wrote: *'And now for the patent of 1847. I am very, very particular about its history, for with great cunning he* (Holden) *tried to show that we were JOINTLY making and patenting improvements in woolcombing. Look at* (James) *Burnley* (page) *299-300. Nothing could be more untrue, as he knew nothing about woolcombing. He had never seen any fine wool combed.'*

Some 19 months later Lister died, thereby putting an end to the affair.

Source: *Sir Isaac Holden and the Square Motion*, Lord Masham (1904)

26 Jun 1857 Bradford-born private is one of first to be awarded the new Victoria Cross in Crimean War.

'Private Matthew Hughes No 1879 Pte 7th Royal Fusiliers was noticed by Colonel Campbell, 90th Light Infantry, on 7th June 1855, at the storming of the quarries, for twice going for ammunition, under heavy fire, across the open ground; he also went to the front, and brought in Pte John Hampton, who was lying severely wounded; and on June 18th 1855 he volunteered to bring in Lieut. And Adjutant Hobson, 7th Royal Fusiliers, who was lying severely wounded and in the act of doing so was severely wounded himself.'

This was the citation for the first Bradford-born soldier to win today the Victoria Cross. Introduced by Queen Victoria for the Crimean War (1853 -1856), it is the most prestigious award, given for gallantry *'in the presence of the enemy'* to members of the British Armed Forces, officers and men without distinction.

This award belonged to the first batch of 62 Victoria Crosses. Uniquely, the batch was also presented by Queen Victoria herself. The ceremony took place at Hyde Park. Tens of thousands of people attended, including Prince Albert. The queen rode on horseback towards the line of men ready to receive their medals, but she did not dismount and awarded the medals from her horse. As each man came forward, his name was read out along with the name of his regiment. The queen pinned the medal to the man's chest.

Private Hughes lies buried in an obscure corner of Undercliffe Cemetery, near to where he was born in Wapping Road in 1822.

In fact, he had a chequered military career. Aged 18, he enlisted in the 7th Royal Fusiliers at Leeds. In the Crimea he was promoted in January 1855 to corporal and then to sergeant nine months later, but then court-martialled and reduced to private, then pardoned. There were several other brushes with military authority. Never confirmed, the reason might have been drink.

He returned to Bradford in 1861, married, became a recruiting sergeant and with his wife ran a pub called the Gardeners Arms until he died in 1882 from cirrhosis of the liver.

Source: www.undercliffecemetery.co.uk

27 Jun 1936   Campaigner Florence White speaks at Great Spinsters' Rally in London.

In 1940 a new law was passed. A woman might now retire at 60, not 65, and claim a pension, providing that she had worked and paid her National Insurance stamps. A man must still wait until he was 65. The reason for the change was Florence White (1886 -1961).

Florence was born in East Bowling, the middle child in a family of three children. Her mother was an illiterate mill worker. Her father was educated, but left the family home in 1889. Florence attended Bowling Back Lane Board School. Although clever, she left school aged 12 and started working a 12-hour day at a local mill. Aged 18 after a breakdown she left the mill. With her sister she earned a living from piano lessons and dress-making. She became engaged, but her fiance died a year later in World War One. Neither she nor her sister were to marry.

Florence became politically motivated and joined the Liberal Party. Canvassing, she came into contact with many unmarried women who suffered real hardship, dying before they reached 65. She became concerned with their lack of financial security.

She decided to start a campaign. In April 1935 she advertised a public meeting at the Bradford Mechanics' Institute. She hoped for 150 attendees, but 600 came. By the end of the evening the National Spinsters' Pensions Association (NSPA) was formed with the demand that spinsters should receive a non-retirement pension of 10 shillings per week at 55 years old, not 65.

By the end of 1935 the NSPA had 16 branches and several thousand members. They described themselves as war spinsters who should have been married, save for the accident of war. Their slogan *'Equity with the Widow'* claimed equality with widows who from 1931 had been able to claim pensions from the age of 55. In 1936 they drew up a Spinsters' Charter.

For four more years they campaigned across the UK and lobbied MPs. Today's rally in central London was one of their largest. The MP for Bradford Central, William Leach, championed their cause and persuaded Parliament to set up a committee to investigate. The campaign stalled until the Chancellor in January 1940 surprisingly announced that pensions were to be paid to insured spinsters and wives of pensioners aged 60.

Not a complete victory, but the NSPA saw it as success.

Source: Florence White (*Oxford Dictionary of National Biography*)

28 Jun 1910   The Fattorini family creates one mail order company, and unintentionally another.

For much of the 19th and 20th centuries Fattorinis was a distinguished name in Bradford. It started with Antonio Fattorini (1797-1859) who came to Leeds from northern Italy around 1870 as a market trader and travelling pedlar at rural fairs.

In 1827 Fattorini moved into a more permanent base in the new central market in Leeds. Four years later he bought his first 'lock-up' shop and focused on jewellery, plate and glassware. In 1841 he opened up another shop in Harrogate and in 1846 a much larger one in Bradford, then rapidly growing with new rail links. This became the base of Fattorini & Sons. He had seven sons, who were all involved in the family business, with one soon moving into a shop in Skipton.

The Bradford shop became very well-known for jewellery, regalia, clocks, watches, musical instruments and luxury goods. Soon two outlets were open on Cheapside/ Kirkgate corner and Westgate. Tony Fattorini, grandson of Antonio, developed a prominent reputation. His knowledge of clocks led him to design the first chess clocks and become a sports timekeeper (eg for the Olympics). He was also heavily involved in local sport. He represented Manningham FC when it broke away from rugby union to league in 1895, and in 1903 when it switched to soccer. Later, Fattorinis were to design the current FA Cup, won for the first time by Bradford City in 1911.

In the meantime, the shop was developing a mail order business based on a much wider range of goods. Today they went one step further to separate completely the new business as a limited company. Empire Stores became one of two large mail order companies in the country. It moved into its Canal Road headquarters, employing about 2,000 people at its height. In 1961 it was listed on the Stock Exchange.

In a strange twist of fate, its main competitor was also from Bradford and also created by a Fattorini. Grattan Warehouses Ltd (later Grattan's) was set up by John Enrico Fattorini who within two years fell out with his cousin Herbert running Empire Stores over a clash of management styles.

Successful, both mail order businesses were eventually bought out by much bigger European retail corporations. Six generations later, Fattorinis' name is familiar in two places as a long-established jeweller, one in Harrogate's main shopping area and the other in the Birmingham Jewellery Quarter.

Source: *A Pedlar's Legacy*, Patrick Beaver (1981)

29 Jun 1968   On the day of a national rail strike the Keighley & Worth Valley Railway reopens as heritage line.

On 9 February 1864 the first sod on the proposed Keighley & Worth Valley Railway (KWVR) was cut by Isaac Holden, its chairman and wool magnate, soon to live in Oakworth. Recognising the need for a rail link from the main network at Keighley for the growing numbers of visitors to the home of the Brontë sisters at Haworth, the Government had passed an Act of Parliament to enable the link in 1862.

This branch line was opened for passengers in April 1867 with stations at Ingrow West, Damems, Oakworth, Haworth and Oxenhope. By the end of 1961 the KWVR passenger service, now unprofitable, was withdrawn, followed by the goods service 18 months later.

Almost immediately a preservation society was formed by rail enthusiasts and local people which bought the line from British Rail. It reopened today in 1968 as a heritage railway, one of the first in the country and still one of the country's only three preserved railways operating a complete branch line in its original form. The first train to leave for Oxenhope was the only train to operate anywhere in the UK because of a national train strike.

Now it has developed into a major tourist attraction with more than 100,000 visitors a year, supported by a few paid staff and hundreds of volunteers.

Steam railways attract film and TV productions and, being one of the earliest heritage lines, the KWVR has developed into a magnet for major films. The most famous film was *The Railway Children* (1970) which exploited the tunnel near Haworth. *Yanks* (1979) also used it as a location, as have episodes from many TV series.

29 Jun 2010   First Cabinet meeting of new Coalition Government takes place at Odsal Stadium.

Prime Minister Gordon Brown started the trend for Cabinet meetings outside London. In 2010 the incoming David Cameron continued it at his first Cabinet today. The whole Cabinet left London and met on this occasion at Odsal Stadium, home of the Bradford Bulls. The away day was intended to show support for hard-hit economies outside the capital. As the new Government's task, however, was to introduce a period of austerity into the public sector, spending £100,000 (eg extra security) on such a meeting attracted much criticism.

Two Yorkshire-born Cabinet ministers, William Hague and Baroness Warsi, took the opportunity to visit the newly built Bradford Grand Mosque.

30 Jun 1643   The Royalists defeat the Parliamentarians at Adwalton Moor in Bradford's only battle.

In December 1642 the Royalists had been repulsed in the first Siege of Bradford.

Six months later in the Civil War they were to face the Parliamentarians again. Nonconformist Bradford was firmly on Parliament's side. Sir Thomas Fairfax was still their leader. The Royalist leader, the Earl of Newcastle, now based in Pontefract, believed that Bradford should be taken, as it was both a troublesome town and critical to supply routes with Lancashire. He set off with at least 10,000 men.

Hearing of this, Fairfax decided to face the Royalists with some 4,000 men outside the town, believing that a surprise start gave them the best chance of another victory. Today they met at Adwalton Moor just inside Bradford's current boundary with Leeds. The Parliamentarians started well and might even have prevailed until a surprise charge by pikemen turned things round. The Parliamentarians fled back to Bradford.

Newcastle followed and stayed over at Bolling Hall, overlooking the town. His men prepared for a second siege in the morning: Fairfax feared for his men. Overnight Newcastle relented and the Parliamentarians were spared. Many believed that Newcastle had seen a ghost that wailed *'Pity, poor Bradford!'*. Only those who resisted were killed.

Although the Royalists came out on top in the West Riding, the Battle of Adwalton Moor encouraged Parliamentarians to regroup, which ultimately led them to defeat the Royalists.

Source: *Bradford*, Joseph Fieldhouse (1972)

30 Jun 1846   The Leeds & Bradford Railway is officially opened.

Since 1830 the case, and choice of routes, for a Leeds/Bradford rail link had been much debated; finally, in 1844 an Act of Parliament was passed. Today nearly two years later was the official opening.

Things did not go well for some of the official guests. Those from Leeds would take the train at noon and arrive in Bradford for a lavish luncheon by the station. The Bradford guests would catch a train from 11am to Leeds to return with the Leeds guests. But the Bradford train was nearly an hour late setting off, crossing the Leeds train at Shipley. When it arrived in Leeds, the station was deserted. All the Leeds guests were now in Bradford enjoying the luncheon which the Bradford guests missed when they finally returned.

It rained heavily all day. It never rains but it pours.

(Note: All 1,000 guests together did enjoy a grand evening banquet in Leeds.)

Source: *Bradford*, Joseph Fieldhouse (1972)

JUNE

BELOW: Brown Muff department commissioned this painting by well-known Bradford artist Percy Monkman to celebrate 150 years of trading (story on 20 Apr).
@: Martin Greenwood

ABOVE: In honour of his hero Edmund Cartwright, who invented the woolcombing machine, Samuel Cunliffe Lister funded Cartwright Memorial Hall, the city's main art gallery (story on 13 Apr).
Credit: Richard Wilson Photography

203

BELOW: Here in Ivegate, one of Bradford's oldest streets, is the 1645 birthplace of John Sharp, Bradford's only archbishop (story on 23 Apr).
Credit: Richard Wilson Photography

ABOVE: The design of the Wool Exchange was famously criticised by Victorian thinker, John Ruskin, but its grand hammer-beam roof helps to make it an architectural gem today (story on 21 Apr).
Courtesy: Waterstone's bookshop
Credit: Richard Wilson Photography

BELOW: Bradford City's main wooden stand is destroyed by fire in Bradford's worst civil disaster (story on 11 May).
@: The Times – News Syndication (2017)

ABOVE: Joseph Jagger, almost certainly the first to 'break the bank of Monte Carlo', was presented with this commemorative key (story on 1 May).
@: Anne Fletcher

ABOVE: Exactly 16 years after it opened, the National Museum of Photography, Film & Television received a major refit and a new name (story on 16 Jun).
Credit: Richard Wilson Photography

National SPINSTERS' PENSIONS Association.
Headquarters at Bradford.

GREAT
SPINSTERS
RALLY

WILL BE HELD IN

THE KINGSWAY HALL
KINGSWAY W. 1, ON

Saturday June 27th, at 3-30
1936

Prominent Speakers including M. P.s

Miss FLORENCE WHITE
Hon. National Organiser and Secretary.

Miss ALISON GARLAND
and Miss Isabel Forsyth, J. P. (NATIONAL CHAIRMAN)

————Meeting will be followed by————

MARCH OF SPINSTERS
Headed by a Full Band, to a
Great OUTDOOR Demonstration
in Hyde Park, The Marble Arch, at 7-30.

Lady Fisher-Smith, J. P. will preside
(PRESIDENT OF THE ASSOCIATION)

RIGHT: Florence White belongs to a strong tradition of Bradford's female campaigners (story on 27 Jun).

1 Jul 1916   Over 1,000 Bradford Pals die fighting at the Battle of the Somme.

The big offensive had been talked about for weeks. For most in the two Bradford Pals battalions it promised to be their first serious action. The report from today was encouraging:

'At 7.30 this morning vigorous attacks were launched by the British Army on a front of about 20 miles, north of the Somme. The assaults were preceded by a terrific bombardment, lasting one and a half hours. The British have already occupied the German front lines. Many prisoners have been taken, and, as far as can be ascertained, our casualties have not been heavy.' (Bradford Daily Telegraph, 1 July).

But then seriously worrying stories filtered through:

'I am indeed lucky to be alive after our terrible experience. I fear very, very many of both Bradford battalions are no more and the same applies to the Leeds Battalion. I walked over our dead in scores both in the open and in the trenches when working my way back ... July 1 will never fade from my memory. I thank God that I am left to live, yet it is really miraculous.' (Private Chapman, 10 July)

By the next week the full horror had dawned and the daily paper expressed the city's dismay:

'The noblest youth of the country walked open-eyed to their death on the ridges of the Somme. The Pals had their baptism of fire and Bradford was a city in mourning.' (18 July)

Under the banner *'Gallant Duty in the Great Advance'*, the *Bradford Weekly Telegraph* published a list of 659 names of men killed, wounded and missing. In addition, 256 photos of the men were shown. The list was introduced with: *'The story of how the Bradford Pals got to grips with the enemy in the big offensive is one which will thrill everybody with pride, even in this hour when the city is stirred with the madness of the sacrifice that has been paid'.* (14 July)

This list was updated every week throughout the summer. By 1 September, some 2,027 names had been listed and 1,576 photos shown. One can only too well imagine the dread that every family in Bradford had of seeing the weekly lists and their relief or agony after they had scanned the latest.

The final death toll for 1 and 2 July is estimated as 1,039. A generation was wiped out.

Source: *Bradford: Remembering 1914-18*, Dr Kathryn Hughes (2015)

2 Jul 1968   The city centre floods yet again, this time with an inch of rain in half an hour.

For anyone who was in the city centre at the time, today was a frightening experience. In the words of the *Telegraph & Argus*:

'Vast thunderclouds massed above the Aire and Wharfe valleys. By 10am the day was going dark. By 10.15am day had turned into night. First came hailstones, the size of walnuts people told us. Then came the rain. It was as though some malevolent power had scooped up part of the Atlantic Ocean and dropped it ... Lister Park weather station reported that within 30 minutes 0.88 inches of rain fell on Bradford.... Water poured into the subway system, filling it like a bucket... Mercifully no one was killed or injured.'

The only way that flood water can flow from the bowl of hills around the city centre is along Canal Road, its name being the only reminder of the route of a waterway long since abandoned. Today the name became dramatically appropriate.

Bradford's geography had caused similar flooding over many years, described by early writers. The city's first historian, John James, documented the first such occasion precisely two centuries earlier. In July 1768 large quantities of cloth and wool were swept away by the flood and a man and boy standing on the church bridge were carried away and drowned. In February 1822 a druggist lost his life examining a watermark by the side of his house after slipping and perishing unseen, his body not found till three days later.

Later, Willam Cudworth recorded another severe flood on 20 December 1837: '(There) *occurred what was described at the time as the greatest and most disastrous flood that had ever occurred in Bradford. In many parts of the streets the water was six foot deep, resulting in great loss of property and drowning of four persons. Rain had fallen continuously for two days previously, but on the day of the flood an intermittent torrent came down the Bowling and Thornton becks, which both became choked on reaching the town...'*

In current times the problems seem to have been solved by the Bradford Beck Alleviation Scheme (1990-1993). This was designed to reduce the probability of flooding in any year to under 2% by building a flood tunnel 3.7m diameter and 1.37km in length at a depth of up to 60m under the city centre.

Source: *Stories of the Century, Telegraph & Argus* (1999)

3 Jul 1963   The City Council votes to demolish Horton Hall.

Bradford City Council in the 1950s and 1960s did not cover itself with glory when it came to making planning decisions for the city centre. The protest against the demolition of Swan Arcade in 1962 was perhaps the lowest point.

On the face of it, today's decision to demolish Horton Hall a year later was equally short-sighted. After all, Bradford was not blessed with too many buildings that could be described as Elizabethan. Many famous old houses such as Bierley Hall and Manningham Hall no longer existed.

The case for the demolition of Horton Hall was different in that it was not part of any master plan to modernise the city centre, unlike most other controversies of that time. It had enjoyed a rather chequered history for at least 100 years ever since it stopped being inhabited by its owner who for some 350 years had been the Sharp family. They had been one of Bradford's most prominent families, giving the city its only archbishop and first eminent astronomer as two of its most famous sons.

Horton Hall was a stone-built manor house probably from Elizabethan times, though its origins are unclear. It was situated in a rural setting on Little Horton Lane, but from the 19th century, surrounded by St. Luke's Hospital, became part of the urban city.

From 1823 the house was mainly let out to a series of tenants until 1918 when fortuitously it started to be used as the home for the new Bishop of Bradford after the diocese was created in 1919. Although intended as a temporary home, it was used by both the first two bishops until 1955. Disliking the hall's gloom, the third bishop and family (Bishop Coggan) moved instead that year to Heaton.

The hall now stood empty and run-down. Although a Grade 1 listed building, the Government lifted the preservation order. The council sought different ideas for using the building, but in the end the cost of restoration was deemed too high. Despite petitions and numerous letters of protest, the council reluctantly agreed to demolish.

Perhaps the saddest loss was Sharp's Observatory, an 18th century extension of the hall's tower by Abraham Sharp to accommodate his need to observe the stars and the only such observatory outside Greenwich.

Source: *Sharp to Blunt: the story of Horton Hall, Bradford,* Astrid Hansen (2000)

4 Jul 1844   The Leeds & Bradford Railway Act finally gives Bradford its train link.

Increasing industrialisation was putting a strain on Bradford's transport network in the 1820s and 1830s, as more goods were circulating. Businessmen preferred the direct route to the slower more circuitous canal route. For example, the *Bradford Courier* in 1828 noted: *'There are no less than fourteen coaches running to and from Leeds daily, able to carry and generally carrying 196 passengers; while forty years previously there was only one coach running between Bradford and Leeds.'* Exponential growth in traffic on the Leeds / Bradford turnpike created wear and tear that made it impossible to keep the road in good condition.

In 1830 the railway came to Leeds with a line to Selby which opened up a route to Hull, thereby speeding the journey to London and the Continent. Pressure was growing for a rail link to Bradford. The issue was debated for 14 years with 14 proposals. Those with stakes in the canal system could see the threat and were on the defensive. The logistics, too, were challenging as some wanted through lines from Bradford to Lancashire that would require expensive engineering to avoid the hills surrounding the town. Once again Bradford's geography was a barrier to its development.

As well as the basic business case, the choice of route complicated matters. Should it be the direct link through Stanningley (nine miles), favoured by the 'short-liners', which meant a steep gradient from Laisterdyke down into Bradford? Or should it follow the longer canal route via Shipley (13.5 miles), which would require six crossings of the River Aire, four of the Leeds/Liverpool canal, a ten-arch bridge at Apperley and a long tunnel at Thackley? The initial costs were similar but the longer route might be cheaper to operate.

Existing railway companies such as the North Midland who ran the Derby to Leeds line could not be persuaded to take on the project, but in 1843 a new one was formed – the Leeds & Bradford Railway Company, with Robert Stephenson, son of George, the engineer in charge. Stephenson chose the Shipley route.

Today at last the Leeds & Bradford Railway Act was passed. Strong opposition to it forced the legal condition that the line should connect at Bradford with a through line to Halifax and beyond. This promise was never kept; the last attempt for a through line was abandoned seemingly for ever in 1920.

Source: *Bradford*, Joseph Fieldhouse (1972)

5 Jul 1956   The Clean Air Act offers a major breakthrough in reducing air pollution.

Cynics might say that it was only when Londoners experienced the Great Smog of December 1952 did Parliament legislate to prevent filthy smoke-filled environments which the country had experienced ever since the start of the Industrial Revolution.

Just consider these statistics from Bradford's Medical Officer of Health in 1960 as, encouraged by the legislation, the city's Clean Air Programme was launched. He talked of the city as a black spot for deaths from bronchitis. Abroad, death rates from bronchitis expressed as numbers per million of population were 33 (Norway) and 44 (Denmark) when the figure for England and Wales was 828. In the West Riding, the figure was 1,121 and in Bradford it rose to 1,690.

The likely correlation between smoke pollution and illness (and death) was thought to be known about for at least 100 years. Ever since Bradford's incorporation as a borough in 1847, bye-laws had been introduced to cover smoke control, However, the issue was never seen as high a priority as sewage and water pollution. Bye-laws were not rigidly enforced and penalties were not a deterrent. Those elected to be in charge of the city, usually mill-owners and merchants, had a clear interest in not rocking the boat. Titus Salt who built smoke-consuming devices into his factories was a shining exception in preventing pollution.

The 1956 Clean Air Act enacted today introduced measures to reduce air pollution, especially by allowing for 'smoke control areas' in some towns and cities in which only smokeless fuels could be burned.

Apart from a much healthier population, the Act also led to a transformed urban environment, as almost all public buildings could be cleaned of black grime to reveal the original warm sandstone underneath.

Source: *Clearing the Air*, Clement Richardson (1986) in *The Antiquary*

5 Jul 1916   Park Avenue footballer Donald Bell wins a posthumous Victoria Cross at the Somme.

Defender Donald Bell helped Bradford Park Avenue win promotion in 1913/14. At the outbreak of war, three months later, he asked to be released to serve. Two years later, now a lieutenant, he became today the only professional footballer to win the Victoria Cross in the war. His bravery on the Somme in throwing a bomb at a critical moment led to the award, but five days later he died dashing across open ground to take out an enemy machine gun.

6 Jul 1768   Entrepreneur Joseph Dawson is ordained.

The Reverend Joseph Dawson (1740-1813) did not conform with anyone's idea of a minister of religion.

When today he was ordained as a Unitarian minister, he could hardly have imagined that he would end up as a respected mineralogist and one of the leading players in Bradford's Industrial Revolution that had a major impact on the town some 30 years later.

After he started his ministry at the Unitarian Chapel in Idle, he was known for eccentricities such as storing in the chapel fodder for cattle he owned and making pens for his poultry among the gravestones in the chapel-yard. To make ends meet, he also worked as a farmer, teacher and doctor, all the while developing his interest in mineralogy from his studies at Glasgow University.

The Royds Hall estate in Bierley had large mineral deposits. Its owner in the mid-18th century, Edward Leedes, was an entrepreneur who gambled with investments that did not work out, eventually became bankrupt and committed suicide in 1787. Aware of the potential of mineral deposits on the estate, Dawson formed a partnership which bought the estate. Using his life savings, he seems to have been the prime mover behind the partnership that included John Hardy, a solicitor and later one of the first two MPs for Bradford in 1832. The Low Moor Ironworks, three miles south of Bradford, was formed in 1789. Dawson's pastoral duties had long since given way to his entrepreneurial instincts.

Low Moor Ironworks was a wrought iron foundry built to exploit the high-quality iron ore and low-sulphur coal found in the area. From 1801 to 1957 it made wrought iron products for export around the world. At one time it was the largest ironworks in Yorkshire, a major complex of mines, piles of coal and ore, kilns, blast furnaces, forges and slag heaps connected by railway lines. The surrounding countryside was littered with waste, and smoke from the furnaces and machinery blackened the sky.

Not only did Dawson leave Low Moor Ironworks as a thriving business which operated for over 160 years, but he left a large collection of over 2,000 mineral specimens. The Joseph Dawson Mineral Collection was donated to Bradford Museums in 1904.

Source: *Round About Bradford*, William Cudworth (1876)

7 Jul 2001   Riots break out across the city.

Summer 2001 saw racial tensions break out in the North of England. Bradford was one city that featured prominently. Riots had broken out in places like Oldham and Burnley, fomented allegedly by National Front rallies. The Anti-Nazi League had responded by organising a rally in Bradford today.

Around teatime violence broke out in the city centre after crowds at the rally discovered that National Front sympathisers were gathering in a nearby pub. Two people were stabbed and many more injured in running battles between white and Asian gangs. Police reinforcements arrived, in full riot gear. The rioters vented anger towards them, throwing broken bottles, bricks and petrol bombs and leaving a trail of damage and disorder in the city. By the evening police had made 18 arrests – 11 whites and seven Asians.

Unfortunately, despite attempts by community leaders to calm things down, this was not the end of the matter. The following night over 1,000, mainly Asians, confronted police in Manningham and surrounding areas. At the height of the trouble police had to call for hundreds of reinforcements from eight outside forces. Two car showrooms were burnt out. Vehicles which were not set on fire were driven at police lines. In one of the worst incidents, a social club with 30 people inside was set on fire; blazing cars were used to block the fire exit before police and firemen mounted a rescue operation.

Further disturbances took place on the third night. Overall, more than 300 police officers were hurt, 297 were arrested, 187 charged with riot and 45 with violent disorder.

Ironically by the end of the week, a major report on race relations called *Community Pride, not Prejudice* was published from Lord Ouseley, former chairman of the Commission for Racial Equality. This had its origins in earlier Bradford riots in June 1995 that had been followed by an internal report widely condemned as ineffective. The Cantle Report into these latest riots was published in December and used much of the thinking of the Ouseley Report.

This time the report seemed to have done the trick with a new theme of 'community cohesion' that addressed a complex mix of issues about social deprivation, segregation, official policy failure and police behaviour. Since then there has been no repetition of the July 2001 rioting.

Source: *The Guardian* (8 July 2001)

8 Jul 1973   The M606, Bradford's motorway, opens.

Connections with the nation's transport infrastructure always arrive as an afterthought for Bradford. In the 18th century plans for Bradford Canal to join the national canal network were developed five years after the plans for the Leeds-Liverpool Canal. In the 19th century the Bradford-Leeds railway link was opened 12 years after Leeds had its first railway.

Now in the 20th century the motorway came to Bradford six years after the M1 reached Leeds and three years after the opening of the M62 crossing the Pennines. Even then the new M606 spur from the M62 to Bradford that opened today still has a feeling of being an unfinished project, nearly 50 years later.

Bradford's motorway, officially known as the Bradford South Radial Motorway, is just three miles long, the third shortest motorway in England. It has three junctions – J1 the start on the edge of Cleckheaton (joining with J26 of the M62), J2 the middle (to Euro Trading Estate only) and J3 the end (joining with the A6177, Bradford's outer ring road, with close links via Manchester Road or Wakefield Road down into the city centre, and also very near to Odsal Stadium).

When the M606 was originally planned, it was intended to go through the city centre, and become the Bradford North Radial Motorway, but this was scrapped and at the opening J3 was left with a half-built motorway junction. Much later this was tidied up, although the start of the provisional route down into the city is still visible beyond the end of the M606.

At the southern end motorists travelling on the M62 from Manchester have a smooth and uninterrupted exit into the M606, but those coming from the Leeds direction have to leave via a large roundabout at the fourth exit point before they drive via a slip road on to the M606. From the south or the east, this does not make for an impressive drive towards the city

The M606 was the scene of a motorway innovation in 2007. Work started to create the UK's first motorway carpool lane (also known as high-occupancy vehicle lane). The one-mile lane scheme was on the M606 southbound and allowed vehicles with more than one person in the car a fast track onto the M62 eastbound at J26. Ten years later this restriction was removed and the innovation abandoned.

9 Jul 2017   The city gives David Hockney an 80th birthday present at the Cartwright Hall.

When he was young, David Hockney spent many hours looking at paintings in the Cartwright Hall Art Gallery – *'It was the only place in Bradford I could see real paintings'.*

It was, then, an appropriate present from his home city to have a permanent gallery dedicated to his work to mark today's 80th birthday. The Cartwright Hall now claims that the David Hockney Gallery exhibits the largest public collection of his earliest work. (A separate privately-owned permanent exhibition of Hockney's mature work already exists in the 1853 Gallery at the Salts Mill art complex opened in 1987 by his friend, Jonathan Silver).

The exhibits include drawings and sketches from Hockney's student days, many of which had rarely been seen in public. One work was *'View of Bradford from Earls Court'* a painting completed just when he was becoming famous in his early twenties that, an ex-pupil, he donated to Bradford Grammar School, and previously was only viewed in the school.

Born in Eccleshill in 1937, Hockney wanted to draw and paint from an early age. He became a familiar figure pushing his easel and paints in an old pram around local streets. As soon as he could, he left school and studied at Bradford Art School from 1953 to 1957. He then spent two years working in hospitals as a conscientious objector rather than go on National Service.

He undertook a three-year postgraduate course at the Royal College of Art (RCA), where he refused to write an essay required for finals, saying he should be assessed solely on his artwork. The RCA relented and he graduated with a gold medal for his year and never looked back.

Hockney quickly developed a national, then an international, reputation after his move to California in 1964. He turned his hand successfully to many facets of art. He is not just a fine artist, but a fine draughtsman, graphic artist, print maker, photographer, set designer and, above all, a fine painter of portraits, landscapes and still life.

His 80th birthday was also marked by a striking piece of public art depicting Hockney by artist Marcus Levine high on an external wall at the corner of Chapel Street and Peckover Street in Little Germany. It was the world's first sculpture made out of painted nails, standing 16ft high and 12ft wide. Its vision and impact are worthy of the subject.

10 Jul 1897   Bradford is granted City status.

Today, just after her diamond jubilee, the mayor of Bradford received a communication from Queen Victoria. It was a Letters Patent, the published legal instrument confirming that Bradford could now become a city.

Nothing changed very much. The Corporation's role did not change and the lives of Bradfordians did not get better as a result. Symbolically, however, it mattered in that after a century of rapid growth Bradford was now on a par with other longer-established Yorkshire cities of Leeds and Sheffield, and further afield Liverpool, Manchester and Newcastle. The Town Hall would now be City Hall. The mayor would have the grander title of Lord Mayor but strangely that was not finally confirmed until 1907.

From a historian's viewpoint, it was a timely upgrade of status. Bradford started its rapid growth about 100 years before; just before half the century was out, Bradford Corporation was created. In 1801 the population of the four townships was 13,244, in 1851 the new borough's population was 103,778 (684% increase) and in 1901 the new city had grown to 279,770 (a further 170% increase). The century splits neatly into half. One of Bradford's two pre-eminent historians of the day, William Scruton (1835-1900) spotted the opportunity with a book of commemoration. Just think of Bradford in 1847 ...

'*Fifty Years Ago!. A long stretch of time surely to look upon when reckoned by the measure of man's life... And certainly it does smack of "by-gone times" when one talks of a period when Bradford had not long had the right of been represented in Parliament, when the Municipal affairs of the town were managed by a few West Riding Magistrates, by the Watching and Lighting Commissioners, and a Board of Surveyors; when there was only one newspaper, and that a weekly, and when the town had just been put in communication with the outside world by the opening of the Valley Line to Leeds, previous to which Bradfordians who wished to visit London had to do so by first taking coach to Leeds, train to Selby, boat to Hull and finally packet to London.*'

And since then ... a charter of incorporation, street improvements, public buildings, churches and chapels, schools, hospitals, parks, villas, warehouses, mills and much more, creating the structure of a city.

Source: *Bradford Fifty Years Ago: A Jubilee Memorial of the Bradford Corporation*, William Scruton (1897)

11 Jul 1981   The police find two crates of petrol bombs left by the Bradford 12.

The summer of 1981 was one of the most torrid in post-war years. Race riots broke out in many inner-city areas across England, eg Brixton (south London), Toxteth (Liverpool), Handsworth (Birmingham), Moss Side (Manchester) and Chapeltown (Leeds). Distrust of the police lay at the root of much of the conflict. Bradford largely escaped the worst until today.

The police received a tip-off that two milk crates with petrol bombs were hidden in bushes behind a nurses' home in Bradford. They removed the petrol from the bottles, replaced it with tea and waited for the offenders to return. Nobody turned up, until 13 days later 12 young Asians were arrested and subsequently charged with:

- making an explosive substance with intent to endanger life and property
- conspiracy to make explosive substances for unlawful purposes.

If found guilty, those charged might receive seven to ten years' imprisonment.

Initially refused bail, the defendants spent a few months in prison before being granted bail on onerous conditions. Three denied any involvement; the others admitted to making the bombs in fear that fascists intent on violence were about to descend on Bradford. The youths (a mixture of Hindu, Muslim, Sikh and Christian) were members of the United Black Youth League, a new group set up ostensibly to protect the Asian community against racial attacks. They quickly attracted strong support from the local community. The case became known as the Bradford 12.

The case came to court in Leeds in April 1982 and lasted 31 days. First, the defence had to fight for a jury that understood the issues of racism. The initial panel of 75 contained only two Asians, none from Bradford. The final jury had seven white and five black persons.

The main line of the defence was that the bombs were intended for self-defence. There had been many recent cases in Bradford and beyond, where the Asian community had not been protected from racial attacks – the police seemed very reluctant to charge those who attacked Asians. The defendants had not intended endangering life or property; they merely set out to deter in response to serious threats of riots fuelled by fascists. The defence also argued that petrol bombs were not explosives because they did not explode on impact. Finally, much of the prosecution evidence was shown to be fabricated.

The jury acquitted the Bradford 12 on a verdict of eleven to one.

Source: http://history-is-made-at-night.blogspot.com/2011/07/short-hot-summer-1981-bradford-12.html

12 Jul 2001 The Ouseley Report on race relations in Bradford is published.

The timing of today's long-awaited report on race relations in Bradford was either extremely unfortunate or extremely providential. It came just a few days after a weekend of the worst violence seen in Bradford for a very long time and indeed in the whole of the UK for many years. On one hand, it was a stark reminder that nothing had improved since the Manningham riots in 1995, despite warnings that problems would escalate. On the other hand, it reinforced the need to do something urgently.

The 1995 riots were first analysed in the Bradford Commission report of November 1996 but this was a report from local agencies which was criticised for not being firm enough with recommendations for actions. Now, with a national profile as former chairman of the Commission for Racial Equality, Sir Herman Ouseley gave an external view of the problems and solutions.

His summary identified *'growing divisions among Bradford's population along race, ethnic, religious and social class lines, and* (the city) *now finds itself in the grip of fear – fear of people talking openly and honestly about problems, fear of leading and managing effective change, fear of challenging wrong-doing because of being labelled "racist", fear of crime, fear of confronting the gang culture and fear of confronting all white and/or all Muslim schools about social and racial integration.*

What is now desperately needed is a powerful unifying vision for the district and strong political, municipal and community leadership. In addition, it needs a people programme that creates social harmony, rejects racial hatred, brings communities together and shows them how to value people of all backgrounds.'

As the July 2001 riots did not just affect Bradford but many other Northern cities and towns, action became a national priority and led to a national report. This was the Cantle Report by Ted Cantle (ex-local authority chief executive) published just six months later in December 2001. It used many ideas in the Ouseley report summarised in a new policy called 'community cohesion' and made around 70 recommendations.

It did lead to a reduction in tension in places like Bradford that 20 years later has seen no repetition of riots.

Source: *Community Pride, not Prejudice: Making Diversity Work in Bradford,* Sir Herman Ouseley (2001)

13 Jul 1931   Bradford holds a Historical Pageant in Peel Park.

Today was the first day of a week-long event called *The Historical Pageant of Bradford*.

The idea of staging such an event had been a response by the city to a major economic depression. In the past four years up to 400 textile businesses had been made bankrupt. Pageants were popular. Other cities had found them highly successful. A pageant about the growth of the wool industry in Bradford might give it a useful helping hand. The Chamber of Commerce, however, disagreed, asserting that *'we have learnt to our cost that the value of exhibitions is of very small importance'*. The event went ahead!

An experienced pageant master was appointed. The plan was to have six episodes, each representing a stage in Bradford's history from the Romans to recent industrial times. Each episode enacted well-known scenes, scripted by a different writer. Man of letters, JB Priestley, and popular local author, Willie Riley, also both contributed positive pieces in the souvenir programme.

There was no attempt to disguise the message. In the Prologue, a shepherdess, standing in the middle of a flock of sheep, sets up the entire narrative inside a textile metaphor: *'As my cloth is woven from the wool I know so well, so today, in this great city of industry, my aim is to weave for you a story that shall be like a beautiful fabric a tapestry of many colours and many figures that will please the eye and linger in your memory – the Living Story of Bradford's Glory'.*

The venue was Peel Park, the action being set against a grassy embankment and trees, where participants could change. It was a big production – 7,500 participants, all volunteers. Costumes, resourced locally, were an obvious advertisement for Bradford textiles – 25,000 yards of material. Big names opened each day's event, starting with Prince George (later Duke of Kent), then David Lloyd George (ex-Prime Minister) and the Lord Mayor of London. The event had wide press coverage; some speeches were even broadcast on the infant BBC.

Heavy showers gave the first day an inauspicious start and continued for much of the week. However, crowds were good (4,000 seats for each performance). There is little doubt that the people of the city were fully engaged (around 30,000 to one estimate). It probably lifted morale, but there is no record of how much it boosted business in the longer-term.

Source: www.historicalpageants.ac.uk/featured-pageants/bradford-pageant-1931/

14 Jul 1904   The Lord Mayor cuts the first sod on the country's only municipal railway.

In order to meet future needs of Bradford's population and businesses the Nidd Valley Scheme was launched in 1891 so that water from the upper reaches of the River Nidd came into the city. After the first reservoir had been built, the Corporation decided to build a light railway to transport workers and supplies to the sparsely-populated land where the second was to be built.

Today, led by the Lord Mayor, a large body of officials travelled by an early morning train to Pateley Bridge to watch him cut the first sod on the proposed Nidd Valley Light Railway. According to the *Bradford Daily Telegraph*: *'The Mayor fulfilled the task with workman-like conviction and expressed the conviction that the railway would be a blessing to the Dales folks and a benefit to the citizens of Bradford'.*

The Corporation had been permitted to build this standard gauge railway on condition that the first six miles should be open to passengers. It equipped the public railway with second-hand locomotives and carriages from the Metropolitan Railway in London.

This became the first municipal-owned railway in the country. Unusually, it operated completely outside the area that the Corporation in question administered.

An official opening took place on 11 September 1907, when a train was hauled from Pateley Bridge to Lofthouse, with two intermediate stops. Although the line remained in operation until Scar House Reservoir was completed in 1936, it closed to passengers in 1929.

Source: *Bradford*, Joseph Fieldhouse (1972)

14 Jul 2019   Two Bradfordians help England win its first Cricket World Cup in sensational finish.

Today for the first time, England won the Cricket World Cup against New Zealand in the most exciting manner imaginable. The main match was tied, only the fifth time in over 450 one-day internationals. The first tie-breaker, the super over, was also tied. The second tie-breaker, the number of boundaries scored, went to England.

Uniquely, two of England's players came from the same place, Bradford – Jonny Bairstow, opening batsman, and Adil Rashid, leg-break bowler. Neither really starred in this game but each played his part. Bairstow scored a solid 36 in a low-scoring game and Rashid bowled an economical eight overs. Integral members of the team, one for his aggressive batting and the other for his wicket-taking, each had played in all the preceding ten games in the tournament.

In January 2020 they were made honorary freemen of Bradford.

15 Jul 1922   The Bradford Canal sees its final barge after years of neglect.

So much energy had been expended in the 18th century in planning its construction. Yet today, nearly 150 years later, it closed as a completely unloved feature of the city.

When the Bradford Canal was opened in 1774, it became a lifeline for new industry and trade. Bradford desperately needed to be part of the new transport infrastructure in the North of England that the canal system provided. It flourished for some 50 years before being overtaken by the railway system.

However, not all was well. Gradually, the canal was becoming a smelly and unhealthy blot on the city. The water was only being replenished by the toxic waters of nearby Bradford Beck. Things finally came to a head in the 1860s. The *Bradford Observer* described it as that *'seething cauldron of all impurity'*. It was finally closed in 1866 as a major public health hazard.

After much debate it reopened in 1873 with a better water supply under different management operating from a new wharf in the city, but it was never as profitable as in earlier years. It entered into gradual decline for the next 50 years until *'River Stink'*, as it became known, saw the last barge make the short journey.

There was very little by way of celebration. The *Bradford Daily Telegraph* showed simply a photo with the words: *'The Bradford Canal is now closed. The last barge to take in cargo at Bradford was the Beta which is seen here making its last trip.'* There were no features or memories to mark the day.

The canal has been largely ignored ever since. However, in 1960 when excavating Forster Square, workmen found the old wooden foundations of the wharf at the canal basin and also the canal bed, which contained thousands of oyster shells from an oyster bar once used by canal workers.

In the 21st century, very little remains of the canal, except for parts of a few bridges and a lock-keeper's cottage at Windhill. The valley route to Shipley is still called Canal Road. Wharf Street just off Canal Road is a reminder of Hoppy Bridge Wharf at the Bradford end, just to one side of St. Peter's Church. All that remains of the canal itself is Dockfield canal basin at the Shipley end, where it joined the main Leeds-Liverpool Canal.

Source: *Stories of the Century, Telegraph & Argus* (1999)

16 Jul 1868   Bradford's first daily newspaper rolls off the presses.

At last after 34 years, the *Bradford Observer* had a competitor. Today, the *Bradford Daily Telegraph* printed its first edition and became Bradford's first daily.

The man behind it was Thomas Shields, a Glaswegian, who had been managing the *North and South Shield Gazette* for four years before landing in Bradford, a boom town with a rapidly expanding population, but only one weekly newspaper.

There is a unique record of the new man's early days in Bradford from an unusual hoard of newspaper cuttings and pictures kept by William Bell, who worked for William Byles at the *Observer*. Under the pseudonym 'Old Stager', he gives an amusing though jaundiced view of the new man on a mission. He recounts how Shields had a few months before taking over at the *Telegraph,* having presented himself at the *Observer*'s office asking lots of questions without revealing his intentions. *'We leave others to give a name to this dissimulation'*, commented Bell.

The new man had immediate impact with both advertising and circulation. You could watch the new four-page daily being printed through the ground floor windows. The autumn 1868 general election was a major boost to the paper. Local MP, WE Forster, was particularly complimentary about the coverage when an entire speech at St. George's Hall was reprinted.

Shields offered the new daily at a halfpenny. Costing just a penny more per week than the weekly *Bradford Observer,* it gave readers an evening paper with all the day's news. Within three months, the *Observer* recognised the competition and became a daily, too. Circulation increased steadily – starting with 6,500 a day in the first year, 13,750 by 1879 and 22,000 by 1885. Premises reflected growth, as the paper moved into a central location in Bridge Street, then five years later Market Street.

Bell wrote of Shields: *'He possessed unbounded confidence: was indifferent as to whether his tactics were foul or fair; he was there as a businessman, without bowels of compassion, sympathy or creed; he would accommodate anybody for a few bawbees.'*

When Shields died in 1887, his own paper was kinder: *'a man of strong character, possessed of rare business abilities, backed by a keen intelligence, great powers of organisation and an almost unique* (sic) *grasp of the possibilities of any case presented him.'*

Source: *Read All About It: The story of Bradford's Telegraph & Argus 1868 -1981* (1981)

17 Jul 1919   After 12 years in Bradford, Swiss baker opens the first Bettys in Harrogate.

Fritz Butzer (1885-1952) was born in Switzerland, the son of a master baker. Sadly, when very young, he lost his mother. Then, when he was five years old, his father died. Now orphaned, he was fostered by a local farmer. As soon as he could, Fritz left his foster home. He trained as a baker and travelled around Switzerland and France, learning to be a confectioner and chocolatier.

In 1907 Fritz decided to come to England. On arriving, he discovered that he had lost the address of his destination. He remembered that it sounded like 'bratwurst' (German for sausage). A helpful person put him on the train to Bradford. On arriving here, he found work at a Swiss-owned confectioners, Bonnet & Sons.

Fritz eventually settled in Harrogate. He changed his name to Frederick Belmont, calling himself a 'chocolate specialist'. He fell in love with and later married his landlady's daughter. Today, with her family's financial support, he opened the first Bettys cafe.

Before long Bettys was establishing its reputation for excellent service, elegant surroundings and delicate continental cakes. It expanded, opening a purpose-built bakery to supply new cafés first in Bradford (1922) – with a ballroom added (1924) – and later in Leeds (1930). In Bradford Bettys occupied a prime location on Darley Street to attract shoppers dropping in after visits to Brown Muff's on Market Street or Busby's on Manningham Lane, both within five minutes' walk. In 1937 Frederick opened up in York, home of chocolate makers, Terry's and Rowntree's.

In 1962 it acquired Taylors of Harrogate, a family tea and coffee merchant company with the brand of Yorkshire Tea.

The combined operation is still a highly successful family-run business managed by Frederick's great-nephew. Currently, it has a craft bakery, cookery school and five café tearooms – two in Harrogate, one in York, one in Northallerton and one in Ilkley – having closed its city centre cafes in Bradford and Leeds.

The Bradford Bettys closed down in 1974. Combined with the loss of its premier stores, Brown Muff's and Busby's, in 1978, this marked the end of an era in the city. Darley Street, in particular, now looks down-at-heel – not the focal shopping point once symbolised by the elegance of Bettys, merely a street to pass quickly up or down.

Why Bettys? Nobody knows! Incidentally, dropping the apostrophe is deliberate – it's the official trading name.

Source: www.bettys.co.uk/timeline

18 Jul 1919   A soldier writes to the *Bradford Weekly Telegraph* the day before Peace Day.

Although World War One came to an end on Armistice Day, 11 November 1918, the Treaty of Versailles was not signed until 28 June 1919. In May the Government announced that 19 July 1919 would be celebrated as Peace Day with a Victory March through London.

Cities and towns prepared their own local celebrations. In Bradford a Peace Committee planned a parade for the day, but a week before several local service organisations such as the Bradford Association of Discharged Sailors and Soldiers declined to take part. The parade was cancelled in protest against inadequate pensions and allowances, and other grievances.

Today, alongside the paper's roll of honour, the *Bradford Weekly Telegraph* published a letter from a soldier that included:

'*It is almost unwillingly that one takes up one's pen to write of those whose names are before us on this sadly happy day. If their names were only names, then words would group themselves in stately periods and march with fitting pomp at these official obsequies. But when memory sets fire to your imagination so that the well-known dead take flesh as you write; when they laugh and jest before you as in many a camp and bivouac; when you hear again the very tones of their voices as they toil, grumbling and indomitable, beside you in the ranks; when you share with them once more the terrible, still excitement of that moment when the barrage crashes down and you wait the signal to mount the ladders; when weeping and cursing, you again roll their poor torn bodies into the shell holes on the Somme, there are no words to express your love, your sorrow and the greatness of your pride.*

A man went home on leave and left us in a front line trench where the water reached our knees and our clothes were sodden to the skin. He travelled slowly from Bradford to Ypres and, when he joined us, the water still reached our knees and our clothes were still sodden to the skin. We had not been dry or warm since he left.

"What is it like at home?" we asked.

"They don't understand" was all he said.'

A Bradford soldier (*Bradford Weekly Telegraph*, 18 July 1919)

Source: *Bradford: Remembering 1914-18*, Dr Kathryn Hughes in association with the Peace Museum (UK), Bradford

19 Jul 1845   Living in Bradford turns German visitor, Georg Weerth, into a communist.

Perhaps the most powerful description of industrial Bradford in the mid-19th century comes from 23-year-old Georg Weerth, a relatively insignificant German visitor writing for *Neue Rheinische Zeitung* in 1846.

'Every other factory town in England is a paradise in comparison to this hole. In Manchester the air lies like lead upon you; in Birmingham it is just as if you were sitting with your nose in a stove pipe; in Leeds you have to cough with the dust and the stink as if you had swallowed a pound of Cayenne pepper in one go - but you can put up with all that. In Bradford, however, you think you have been lodged with the devil incarnate. If anyone wants to feel how a poor sinner is tormented in Purgatory, let him travel to Bradford.'

Weerth came from a comfortable middle-class family in Detmold in Westphalia, Germany. Many young Germans with similar backgrounds had come to Bradford to build new lives from the business opportunities in manufacturing and commerce offered by a city that was growing rapidly.

Without any known political views, arriving in 1843 in order to widen his business experience, he became within less than two years a radical thinker, friend of Karl Marx and Friedrich Engels and so, not surprisingly, a communist. Today he wrote to his mother about that transformation. He compared his experience with Engels who had just published a book *The Condition of the Working Class in England,* based on personal observations and research in English cities, largely Manchester. Engels had visited Bradford, describing it memorably as *'a stinking hole'.*

Engels' family had disowned him. Weerth asked his mother not to do the same.

Weerth left Bradford in 1846 and went to live in Brussels, where Karl Marx had his home. In 1856 he died of tropical fever on a business trip to Cuba, predicting that Cuba *'would be the field where the great conflicts of the new world would be fought out first'.*

Source: *Little Germany: German Refugees in Victorian Britain,* Rosemary Ashton (1989)

20 Jul 2011   Bradford City fire hero is honoured with doctorate by the University of Bradford.

Today Professor David Sharpe received an honorary degree from the University of Bradford where he had established a world-class unit in dealing with burns following the Bradford City fire disaster at Valley Parade on 11 May 1985. He was presented with a Doctorate of Science for his pioneering work and for developing the next generation of plastic surgeons. It was a very appropriate professional recognition for someone who responded so impressively to such a disaster and then dedicated the rest of his career to helping others who suffered from burns injuries.

There were many heroes on that dreadful day. Sharpe, a consultant plastic surgeon for just five months when he was on call, would have been near the top of everybody's list. He treated many in the immediate aftermath and went on to treat more than 200 patients who suffered burns, mainly to the hands, scalp and back of legs. On the Monday after the fire Sharpe and his team operated on some 25 cases. That week they handled 80 skin grafts.

He found it crucial to keep the swelling down by keeping the hand elevated. But conventional fabric arm slings did not do this when a patient was lying in bed with other injuries. He invented what became known as the Bradford sling. It was a simple design, made from foam and velcro straps, ensuring even pressure over the arm, and can either be suspended beside the bed of the patient or held against the patient's body. It is now used after every hand operation and revolutionised the management of hand injuries or operations world-wide.

He helped found the Plastic Surgery and Burns Unit at the University of Bradford, making the city a pioneer in plastic surgery, now recognised as one of the top research units in the country for skin healing and wound research. He was its director from the start till he retired in 2013. The unit was established from public donations and royalties from the Bradford sling, and continues to benefit from such funds.

The unit is both a practical and fitting legacy of the disaster. It was equally appropriate that three years later on 26 April 2014 to mark his retirement Professor Sharpe was presented with a book of testimonials on the pitch at Valley Parade. It was an emotional occasion for him, the club and the fans.

Source: www.theargus.co.uk/news/9150681.amp/

21 Jul 1914 — *Yorkshire Post* promotes tomorrow's opening of Great Yorkshire Show at Bradford Moor.

The Great Yorkshire Show is the largest agricultural show in England. Since 1951 it has been sited permanently just outside Harrogate, but before then it moved from year to year around the county. It visited Bradford five times – Four Lane Ends (1891), Dudley Hill (1901), Bradford Moor (1914) and Thornbury (1925 and 1934).

Today, the *Yorkshire Post* gave the 1914 event a good promotion, setting out what visitors might expect. It stressed how easy it was to get there – just a 15 minute tram ride from Forster Square. Once arrived, people would find their way around very easily. All preparations were well advanced. The article covered the agricultural and horticultural exhibitions and competitions. With fine weather the organisers were confident of record crowds.

The weather did turn out well. The attendance was good at 82,461 over three days, but not quite good enough to beat the 1891 record of 86,143. It would still show a substantial profit of over £1,000 from a turnover of £5,390.

One talking point that the advance publicity failed to cover was the mode of arrival of the respective Lord Mayors of Bradford and Leeds. The Bradford party arrived by stage-coach, but from the tone of the report was upstaged by the Leeds party arriving by aeroplane. In fact, the newspaper devoted a full column to this *'novel visit'* to the show. Watched by large crowds, the pilot, *'an experienced aviator'* set off in a *'Blackburn monoplane'* from Roundhay to Quarry Gap Field, *'an aerodrome',* near the showground – a journey of about 11 miles.

However, not all went smoothly: *'The powerful engine of the monoplane declined its office, and refused to be coaxed into obedience. Mechanics applied themselves diligently to the task of diagnosing the trouble, and at length it was found that the fault lay with the sparking plugs. These were quickly removed and replaced by one taken from convenient motor cars on the ground, but even so there had been a delay of an hour and a half.'*

Some two weeks later the country was at war. How many of that 82,000 crowd were to find themselves within weeks in khaki and preparing to fight? We will never know. For many certainly this show would have been their final day out with family and friends for a long time and, for some, forever.

Source: *Yorkshire Post* (21 July 1914)

22 Jul 1844   Those convicted of manslaughter in the Irish riot case return to court for sentencing.

The mass influx of Irish immigrants in the 1840s also brought some of their conflicts. There were occasional skirmishes between Protestant and Catholic gangs. The most serious took place in May 1844.

Today should have seen the last act of the case being acted out as five Catholic labourers returned to court after being found guilty of manslaughter on 18 July of the death of Benjamin Gott, a participant in an Orangemen's march through Bradford.

On 30 May 1844 the *Bradford Observer* had reported the march, the men drinking as they sang Protestant songs through Catholic areas. A group of some 200 men responded with *'a violent and cowardly attack upon the few unarmed, but, perhaps, foolish and ignorant men. The Orangemen commenced a retreat; but they were so kicked and cuffed, knocked down and cudgelled, that few of them escaped without broken heads or broken and bruised skins'.* Benjamin Gott's skull was so badly fractured that he died two days later.

Now the local judge referred the case for sentencing to Westminster Hall. *The Bradford Observer* gave a measured, but wise commentary, befitting a liberal newspaper:

"It was quite impossible," the learned judge said, "for any person acquainted with human nature to suppose that a party of men should march through a populous town like Bradford, exhibiting party colours, and playing tunes of a party and offensive character, without producing serious riot, and even bloodshed." So it appears that the learned judge is clearly of the opinion that the Bradford Orangemen are morally guilty of the death of poor Benjamin Gott. "It was impossible to doubt," he said, "that the tune of the Boyne Water was played for the purpose of exhibiting some sort of triumph over a certain class of the inhabitants of Bradford." This is exactly the view we took of the matter... We hear that our Orangemen have resolved to walk in procession to the churches in the district on Sundays, for the purpose of raising contributions for the widow and children of Benjamin Gott. If they think that they are morally bound to support the widow and children of this poor man, we think so too, but, when they walk in procession to the churches, we think that sackcloth and ashes would suit them better than their usual party colours.'

The men were sentenced for transportation.

Source: *Bradford Observer* (25 July 1844)

23 Jul 1914   Alfred Angas Scott writes in *Motor Cycle* magazine about the benefits of a two-stroke bike.

Today Alfred Angas Scott (1875-1923) wrote in an enthusiasts' magazine about the main achievement of his life – the twin-cylinder engine that was the trademark of the classic Scott motorbike.

Growing up, Manningham-born Scott moved with his family to Scotland and then Staffordshire, where he studied engineering and design. Then he practised his trade in Kirkcaldy and Gloucester. He came back to Bradford.

Here, he designed and patented the first six Scott motorcycles, manufactured by his friends, the Jowett brothers. This design, which used a home-made twin-cylinder engine installed into the steering head of a modified bicycle, had a quite modern look. These features were to remain an integral part of the Scott motorcycle for the next 70 years.

In 1908 Scott formed the Scott Engineering Co. based in Saltaire in order to manufacture the new motorbike. He raced it very successfully. No manufacturer of the period could achieve full publicity until they had competed in the Isle of Man Tourist Trophy (TT) races. Scott competed several times in the pre-war years. In 1910 his was the first two-stroke motorcycle to complete a full TT course under race conditions. Each year from 1911 to 1914 a Scott bike had the fastest lap; in 1912 and 1913 he won the event.

When World War One broke out, Scott's company supplied armoured motor cycles for the use of the troops. They were fitted with Maxim guns, fixed for high-angle firing to deal with aircraft, as well for other kinds of military work.

By the end of the war Scott left his company to start a new one, Scott Autocar Co. based in Lidget Green, in order to build the 'Scott Sociable', an innovative, half-sidecar, half-car, three-wheeler. This had a rather strange appearance, looking like a small car with the front left wheel missing, built on a triangular tubular chassis. It was not a success; only 100 to 200 were made.

In 1923 Scott died of pneumonia at home in Heaton contracted from driving a Sociable in wet clothes. His name, however, lived on through his first company which built bikes that continued to appeal to dedicated enthusiasts. The Scott bike achieved cult status in the inter-war years with models such as the legendary Squirrels, Super Squirrels and Flying Squirrels – a status on a par with the Jowett cars, also made in Bradford by his friends.

Source: www.undercliffecemetery.co.uk/about/history/alfred-angas-scott/

24 Jul 1937   The foundation stone is laid for the new Bradford Grammar School building in Frizinghall.

Today at last work started in earnest for the building of the new school on a prime site opposite Lister Park, a couple of miles from the city centre. Sir Henry Price, a major donor, performed the ceremony, the Archdeacon of Bradford did the consecration, and William Edwards, the recently retired headmaster, presided.

For Edwards in particular it had been a long haul. In 1918 he had taken over from the legendary Rev WH Keeling who had established the school's academic reputation. In 1818 the governors had chosen a new site for the school just off Manor Row on the edge of the town near where middle class families then lived. But 100 years on, as pupil numbers increased, it was no longer fit for purpose. It was surrounded by slums and businesses, and its playground overlooked railways lines near Forster Square station. It was not a pleasant location for a school. In his 1918 report to governors, Edwards made this clear: *'The school is now full.... What is really needed is a new school.'*

Choosing a suitable site took two years, buying it another five years and finding the money to pay for the building another ten years. This involved the launch of an appeal fund for £185,000, including lengthy negotiations with the Corporation for a grant. By the time Edwards cut the first sod for the foundation stone in 1936, he had retired.

Yet it would be another 12 years before the school was formally opened.

The building was nearly complete when World War Two was declared. Immediately, the army commandeered the building and occupied it for six years. In the meantime the Butler Education Act had been passed in 1944 which prompted a major debate about the status of the school. Should it remain private or become a new direct grant school with funding from central government, so providing access for sons of poorer families? The governors chose the latter option.

Finally, on 12 January 1949 the school was formally opened by the young Duke of Edinburgh, the future queen's husband in his naval uniform. Crowds cheered his arrival through Lister Park and 2,000 in the brand new Price Assembly Hall listened to the speeches.

Since Edwards' recommendation, it had taken 31 years before the new school opened its doors for lessons.

Source: *Hoc Age - Bradford Grammar School 1818-1996*, Tony Moxon (1999)

25 Jul 1877 The public funeral takes place for philanthropist Charles Semon.

Judge the man by his funeral procession!

Today the city prepared to honour Charles Semon, a most generous man, one who had emigrated from Germany when a young man and prospered in Bradford. After his family, the cortege comprised employees of his two main companies and then representatives from the Chamber of Commerce, the Board of Guardians, Bradford Infirmary, the Eye and Ear Hospital, the Fever Hospital, the Nurses' Training Institution, Royal National Lifeboat Institution, the Tradesmen's Benevolent Institution, the Tradesmen's Home, the Spinsters Provident Fund, the Society for the Prevention of Cruelty to Animals, the Mechanics' Institute, Friends, Church Institute, Grand Order of Oddfellows, borough magistrates, the Mayor and Corporation and members of the Jewish Association. Then there appeared a procession of over 20 carriages for friends.

The mourners gathered in Market Street in the centre and made their way to Scholemoor Cemetery some three miles away, where the burial was the first in the new Jewish enclosure. Crowds lined the streets all the way.

Born in the German port of Danzig in 1814, Charles Semon came to Bradford to build a textile export-house, dealing in yarn, stuffs, worsted and woollens. He supplied goods to all over Great Britain and exported to Australia, the USA and Europe.

As well as being a successful businessman, Semon became heavily involved in municipal affairs and the cultural life of the city. He helped to found the Chamber of Commerce in 1852, he was the first Jewish and foreign-born mayor of Bradford, he was a Justice of Peace and Deputy Lieutenant for the West Riding, and he built and endowed a convalescent home in Ilkley to be handed over to the Corporation for its long-term upkeep. He left £35,000 for the city's educational institutions (over £3.3 million at current prices).

Source: *Bradford Daily Telegraph* (25 July 1877)

26 Jul 1949   Brian Close becomes the youngest ever cricketer to bat for England.

When today the 18-year-old Brian Close went out to bat at Old Trafford in his first Test for England, he could never have imagined that 27 years later he would walk out on the same ground to open the batting against the dangerous West Indies in his final Test.

Unfortunately, talented as he was, it did not work out for him as a Test cricketer. He did play in 22 Tests, but missed opportunities, unsupportive management and an attraction to controversy all got in the way. His was a stop-start career, his appearances coming in short sporadic bursts.

Perhaps the pivotal moment occurred in 1961. Brought back to stiffen the batting, he came in to bat against the Aussies. Victory was in the air. Caught out from a wild shot, he was widely blamed for the unexpected defeat in the match and the series.

Five years later, he came back as captain against the dominant West Indian team for the last match in a lost series. With brave, confident captaincy Close secured a surprising victory. Next year he led England to two series wins. Certain to lead the 1967/68 West Indies tour, he was accused of timewasting in a county match and was punished by being dropped. With six wins out of seven he was statistically England's most successful captain.

An attacking left-handed batsman, an extremely useful bowler of swing and spin, one of the bravest close fielders of all time, Close had an impressive county record as all-rounder in the 1950s and then as captain in the 1960s, winning the championship for Yorkshire four times. He was unceremoniously sacked in 1970 for his disapproval of the new one-day cricket and snapped up by Somerset whom he built into a strong team in the 1970s.

Born and educated in Rawdon just outside the Bradford boundary, he was a teenage star for Yeadon playing in the strong Bradford League. He lived most of his life in Baildon, where a street was named the Brian Close Walk in his memory and where in retirement he played a few games, again in the Bradford League.

The final image of his professional cricketing life is that day in 1976. Facing a fearsome quartet of West Indian fast bowlers, with no protective head gear, a 45-year-old opener who rarely opened, taking balls on his body, he was the only English cricketer capable of standing up to the barrage.

27 Jul 1766   Rev John Wesley writes about the new Octagon Chapel on Horton Lane.

Today, the famous Methodist preacher John Wesley (1703 -1791) spoke at Bradford's first Methodist chapel, newly built on Horton Lane. It was an octagon shape, which for some years in the late 18th century became quite fashionable.

Of the day Wesley wrote in his journal: *'There was so large a multitude, and the rain so damped my voice, that many in the skirts of the congregation could not hear distinctly. They have just built a preaching-house in a square of 54 feet, the largest Octagon we have in England, and it is the first of the kind where the roof is built with common sense, rising only a third of its breadth, yet it is as firm as any in England: nor does it hurt the walls. Why then should any roof rise higher?'*

Wesley seemed to like octagon chapels, also praising highly the most famous one of all at Norwich, still standing and built in 1757.

Unfortunately, the new chapel in Bradford was structurally unsound and only lasted until 1810 when the congregation moved to Kirkgate Chapel in May 1811. Some say that the design of such chapels was inherently unsafe, but the survival of a similar chapel built in 1764 at Heptonstall on the other side of Halifax suggests otherwise.

Wesley spent the last 50 years of his life travelling across the country preaching Methodism, sometimes twice or three times a day. Inevitably he visited Bradford several times. His first visit had taken place on 17 June 1744. He visited again on 27 April 1747 when he preached on the green at Low Moor. This time he was accompanied by John Nelson, who had already established a reputation locally, as indicated by a plaque on Ivegate commemorating his imprisonment in 1744: *'John Nelson of Birstall. Stonemason and Methodist preacher. Helper of John Wesley. Was lodged in a dungeon near this spot, May 5 1744.'*

Wesley then preached at the Cockpit in 1757, a building that had been a hotbed of drinking and gambling before one room was let for some years to the Methodists until they built their new Octagon Chapel.

Another blue plaque also recorded a later visit, this time to Baildon: *'On 22 July 1786 John Wesley Anglican Minister and Founder of Methodism preached from this window on the text, Mark 3v35.'*

Source: *Pen and Pencil Pictures of Old Bradford,* William Scruton (1890)

28 Jul 1954   Bradford's man of film, Steve Abbott, is born.

Few Bradfordians since the millennium have done more to put their home city on the country's map in terms of reputation and business. Today Steve Abbott was born in Barkerend where he was brought up.

After an unusual and varied career, Abbott was approached in 2007 to lead the bid for Bradford to build on its rich film heritage and become the world's first UNESCO City of Film. Two years later he succeeded and for the next decade was its chairman. Just in 2018, 35 film and TV productions were made in and around the city, including *Peaky Blinders, Victoria* and *The ABC Murders.*

Abbott won a scholarship to Bradford Grammar School, from where he gained an open scholarship to read mathematics at Cambridge University. Here, he developed a passionate interest in cinema. On graduating, ideally he wanted a career in film, but settled initially for training as a chartered accountant.

On the day he qualified, he found himself being interviewed for a job with Handmade Films, set up by ex-Beatle George Harrison to rescue Monty Python's *Life of Brian.* Within 18 months he was joint business manager for the Pythons. It is perhaps no accident that the Python film *Meaning of Life* (1983) contained scenes filmed in Bradford at Norfolk Gardens and Lister Park, or even that this was where he spent his first-ever day filming on location.

With the Pythons he founded Prominent Features, which made popular award-winning films such as *A Fish Called Wanda* (1988), *American Friends* (1991) and *Brassed Off* (1996), all of which he also produced. They also founded Prominent Television, which made all Michael Palin's BBC travelogues.

From 2002 he was appointed chairman of Screen Yorkshire, created to build a sustainable film industry in the county. Its role covers investment, building of studios, promotion of film locations and, above all, development of talent. When government funding was removed in 2010, he was instrumental in turning it into the only self-sustaining regional film agency in England from nine originally created. His role for UNESCO City of Film at Bradford has built on this.

Abbott has demonstrated his passion for Bradford. The city has recognised this three times – making him Honorary Doctor of the University of Bradford in 1998, Honorary Fellow of Bradford College in 2012 and in 2019 presenting him with a 'Brafta' at a special civic reception at City Hall.

Sources: Several Youtube interviews

29 Jul 1929 JB Priestley publishes *The Good Companions,* an instant success.

Today witnessed a publishing sensation and a breakthrough moment in JB Priestley's rising literary career. It saw the long-awaited publication of *The Good Companions,* a long picaresque novel. It tells the story of three travellers cast adrift from their usual lives who fall in with a concert party, the Dinky Doos. Renamed The Good Companions, the troupe have many adventures, odd encounters, successes and failures and happy endings at last.

It had been trailed locally for months. The *Bradford Daily Telegraph* ran a piece on 6 March about the 250,000 word novel (80,000 words being the norm): *'This will be a return to the practice of the great 19th century novelists. Anyone who is acquainted with Mr. Priestley's previous books will anticipate that, though the new one may be long, it will not be tedious.'*

The *Yorkshire Post* printed a long article today:

'The book is a frank return to an older technique of fiction than that most commonly employed by contemporary novelists since the war years. It is a picaresque story, deriving from Smollett, Dickens, and Wells, but remaining always characteristic of its teller.

The story moves at its ease from adventure to adventure about the roads and townships of North and Mid-England. It tells of how Jesiah Oakroyd left his angular wife and little house in the Yorkshire manufacturing town of Bruddersford, of how Elizabeth Trant made holiday from the sedate respectability of the village of Hitherton, having let the Hall on her father's death, and of how Inigo Jollifant, teacher in Mr. Tarvin's school, had a glorious "bust-up" with Mr. and Mrs. Tarvin, and took to the road with his haversack. It tells of what singular happenings that befell them until they met, by the workings of fate, in the station refreshment rooms at Rawsley...'

The new novel was an instant success. An initial print run of 7,000 copies, itself quite unusual and risky, was repeated 25 times in two years. Bradford's Public Library obtained 120 copies. It transformed Priestley's life and literary career, in particular freeing him financially to explore the new challenge of writing for the theatre. Critically, it was well received, winning the James Tait Black Memorial Prize for fiction then in its tenth year, now over 100 years old.

Source: *Stories of the Century, Telegraph & Argus* (1999)

30 Jul 1898   New electric trams start to replace horse and steam trams.

The ride took less than 15 minutes, but it was deemed important enough for a civic opening. The Tramways Committee and guests boarded the two tramcars in Forster Square, watched by a large crowd, and rode along Bolton Road to the city boundary. They got off for 'a light luncheon' at a nearby villa owned by a former councillor and returned to the Town Hall where they 'dined'. They finished with a toast to *The success of the Bolton Road Tramway*.

The *Bradford Daily Telegraph* recorded the whole occasion.

The new transport reduced the journey time from three quarters of an hour to go by tram (horse or steam) or cab to under a quarter of an hour. It was believed that the potential for the district was great. Trams had already been in operation for some 16 years in parts of the city, first horse-driven and then steam-driven.

The Corporation had gained powers under the Bradford Corporation Tramways Order, 1881 to construct its own tramway system. The first route from Rawson Square in the city centre, to Lister Park Gates opened to the public on 2 February 1882 with a half-hourly service from 8am to 11pm. A fleet of six horse-drawn open-top 38-seat double-deck tramcars were used. The fare was twopence.

On August 8 1882 a line was opened along Leeds Road to Stanningley using steam traction because of the gradients. Next year a steam tram service started from the city to Allerton. Later, a route to Tong Cemetery and an extension of the horse-driven route to Undercliffe from Manningham followed. In 1884 a new line was constructed from the Town Hall Square to Shelf. From 1892, steam trams from the city travelled as far as Wyke via Manchester Road and Odsal.

Electric trams signalled an end for horse and steam. On 31 January 1902, the pioneering horse trams on the Manningham Lane service were finally retired. On 1 April 1903 the last steam tram ran on the Shelf service. The Bradford tramway system was now all-electric, but it would not be long before trams would be threatened by the new trolley-buses.

Source: *Bradford Daily Telegraph* (30 July 1898)

31 Jul 2006 Professor David Rhodes announces his retirement as Filtronic's chief executive.

'David Rhodes blends the talents of an outstanding engineer with the achievements of a highly successful entrepreneur and businessman.

David graduated from Leeds in 1964 and was awarded his PhD in 1966. He had a short but distinguished period in the United States which established his reputation in microwave engineering, returning to Leeds in 1969 as a Lecturer in Electrical Engineering. He was promoted rapidly: to a Readership in 1972 at the age of 28, and a Personal Chair in 1975.

In 1977, David founded Filtronic Components Ltd, building on his own research. After two years working from his own home, he moved into dedicated premises and hired his first engineers – Leeds graduates of course! … The advent of mobile communications presented new opportunities and Filtronic Comtek was founded in 1992; it was successfully floated in 1994. International growth followed and in 1998 Filtronic acquired a number of companies, including a compound semiconductor capability. Today, Filtronic plc embraces wireless telecommunications, and defence businesses, employing over 3,500 staff worldwide in 17 facilities. In 2003, the company made over 400,000 base station units and over 120 million handset antennae. It is the UK's most successful university spin-out company.

David remains a powerhouse of technical innovation, driving the development of new products based on highly innovative engineering solutions. His interest in the fundamentals of engineering, especially mathematics, remains his passion, and aside from his stalwart support for Bradford City Football Club, occupies whatever spare time is available to him …. His world-leading excellence in his field continues to be widely recognised with the award of the most distinguished prizes from learned societies including the Royal Academy of Engineering, the Royal Society and the IEEE … He was elected to the Royal Society in 1993.'

In 2004 a close colleague gave this presentation at Leeds University when Professor David Rhodes received an honorary doctorate in engineering. Over two years later Rhodes announced his retirement from the company Filtronic that he had founded.

Rhodes was a man from Leeds, but he had two important connections with Bradford. First, his company located to Saltaire in 1995 when Jonathan Silver was energetically rebuilding it with new technology companies. Second, he was director of Bradford City AFC at the best and worst of times when they reached the Premier League and then plunged twice into administration. Without his support they might well have folded.

Source: www.leeds.ac.uk

AUGUST

1 Aug 2000   On Yorkshire Day, Dr Arthur Raistrick is commemorated as 'Dalesman of the Millennium'.

Bordering to the north with the more rural parts of Bradford district (beyond Ilkley, Keighley and Haworth), the Dales can naturally be thought of as Bradford's hinterland – the place that Bradfordians go for days out in the countryside and, in less prosperous times, went for their week-long family holidays.

Nobody symbolises this link better than Dr Arthur Raistrick (1896-1991), born in Saltaire and educated at Bradford Grammar School, whose life straddled almost the entire 20th century. No date was better to remember him than the first Yorkshire Day in the new millennium. No place was more appropriate than just outside Grassington overlooking the village of Linton where he made his home. Today the Yorkshire Dales National Park Authority, supported by many other organisations closely associated with him, commemorated Dr Raistrick with an appropriate sculpture – a limestone bench, complete with key themes from his full and active life.

He had been a leading geologist, industrial historian, archaeologist, National Park campaigner, pacifist, socialist, Quaker and one of the true founders of the National Park movement in Britain.

This career developed naturally from his background. His mother, aunts and uncles had worked at Saltaire Mill. His father had been a founder member of the Independent Labour Party, which started in Bradford. His four grandparents came from four different dales as farmers and lead miners. He left school at 16 to be an engineering apprentice, but spent three years of World War One in prison as a conscientious objector.

Resuming his education at Leeds University, he graduated in civil engineering and took a PhD in geology. He became a prolific academic writer in geology, carrying out research in industrial archaeology, for example lead-mining in the Dales. He taught extensively in adult education.

His interests took him beyond the Dales. As a Quaker he studied Quaker history and involvement in science and industry. With a close friend this led him to produce a seminal work on the Darbys of Coalbrookdale, and their role in the cradle of the Industrial Revolution. This led eventually to the recognition in 2011 by UNESCO of Ironbridge Gorge as a World Heritage Site.

Raistrick received honorary doctorates at Leeds and Bradford Universities. Appropriately he bequeathed to the latter his extensive library of writings, books and maps.

Source: *The Yorkshire Dales Society: 1981-2006: The Story So Far: A Personal Account*, Colin & Fleur Speakman (2006).

2 Aug 1773   The new Piece Hall opens for business.

Growth in the wool business was being hampered by the lack of a single place where pieces of cloth could be traded. Clothiers had to use the White Lion Inn on Kirkgate where each had lock-up closets, or else they simply sold pieces on the street. Businessman John Hustler energetically led the case for a Piece Hall. As a result wool traders today had a new place for doing business.

The new Piece Hall stood next to the old Talbot Hotel in Kirkgate, opposite the bottom of Piccadilly. Running down towards the centre from where the building stood, Piece Hall Yard is now its only reminder. In its day it was an impressive structure, built like a barn, with a belfry and a flight of steps on each side, leading up to a stone balcony which formed the main entrance. This commanding position was found very useful for outdoor speakers at elections and other times, there being plenty of space for a large audience. It was Bradford's first regular market place for wool traders from surrounding districts and one of the first symbols of Bradford's commercial prosperity.

Its design did have some drawbacks. The main one was lack of privacy. Inside it was divided into stalls where terms of business agreed in one stall could be clearly overheard by neighbouring buyers and sellers. There were firm rules for participating, covering opening times, arrangements for horses, starting and closing times for trading (backed by fines), false claims of ownership, encroaching of space and disputes over measurement..

There was no doubt, however, that it was a successful venture and an extension was soon added to the premises. Trade eventually overflowed into the old Market Hall on the site of the present Wool Exchange. John Hustler proposed to build a Market Hall with shops behind Piece Hall, but William Rawson, lord of the manor who owned the market rights, objected.

Eventually, as the volume of pieces increased dramatically from machines replacing handwork, the bigger merchants started to display their pieces in their own warehouses, often in the expanding Little Germany. Piece Hall became less useful.

Eighty years after it had been hailed as a major success, the Piece Hall was finally closed for business. It became a private establishment and was used as a drapery.

Source: *Pen and Pencil Pictures of Old Bradford*, William Scruton (1890)

3 Aug 1914   Thirty young German Bradfordians leave Bradford to fight for Germany.

Britain declared war on Germany at 23.00 hours on 4 August 1914. On the same day the *Bradford Daily Telegraph* reported: *'Over the weekend quite a number of young Germans residing in Bradford left the city in order to re-join their regiments. Yesterday about thirty departed for London on the 2.50 pm train. They were seen off by friends and the German pastor.'*

All people of German nationality, and their British-born wives and children, had to be registered by 20 August, after which they were denied the use of a motor car or a telephone, and their mail was scrutinised. Some were later arrested and interned on the Isle of Man for the whole war.

The declaration of war posed many problems for Bradford's small but influential German community that had taken root from the mid-19th century. There are no official figures as to its size, especially as there could have been up to three generations for some families. We can surmise that there might have been up to 5,000 individuals by 1914, as estimates of the first wave usually refer to around 500 families. Many had been naturalised but bore obviously German names. The group of 30 who left immediately represent one reaction.

For most, loyalties might have been split. Certainly stories from the first few weeks also reflect ambivalence on the part of Bradford's native population.

Most German emigres were middle class businessmen. One German group that was different, and not just in Bradford, were pork butchers. Although they did not speak English well, they were liked and expert in their food knowledge. They became targets. The *Leeds Mercury* reported (Monday 31 August) that in Keighley on Saturday evening a shop belonging to a pork butcher *'and non-naturalised alien'* and *'in business for some years',* had its windows stoned. Police were called to quell a crowd disturbance.

Even if not attacked, Germans were treated differently. Albert Munz, 19-year-old son of a pork butcher and naturalised British citizen, died in 1918 fighting for the Middlesex Regiment, known as the Kaiser's Regiment, who were kept away from the front-line to avoid perceived conflicts of interest.

In the Bradford area these were isolated incidents. Most Bradfordians were broadly sympathetic towards the significant German contribution to civic life and philanthropy for the past three generations.

Source: *Little Germany: A History of Bradford's Germans,* Susan Duxbury-Neumann (2015)

4 Aug 1928   Local boy made good opens the Brontë Parsonage Museum.

It was a long-awaited event for all Brontë devotees. Ever since the Brontë Society was formed in 1893 and, five years later, a small museum opened in the centre of Haworth, they had dreamed of the day when the parsonage, home to the Brontë family for most of their lives, would become a literary shrine. The person who made this possible was local boy Sir James Roberts (1848 -1935), now owner of Saltaire Mill and village after Sir Titus Salt and his family. Today he presented the parsonage and deeds to the Brontë Society as a permanent home for Brontë memorabilia at a gathering of over 1,000 visitors. The *Yorkshire Post* reported:

'Handing over the deeds, Sir James said he was born in that parish during the week which the unhappy Branwell died; an event followed at intervals of distressing brevity by the deaths of Emily and Anne.

"It is to me a somewhat melancholy reflection' said Sir James 'that I am of the fast narrowing circle of Haworth veterans who remember the Parsonage family. I heard Mr. Brontë preach in the pathetic blindness of his old age. Mr. Nicholls (ie Charlotte's husband) *frequently visited the schoolhouse as children ate the midday meal in the interval of our elementary studies, while Martha Brown, the faithful servant to whom Mr. Brontë gave the money box, the contents of which she was to keep ready for a time of need is still a well-remembered figure. Above all these memorabilia, there rises before me the frail, the unforgettable figure of Charlotte who, more than once, stopped to speak kindly words to the little lad who now stands a patriarch before you. I remember her funeral one Eastertide, and some six years afterwards that of her father.*

The presentation of the title deeds is to me an act of homage, alike to the genius of the Brontë sisters, and the nobility of their courageous lives."

Built in 1779, the parsonage was from 1820 till his death in 1861 the home of Patrick Brontë, a man of books and incumbent of St Michael and All Angels' Church, Haworth, and his family of wife and six children who were all to die before him. The moorland setting and their father's library had a profound influence on the writing of the three literary sisters, Charlotte, Emily and Anne.

Source: *Yorkshire Post* (6 August 1928)

5 Aug 1873   The Halifax, Thornton & Keighley Railway Act is passed.

The terrain west of Bradford is hilly, rising to 1,000 feet above sea level with several steep-sided valleys. Today was passed a most ambitious railway act, linking the towns of Bradford, Keighley and Halifax. It posed severe engineering challenges. Looking back now, one wonders how its construction was ever justified.

It was built and opened in stages over the 1870s and 1880s, work undertaken by Great Northern Railways.

The first stage was a line over five miles from Bradford to Thornton opened in 1878. One important aim was to provide a rail link to Queensbury, where local wool magnate John Foster required transport for coal for his Black Dyke Mill. The line connected Bradford, Great Horton, Clayton and Thornton. It ran past Queensbury, but no station could be built. Beyond Clayton, the line required a 1,000 yards long tunnel and coming into Thornton, a massive 20-arch viaduct.

Next, Halifax was connected with Thornton. It built from an existing link at Ovenden, two miles north of Halifax, to Holmfield and Queensbury, then linking with the Bradford to Thornton line. It opened in 1879. Queensbury still did not have a station, but now it had a tunnel. Queensbury Tunnel was over 2,500 yards long, took four years to build and cost ten navvies their lives.

The final stretch just under ten miles from Thornton to Keighley was the most difficult. It required another major viaduct, at Hewerden, 17 arches, 123 feet high, and two more tunnels. New stations included Denholme, Wilsden, Cullingworth and Ingrow East. It opened in 1884.

Finally, in 1890 Queensbury's station opened – still one mile downhill from the village. It was a most unusual triangular station: only two similar exist in the country, curiously one at Shipley not far away. Each of the three lines leaving the station enters a lengthy tunnel, or series of tunnels.

Passenger services on these lines ran for around 60 years. However danger signs commercially were emerging. The hilly Bradford-Halifax and Bradford-Keighley routes were always much slower than the alternative valley routes. Trams competed with the train to Thornton. Buses everywhere started to compete.

Gradually, the network disintegrated in the 1950s as routes were scaled back and stations closed. When the 'Beeching axe' was swung in 1963, there was little left to cut. What remains are a rich heritage, splendid viaducts and a few scenic footpaths instead of railway lines.

Source: www.lostrailwayswestyorkshire.co.uk

6 Aug 1875   Queen Victoria approves the endowment of the new Bradford Girls' Grammar School.

In 1662 King Charles II gave a royal charter to Bradford Grammar School. This was, of course, for boys; it took more than 200 years before people started to think about girls.

The charter had expressed the purpose of the school as: *'That there shall bee One Free Grammar School of King Charles the Second at Bradford, for the teaching, instructing, and better bringinge upp of children and youth in Grammar and other good Learning and Literature.'*

By 1870 the political climate towards education was changing. That year WE Forster, the Education Minister, had brought in his Elementary Education Act, guaranteeing basic education for all children to the age of 14. The governing body for Bradford Grammar School made a case for a joint endowment, based on the point that the phrase in the charter *'children and youth'* included girls. The Commissioners of the Endowed Schools Act in 1869, also brought in by WE Forster, accepted this case in 1875 and agreed a new scheme that laid down that *'this foundation shall consist of two branches, one for the education of boys and the other for the education of girls'.* Remarkably for the time, the scheme also allowed for an equal number of men and women on the governing body of eight representative and four co-opted governors.

So, today Bradford Girls' Grammar School became the first school in England of the *'high school type offering education of the highest grade to girls from seven to nineteen years of age'.* Term started for the first time with 109 pupils on 29 September 1875 with a formal opening by Lady Frederick Cavendish, wife of a prominent national Liberal politician. The first location of the school was the already cramped Hallfield Road School, a soot-blackened, converted building, which, later, was attached to Busby's department store just off Manningham Lane.

One of the first pupils to make a name was Marion Greenwood, who won a scholarship to Cambridge University aged 17. From there she became a distinguished physiologist and the first woman to have a paper presented to the Royal Society in 1893. A strong role model for Bradford girls, she still had to allow a man to present that paper to a society that did not admit female members.

There were still many battles to come for a more equal society for women.

Source: *Bradford Grammar School 1662 to 1912*, Rev WH Keeling (1912)

7 Aug 1976   Kiki Dee and Elton John complete six weeks with a No 1 single.

'Don't go breaking my heart' – the song was Kiki Dee's claim to fame and the song with Elton John that forever defines her, the first Bradford-born singer to reach number one. Intended as an affectionate pastiche of the Motown style and composed by Elton John and Bernie Taupin, it hit the top on 3 July 1976 and stayed there for six weeks, last appearing today. For both singers it was their first No 1 appearance in the singles charts. For four weeks it was also No 1 in the US charts. Many years later in 1985 they also performed live at Wembley for Live-Aid.

Kiki Dee's success was a far cry from her modest background. Born Pauline Matthews in Little Horton in 1946, she had a natural singing talent: *Twelve-year-old Pauline Matthews loves singing and wins prizes for it, too, but she has never had a lesson. Her most recent successes were at Cleethorpes last week while on holiday with her father. She won first prize in two talent competitions run at the Pier Pavilion'* (18 August 1959).

Her first job as a 16-year-old was as a shop girl in Boots. As a teenager she sang with a local dance band at the Mecca ballroom. In October 1962, she had a lucky break. The American singer Donna Douglas was performing at the Alhambra and fell ill. Pauline was invited to audition as a replacement and replaced the star at an hour's notice. Despite understandable nerves and inexperience, she carried it off to great applause.

Soon down in London, she began as backing vocal for Dusty Springfield before releasing her own first single in 1963 – *Early Night*. In 1970 she went to the USA and became the first UK female singer to sign with Motown's Tamla Records. On her return she signed up with Elton John's Rocket Records label.

No one-trick pony, Kiki Dee has had a long singing career - 40 singles, 12 albums and many live shows plus an appearance in *Rocketman,* the 2019 Elton John biopic.

Source: *Telegraph & Argus* (25 October 2010 and 28 June 2018)

8 Aug 1866   Another Illingworth marries another Holden.

The Illingworth and Holden families were already rich and powerful in mid-Victorian Bradford.

Today's marriage between the Illingworth son, Alfred, and the Holden daughter, Margaret, increased even further the wealth and influence of their families. Moreover, his younger brother Henry had married six years previously another Holden daughter, Mary. To complete the connections, an Illingworth daughter, Margaret, married a Holden son, Angus. The Illingworth boys and their wives lived next door to each other in Allerton and owned mills close to each other in Bradford. Together, the families employed thousands of Bradfordians in their businesses. Four of their sons were also to take over the family business.

Daniel Illingworth (1792-1854) and his brother Miles established their first factory at Prospect Mills in Bradford. They bought another which became known as Providence Mills and which Daniel's younger son Henry operated till his death in 1895.

Daniel's elder son Alfred (1827-1907) was educated at Joseph Hinchcliffe's Academy in Horton that took in sons of middle-class nonconformist families. He then attended Huddersfield College for a business education. Afterwards at the age of 16 he joined his father's business at Providence Mills together with his brother Henry.

After Alfred's marriage, the brothers built Whetley Mills, one of the largest spinning mills in Bradford. It operated under the name Daniel Illingworth & Sons. The mill was directly opposite Alston Works, which the Holden family had just completed in 1864.

While Henry Illingworth managed the mills, Alfred went into politics and became a powerful local and national player. He took over as Liberal MP for Knaresborough in 1868 from his father-in-law, Isaac Holden, and held it until 1874. He then represented Bradford from 1880 to 1895.

Alfred was a strong believer in freedom for individual action. He supported the disestablishment of the Anglican church, believed in free trade and opposed military action. Interestingly, he did not support fellow Bradford Liberal MP, WE Forster, over education reform, despite accepting the need for more technical education.

Although he supported workers' rights, he did not welcome interference in the employer-employee relationship. His strong views had the unintended effect of contributing to the rise of the new Independent Labour Party. He left politics in 1900, somewhat disillusioned.

His vault is the most impressive monument in the whole of Undercliffe Cemetery.

Source: Alfred Illingworth (*Oxford Dictionary of National Biography*)

9 Aug 1864   Lord Palmerston lays foundation stone for Wool Exchange.

Henry Ripley, chairman of the Exchange Company, invited Lord Palmerston, Prime Minister and the most prominent statesman of the day, to lay the foundation stone for the new Wool Exchange. Like St. George's Hall (1853) and later the Town Hall (1873), this was another step in Bradford marking its new prosperity with fine civic buildings. There had been much controversy about the design, which eventually was awarded to Lockwood and Mawson. It was described as Venetian Gothic.

Today, the Corporation pulled all the stops for their distinguished visitor. It was made a public holiday. Some 100 carriages formed a long procession from Peel Park where there was a 19-gun salute. A large platform was erected by the Market Street site with ticket-only access for up to 1,000 people. The *Bradford Observer* estimated at least 50,000 people on the streets.

In the evening Palmerston was the guest of honour at a grand dinner held in St. George's Hall, where the Bradford Choral Society greeted him with *'See the Conquering Hero'*.

Not all went well. Many of Bradford's working men greeted their visitor in silence. Without a vote in elections, they saw him as a major barrier to their enfranchisement. The right to vote had returned in the 1860s as a major grievance. Placards had been displayed around the centre with the words: *'Working men of Bradford, don't be Ripley-ridden; don't cheer Lord Palmerston'*.

Source: *Bradford Observer* (11 August 1864)

9 Aug 1965   Harry Corbett and Sooty appear on *Desert Island Discs*.

Every celebrity looks forward to an appearance on *Desert Island Discs*. Today the accolade belonged to one of the nation's favourite entertainment acts in the 1950s and 1960s. Harry Corbett (1918 -1989) was born into a well-known Bradford family. His uncle was Harry Ramsden of fish 'n chips fame. With deafness in one ear Corbett could not pursue ambitions to be a concert pianist, but he did play the piano in his uncle's restaurant.

Sooty appeared sometime after Corbett had bought a puppet to entertain his family on holiday in Blackpool. He blackened the ears and nose with soot and called him Sooty. In 1952 they first appeared on TV in BBC's show *Talent Night*. Thereafter, they were regulars on television. Each appearance would finish with the catchphrase: *'Bye-bye, everybody! Bye-bye!'*

Corbett's eight records were a mixture of classical and popular, reflecting perhaps his early ambition and his later achievement.

10 Aug 2002   The Geoffrey Richmond rollercoaster ends in resignation.

Today was the sad and predictable end of an era that was great fun while it lasted in the life of any Bradford City supporter. The flamboyant chairman resigned. Nearly two years later he was declared bankrupt.

Leeds-born Geoffrey Richmond was a 'larger than life' chairman for eight years from 1994 to 2002. He was more successful than any other since the first eight years when Bradford City won the FA Cup. Any long-suffering fan brought up after those golden years had to support a club with little ambition and little investment. It remained in the doldrums, 'yo-yoing' between the old Third and Fourth Divisions, with little prospect of any real success. For such a large city, the club underachieved on a massive scale.

Then along came Geoffrey Richmond with money, charisma, ambition and a liking for controversy. He claimed to everyone's disbelief that the team would be in the Premier League (then two years old) within five years.

His crowning moment was to achieve this ambition in May 1999, the first time City had played in the top division for 77 years, and then to escape relegation in their first season back, both achievements being secured with exciting wins on the last day of the season against Wolves (away) and Liverpool (home) respectively.

Having sacked three managers in four years, he achieved this with a rookie in Paul Jewell, but the price was high. After a disagreement with the chairman Jewell departed to another club. Richmond overstretched himself and the club in *six weeks of madness* (his words) signing players who were unaffordable, especially Italian star Benito Carbone rumoured to be on £40,000 per week, at the time one third of the club's total wage bill.

The team were relegated in April 2001 and the club was in freefall into administration in May 2002. It took ten years to recover from this blow.

10 Aug 1997   The new Bradford Bulls take the Super League with 18 straight wins.

Rarely can a professional team in any sport in any part of the world have had such a successful run as Bradford Bulls in 1997. This was the second 22-match season of summer Super League and the first since Bradford Northern became the Bulls.

Today, winning 32-21 at Sheffield Eagles they became champions with their 18th consecutive victory. In only four matches was the margin of victory less than 10 points.

11 Aug 1869   Magistrates tighten up the licensing of beerhouses.

In March 1849 Mayor Titus Salt had received the report he had commissioned into the moral state of Bradford. One of its key findings was the state of the town's 150 beerhouses, almost none 'decent and orderly'.

Just over 20 years later, Mayor Henry Brown believed that the beerhouses should be brought under much greater control of local magistrates after the liberalisation of licensing encouraged by the 1830 Beerhouse Act. He was not alone. In 1869 a Tory's private member bill led to a new Wine and Beerhouse Act which took effect from 15 July.

This Act introduced the need for a magistrates' certificate for the sale of beer for consumption on or off-site. There would now be four grounds for an applicant's licence to be rejected:

- failure to produce satisfactory evidence of good character
- previous forfeit of a licence for misconduct
- owning, or occupation, of a house, or adjacent house of a disorderly character, or frequented by thieves, prostitutes or persons of bad character
- lack of qualification by law.

Today, the *Bradford Observer* reported on the steps that the town's magistrates were taking in preparation for the first licensing session to be held at the end of the month. The police would produce a return of the names of the beerhouse keepers in the borough who had been fined, reported for harbouring prostitutes, keeping irregular houses, etc. The mayor and magistrates were about to make a tour of the premises for which licenses were sought. In 1867/68 the borough had 409 beerhouses with a further 134 places licensed to sell beer and 15 to sell wine. With an expected 15% increase in beerhouses, there might be between 600 and 700 applications this time to check.

In the event 90 cases out of 626 (14%) were refused a licence, mainly on grounds of character. This included 18 out of 29 (60%) applications from those new to the trade. Almost all refusals related to premises in the slum areas in the centre of the town. The chief constable and magistrates expressed themselves well satisfied with the outcome which would encourage better conduct in all beerhouses.

Source: *The Public House in Bradford, 1770 -1970*, Paul Jennings (1995)

12 Aug 2014   Timothy Taylor's Boltmaker wins the annual Champion Beer of Britain award.

Today, the only independent brewer in the Bradford area won the Supreme Champion Beer of Britain title presented by the Campaign for Real Ale (CAMRA), at its annual Great British Beer Festival. The beer that won the title for Keighley's Timothy Taylor was its Boltmaker brew. It was described as a *'well-balanced, genuine Yorkshire Bitter, with a full measure of maltiness and hoppy aroma'*.

Since the competition was instigated in 1978, Timothy Taylor had won it four times earlier in 1982, 1983, 1994, 1999 with its Landlord beer, a classic pale ale. No brewer has won it more times and only five others out of 30 previous winners have won it more than once. By this measure Timothy Taylor is the best independent brewer in Great Britain. The assessment is carried out in three stages – a series of local CAMRA tasting panels, regional beer judging competitions and, finally, the national judging at the annual festival.

It was a special victory, being the first time that Timothy Taylor's had won with a different beer than Landlord, created in 1952, which had always been the beer that outsiders associated with the brewer. The bitter was re-named in a 2012 competition after one of its licensees came up with the name to celebrate the town's engineering tradition. Boltmaker was the brewer's favorite beer, sold well in the brewer's own pubs and, after the name change, had been more prominent outside Yorkshire. It was also special for managing director, Charles Dent. After 20 years of success and a period of significant investment he had decided to retire. This was his crowning moment.

Timothy Taylor's has been a family-owned business since Bingley-born Timothy Taylor had opened his brewery in Cook Lane, Keighley in 1858. Five years later he moved to its present site at the Knowle Spring. Taylor's grandson took over in 1894 and instigated major improvements such as a deep artesian well and a new brewhouse. The way Timothy Taylor brews true cask ales now is the same way as it did then with a strong emphasis on quality and use of the best ingredients.

It is now the only such independent brewer in West Yorkshire. Many drinkers in the Bradford area can sup the nation's best brew in several pubs that it owns at Bingley, Haworth, Keighley, Oakworth, Oxenhope and Thornton.

Source: *Telegraph & Argus* (27 August 2014)

13 Aug 1850   A public meeting agrees the idea of a public park to commemorate Sir Robert Peel.

Sir Robert Peel, former Prime Minister, died on 2 July 1850. He was a great supporter of the Free Trade Movement, which had made him very popular with Bradford's businessmen who were rapidly expanding their wool trade. There was a strong groundswell of opinion that he should be commemorated.

During the 1840s access to public spaces had become a social issue ever since a Government Select Committee (1840) had investigated the health of towns; Bradford had often been picked out as extremely unhealthy.

Today, Bradford's establishment attended a public meeting at the Temperance Hall to consider a public park as memorial to Peel. They included Titus Salt, William Byles and the Reverend Jonathan Glyde. As mayor, Salt had led an investigation into Bradford's moral condition that recommended just a few months earlier a large recreational public space.

Glyde had also been a passionate supporter of a public park and now he spoke up: *'Nothing had pressed so much upon his mind during the last two years as the importance of having a public park or a place of recreation. He rejoiced that now this movement was to be associated with Sir Robert Peel. This was a proud day for the working classes. Sir Robert Peel sprung from the people ... ' (Bradford Observer).* Later Glyde wrote a letter to the same paper (5 September) confirming the success of Peel Park, Salford, since its opening in 1846. Peel, a Lancastrian, had been a prominent subscriber.

Peel Park, between Bolton and Undercliffe, was open in 1853. It held several galas in the early years to pay off the mortgage on the land purchase before the Park Committee handed it over to the Corporation in 1863. It became the blueprint for four more public parks, situated like Peel Park on the slopes overlooking the town centre: Lister Park, Horton Park, Bowling Park and Bradford Moor Park. The blueprint comprised promenade, flower gardens, seating areas, greenhouses, refreshment area, drinking fountains, bandstand, lake, park-keeper's lodge, gates and walls.

In criticising Roundhay Park (Leeds), the *Leeds Times* (1 September 1883) looked across approvingly to Bradford: *'Those who want to see how admirably public parks can be kept should visit Bradford before the bloom of the flower gardens is gone, and we can promise them a surprise and a treat.'*

Source: *Some Bits of Bradford History*, Janet Senior (2018)

14 Aug 1842   A Chartist camp meeting at Bradford Moor triggers four days of riots across Bradford.

The fiasco of the first Chartist uprising in Bradford in 1840 had applied a brake to the momentum behind Chartism. The next year it revived. Feargus O'Connor, one of the national Chartist leaders and based in Leeds, was released from prison to much celebration. He came to address a crowd of some 6,000 in Horton and urged a new Chartist petition to Parliament.

The People's Charter called for six reforms to make the political system more democratic:

1. A vote for every man twenty-one years of age.
2. A secret ballot to protect the elector.
3. No property qualification for Members of Parliament.
4. Payment of MPs, enabling men of modest means to stand for Parliament.
5. Equal-sized constituencies.
6. Annual Parliamentary elections (the only reform not eventually implemented).

A severe economic recession in 1841/42 led to major unrest and a petition signed by over three million, of whom 26,000 from the Bradford district (a significant percentage of the local population). However on 2 May Parliament rejected the petition out of hand.

The working classes of the north reacted with a series of strikes. In Bradford today they held a Chartist camp meeting on Bradford Moor. This led the next day to a march across the town and mills came to a halt. An eye-witness recalled: *'I well remember the savage appearance of that huge crowd of men as they marched through Horton to Bradford. The sight was just one of those it is impossible to forget. They came pouring down the road in thousands, taking up its whole breadth – a great, famished-looking, desperate multitude, armed with heavy bludgeons, flails, pitchforks and pikes – and hundreds and hundreds with their coats in rags and tatters.'*

The marches and strikes continued for a couple of days but, when the magistrates ordered the military to clear the town on 17 August, the disturbances fizzled out.

Nevertheless, the magistrates reported to the Home Secretary that the *'present military force is quite inadequate for the preservation of the public peace'.* It was another two years before the Treasury finally gave the funds for the building of the first barracks in the town at Bradford Moor.

Source: *The Chartist Risings in Bradford,* DG Wright (1987)

15 Aug 1907   Inquest cannot explain a mysterious, tragic death in Thackley Tunnel.

It was a complete mystery.

A platelayer gave evidence today. Two days earlier, walking through Thackley Tunnel on the Shipley to Leeds railway, he discovered a body by the track side not far from the Shipley entrance. One leg and part of the head was badly severed. Evidently a train had run over the man.

In his pocket the man had a gold watch, still working. It had an inscription: *'Presented to JH Bell, Esq, by the woolsorters of Bradford and district, as a token of services rendered in the woolsorters' disease, Bradford 9 April 1881.'*

The Shipley station master confirmed that all the train doors were fastened when the train left. His Apperley Bridge counterpart testified that he did not notice any doors open when it arrived at the next station.

The inquest found that the man had been run over by the train, but no evidence indicated how he came to be on the line.

The man was a distinguished economist, Henry Gibbins (1865 -1907). Born in South Africa, educated at Bradford Grammar School and Oxford University, he had been a teacher, headmaster and priest. He had also written several books on economics. He had married the daughter of a distinguished Bradford doctor, whose home he was visiting when the accident happened.

Source: *The Tales of Thackley's Tunnels*, Norman Alvin (2016) in *The Antiquary*

15 Aug 1971   Harvey Smith gives a V sign to show-jumping judges.

Equestrian sports do not figure much in Bradford life. The main exception is Harvey Smith from Eldwick on the moors' edge. Although his show-jumping career was distinguished, he is remembered for one famous incident that took place today and was captured clearly on television, replayed endlessly.

He was seen to make a two-fingered V-sign towards the judges after winning the British Show Jumping Derby at Hickstead. The rider protested his innocence, claiming the judges mistook his gesture. *'It was a straightforward V for victory. Churchill used it throughout the war'*, he claimed. The judges disagreed; he was stripped of his £2,000 winnings and a major show jumping title. After huge public backing for the rider, the disqualification was reversed two days later. However, he did admit afterwards that he was making an obscene sign at the judges. The publicity even led to *'doing a Harvey Smith'* creeping into the English language.

Smith had the reputation of being controversial, rebellious and plain-speaking.

16 Aug 1791   The first casting takes place at Low Moor Ironworks.

Today, the Low Moor Ironworks started production with its first casting of iron. We do not know if this prompted any act of celebration, but we do know that in subsequent years the event was commemorated by the forgemen 'blowing in ale' provided at the company's expense.

The company was established by Hird, Jarratt, Dawson and Hardy to exploit the high-quality iron ore and low-sulphur coal in the area. It was one of five such businesses in the area of South Bradford that opened over some 20 years. Low Moor Ironworks (founded 1790) became the largest, employing up to 3,500, and outlasted the others – Emmetts at Birkenshaw (1782), Bowling Ironworks (1788), Shelf (1792) and North Bierley (1811).

It manufactured a whole range of domestic and industrial iron products that supported a period of rapid industrial growth in Britain and across the developed world. Business boomed in times of war. The Napoleonic Wars and the Crimean War in particular both saw the manufacture of guns, cannons and shells.

The local poet John Nicholson described the impact of this growth:

White as the sun and metal runs   *The carronade, the pond'rous ball;*
For horse shoe nails or thund'ring guns   *The place where steam moves his wings*
The trembling hairspring of a watch   *The nails in beggars' shoes and kings'*
An anchor or a cottage latch –   *The anchor's chain, the fisher's hook*
Most implements the farmers have   *The sword – the latchet– and the crook*
And those of steamers in the wave   *The sounding anvil, all the blades*
The tailor's needle or the shell   *The cause of many thousand trades;*
That levell'd once where princes dwell   *No pen can write. No mind can soar*
The engine, boiler, cobbler's awl   *To tell the wonders of Low Moor.*

Source: *The Low Moor Ironworks, Bradford,* Charles Dodsworth from *Industrial Archaeology,* (May 1971)

16 Aug 1964   Barry Watson becomes the fastest person to swim the Channel.

Today, Barry Watson (1938-2020) from Bingley broke the record for swimming the English Channel from France to England in 9 hours and 35 minutes at the age of 26 – one hour faster than the previous best. His record was to last 13 years. He repeated the swim with longer times in 1968, 1969 and 1970. He also set records swimming Lake Windermere, Loch Lomond and from Fleetwood to Morecambe. Although swimming into his 70s, he failed in

17 Aug 1982   Actor Bernard Hepton achieves a life-long ambition.

An electrician's son from a family of mill workers, Bernard Heptonstall (1925-2018) grew up in Saltburn Place just off Toller Lane, Bradford. This was the same street where writer JB Priestley had grown up 25 years earlier.

He was introduced to acting in his teens when, as a fire-watcher in wartime, the boredom was relieved by some one-act plays brought along by the woman in charge. This encouraged him to join the Bradford Civic Playhouse, then a thriving amateur theatre, whose president was JB Priestley.

A further lucky break was the arrival of a new artistic director in Esme Church, an experienced actress with a national reputation, who used the opportunity to set up the Northern School of Drama in 1944. For a few years this became one of the best places in the country outside London to learn the trade of acting and for Bradfordians the best time in the 20th century to do so.

Esme Church's first student was known as Bernard Hepton. He was joined by many others who became national names, eg Tony Richardson, Billie Whitelaw and Sir Robert Stephens. Stephens was to say about Hepton: *'Immediately you could see that he was brilliant'.*

It is small wonder that with these local connections Hepton developed an ambition to land his dream part, written by the celebrity from his street and the playwright revered by his local theatre - JB Priestley's most famous play *An Inspector Calls.*

Before this ambition could be realised, he had to develop his own acting reputation. He worked in repertory in York and Birmingham. However, he became most well-known for his work in prominent TV drama series. For example, he played Thomas Cranmer in *The Six Wives of King Henry VIII* (Keith Michelle the lead) and *Elizabeth R* (Glenda Jackson the lead); the German Commandant in three years of *Colditz*; Pallas, the Greek freedman, in *I Claudius* (Derek Jacobi the lead); intelligence officer Toby Esterhase in *Tinker, Tailor, Soldier Spy* and *Smiley's People* (Alec Guinness the lead both times). All these and many others were high-class productions of what became vintage television drama.

Playing a wide range of significant supporting parts, Hepton was rarely the star. The moment when he finally took the lead role came today in the first of a three-part BBC TV mini-series as the mysterious Inspector Goole in *An Inspector Calls.*

Source: Obituary,*The Guardian* (30 July 2018)

18 Aug 2016   The Brownlee brothers win gold and silver in the Rio Olympics triathlon.

The modern triathlon is arguably the toughest Olympic event. It covers three disciplines, in a single continuous race – swimming (1.5 km), cycling (40 km), running (10 km). Or put differently, 32.1 miles of strenuous physical activity, just over 20% longer than the marathon.

To win an Olympic gold medal for such an event puts you on the highest pedestal for a long-distance sport. For your nearest rival to be your brother makes for a special pair of brothers unparalleled in Olympics history. Today the Brownlee brothers, Alastair (b.1988) and Jonny (b.1990), achieved this accolade at the 2016 Rio Olympics, having come one-three at the 2012 London Olympics.

Born in Dewsbury, they were both educated at Bradford Grammar School and both are members of Bingley Harriers. They practised the three triathlon disciplines from an early age. Just going to school was great for practice. Living in Horsforth just outside the Bradford boundary, they cycled to school along the Leeds-Liverpool Canal towpath – ten miles and 40 minutes each way, no hills, little traffic.

When they got to school, they found the running culture supportive of their ambitions. Their teacher who organised cross-country running had been at the school when Richard Nerurkar had shown the talent that led him to two Olympic marathons. The school allowed them to go every day on training runs at lunch breaks. As the school running club was a registered club, the brothers were able to compete in strong amateur competitions, not just school races.

When it came to early morning swimming practice at the Leeds International Pool, they had barely the time to get to school in Bradford, often having to run from the station to school.

Such an upbringing was critical to their success.

From their early 20s the brothers have dominated triathlon at elite events. As well as two Olympic gold medals, Alastair has won gold at two world finals, three European and one Commonwealth games and come first at 25 world series events. As well as his Olympic silver and bronze, Jonny has won 13 world series events. On ten occasions they have come first and second with Alastair winning eight and Jonny winning two.

Postscript: In the 2020 (2021) Tokyo Olympics with Alistair unfit, Jonny came fifth. However, in the inaugural triathlon mixed relay he finally won an Olympic gold in his last Olympics appearance.

Source: *Swim, Bike, Run*, Alistair & Jonathan Brownlee (2013)

19 Aug 1920   Two young girls hoax the world with photos of the Cottingley fairies.

Sixteen-year-old Elsie Wright, studying art, had some experience of photography. She borrowed a camera from her father and had access to his dark room. She took her 10-year-old cousin Frances Griffith to the beck that ran along the bottom of her Cottingley cottage garden. That day she took one shot of Frances half-smiling and leaning on a mossy rock. They often played around that beck. When asked by her mother why she spent so much time there, she said *'I went to see the fairies'*.

Elsie had an idea. Why not draw some fairies and cut them out in cardboard, stick them in the grass and take a photograph? When she developed the photo with her unsuspecting father in the dark room, she saw the life-like photo emerge. A few weeks later Frances took a second photo of Elsie playing with a gnome-like creature, after which, thinking it just a prank, her father banned them from using the camera. Elsie's mother, however, believed the girls.

By chance, the girls' mothers were developing an interest in theosophy, becoming popular as a form of religious thought based on a mystical insight into the divine nature. At a Theosophical Society meeting in Bradford the speaker talked about fairies. Elsie's mother mentioned to him the fairy photos. The speaker used this at the society's annual conference months later. A leading member, Edward Gardner became very interested. He checked the authenticity of the photos with experts.

Gardner then told Sir Arthur Conan Doyle, a leading contemporary literary figure who had recently converted to spiritualism. He persuaded Gardner to obtain more photos. Visiting Cottingley today, Gardner encouraged the girls to take more. Left alone, they produced three photos.

Intrigued, Doyle wrote an article about the Cottingley fairies in an illustrious London magazine. It sold out in days and the whole world knew about the story. Later he wrote a full book – *The Coming of the Fairies.*

Eventually, the furore died down. The girls got married and had families. Fifty years later interest was reawakened. At first, the now elderly ladies were enigmatic about the fairies, until in 1983 one admitted in a magazine that the photos were fake.

Elsie died in 1986, Frances in 1988. They never lived to see the 1997 film, set in Cottingley – *Fairy Tale: A True Story.*

Source: *The Case of the Cottingley Fairies,* Joe Cooper (1998)

20 Aug 1917   Jimmy Speirs, Bradford City's FA Cup hero, is killed at Passchendaele.

With daily news of casualties during World War One, the names that caught the eye were often sporting heroes. One such was Jimmy Speirs, captain and scorer of the winning goal in Bradford City's FA Cup winning team in 1911. In late summer 1917 news filtered through that he was wounded and missing in the Battle of Passchendaele. Today was later confirmed as the official date of death.

Gradually, the story of his war was pieced together. After the end of the 1914/1915 season, he enlisted as a volunteer with the Cameron Highlanders. Had he waited for conscription nine months later, he would have been exempt through being married with a young family. In March 1916 Corporal Speirs was posted to France. Six months later, he was wounded on the Somme, but recovered to fight again. He won the Military Medal for bravery in May 1917, but unfortunately the citation has not survived.

He came home from leave in June 1917, visiting friends and family in Bradford, Leeds and Glasgow before returning. The fatal news soon followed. He is buried near Ypres. Some 245,000 men died in this battle.

He was not the only City player in the FA Cup winning team to die in World War One. Bob Torrance, central defender and another Scot, was to lose his life nine months later. In all, four serving and six former City players died fighting for their country.

Like many promising Scottish footballers of the day, the Glaswegian Speirs went down south after four seasons (three with Rangers) and came to Valley Parade. Here he spent three and a half seasons scoring 34 goals in 96 matches. Season 1910/11 was the highlight, not just for the FA Cup win, but for finishing fifth in the First Division, City's highest ever position in the Football League. In December 1912 he was reluctantly sold to an ambitious Leeds City for the high fee of £1,400, at the time a record for both clubs.

Postscript

In 2003, Speirs' family auctioned his FA Cup winning medal with his Military Medal and service medal. The FA Cup medal was sold for £26,210, a record for such an item. It was bought by Bradford City fan Mark Lawn, who later became the club's chairman and allowed it to be shown in the club's museum.

Source: www.footballandthefirstworldwar.org/jimmy-speirs/

21 Aug 1916 Forty people are killed by explosion at Low Moor munitions factory.

With bad news from the Battle of the Somme, summer 1916 was not a good time for Bradfordians. In normal times yesterday's news would have dominated the papers. The *Bradford Daily Telegraph* (22 August 1916) reported:

> *YORKSHIRE DISASTER*
> *EXPLOSION IN A MUNITIONS FACTORY*
> *SERIOUS LOSS OF LIFE*

'The Press Bureau issued the following communication at eight o'clock last night: An explosion took place this afternoon at a munitions factory in Yorkshire. Full details are not yet to hand, but the loss of life appears to be serious. Assistance has been sent from neighbouring towns. A further statement will be issued as soon as possible.'

The *Yorkshire Post* carried the same uninformative story tucked away with lots of other news, much of it about the war.

The next day the press carried more news from the Press Bureau, but it just prompted further questions. Loss of life was not as serious as first thought, but no details were given. The explosion started with a fire outside one of the magazines of shells, which led to further explosions, but no indication was given about the source of the original fire. And still there was no indication where in Yorkshire the explosion took place. Questions that day were asked in the House of Commons of the Minister of Munitions. He admitted that 20 bodies had been recovered so far, but refused to say where the factory was.

Clearly, the Government wanted to keep the information as low key as possible and control the narrative, preventing any on-the-spot reporting, interviews and photographs, as would be expected in peace time.

In 1914, the British Army had soon realised that it needed high-explosive shells for trench warfare. With experience of using picric acid instead of gunpowder, the Low Moor Munitions Company had become one of the major suppliers of the explosive. Today, a drum containing the chemical had caught fire when some of the magazines of shells were moved.

It emerged much later that 40 people were killed, including six firemen and one policeman, with over 100 injured. Moreover, 50 houses were so badly damaged by the debris that they had to be rebuilt and 2,000 suffered minor damage. The fatality list made it Bradford's second worst-ever disaster at the time, only exceeded by the 1882 Newlands Mill disaster (and later the 1985 Bradford City disaster)

Source: *Stories of the Century,Telegraph & Argus* (1999)

22 Aug 1918 — Government finally accepts Friedrich Eurich's recommendations for preventing anthrax.

Woolsorting was a critical early step in producing woollen goods. It aimed to identify the correct quality of fleece for a specific cloth to ensure the highest quality. Woolsorters discarded badly soiled pieces of wool before sorting the rest by sight and touch. The task was unpleasant, made worse by the threat of a deadly disease. For years this was thought to be just a heart attack, not linked with woolsorting.

Bales of wool were often contaminated with blood or skin and sometimes contained the anthrax bacillus. This created open sores on the skin and a sudden painful decline in the victim, leading to death. With tens of thousands of woolsorters working in 19th century Bradford, it was no surprise that it was known as the 'Bradford disease'.

Born into a Jewish family in Germany, Frederick Eurich (1867-1945) moved to Bradford with them, when aged seven. Educated at Bradford Grammar School, he studied medicine at Edinburgh University where he won a gold medal for his doctorate.

In 1896, he established a GP's practice, giving a free morning surgery at the Bradford Royal Infirmary. Here he came across the painful cases of pulminary anthrax. The Corporation opened up a Pathological and Bacteriological Laboratory and appointed Eurich as the chief bacteriologist.

In 1905 the Home Office, in co-operation with the Bradford Chamber of Commerce, founded the Anthrax Investigation Board for Bradford and District and appointed Eurich as bacteriologist. The investigation involved the painstaking analysis of about 14,000 samples of wool and hair. The virulent nature of the anthrax bacillus put him in serious danger.

Eurich was the first to cultivate anthrax organisms from the wool. He also found unexpectedly that wools might be as dangerous when clean as dirty. He discovered that the blood stream of animals carried the infection; their blood stain could be found on the wool. He also found that many varieties of wool and hair were liable to infection and listed them roughly in order of danger. Finally, he found a way of killing anthrax spores and bacilli with no side-effects on associated processes such as spinning and dyeing. Today, the Government's official investigation supported his findings in its final report.

Workers in wool owe a large debt of gratitude to him for his long-sustained work on the dreaded 'Bradford disease'.

Source: *Frederick William Eurich: 'Conqueror' of Woolsorters' Disease*, Stella H Carpenter (2005) in *The Antiquary*

23 Aug 1849   Titus Salt creates the tradition of the works outing.

Today, proclaimed the *Bradford Observer*, it was quite a factory turnout. The story was not the usual kind of turnout, say a strike or Chartist riot, that had been a feature of the 1840s. It was a works outing of the sort that Titus Salt pioneered and was to repeat on several occasions later.

The previous Saturday, around 2,000 employees gathered at Bradford Midland station to catch one of two long trains that set off on the new railway line opened that year for the seaside resort of Morecambe. Titus Salt, his eldest son and some friends occupied the first-class carriage at the front. Four musical bands played before the first train set off at one o'clock, the other shortly after.

The packed trains took them to Skipton and then to the small station in the hamlet of Bell Busk, gateway to Malhamdale. Here at a quarter-past two they alighted. Most relaxed in the surrounding countryside, but despite some heavy rain showers some 200 to 300 walked the five miles to Malham and beyond to the local beauty sport of Gordale Scar. Here, the bands that had accompanied them struck up a well-received musical interlude. The grandeur and sublimity of the location made a strong impression on those who had tramped there.

The whole outing was very well organised. The paper reported that *'not a single accident of the slightest kind occurred to mar the pleasure of the day'*.

After the turmoil of recent years, this marked a new approach to employer-worker relationships that was the stamp of Titus Salt.

Source: *Balgarnie's Salt,* Robert Balgarnie (2003)

23 Aug 1875   The Star Music Hall opens as first stage of new entertainment complex.

At the bottom of Manchester Road, opposite the site of the future Bradford Alhambra, the first phase of a two-storey entertainment complex was opened today. This was the Star Music Hall, accommodating some 2,100 patrons. Eight months later the second phase opened for the Prince's Theatre built for over 2,800 patrons.

The Star Music Hall became the People's Palace and then the Palace Theatre that closed in 1938. The Prince's Theatre closed in 1961. Eventually, both buildings were demolished in 1964. Behind the site was later built what is now the National Science and Media Museum.

Source: http://www.arthurlloyd.co.uk/BradfordTheatres/PrincesTheatreBradford.htm

24 Aug 1847   Emily and Anne Brontë have Charlotte to thank for getting their first novels published.

By any standards the years from 1846 to 1849 were a period of great creativity and tragedy in the Brontë household at Haworth.

In 1846 under male pseudonyms – Currer, Ellis and Acton Bell – the three literary sisters had published, with their own money from their aunt's legacy, a collection of poetry, which had sold few copies. Undeterred, all three embarked on novels that have left a lasting legacy in English literature.

Charlotte completed her first (*The Professor*), Emily her masterpiece (*Wuthering Heights*) and Anne her first (*Agnes Grey*). Finding publishers was the next task. They approached several without success, until on 19 July 1847 Thomas Newby agreed to publish Emily and Anne's works together in one volume on condition that they contributed £50 to the cost for the first edition refundable in the event of a second. They paid the money and then waited. Newby appeared to lose interest.

In the meantime Charlotte had received a courteous and thoughtful rejection letter from Smith Elder & Co, which encouraged her to get on and complete her second novel *Jane Eyre*. Today she sent this full manuscript to this publisher, who immediately received enthusiastic feedback from a couple of readers. By 16 October it was published and became an instant success.

Charlotte's break was excellent news for her sisters, too. Newby decided that he might now cash in on this new writing family called Bell. *Wuthering Heights* and *Agnes Grey* were published on 6 December. *Wuthering Heights* did run to a second edition. Newby approached her about a second novel, but Emily fell ill in October 1847 and died of tuberculosis in December.

Anne was initially not successful. Critics felt that *Agnes Grey* was a pale imitation of *Jane Eyre,* both being about the lives of governesses. Anne, however, wrote a second novel. *The Tenant of Wildfell Hall,* published in June 1848, was immediately successful, being sold out in six weeks.

Her joy was cut short by the sudden death, probably from tuberculosis, in September of the girls' much loved brother Branwell, and then Emily. The family tragedy continued in May 1849 with Anne's own death, again from tuberculosis.

Within 21 months, each sister had published what turned out to be a classic novel. Within the next 18 months the two youngest who had published together had died, along with their brother. Their story is surely unique.

Source: http://englishmatters.gmu.edu/issue8/lathbury/lathbury_body.htm

25 Aug 1888   Bradford's great mathematician George Adolphus Schott wins important chess game.

George Adolphus Schott (1868 -1937), Bradford's most distinguished mathematician since 1900 at least, was no mean chess player. In his twenties, he was an active member of Bradford Chess Club. He played in county and British amateur championships with some distinction. For example, he won first prize at the West Yorkshire Chess Association meeting when it came to Bradford at the Talbot Hotel (*Bradford Daily Telegraph,* 30 April 1888).

Today, later in the same year, saw probably his best victory, when he was captain of Cambridge University Chess Club. The *Leeds Mercury Weekly Supplement* (25 August 1888) commented that *'great credit is due to the captain of the University Chess Club for his achievement'* (in beating Guest). Guest was clearly the man to beat, but we have no further information about Schott's illustrious opponent!

A good chess player, Schott was undoubtedly a great mathematician. Born to German parents who had emigrated to Bradford like many others to work in the wool business, he was educated at Bradford Grammar School and Trinity College, Cambridge where he gained a double first in natural sciences. He went on to become a Doctor of Science at London University with a thesis about electron theory before joining the staff of Aberystwyth College in 1893 as a lecturer in physics.

He became its Professor of Applied Mathematics from 1909. That year he was also awarded the prestigious Adams Prize at Cambridge University that commemorates the role of a John Adams in the discovery of Neptune. This prize is awarded each year by the university to a UK-based mathematician for distinguished research in mathematical sciences. Schott's specialist area was electromagnetic radiation. His classic work on electronic radiation predicted blue light near synchrotron particle accelerators, called 'synchrotron radiation'. This was not observed experimentally until ten years after his death.

Schott's final academic accolade was to be made a Fellow of the Royal Society in 1922.

He lived a quiet life in mid-Wales, marrying in 1913 in his forties a German lady. He did not hide his German connections. This led to a few difficult days when he became the subject of anti-German feelings at the outbreak of war. He had to face down ugly scenes with a mob outside his house. The problem did not return and he remained the rest of his life in Aberystwyth.

Source: www.manchess.org.uk (Yorkshire Chess History)

26 Aug 1946   Captain Brian Sellers leads Yorkshire CCC to sixth county cricket championship.

Today, down at the Saffrons in Eastbourne, one of cricket's iconic grounds, Yorkshire completed a regulation victory in two days against Sussex by six wickets. They became champions for the first post-war season and for the sixth time in nine seasons under the leadership of Brian Sellers, adding 1946 to 1933,1935,1937,1938 and 1939.

Although the legendary Lord Hawke won eight championships for Yorkshire in the pre-World War One era, Sellers was considered by most observers the better captain. Unlike Hawke, he never came near to Test Match status; he was picked as a captain, being only a modest batsman going in at number 7 and a very occasional bowler. He did, however, set a very good example as a fielder. In 1940 he was one of Wisden's five cricketers of the year, proclaimed to be the *'most successful county captain of all time'*. In nearly 75 years since this last championship, his record has never been bettered.

A son of a Yorkshire batsman, he was born to lead. He was captain of his school team at 16 and at 24 of his home town club team, Keighley in the tough and extremely competitive Bradford League. He was the epitome of determination and notoriously spoke his mind. *'We are out to win; if we cannot do so, good luck to our opponents, but we are not going to give them a chance if we can help it'*, he claimed. Force of personality allowed him to mould a team of England stars to county success, including Bill Bowes, Len Hutton, Maurice Leyland, Herbert Sutcliffe and Hedley Verity.

He became the county's chairman in 1959 and in that role he oversaw Yorkshire to another decade of success in the 1960s with seven championships in ten years (four under the equally competitive Brian Close).

Unfortunately his time at the helm is also remembered for much strife. In a succession of controversies he was unceremonious in allowing key stars such as Johnny Wardle (1959), Ray Illingworth (1968) and Brian Close (1970) to leave while they had some years left in their careers. Finally, he was himself forced to resign in 1977 after some years of strife under captain Geoffrey Boycott.

Source: *Brian Sellers: Cricket Tyrant*, Mark Rowe (2017)

27 Aug 2009   Adil Rashid becomes first English international cricketer from Pakistani family.

Since the 1960s more Pakistanis have settled in Bradford than almost anywhere else in Britain. Pakistanis are passionate about cricket, their national sport. The Bradford League is traditionally one of the strongest centres of cricket in Yorkshire, if not the country. It is, therefore, surprising that it had taken so long for a Bradford-born Pakistani to become a regular Yorkshire player, let alone an English cricket international.

Today, Adil Rashid, leg-spinner, born in Heaton, became the first such player not just from Bradford, but from England when he was selected in the one-day international against Ireland in Belfast. He was in and out of the one-day side for several years, not becoming established as a valued leg-spinner until around 2015, in what became the World Cup winning team of 2019. Although he was selected for Test Match squads from 2010, he did not play his first Test until 2015 and rarely played a full series thereafter.

There is little doubt that, despite being in desperate need of home-grown talent, Yorkshire County Cricket Club did little to positively encourage boys from Asian families to represent them until the turn of the century. The main factor in Rashid's success was undoubtedly his father who gave his three sons great support in playing cricket from childhood.

Source: *The Daily Telegraph* (6 August 2006)

27 Aug 1908   Emmeline Pankhurst reports on a mass rally of suffragettes on Shipley Glen.

Shipley Glen was an ideal venue for mass meetings. Writing today in *Votes for Women,* the leader of the suffragette movement, Emmeline Pankhurst, reported on such a rally held earlier on 31 May where she had spoken with her three activist daughters. It was attended by up to 100,000 supporters (the local *Shipley Times & Express's* estimate was 60,000) and described by one daughter as *'a great triumph for our cause'.*

In a full account Emmeline herself wrote: *'For weeks past all Bradford has been talking about the Yorkshire Suffrage Sunday... a never-ending stream of people on foot wended their way to the picturesque glen, the property of the people of Bradford, about three miles away from the city itself. The vast audience of orderly and attentive persons prevented any effective disturbance and at five o'clock a resolution calling upon the Government to enfranchise the women of this country was carried with practical unanimity.'*

Source: *Bingley: A Living History,* Alan Cattell (2016)

28 Aug 1854 After consecration of half of Undercliffe Cemetery, a message of thanks is sent.

Today, a grateful citizen wrote a letter to the *Bradford Observer*: '*My heart rejoiced that such a decent provision had been made for the reception of the dead. I cannot but express my thanks in this public way to the parties, who have been the means of establishing it … I thank them all from my very heart, for when death invades our families, it is a great relief to know we can deposit their earthly remains in such an appropriate place'.*

In the first 50 years of the 19th century the population of the borough of Bradford's four townships increased nearly tenfold from 13,264 to 103,778. This led to overcrowding, not just in terms of housing for those living, but also burial space for those dying. Burials could no longer be restricted to churches and chapels. Bradford needed a cemetery, unattached to a place of worship, as was starting to appear in other urban centres; new laws had just been passed to allow for this.

A group of businessmen came together in 1849 to form the Bradford Cemetery Company, including men such as Robert Milligan, Titus Salt and Henry Brown, all mayors of Bradford. In 1852 they received a licence to operate as a private company with those to be buried paying fees for their plots. They identified 26 acres of land on the crest of Undercliffe Hill overlooking the town and bought the site at an auction. They appointed as registrar and designer William Gay who had designed an impressive cemetery in Leicester.

The new cemetery was divided into two: the western side for Anglicans and the eastern side for nonconformists. Although the site was open for burials from March 1854, it was not till 25 August that the Bishop of Ripon (Bradford's diocese at the time) consecrated the Anglican half, a ceremony attended by 4,000.

Some of the largest plots contained striking memorials such as the Jacob Behrens Memorial and the Mausoleum for Alfred Illingworth's family, considered to be the cemetery's showpiece. They make a stark contrast with the Quakers who bought 197 plots in 1855 after their previous burial ground was sold. Their area is notable because all their gravestones are laid flat in the ground, not upright, 'no man being above another'.

Source: *In Loving Memory – The Story of Undercliffe Cemetery,* Colin Clark & Reuben Davison (2004)

29 Aug 1853   St. George's Hall opens with a three-day music festival.

Today's opening of St. George's Hall was a landmark in Bradford's development in the 19th century. It was its first major investment in a grand public building, although funded by private persons, not the new Corporation. The feeling of civic pride is captured by the *Bradford Observer:*

'*Yesterday was a proud day for Bradford. Long will the remembrance thereof live in the hearts and memories of all who witnessed the glorious opening of St. George's Hall ; long will the strains of the spirit-stirring music, which were so wonderfully performed, vibrate in the minds of all who were fortunate enough to be present ; and often may our townsmen have the high gratification and privilege of listening to such a glorious phalanx of executants as those who yesterday for the first time performed in the orchestra of our splendid Hall!'*

One correspondent from the *Illustrated London News* on a visit north that year suggested that the city had emerged out of the shadow of its neighbour: it was now '*Leeds near Bradford*', he proclaimed.

With hindsight such a building was a luxury when so many people were living in appalling squalor with high risk of disease and illness. Yet there was a real shortage of public buildings for any entertainment or large meetings. One could only use the upper room of the Old Exchange building, the old Mechanics' Institute, the Temperance and Oddfellow Halls. St. George's Hall with its 3,500 capacity could now be used not just for concerts orchestral and choral, but also mass meetings, lectures, performances, banquets and assemblies of all kinds.

The idea had first surfaced publicly when Mayor Titus Salt had commissioned a review into the town's moral condition. Other influential businessmen supported it such as Jacob Behrens, keen to see concerts, as in his native Germany. Latterly, Mayor Samuel Smith made it happen by securing £16,000 through £10 shares. Designed by Lockwood and Mawson, St. George's Hall was described by Smith as '*the best means of removing the vice and immorality so prevalent in our population. In such a large public hall, thoroughly good concerts could be provided at a cheap rate, and would have the effect of drawing away people from beer-houses and other low places.*'

It is now the third oldest concert venue in Europe.

Source: *Bradford Observer* (1 September 1853)

30 Aug 1979   Busby's famous department store burns down.

February 1978 was a sad month for Bradford's two once-famous department stores. Brown Muff's down in the city centre had sold out to Rackhams. A week earlier Debenhams had finally closed its store on Manningham Lane, taken over in 1958 after founder Ernest Busby had died. The writing had been on the wall ever since March 1973 when Debenhams announced a re-branding – all references to Busby's were to be replaced with Debenhams. Both famous Bradford names from its prosperous past had now disappeared into the anonymity of national chains.

The fate of the two buildings, however, was to be quite different. Rackhams survived for another 17 years before closing down and the building became semi-derelict, still used only for small featureless outlets on the ground floor. In contrast, after lying empty for months, Debenhams suddenly disappeared in an almighty blaze.

Today, at teatime, a dramatic fire destroyed the former Busby's. Nearly 100 firemen from all over West Yorkshire attempted to tackle the blaze, but could not prevent leaving the Victorian-style listed building in a heap of smouldering rubble. At the height of the blaze a third of the facade crashed into Manningham Lane, hurling huge chunks of masonry across the road. As thousands of people gathered, smoke and flames billowed high into the sky until the building was a twisted pile of hot rubble – leaving for Bradfordians only memories of a once-loved store.

The following year, Eric Busby (one of Ernest's three sons) wrote: *'So the famous Victorian building was burnt to a mass of twisted metal and rubble in less than three hours. I cannot dwell on this sad ending except to say that it was less distressing than the empty building had been. And mind you, I did think that as a fire it was the best ever! A dramatic, super-magnificent finale.'*

The remains of the building had to be demolished. The Manningham Lane Retail Park stands on the site, offering no memorable retail experience and no reminder of the past.

On 14 April 1980 local MP, Bob Cryer, asked the Home Secretary in the House *'if he will call for a report from the chief constable of the West Yorkshire police on the fire which destroyed the former Busby's department store in Bradford'.* The reply was *'No. We know of no reason to do so'.*

Source: *Telegraph & Argus* (30 August 1979)

31 Aug 1940   The Luftwaffe carries out its most serious night of bombing the city in World War Two.

Bradford was devastated by losses incurred in Northern France in World War One. In comparison it escaped lightly in World War Two. Unlike many cities, it only suffered four nights of bombing, but on just one night it did suffer a death and that was tonight.

The context for the first three nights was the Battle of Britain taking place over the skies of the south-east following the fall of Holland, Belgium and France. Only Britain stood in the way of a complete German victory over the Allies. The Luftwaffe could now strike the ports and manufacturing cities of the north.

The first day of bombing was 22 August, three bombs landing in Heaton Woods. The second occurred on 28 August with four bombs in the city centre and one slight casualty.

The third day (tonight Saturday evening and Sunday morning) was much more serious. Starting at 11.13pm and ending at 2.40am. 116 bombs landed causing major damage in different parts of the city with one woman dying and 111 treated for injuries.

On Monday 2 September the *Telegraph & Argus* was not able to cover the events in any detail because of reporting restrictions. It could not name locations affected or buildings hit, merely saying that a north-east town had suffered bomb damage. However, its leader columns were defiant: *'If the Germans think they are going to win the war by setting departmental stores on fire and dropping bombs in shops, then they are going to be very much mistaken ...Why play the German game by magnifying the effects of an attack which, taking into account its duration and severity, caused comparatively little damage?'*

Later it was confirmed that the biggest fire had gutted Lingard's department store and adjoining Kirkgate Chapel. A bomb tore through the roof of the Odeon cinema. Five storeys were sliced out of a warehouse off Manchester Road. Part of Rawson Market was damaged. Everywhere windows were smashed, tramlines and phone lines out of action. Rubble and smoke confronted Monday morning commuters arriving for work.

The final night of bombing was 14 March 1941. Invasion was no longer a threat. Some 595 bombs were dropped, but damage was relatively slight. Two houses were demolished, eight more damaged. There were few casualties.

That, thankfully, was the limit of Bradford's war the second time round.

Source: *Stories of the Century, Telegraph & Argus* (1999)

SEPTEMBER

1 Sep 1903   Bradford City play their first professional match in the Football League.

After six months of hectic preparations, Bradford City's first-ever match today was undistinguished. Playing away at Grimsby Town, they lost 2-nil. Nobody could have predicted twelve months earlier that the rugby league side of Manningham FC would be soon replaced by a new professional soccer team, starting this season in Football League Division Two.

For at least 30 years rugby had been a stronghold of sport in Bradford and the West Riding. Yet, at the start of 1903 meetings started to discuss the formation of a Football League club for the city. By the end of March Manningham FC, struggling for money, agreed to allow a new soccer club to play at their Valley Parade ground.

On 25 May, after much lobbying, the Football League voted to accept Bradford City by 30 votes out of 35 to replace Doncaster Rovers. Three days later some 160 members of the new club heard at the Belle Vue Hotel on Manningham Lane how the new team had become a member without ever having played a single match.

In five years' time they were to be promoted to Division One and three years after that finish fifth in that division and win the FA Cup, achievements that have since been well beyond them to the current day, over 100 years later.

Source: *Bradford City: A Complete Record, 1903-1988,* Terry Frost (1988)

1 Sep 2019   Bradford Bulls play their last game at Odsal Stadium (or do they?).

Today was a sad day for Bradford sport. A crowd of 7,531 saw the Bradford Bulls play their last game at the famous Odsal Stadium. The stadium's high overheads and maintenance costs, a burden for so long, proved too much after seven years of financial difficulties, during which time the Bulls were relegated from the Super League. They moved to Dewsbury's much more compact stadium for two years at least, before hopefully returning to a new Bradford home.

From 1934 the old Bradford Northern had made it their permanent home for 62 years. The Bulls took over in their inaugural record-breaking season of 1998, winning the Super League in its second season after their 18th straight win by 32-12 at Sheffield Eagles. Now they comfortably beat them again with the similar score of 30-10, but this time in the Championship.

Odsal had been Bradford's home of Rugby League for 85 years.

Postscript: The Bulls returned to Odsal on 30 May 2021!

2 Sep 1868   William Stansfield of Esholt Hall complains about excess sewage in the River Aire.

'The Corporation should be restricted from causing or permitting to pass any sewage or other offensive matter into Bradford Beck in such a manner that the same may pass into the River Aire to the injury of the plaintiff, or to the pollution of its course, past Esholt Hall estate, or into the river at all.'

William Stansfield of Esholt Hall secured this injunction today from the Court of Chancery. The Corporation had to improve the sewage system in order not to pollute Bradford Beck, which at Shipley flowed into the River Aire, which in turn three miles downstream passed by the village of Esholt.

The town's sewage system quite simply could not cope with the rapid growth of population in the early and mid-19th century. Ever since the new Health of Towns Commissioner reported in 1843 that Bradford was *'the dirtiest, filthiest and worst regulated town in the kingdom'*, the warning was clear.

After its creation in 1847, the Corporation had taken some measures (eg a main trunk sewer started in 1853), but all its actions depended on using the river as the natural place to deposit the sewage. The more efficient the town's drainage, the worse became the condition of the beck and the river.

An 1867 report from the Rivers Pollution Commission stated that the Rivers Aire and nearby Calder were *'poisoned, corrupted and clogged by refuse from mines, chemical works, dyeing, scouring, and fulling, worsted and woollen stuffs, skin cleansing and tanning, slaughter-house garbage and the sewage of towns and houses'*.

As a solution the Corporation settled on a proposal for sewage works at a 38-acre site in Frizinghall (between Bradford and Shipley), but it turned out to be only a partial solution. It came to realise in the 1890s that a long-term solution was essential, requiring a much larger sewage works built on a much larger piece of land.

The sting in the tail was that the nearest suitable place for such a facility was the 1700 acres of Esholt estate! The Corporation would have to make a compulsory purchase from its owner, two sisters from the same Stansgate family. After protracted negotiations, the Esholt estate was sold to the Corporation in February 1904 for £239,742, but it would be several years before Esholt Sewage Works started operation.

Source: *Esholt Sewage Disposal Scheme*, Bradford Corporation (1912)

3 Sep 1999   Council leader gives total support for the plans to build new Bradford Grand Mosque.

'I am strongly in support of the Mosque being constructed on Horton Park Avenue by Suffa-Tul-Islam... I have strongly supported it through the planning process both as local member and as Leader of Council.

It is my view that Suffa-Tul- Islam are the most professional, well-organised group that I have had the pleasure to deal with in respect of Mosque construction and I have had dealings with many. The mosque itself has a design which will be a considerable enhancement to the district as a whole and ... a focal point for Islamic culture within the district... the associated community facilities will also be a considerable benefit for the local community... When this project is completed, it will clearly be one of the largest, most prestigious mosques in Europe and will demonstrate ... that the Islamic community within Bradford ... has developed a massive degree of self-confidence in its future.'

Today's letter from Councillor Ian Greenwood represented an important step in the new Bradford Grand Mosque to be built opposite the ruins of the old Park Avenue football ground and on the site of Horton Park station on the old Bradford to Keighley railway. Greenwood was a highly respected Leader of the Council for many years. His statement was a valuable endorsement that such a mosque would enhance the city.

Its founder was Shaykh Mohammad Habib-Ur-Rehman Mahboobi, a Sunni and world-renowned Islamic scholar. Coming to the UK in 1978 as a 25-year-old, he founded the Suffa-Tul-Islam UK Association in 1983. It converted a four-storey disused mill in Sunbridge Road into a mosque, community centre, madrassah and after-school club. By 1998 its numbers had grown so quickly that it required new purpose-built premises. The founder's qualities of sincerity, selflessness and dedication gave him community leadership. The symbol of their confidence is the high percentage of 'huffaz', the 150 Muslims who have memorised the Quran's 114 chapters (over 77,000 words).

With its pink-red sandstone the mosque has a striking appearance. It has three domes (two green, one gold) and 12 minarets (two higher than 90 feet), all crowned with a crescent moon and star, symbol of Islam and also part of Pakistan's national flag.

Up to 60 years ago the city's skyline was dominated by mill chimneys belching smoke. Now it is the domes and minarets of new mosques that rise into the sky.

Source: Information supplied by Suffa-Tul-Islam

4 Sep 1952　　Bolling Hall is designated a Group 1 listed building.

It was only a formality that Bradford's oldest surviving building was listed today as a 'building of exceptional interest' (the definition of a Group 1 listing). The listing process was covered by a provision in the Town and Country Planning Act 1947.

The full description in the official entry states (bullet points added):

- *A large hall, the most substantial surviving in Bradford.*

- *It is also the earliest in structural origin being an enlargement on the basis of two medieval probably 14th century towers. Sandstone and gritstone rubble. The towers with parapet copings and stone slate roofs.*

- *The main south front between the towers is mid-17th century, circa 1660 and has a remarkable variety of fenestration and motifs: cross mullioned windows, semi- circular and circular mullioned windows, two canted bays through two-storeys of eight lights and a vast hall window of five plus five lights with two transoms.*

- *Rising from the lintel of the hall window is a three light semi-circular window and three light ogee window, above this there is also a Victorian canted bay window next to the right hand tower.*

- *The rear elevation has projecting wings, the west one is the only ashlar faced part of the hall and has plain mullioned windows but there is a probably reset medieval window of three ogee headed lights on the top floor.*

- *The east wing has mullioned and transomed windows.*

- *Inside the hall has an 18th century ceiling and a gallery to the rear.*

- *One room on the first floor retains lively original plasterwork consisting of broad bands of foliage and birds contained between them.*

In truth, the old hall – part castle, part manor house – is a hotch-potch of different styles going back to its 14th century origins.

It enjoyed a moment of fame in 1643 during the second siege of Bradford in the English Civil War. The house was a Royalist base and the Royalists took the town, which had strong Parliamentarian sympathies.

After being owned by the Bollings (till late 15th century), then the Tempests (till 1649), and many others for much shorter periods, it was finally sold to Bradford Corporation in 1912 and opened in September 1915 as a museum free to all visitors.

Source: historic.england.org.uk

5 Sep 1993   Play about the Airedale Poet has its 'world premiere' at Salts Mill.

At the end of June 1993, over a meal, Leeds poet Tony Harrison accepted a challenge by entrepreneur Jonathan Silver to write a play for Saltaire and to do it in two months. They agreed that John Nicholson, the so-called 'Airedale poet' (1790-1843), might be a suitable subject. Passionate about poetry, Nicholson led an eccentric life with a tragic end when he slipped and drowned, crossing the River Aire near Salts Mill where he had also worked as a woolcomber.

The play, *Poetry or Bust,* had its premiere tonight in the same mill that had now been redeveloped by Silver into an arts complex. The book of the play had a cover designed by their mutual friend, David Hockney. The whole venture was sponsored by Pace Micro Technology, the new company that had become very successful from the regeneration of Salts Mill.

Brought up in Eldwick, Nicholson had one year's education at Bingley Grammar School. He became a woolsorter at his father's Eldwick mill, but his main interest was poetry. His volume of poetry, *Airedale in Ancient Times,* was very popular. His funeral at Bingley was attended by over 1,000 mourners.

Source: *Poetry or Bust*, Tony Harrison (1993)

5 Sep 1899   Christopher Spencer submits his patent for the Spencer (slipper) track brake.

In 1898 Christopher Spencer became general transport manager in Bradford and developed into the city's most important person for managing the public transport system of trams and trolley-buses during the 20 years before the end of World War One. The same year he saw the opening of the first electric trams in the city, followed in 1909 by the invention of a unique dual-gauge tramcar design between Leeds and Bradford and in 1911 by the introduction of the first trolley-bus service in the country.

He also gave his name to an innovation for which he submitted a patent application today that was approved 10 months later.

The Board of Trade had imposed special conditions for trams being used on steep hills, one being the use of some form of slipper brake. All the main routes into Bradford were hilly. Hence, he designed this slipper brake, which was a wood-faced track brake shoe, pressed on to the track as the tram descended hills. It was used on many tramway systems across the country.

Source: *A Century of Public Transport in Bradford, 1882-1982*, DJ Croft (1982)

6 Sep 1851   German-born Fanny Hertz marries a yarn merchant from Bradford.

Today the accident of marriage brought to Bradford its first influential female educationalist.

Born into a Jewish family in Hanover, Fanny Hertz (1830-1908) came to London as a child when her father, a diamond merchant, moved there. Not yet 21, she married her cousin, William Hertz, at Westminster. He was a yarn merchant who owned a mill in Bradford, where they settled down and brought up a family.

Their homes in Horton, then Vicar Lane, became a meeting place for writers, artists, and thinkers, and those with an interest in radical causes.

Fanny Hertz was a passionate feminist and proponent of women's education, fighting what she called *'the deeply rooted prejudice that woman has neither the same powers nor the same aspirations as man'*. In particular, she championed the cause of working-class women who were not eligible to study in Mechanics' Institutes. In 1857 she helped found Bradford's Female Educational Institute. Within five years it had around 500 students attending its evening classes who almost all had already spent up to 12 hours working during the day. They included factory workers, nursemaids, domestic servants and others living at home. Many were totally illiterate, some could just about read but not write and only a few could do simple sums.

In 1859 she spoke at the third National Association for the Promotion of Social Science that met in Bradford. Here, she condemned the narrow and utilitarian perspective which saw the purpose of women's education as preparation *'for the duties of wives and mothers, of mistresses and servants'*.

She became involved in a national movement to further the education of women and represent Bradford on the North of England Council for Promoting the Higher Education of Women. By 1871, she was a committee member of the National Union for Improving the Education of Women of All Classes, founded by Maria Grey.

She set up the Bradford Ladies' Educational Association in 1868 with Jane Forster, the wife of WE Forster, Bradford MP, whose 1870 Elementary Education Act revolutionised state education. They organised for several years programmes of high standard lectures. They also helped to create Bradford Girls' Grammar School on the same basis as the recently-reformed boys' school. The new girls' school opened in September 1875, after Hertz and others secured the £5,000 funding by donation for its new building in Hallfield Road off Westgate.

Source: Fanny Hertz (*Oxford Dictionary of National Biography*)

7 Sep 1936   On his birthday Sir Anthony Gadie completes topping-out for Scar House Reservoir.

Nobody could begrudge Sir Anthony Gadie (1868-1948) his 68th birthday present. Today he ceremoniously placed the last stone in position on Scar House Reservoir, the largest-ever engineering project that Bradford Corporation had undertaken.

A self-made man, Gadie had been a councillor from 1900 to 1945, then the Lord Mayor in 1920 and 1921, and finally the Chairman of the Corporation's Water Committee. He himself had cut the first sod as Lord Mayor 15 years previously in 1921. Over its duration he had to defend the project from critics who saw it as a waste of money, calling it 'Gadie's Folly'.

The Corporation had been planning reservoirs in Nidderdale to supply the growing population of Bradford since 1891 when the Nidd Valley Scheme was launched. Two reservoirs were planned initially – a compensation reservoir at Gouthwaite (completed 1901), and a storage reservoir at Angram (completed 1915) To connect the reservoirs to the treatment works at Chellow Dean in Bradford an aqueduct was built comprising a pipeline and tunnel. As a result of the difference in heights the water could be supplied by gravity and no pumping required.

The final stage was a third reservoir at Scar House, just downstream of Angram. It would increase the total storage capacity of the Nidd Valley Scheme to 3.3 billion gallons. Without the Scar House project the Corporation could not meet demand at peak times and in times of drought.

Born in Skipton, Gadie moved when a young boy with his family to Bradford. He was a 'half-timer' until he was eleven. He attended evening classes at Bradford Church House and worked as an invoice clerk and secretary at the Bradford Brick and Tile Company. This may have brought him into contact with builders. He then started his own business as a builder and made his mark developing 'Gadie's garden suburb' at Allerton.

He was also an enthusiastic military volunteer from 1886. When war broke out, he was a captain; by the end, a lieutenant-colonel mentioned in despatches. After the war he set up in business as an auctioneer. He was also elected Conservative and Unionist MP for Central Bradford from 1924-29. In 1935 he was knighted for political and public services.

The final and much-deserved honour that Gadie was to receive was being made freeman of the city on 31 October 1944.

Source: https://www.undercliffecemetery.co.uk/about/history/anthony-gadie/

8 Sep 1902   Francis Laidler steps into theatre management at the Prince's Theatre.

The career of Bradford's famous impresario Francis Laidler (1867-1955) started today, when under new management the Prince's Theatre launched a new production. The new management was a partnership between Walter Piper, the theatre's general manager, and Francis Laidler, then the 35-year-old secretary of the Bradford Brewery Company. Laidler was to be responsible for the theatre's financial affairs, while Piper concentrated on the productions. This would be a part-time role, enabling Laidler to keep his main role at the brewery.

Laidler had no previous experience of the theatre. Born and bred in Teesside, he was first apprenticed to the National Provincial Bank. He moved to Bradford shortly after his marriage as a 21 year old to become a clerk at one of the wool trade's leading houses before moving to the brewery.

The Prince's Theatre had had a chequered history. Built as part of an entertainment complex above the Star Music Hall, it opened in 1876 and was badly damaged by fire in 1878. It reopened in 1879 and struggled through the 1880s. Its fortunes improved somewhat under a new proprietor who focused on melodramas by touring shows.

Under Piper and Laidler the theatre straightaway had a major success with the innovation of a pantomime, *Red Riding Hood*. It seemed to make a big impression not just on the audience, but on Laidler himself who soon had to face a big decision.

Within six months of Laidler's involvement, Piper died. Should Laidler take the gamble of becoming the new proprietor and leave his secure job? Ironically, Piper had taken out a large insurance policy against Laidler's death and advised his new partner to do the same. Laidler declined and so had no financial cushion against the risk.

He decided in favour of the theatre. If the success with the pantomime could be repeated, he would make enough money to offset losses of other shows in the year. This was to become his guiding principle for the next 50 years of theatre management.

He was, however, not content to rest on his laurels. Another big decision was to present itself ten years later when he eyed up an empty piece of land across the road that might be the site of a much grander theatre - the Bradford Alhambra.

Source: *Domes of Delight: The History of the Bradford Alhambra*, Peter Holdsworth (1989)

9 Sep 1873   Bradford's new Town Hall is opened.

Today was an important landmark in Bradford's development with the opening, finally, of the new Town Hall.

Ever since 1851 there had been much debate about its cost and, more recently, its location. Eventually, a triangular site was purchased with frontages on Market Street, Chapel Lane and Leeds Road. From 32 submissions, leading Bradford architects Lockwood and Mawson yet again won a major competition for designing a town hall to rival those of Leeds (1858) and Halifax (1863).

The opening was marred by torrential rain. The feature of the ceremony was a procession representing all branches of Bradford trade, reminiscent of past processions commemorating Bishop Blaise, patron saint of the worsted trade (last held in 1825). Mayor Matthew Thompson led the procession from Lister Park to the new building. Large crowds lined the streets, enjoying the day off granted for the event. The mayor threw a banquet at the Victoria Hotel and the next evening a grand ball.

From afar, the most striking feature of the Town Hall is the clock tower rising 220 feet, inspired by the Palazzo Vecchio in Florence. It has 13 bells which first rang at today's opening.

The other unusual feature can only be seen much nearer. Clearly visible from the street, 35 statues of Britain's monarchs are mounted around the walls. Unexpectedly they include Oliver Cromwell, Lord Protector in the 1650s, marking the support by Bradford's leading families of the Parliamentarian side during the English Civil War.

It was rumoured that Irish workmen charged with hauling the statue in place would drop it 'accidentally on purpose' so that the statue of the man hated by the Irish would smash to pieces. However, the Corporation caught wind of this and replaced the gang with English workers.

Source: *Historical Notes on the Bradford Corporation* (William Cudworth, 1881)

9 Sep 1917   3,000 women in the Bradford Women's Humanity League hold an anti-war protest.

In one of several anti-war protests 3,000 women marched today from Westgate across the city in protest against the slaughter of their menfolk in World War One. Three years of war with unremitting headlines of death, injury and family loss had taken their toll. It was a peaceful demonstration, but one woman was charged and fined for 'slandering young soldiers'.

A plaque on the Textile Hall in Westgate marks the place where this remarkable demonstration started.

Source: *Struggle and Suffrage in Bradford*, Rachel Bellerby (2019)

10 Sep 1992 Conference paves the way for Bradford's unique Peace Museum.

Today was the opening day of the first international conference for museums of peace that took place at the University of Bradford. It was arranged by the British Give Peace a Chance association, bringing together, for the first time, the management and staff of peace museums, anti-war museums and similar institutions worldwide. Over 30 representatives from 10 countries met up to exchange experiences and make a start on future cooperation.

Museums for peace are non-profit educational institutions that promote a culture of peace through collecting, displaying and interpreting peace-related material. They inform the public about peace and nonviolence, using illustrations from the lives of individuals and from the work of organisations, campaigns and historical events.

Ever since 1992, the conference has been held every three years. In 2005, it changed its name to the International Network of Museums for Peace, with an extended definition that now includes more peace-related sites, centres and institutions. In 2008, the secretariat was established in The Hague.

One achievement that arose out of the international conference was the establishment of a peace museum in Bradford in 1994. This was made possible by a five-year grant from the Joseph Rowntree Charitable Trust (established by the celebrated Quaker). Initially, it operated out of a temporary site in the Wool Exchange before moving in 1998 to its present site on the top floor of 10 Piece Hall Yard.

It is the only museum in the UK dedicated to the collection, conservation and interpretation of material relating to the history and development of peace, nonviolence and conflict resolution. The museum draws on a growing collection of thousands of peace-related artefacts from around the world. Part of its gallery is devoted to the peace history of Bradford. It has produced an attractive and informative 34 page leaflet called *Bradford Peace Trail, a walk around Bradford City of Peace* with brief descriptions of the city's many champions and initiatives for peace.

The museum is also a leading provider of learning for young people, working alongside partners in its own gallery or in the community. These sessions explore issues of equality, diversity, cohesion and inclusion. Finally, it publishes high-quality story books and resources for teachers, including *The Peace Challenge: Stories of Bradford Peacemakers*.

Source: www.https://peacemuseum.org.uk

11 Sep 1948   Sir Learie Constantine plays his final match in the Bradford League.

Formed in 1903, the Bradford Cricket League (approximately 20 teams) has always been considered one of the strongest leagues in England. It has nurtured many famous Yorkshire cricketers. For example, three became England captains – Sir Len Hutton (Pudsey St Lawrence), Ray Illingworth (Farsley), Brian Close (Yeadon). Coincidentally, they all played for teams technically in Leeds just outside the boundary of Bradford, but those teams chose to play in the Bradford League.

One of the League's strengths was the use of overseas players who in their winter came to make money in England. Each club was allowed one such professional. This helped to improve standards and attract bigger crowds. No professional was more popular and successful than Learie Constantine from Trinidad (1901-1971).

He was the first star player from the West Indies – a stirring fast bowler, thrilling batsman and brilliant fielder. Initial success on the first West Indies tour of England in 1923 (he took the first ever West Indies Test wicket) and again in 1928 encouraged him to seek a career as a professional cricketer in England. He spent ten years playing at Nelson in the Lancashire League before crossing the Pennines.

He played during World War Two for Windhill and at the end of his career had three post-war seasons with Windhill, topping the league's bowling averages in both 1947 and 1948.

In 1948 Sir Learie, aged 48, finished his career in the Bradford League in style. Today, on his last appearance for Windhill he claimed a wicket off his last ball against Keighley. Then in his final innings he took the chance to lead his side to victory. This made them league champions for the sixth and final time. He commented: *'I went in for my farewell innings. I had to do something to mark the occasion, and despite fine and steady bowling, I managed to notch up 69 not out, winning the match with a final four that went humming to the boundary as clean as any ball I have ever hit.'*

Taking advantage of his reputation as a sporting star, his career developed into law and politics. In 1961 he was appointed Trinidad and Tobago's first High Commissioner in London. Next year he was knighted and in 1969 made a life peer. When he died in 1971, he was granted the honour of a memorial service at Westminster Abbey.

Source: *Learie Constantine* (Gerald Howat, 1975)

12 Sep 2015   An Open Day is held at the unique archaeological site of Park Avenue football ground.

It was once called the People's Palace with a state-of-the-art football stadium alongside an iconic cricket ground. Now most of it is an overgrown, derelict piece of ground in a downtrodden part of the city and overlooked by the splendid new Bradford Grand Mosque. Bradford Park Avenue has seen better days.

Today an enthusiastic group of nostalgic folk held an Open Day to share memories prompted by findings from a unique archaeological dig and documented in an unusual book.

The ground was first used in 1880 for cricket and rugby union. Rugby league replaced rugby union in 1895. Under pressure from Bradford City's early success in 1903, the club switched controversially in 1907 to association football to become Bradford (Park Avenue). A year later it joined the Football League.

The ground was transformed in 1907 by a major development by the most celebrated stadium architect of the day, Archibald Leitch. The new football stadium was designed for 40,000 spectators (12,000 seated). It had several notable features, including a distinctive new pavilion and a double-decker grandstand with three special gables, the central one having an innovative design and crest. The whole effect was to put to shame the club's rivals across the city at Valley Parade.

Some 70 years later with Park Avenue relegated from the Football League and fearing bankruptcy, the ground was sold. After one year's ground-sharing at Valley Parade the club was finally wound up.

In 2013 archaeologist Jason Wood and artist Neville Gabie conducted at the old ground the first-ever excavation of a football goalmouth. This generated great interest and led to a much broader excavation in 2015. Today's Open Day shared the findings with Avenue fans returning to the hallowed turf.

The Kop's concrete steps were clearly visible among the overgrown trees and the perimeter wall still survived, complete with bricked-in recesses where turnstiles had been installed. Many interesting items were found, such as marbles in the goalmouth that had been thrown at goalkeepers. One of the strangest was a nappy pin, unearthed next to one of the ground-hooks behind the left-hand goalpost. A star goalkeeper's daughter came to explain that one day the elastic on her father's shorts had snapped during a match. The trainer had to perform an emergency repair. Thereafter, he was regularly showered with pins when he kept goal!

Source: *Breaking Ground: Art, Archaeology and Mythology*, Neville Gabie & Jason Wood (2015)

13 Sep 1845   Irish newspaper announces the arrival of potato blight.

'We stop the Press with very great regret to announce that the Potato Murrain has unequivocally declared itself in Ireland. The crops around Dublin are suddenly perishing.'

Today's *Gardeners' Chronicle's* notice was one of several newspaper alerts this month announcing the potato blight. Ireland depended totally on the potato for food and jobs. One third of the crop was lost in 1845 and three quarters in the next two years. It is estimated that as a result at least a million people died and another million emigrated.

Large numbers fled to Yorkshire and to Bradford in particular. By the 1851 Census Bradford's population had increased in 50 years from 6,393 to 103,778, a large proportion being immigrants from outside Yorkshire. By 1851 Bradford had 9,581 Irish (10%) rising from 1,868 (5%) in 1841. By 1851, a larger percentage of Irish were born in Bradford (26%) than anywhere else in Yorkshire.

The Irish came largely from specific areas, eg 33% from Queens County in the centre of Ireland and from the counties of Mayo (14%) and Sligo (11%) in the west, where there was a tradition of textiles. This might well have encouraged immigrants to move to Bradford, the new home of textile manufacturing. Many, it is thought, could only speak Irish.

Unsurprisingly, the Irish congregated in crowded slums near city centre mills, places like Wapping, Goit Side, Broomfield, Black Abbey and White Abbey, names that have largely disappeared from the map. For most, living conditions were dire, wages low and life a struggle.

Irish immigration was not popular with Bradfordians. The Irish accepted lower wages than other workers. Reports from the Chief Constable and the *Bradford Observer* provide ample evidence of delinquency, drunkenness and brawling in Irish areas.

Detailed research about Irish immigration was published in 1968 as immigration from Pakistan was becoming a controversial issue in the city. It concludes with this observation:

'We have seen that the Irish migration to Bradford was an important episode in its urban and industrial development. It is worth noting that their mode of settlement and the forces which shaped the settlement patterns, have many parallels with the present-day immigrant situation, whether we are thinking of the development of geographically differentiated social zones, or the behaviouristic patterns of the host and immigrant communities which influenced their evolution.'

Source: *Irish Settlement in Mid-Nineteenth Century Bradford*, C Richardson, *Bulletin of Economic Research* (May 1968)

14 Sep 1870   James Hanson places advertisement for private evening classes.

'Advanced Classes – James Hanson proposes forming evening classes for the study of English Language, English Literature, English Constitutional History, Political Economy, History of Philosophy.'

Today this unremarkable advertisement appeared in the *Bradford Observer*. It gives little away about its author who, a life-long advocate for education, was one of the most important and energetic figures in Bradford's educational circles during the second half of the 19th century.

Born in Huddersfield, James Hanson (1815-1895) stopped formal education when, eight years old, he was sent to work full-time in his father's mills. He was said to have *'a profound thirst for knowledge'*, evidenced by his interest, when 14, he taught his father's employees to read during their breaks. Evening classes then paved the way for him to become in 1834 a teacher in a school near Huddersfield.

In 1840 he moved to Bradford and purchased a private school near Manor Row. *'In a low condition'* with just ten pupils, its roll increased to 50 after his ten-year tenure. He returned to Huddersfield where he worked four years in his brother's woollen business before restarting as a teacher. In 1857 he came back to Bradford to set up *The Bradford Review*, a four-page Saturday journal aimed at the radical wing of the Liberal Party. Widely read but not a financial success, it lasted 12 years (January 1858 to February 1870).

1870 was the most important year in Hanson's life, because it saw the Forster Elementary Education Act. This led to him joining the new Bradford School Board in November. From the outset he chaired its influential School Management Committee. He was extremely 'hands-on', visiting all board schools each week. He was particularly interested in school attendance. The Committee oversaw the building of eight Elementary Board Schools, including one at Feversham Street which also developed into the country's first mixed local authority-owned secondary ('Higher Elementary') school.

In 1888 he became Chairman of the Board for six years, when he retired, dying a year later. The minister at his funeral described him as *'an active public servant of eminent ability and unflinching devotion ... content with a small house and a moderate fee he could be, but content with an ill-informed mind and shallow interests he could not be'*.

His name has lived on. Feversham Street Board School became the Hanson Grammar School, then the Hanson School and now the Hanson Academy.

Source: https://www.undercliffecemetery.co.uk/about/history/james-hanson/

15 Sep 1855   The Black Dyke Mills Band is formed.

Today the *Halifax Courier* reported: *'Queenshead Band formed early in the century by residents came into difficulties. John Foster & Son, having lately become acquainted with the depressed state of the band determined to make an effort themselves to raise it up again. Accordingly they have purchased from that eminent maker, Mr. Joseph Higham, of Manchester, a new set of instruments which have this week been delivered to the band, which in future is to be denominated Black Dyke Mills Band. A new and talented leader, as well as several performers, have been added to the band which now comprises 18 musicians. Messrs. Fosters have provided for them a comfortable room in which they will meet for practising.'*

The village of Queensbury (previously Queenshead, after its main public house) became synonymous with John Foster and the Black Dyke Mills that he owned from 1825, where most of the local population worked. From now they became closely linked with the Black Dyke Mills Band, which was to develop and sustain an international reputation.

The band formed today was not in fact the first such band linked to Queenshead. In 1816 Peter Wharton founded a brass and reed band, in which John Foster, founder of Black Dyke Mills, played French horn. After it went out of existence through loss of members, a new band was formed in 1833, called 'Queenshead Band', which may have contained players from the former band. Today's announcement seems to have reconstituted that band and is considered the founding date of the now famous band. It was fitted out with uniforms made from the mill's own cloth.

Most of its musicians have both lived in Queensbury and worked at the mill, reinforcing the close link between the band and the community which remains to this day. The band has always been one of the leading brass bands in the world. In 1904 it made one of the earliest brass band recordings. Two years later it embarked on a five month tour of Canada and the United States, playing in over 200 concerts.

The band has been European Champion 13 times and won numerous other awards. One special achievement was the award of Honorary Freedom of Bradford by the City Council in 1977, the first such group to be so awarded.

Source: www.blackdykeband.co.uk

16 Sep 1963   Filmed mainly in Bradford, *Billy Liar* opens on general release.

The film that put Bradford on the map as a movie-making location opened today outside London.

Billy Fisher is a lazy, irresponsible 19-year-old clerk in the provincial north with a dead-end job as a clerk in an undertaker's office. He lives in his imaginary world called Ambrosia where he is the heroic leader. Acquiring three girl-friends who all accept his proposal of marriage, he alienates his friends and family with a string of fantasies, stories and lies. Eventually, they all catch up on him and he agrees to escape to London with Liz, the one who best understands his fantasies. Or does he escape?

The story is set in an imaginary industrial town in Yorkshire, but it is generally associated with Bradford which provided many of the locations. Important scenes take place at Undercliffe Cemetery ('somewhere quiet' for a romantic walk with one of Billy's fiancees), Bolton Woods quarries (for dumping stolen calendars), the Mecca ballroom on Manningham Lane (where things come to a head with Billy's three fiancees) and in the background the actual demolition of the iconic Swan Arcade. Billy's family lives in a semi-detached house in the lower end of suburban Baildon.

Directed by John Schlesinger, the film secured six BAFTA nominations in 1964: best British actor (Tom Courtenay as Billy), best British actress (Julie Christie as Liz in her film debut), best British cinematography in black and white, best British screenplay, best British film and best film from any source. It failed to win any BAFTA, but was rated by the British Film Institute as number 76 in its top 100 British films of the 20th century.

The film also had important supporting roles for a young Rodney Bewes as Billy's fellow clerk (from Bingley, destined for *The Likely Lads*), a youngish Leonard Rossiter as Billy's undertaker boss (destined for *Rising Damp*) and a much older Wilfred Pickles as Billy's father (from Halifax, character actor and radio presenter of *Have A Go, Joe*).

Billy Liar was an important film in the first phase of the British New Wave. Many novels, plays and films of the 1960s reflected a post-war period when there were more educational opportunities for working-class children (Billy had gone to grammar school, unlike his father). It was a 'kitchen sink drama', viewed as being socially or morally realistic, and created a distance from the parents' generation who had lived through the war.

17 Sep 1864   Emma Sharp sets off to be the first woman to walk 1,000 miles in 1,000 hours.

In the 19th century, competitive walking, or pedestrianism, as it was known, was a popular spectator sport.

In 1809 Captain Robert Barclay made a 1,000 guinea bet with one of his rivals that he could walk 1,000 miles in 1,000 hours. He calculated that, if he walked back-to-back miles with 90 minute rests, he could complete this in around 42 days. It worked. He completed the walk in July 1809. The feat became known as the 'Barclay Match'.

Just walking at a leisurely pace may sound easy, but walking 1,000 miles in 1,000 consecutive hours does not just take a physical toll on the body. Constant walking in circles and the lack of regular prolonged sleep over a six-week period takes a major mental toll.

Women tried this challenge, too. When Emma Sharp from Bradford in her early thirties heard that an Australian woman had just failed, she became interested. Despite lack of training and also without her husband's support, she secured the help of the landlord of the Quarry Gap Hotel, at Laisterdyke. He was keen to offer his grounds as the location for the walk. In exchange, he would receive a percentage of the ticket sales, and no doubt also do good business from spectators. A woman attempting the challenge would add to the interest.

Today, Sharp took the first step of her 1,000 mile walk. She followed a roped-off course of 120 yards with 90-minute breaks every two miles. Walking day and night, she continued this routine for six weeks, until she completed her last mile.

As no women and few men had ever successfully completed this, her progress was widely reported and closely watched by the public. Many started making bets. Gradually, some tried to encourage her to quit by jeering, or worse. In the final days, the police had to protect her. Emma herself walked the final two days with a pistol, which she had to fire in warning to ward off unruly spectators.

Despite all the aggravation, on 19 October Emma Sharp did become the first woman to complete the Barclay Match. Some 100,000 people were estimated to have watched her at some time during the walk. Locals celebrated her success by organising a band on her final day and roasting an ox in her honour.

Source: www.http://www.todayifoundout.com

18 Sep 1978   *The Times* commends Lord Asa Briggs' appointment as Chancellor of the Open University.

For most academic high-flyers, being appointed Chancellor of the ground-breaking Open University would be the pinnacle of a career, but Keighley-born Lord Asa Briggs of Lewes (1921-2016) was no ordinary high-flyer. This was merely just another in a list of outstanding contributions to public service throughout his long life.

His prodigious ability and energy were apparent from the beginning. He was educated at Keighley Grammar School and as a 17-year-old started at Sidney Sussex College, Cambridge where he gained a first in history. Without disclosing this he also enrolled at the same time as an external student at the London School of Economics and gained a first in economics! During the war he worked as a code-breaker at Bletchley Park alongside Alan Turing.

The war over, he became a fellow at Worcester College, Oxford before coming back to Yorkshire as a professor. Aged only 34, he was made Professor of Modern History at Leeds University.

Six years later he was appointed Dean of the School of Social Studies at Sussex University, one of the seven new wave, 'plate-glass' universities that opened in the early 1960s. Here he shaped a new type of history curriculum and introduced an Oxbridge-style tutorial system that had never been operated by the older redbrick universities. He also found time to publish *Victorian Cities* (1965), which contains a valuable summary of Bradford's 19th century development.

Becoming Vice-Chancellor in 1967, he positioned Sussex over the next nine years as the leader of the new universities. In 1976 he returned to Oxford to become Provost of Worcester College for 15 years.

In the meantime the BBC commissioned him in 1958 to write its history in five volumes. In 1970 he chaired an independent review of the nursing profession. He was also an active governor of the British Film Institute, President of the William Morris Society, President of the Victorian Society and the founding President of the Social History Society. Never one to forget his Yorkshire roots, he was President of the Brontë Society from 1987 to 1996.

Today, *The Times* described his recent appointment to the Open University as an ideal fit. He was a leading thinker and achiever in university education; he was an authority on broadcasting and a long-term advocate of part-time education. Finally, he had sat on the planning committee that led to the creation of the Open University.

Source: *The Times* (18 September 1978)

19 Sep 1988   Adrian Moorhouse wins the 100m breaststroke at the Seoul Olympics.

Today was the culmination of 10 years' hard practice and determination. Adrian Moorhouse became the first-ever Olympic gold medallist from Bradford (100m breaststroke), only the fifth swimmer from Great Britain to win Olympic gold and the only British individual gold medallist at the Seoul Olympics in any sport. Later that year he was runner-up in the BBC's Sports Personality of the Year.

His initial inspiration came as a 12-year-old watching David Wilkie win gold at the 1976 Montreal Olympics. By the age of 14 he was committed to a tough and highly disciplined training regime.

Having gone to bed at 9.30pm, every day he got up at 5am to be driven 16 miles to Leeds by his father from Bingley where the family lived. Here, Moorhouse swam for two hours, before being driven to Bradford Grammar School for a 9am start to his day's education. Later in the day he completed another two and a half hours' training in the afternoon or evening, depending on whether it was term time.

Once he started competing in international events, he had some reward for his commitment. When 15, he was chosen for the national senior squad, number two to Duncan Goodhew, gold medallist at the 1980 Moscow Olympics. A year later he became Britain's number one breaststroke swimmer, winning the European bronze. He then won three golds at the next three European Championships (1983, 1985 and 1987) and the next two Commonwealth Games (1982 and 1986).

Although overall he made good progress to his ambition of Olympic gold, not everything went right for Moorhouse. At the 1984 Los Angeles Olympics, he was tipped for a gold medal in the 100m breaststroke, but missed out completely, coming fourth to a new world record holder. He seriously considered giving up, but an important victory in April 1985 led to a second European gold and his career was back on track.

Going into the Seoul Olympics, Moorhouse was clear favourite for gold, but the race did not go to plan. By breakfast time, Britain was waking up to one of the most dramatic races in Olympic swimming history as he recovered from sixth place at the turn of the two-length race to win by just 1/100th of a second.

Source: *Stories of the Century, Telegraph & Argus* (1999)

20 Sep 1853   On his 50th birthday Titus Salt's new mill at Saltaire opens.

After working in his father's textile firm for ten years, Titus Salt started his own firm in 1834. By 1850 he owned five of his own mills in the centre of Bradford. He became increasingly concerned about the city's growing pollution. As mayor in 1948/49, he had failed to persuade fellow factory owners to adopt a special smoke burner that he had introduced in his own.

He decided to move out of the city to a green field site of several acres alongside the canal and the railway. The location was ideal for communication to London and Scotland and across to Hull and Liverpool. Designed by Lockwood and Mawson in the Italian style, the new mill was light and airy for the time. It was six storeys high and nearly 550 feet long. It was built for a workforce of over 3,000.

Today, the workforce celebrated the mill's opening with a magnificent banquet in the new combing shed.

Now work would start on the new village of Saltaire where the workforce would live.

Source: *Bradford*, Joseph Fieldhouse (1972)

20 Sep 1873   On his 70th birthday Titus Salt has his best-ever celebration.

By this time in his life Titus Salt had hosted many events for his workforce, but today's 70th birthday celebration was the finest.

Now he took 4,200 employees on three special trains from Saltaire to his country home of Crow's Nest at Lightcliffe. At two o'clock everyone set down to dinner in an enormous marquee (4,200 square yards) shaped in the letter 'T' like Saltaire Mill itself. Entertainment was provided by three bands, a Punch and Judy show, sports, games and dancing.

One guest stood up to congratulate Sir Titus on the 20th anniversary of the mill and on his 70th birthday. He responded with *'I hope to see you many times yet, if I am spared'*.

He was to survive just three and a quarter more years.

Source: *Balgarnie's Salt*, Robert Balgarnie (2003)

20 Sep 1873   Saltaire Congregational Church is completed.

Although this unusual church in the model village of Saltaire had been open for services for over 17 years, the final building was only complete today with the opening of the attached Sunday School. With a classical design by Lockwood and Mawson rarely found in a non-conformist church, it is the only church in the Bradford area selected by Simon Jenkins in his *England's Thousand Best Churches*.

21 Sep 1962   Tony Richardson's film *The Loneliness of the Long-Distance Runner* is released.

In 1999 the British Film Institute (BFI) invited 1,000 people from the world of British film and television to produce the list of the 100 greatest British films of the 20th century. Only four other directors achieved more than the three entries directed by Tony Richardson (1928 -1991). The films dated from a particularly creative period in his life – the early 1960s. Released over three consecutive years, they comprise *A Taste of Honey* (1961), *The Loneliness of the Long-Distance Runner* (1962) and *Tom Jones* (1963). This last film won four Oscars, including Best Film and Best Director.

His close friend and fellow director Lindsay Anderson described these three films as *'changing the face of British cinema'.* Two of Anderson's own 1960s films also appeared in this list – *This Sporting Life* (1963) and *If* (1968).

From some 20 films and 40 plays that he directed, Tony Richardson selected as title of his memoir *Long-Distance Runner,* suggesting that this film released today had special resonance for him. Starring up-and-coming Tom Courtenay in the title role (for which he won a BAFTA for best young actor), the film is based on Alan Sillitoe's short story about a rebellious youth sentenced to an approved school for burgling a bakery, who gains privileges in this institution through his ability as a long-distance runner.

Shipley-born, Tony Richardson had largely negative memories of his childhood. His home was above the pharmacy between Shipley and Saltaire. His father was a hard-working chemist, but remote from his only child. His mother had little life beyond the kitchen. The wider family was dysfunctional. He hated school and had few friends.

He enjoyed the company of Bob, the family sheep-dog, and their walks upon the nearby moors. *'They were the testing ground, the moors, testing your manhood and growing up by the distances you could gradually master, the weather you could endure in an exhilarating loneliness – your only companions sheep and grouse, curlews and lapwings , larks and plovers. From them came strength and independence and freedom.'*

He fondly remembered childhood visits to the Bradford Alhambra. He attended theatre classes at the Bradford Civic Playhouse (but his memoir makes little mention of his time there). Then he went to Oxford University where his life suddenly blossomed, He started directing, which he continued for the rest of his life with great energy and creativity.

Source: *Long-Distance Runner, A memoir,* Tony Richardson (1993)

22 Sep 1930   The New Victoria cinema becomes the largest cinema outside London.

Today at 2.30pm the Lord Mayor opened the New Victoria Cinema in the city centre on the site of an old brewery. Designed in an Italian classical style by the Bradford architect William Illingworth, the 3,500 capacity cinema auditorium was believed to be the largest in Britain outside London.

The opening ceremony featured the London Symphony Orchestra and naturally included a showing of some of the latest films, including the British comedy *Rookery Nook* and a Mickey Mouse cartoon *Barnyard Concert*.

An important feature of the auditorium was its excellent acoustics compared with many older cinemas that had poor acoustics. The new auditorium was specifically designed with talking pictures in mind. The building also contained a well-appointed restaurant and a ballroom.

In 1950 the cinema became the Gaumont. Its large capacity made it ideal as a concert venue for world-famous performers. For example, it hosted Bill Haley and the Comets (1957), Buddy Holly (1958), the Beatles (1963, twice, and again in 1964), the Everly Brothers (1963) and the Rolling Stones (1965).

In 1969 the cinema changed its name again and became the Odeon. Instead of one large auditorium, it was now split so that several films could be shown at the same time. It closed as a cinema in 2000.

Since then its future has been in jeopardy, embarrassingly in view of Bradford's status as the first UNESCO City of Film. Currently, there are exciting plans to restore it as a live music and conference venue.

22 Sep 1930   Future Wurtlitzer organist, Arnold Loxam, watches the opening night at the New Victoria.

The new cinema today made a lasting impression on a 14-year-old Arnold Loxam sitting in the audience. He had already performed in Bradford as a child pianist from 1925. After World War Two he came back to the cinema to play the Wurlitzer theatre organ for the next 16 years, performances often being recorded for BBC Radio. He then played theatre organs all over England and abroad for the rest of his life into his nineties, becoming one of the last great theatre organists in the country.

He had another good reason to remember the cinema with fondness, because there in 1948 he met his future wife working as an usherette.

23 Sep 1940 Bradford's celebrity hotel marks visit of George Formby.

When you enter the foyer of the Midland Hotel, you see these words in a plaque, proudly hanging on the wall.

'George Formby and his wife stayed here from 23 to 28 September 1940'.

When the Midland Railways Company invested in this hotel between 1885 and 1890, it intended the place to be a showpiece to attract the wealthy and famous, typically stepping off the train from London at the Midland Station and walking the 100 yards or so. The station, but not the hotel, was renamed in 1924 as Forster Square Station. The hotel's main claim to fame was indeed the name of those who came. Paul Robeson, Laurel and Hardy, The Beatles, The Rolling Stones and almost every Prime Minister till Harold Wilson stayed there.

And so did ukulele-playing film star, George Formby (1904-1961) – the only one of this A-list of celebrities to merit a plaque. Born and bred in Wigan, he became the best paid entertainer of the day with a universal appeal. Moreover, his stock may have been particularly high on this occasion and his presence more than welcome in the dark days of the Battle of Britain. We know from newspaper reports that audiences that week at the Bradford Alhambra enjoyed his saucy songs and cheeky style. One song that they did appreciate from a Lancastrian was *'Down in the "ol coal 'ole"* chosen for his Yorkshire audience, not perhaps one of his most well-known pieces like *'Mr Wu'*.

Those days are long gone. The hotel gradually fell into disrepair from the 1970s but new management and new investment in the 1990s helped to restore its appeal. Even though the cachet of staying at the Midland has been lost for ever, one suspects, one can still see many of the original features. The French Ballroom, for example, retains its high ceilings, glittering chandeliers and quality ornate plasterwork.

A short distance across the city, the same cycle can be seen in the other prestigious Victorian railway hotel, the Victoria (now Great Victoria) attached to the old Exchange Station – older (1867), grander, but a little less impressive.

Source: http://www.historichotelsthenandnow.com/midlandbradford.html

24 Sep 1848   Branwell Brontë leaves as his legacy the only portrait of the Brontë sisters.

Today, Branwell Brontë (1817 -1848), the fourth child and only son in the Reverend Patrick Brontë's family of six children, died suddenly at the family home in Haworth, aged 31. The cause was not known, but in a place where, and at a time when, the average life expectancy was just twenty-five years his early death seemed unremarkable. Indeed, his oldest two sisters had both died, aged 11 and 10, and his youngest two adult sisters, Emily and Anne, were to die within the next eight months aged 30 and 29 respectively.

Moreover, Branwell had lived a dissolute life, frequently drunk and known to take opium. In fact, his addiction was such that in Branwell's later years he slept in his father's room so that Patrick could watch over his son, seen as a danger both to himself and his family.

With his other sister Charlotte already making a big name with her first novel *Jane Eyre* and his two younger sisters completing their first novels, Branwell was known to lament that in all his life he had done *'nothing great or good'*.

Nevertheless, he had shown potential as a portrait painter. When he was around 19 years old, his father had arranged for him to seek admission at the London Royal Academy School of Art, providing him with money and letters of introduction. This had, however, not worked out and he returned with a story about being set upon by thieves.

Branwell may have cut a frustrated figure all his adult life, but he did unquestionably leave an important legacy. His portrait of his famous three literary sisters remains the only image of the three of them together. For more than 100 years it has hung in the National Portrait Gallery after being rediscovered rather fortuitously, folded in a cupboard, after the death of Charlotte's husband in Ireland in 1906, over 50 years after her death in 1855.

The portrait is now frequently used in books, exhibitions and other Brontë memorabilia. It shows, on the left, Emily and Anne looking slightly to the right and, on the right, Charlotte a little apart from them and looking slightly to the left. The portrait initially showed Branwell between Emily and Charlotte, but was later removed by him, leaving just a dim shadow. It also shows the fold marks left by years of neglect.

Source: Brontë Parsonage Museum

25 Sep 1886   Valley Parade sees its first sporting action with rugby union.

Today saw the first match ever to be played at the new Valley Parade ground. However the game was not association football, nor even rugby league that preceded it. On what turned out to be a historic debut at a venue, always to be connected with Bradford City, Manningham FC played Wakefield Trinity at rugby union, losing narrowly in front of 8,000 spectators.

It also marked a new stage in the developing rivalry with rivals Bradford FC. The upstart Manningham club now had a new and much larger base. The tussle would grow for the next 30 years.

The year 1880 when Bradford FC was formed with a new base at Park Avenue also saw the start of Manningham FC. It acquired a lease on land at Carlisle Road for its ground. This may not had the facilities of the new Park Avenue, but it had a better location in the centre of Manningham. Carlisle Road was basic, often muddy, with wooden viewing platforms capable of holding up to 3,000 spectators. In 1885 it invested in a new grandstand at one end of the ground, which immediately seemed bad timing.

Suddenly the club had to find a new ground and in haste. The Bradford School Board made a compulsory purchase of the ground for the proposed Drummond Road School. The last game at Carlisle Road was played on 24 April 1886.

Fortunately, a new ground was quickly found at a site, which involved carving a platform out of the hillside down towards the railway from Manningham Lane. The location was ideal, near routes into the city centre and not far from Bradford Midland and Manningham train stations. It was cheap, needed much development, but had potential with a capacity of at least 15,000. The pitch could be quickly hacked out of the hillside. The new grandstand could also be transferred to the new ground. If the club wanted to grow, there was no choice but to invest in this ground.

Most of the £1,070 cost was related to levelling and excavating. It was one tenth of the cost of developing Park Avenue six years before, although that did include a cricket ground. The contract to build was signed on 11 June and the ground ready for use in mid-September. By any account it was an impressive achievement.

This became Valley Parade.

Source: *Room at the Top*, John Dewhirst (2016)

26 Sep 1912   Willie Riley moves easily from one career to another with first-time best seller.

Willie Riley (1866-1961) lived well into his nineties, his working life split neatly into two unusual and unconnected parts.

Born in Laisterdyke, he attended Bradford Grammar School. His father bought him and his brother a magic lantern for showing pictures. They set up a lantern slide business. They also developed the Kineoptoscope projector and started to produce some early films. Ultimately, this business collapsed.

Just before it did, Riley wrote a novel to amuse friends. They persuaded him reluctantly to publish. It attracted several positive reviews, including today's piece in *The Standard:*

'It is not often that the first book to be launched by a new publishing house is from the pen of an unknown writer. But the new house of Herbert Jenkins shows signs of being inclined toward novelty and enterprise in publishing, and that in a manner which looks like making for prompt success. The first book under the new imprint is one easy to enjoy, but hard to classify. Its title is "Windyridge", and its author's name is given as W. Riley.

Its irony is gentle to the point of tenderness, its sentiment is of the kindliest and most delicate, and the supposed narrator – the book is written in the first person singular – is a woman. Be that as it may, here is a book about which one prophecy may be made with safety: it will be read, quoted, and enthusiastically admired by a multitude of people; and that for the simple reason that it will reach the hearts of a multitude. It is that – sufficiently rare – kind of a book; unpretentious, vitally human, rich in kindly, gentle humour, and withal, mellow understanding. It was originally written, we gather, not for publication, but to cheer and divert friends in trouble. Perhaps that accounts for its direct human appeal. "Windyridge" will be much talked of and much read this autumn; and its publishers are to be congratulated upon the very auspicious start they have made.'

The reviewer was right. *Windyridge* (based on Hawksworth between Bradford and Ilkley) was an immediate best seller, up to 500,000 copies bought. Published in 1912, as Riley's first business was failing, it was perfectly timed. Over the next 47 years he was to write 39 books, including 30 novels, nearly all set in the Yorkshire Dales.

Now, *Windyridge* and its writer are barely remembered.

Source: *The Standard* (26 September 1912)

27 Sep 1921   Julia Varley (with another) becomes first woman elected to the TUC General Council.

The report of today's ground-breaking election just gave the facts. Julia Varley of the Workers' Union (WU) was elected as one of two delegates for the new Women's Section in the General Council of the Trades Union Congress (TUC). Now that women over 30 had the vote and could stand for election to Parliament, the TUC followed suit in allowing women into its highest echelons.

There could have been no more suitable candidate to break through this barrier. All her life Varley (1871-1952) was a tough fighter and passionate campaigner for women's rights.

Born to millworkers in a back-to-back in Horton, she learnt as a child that her great-grandfather had been a protestor at Peterloo and her grandfather had been active in Chartist riots in the 1840s.

When she was 12, she inevitably started work in a local mill – a 'half-timer' going to school but also working. A full-timer when 14, she joined the General Union of Textile Workers and soon took on a role of full-time organiser. In 1891 she witnessed at first hand the bitter strike at Manningham Mills. She later became the first woman elected to the Bradford Trades Council.

When 24, she deliberately lived for six weeks as a tramp walking from Leeds to Liverpool to experience what it was really like to live on Poor Law handouts. This must have been invaluable when from 1901 to 1907 Varley was one of few women to be elected a Guardian of the Bradford Poor Law Union.

It is no surprise that she was also a prominent suffragette. On one famous occasion in 1907 suffragettes tried to break into the Houses of Parliament. She was imprisoned for 14 days, one of seven from the Bradford area in a group of 57 so punished.

Two years later Varley moved to Birmingham as a trade union organiser, principally for the WU. Here she established a reputation for helping workers win many disputes over many years.

After today's elevation, her reputation became national and international. When the WU amalgamated with the TGWU she was appointed its Chief Women's Officer. Her campaigning led to an OBE in 1931 and a good friendship with the Duke of York (later King George VI).

She retired in 1935 and returned to Bradford to live with her two sisters.

Source: *Julia Varley – Trade union organiser and fighter for women's rights*, booklet by UNITE (2015)

28 Sep 1830 Factory-owner John Wood persuades Richard Oastler to campaign against child labour.

Today was a turning point in the life of Richard Oastler (1789-1861), the so-called 'Factory King'. For the rest of his life he championed the cause of better working conditions in factories.

A land agent from near Huddersfield, Oastler visited today his friend John Wood who lived at Horton Hall, owned two spinning mills in Bradford and opened a school nearby. Both were active campaigners against the slave trade. He asked Oastler why he had never campaigned against child labour in factories. Surprised, Oastler listened to an account of the evils of this system. Children worked fourteen hours a day and sometimes had to crawl under moving machinery where adults could not: this often led to children being severely injured and even worse.

The next morning, Oastler gave a solemn vow to his friend that he would campaign to end these cruel practices. That day he wrote a letter to the *Leeds Mercury* headed *Yorkshire Slavery*:

'Thousands of our fellow-creatures and fellow-subjects, both male and female, the miserable inhabitants of a Yorkshire town are this very moment existing in a state of slavery, more horrid than are the victims of that hellish system of colonial slavery. These innocent creatures drawl out, unpitied, their short but miserable existence, in a place famed for its profession of religious zeal, whose inhabitants are ever foremost in professing temperance and reformation ... The very streets which receive the droppings of an 'Anti-Slavery Society' are every morning wet by the tears of innocent victims at the accursed shrine of avarice, who are compelled (not by the cart-whip of the negro slave-driver) but by the dread of the equally appalling thong or strap of the over-looker, to hasten, half-dressed, but not half-fed, to those magazines of British infantile slavery, the worsted mills in the town and neighbourhood of Bradford.'

Oastler threw himself into a battle much nearer to home than the colonial slave trade. A fine orator as well as letter-writer, he turned factory reform into a pressing national issue. He organised workers to pledge for a universal ten-hour day. However, the campaign had several setbacks, and he fell into debt, was imprisoned, and only rescued by the support of his friends over three years later.

It was not until the 1847 Factory Act was passed that his campaign had a successful outcome.

Source: *Leeds Mercury* (16 October, 1830)

29 Sep 2008   We say goodbye to Mr Bradford and Mr Bingley.

Today's announcement was the death of two very familiar figures in national life. For 30 years Mr. Bradford and Mr. Bingley had represented one of the country's most successful and recognised building societies – the Bradford & Bingley. The logo of the two bowler-hatted gentlemen in silhouette would no longer be the outward face of the institution.

The Bradford & Bingley Building Society was formed in 1964 when the Bradford Equitable Building Society and the Bingley Permanent Building Society merged. Both had been established in 1851 with the simple idea that those who had money could save at an attractive rate and the money they deposited could be used to provide loans for the less well-off.

Today, the Spanish Santander Group acquired all Bradford & Bingley's £20 billion (2.7 million customers) savings business, 197 branches and 141 agencies. The mortgage book, personal loan book, headquarters, treasury assets and its wholesale liabilities were taken into public ownership and closed to new business.

Understandably, people reacted: *'I told you so!'* Back in December 2000 the building society had officially demutualised and floated on the London Stock Exchange with former members of the society, each receiving a minimum of 250 shares worth £567.50 at the time, and savers with more savings receiving more shares worth up to £5,000 each.

Eighteen months earlier when this intention was revealed, the *Telegraph & Argus* commented: *'The tragic victory of the carpet-baggers over the future of the Bradford & Bingley Building Society casts a shadow over the whole community, not just in Bradford district but right across the country. Yet again, simple greed has won the day. Those who sought to make a quick killing will find themselves a few hundred pounds better off – potentially at the expense of hundreds of jobs.'* (27 April 1999).

With today's news, more than 150 years of history ended as a mere footnote in the annals of the financial crisis of 2008. The old building society had registered more than 100 separate trademarks featuring the bowler hat, its long-running logo. It had even purchased a bowler hat in 1995 for £2,000, which had formerly belonged to Stan Laurel.

The area also lost a good sponsor. Before its collapse the Bradford & Bingley had sponsored Yorkshire CCC, Bradford & Bingley RFC and Bradford City AFC, including the Valley Parade stadium. Indeed it was a sad day.

Source: *Telegraph & Argus* (29 September 2008)

30 Sep 1920   The Bradford Through Lines Act reaches the end of the line.

One condition of the 1844 Leeds & Bradford Railway Act was that the new rail link to Bradford should provide a through line to Halifax and beyond, but that condition was quietly forgotten.

'Bradford's railway circumstances are singularly unfortunate because of a series of historical quirks. As a result... we have two railway stations, both termini: the Interchange, which is modern, bleak and inadequate, approximately nine miles from Leeds, and Forster Square, approximately three miles from Shipley—which can be seen to have an air of faded grandeur, when it is possible to burrow behind the buildings and find out where it is.

Yet another opportunity arose in the early 1880s when reconstruction of Bradford Exchange station was in an advanced state of planning. A leading local architect was hired by a group of prominent Bradford businessmen to prepare plans for a central station on a through line and the cost was put at £300,000. But, after conferring on the scheme, the three railway companies, which already had local interests ... sent a sharp rebuff to the promoters saying that the project was unrealistic. One of those railways—the Midland—13 years later drew up its own proposals for a Bradford through line, at an estimated cost of £2.1 million; and the scheme was authorised by the Midland Railway (West Riding Lines) Act 1898. The House was so keen to endorse Bradford's view that it gave its consent for the extension of time to promote the scheme to build the railway in 1901, 1904 and 1907. But the local authority rightly suspected that the Midland Railway was dragging its feet, and so eventually produced yet another scheme.

The Bradford Through Lines Act received the Royal Assent on 25 July 1911. But before anything could be done, the First World War intervened in 1914, and in the post-war recession the scheme was again put to one side and forgotten.'

The words belong to Bob Cryer (Labour MP for Bradford South), who always spoke with ardour about local matters. In 1988 he was lobbying hard for yet another doomed attempt at a 'through line' linking Bradford's two separate stations.

Footnote:

On 18 November 1919 the Midland formally abandoned the Bradford Through Lines plan. Today all the property in the central area which had been acquired for demolition for the 1911 venture was sold to Bradford Corporation.

Source: *Hansard* (22 June 1988)

BELOW: Celebrating the unique Brontë sisters, the Parsonage Museum is a literary shrine for hundreds of thousands each year (story on 4 Aug).

ABOVE: In celebration of his 80th birthday, a wall sculpture of David Hockney looks out over Little Germany (story on 9 Jul).
Credit: Richard Wilson Photography

BELOW: The opening of the new cemetery at Undercliffe was an important landmark in the rapid growth of Bradford (story on 28 Aug).
Credit: Richard Wilson Photography

ABOVE: When Lord Palmerston came to the city to lay its foundation stone, the new Wool Exchange attracted great attention (story on 9 Aug).
Credit: Richard Wilson Photography

BELOW: One of Bradford's most striking mosques is Suffa-Tul-Islam near Horton Park, also known as Bradford Grand Mosque (story on 3 Sep).
Courtesy: Al-Jamia Suffa-Tul-Islam Grand Mosque

ABOVE: St. Georges Hall was Bradford's first public building and is now one of the oldest concert halls in Europe (story on 29 Aug).
Credit: Richard Wilson Photography

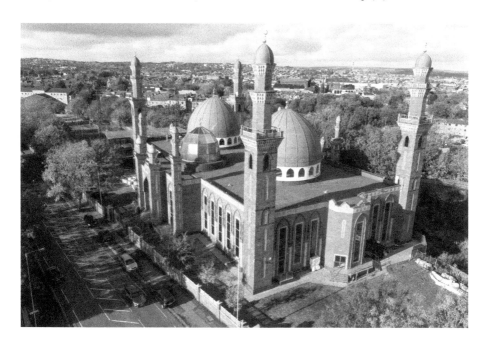

BELOW: In his new village at Saltaire, Sir Titus Salt built the Congregational Church, one of the nation's most distinguished nonconformist churches (story on 20 Sep). *Credit: Richard Wilson Photography*

ABOVE: All the nation's monarchs (plus Oliver Cromwell) decorate City Hall (story on 9 Sep). *Credit: Richard Wilson Photography*

1 Oct 1847   Bradford Corporation hosts its first mayoral dinner.

Over five months since it received its charter, the new Bradford Corporation celebrated today with its first mayoral dinner. Some 200 guests sat down in the Exchange Buildings (they would have to wait another 26 years for their own Town Hall). The new mayor sent out invitations to guests irrespective of their political beliefs, an action that helped to put behind them the controversy leading up to the charter.

The borough's first mayor and also chairman of the new borough magistrates was Robert Milligan (1786-1862). His dramatic rise reflected the times. Born to a tenant farmer in the Scottish Lowlands, he moved to Crosshills (between Keighley and Skipton) around 1802 as a 'travelling Scotchman' working as a door-to-door salesman. By 1810 he had opened a draper's shop in Westgate, eventually becoming a buyer for Leo Schuster & Co. of Manchester and through that job met Henry Forbes. Together they formed Milligan, Forbes & Co, Stuff Merchants that became synonymous with the stuff trade of Bradford (ie worsted wool). It was housed in impressive new premises, built in 1853 on Hall Ings, unusually for the city centre on level ground (eg warehouses in Little Germany were on a slope). It was considered Bradford's first 'palazzo', which from the 1920s became the headquarters of the *Telegraph & Argus*.

From 1851 to 1857 Milligan was elected Liberal MP for the borough in three successive Parliaments.

His lasting monument, however, is an impressive pillar, 20 foot high, in Undercliffe Cemetery. He had been a founder member of The Bradford Cemetery Company and secured a prime position for his memorial in the city's newest cemetery. It is accompanied by fulsome praise in a description of his life.

'Born in Scotland, he became a resident of Bradford in 1808. His talents and industry guided by integrity and honour raised him to a high distinction as a merchant. He was the first Mayor of Bradford. . He represented the town in two successive parliaments with fidelity and distinction. He was generous and warm hearted in his hospitalities, liberal in his support of religious and other benevolent institutions. He departed this life in faith and hope of the gospel July 1 1862 aged 75.'

Source: *Historical Notes on the Bradford Corporation* (William Cudworth,1881)

2 Oct 1911   The new Bingley Teacher Training College for Women receives its first students.

In the 19th century, the training of teachers was largely carried out under a pupil-teacher system, success depending totally on the quality of the teacher doing the mentoring. At the same time, women's education was regarded as lower priority than men's education. The Education Act 1902 allowed the newly-created education authorities to introduce teacher training colleges.

The opening of the first such college specifically for women in the West Riding was a landmark event. The county employed 6,000 teachers, 75% of whom were women. Today the Bingley Teacher Training College for Women opened its doors to its first 122 female students.

West Riding County Council had received funds for its first such college. It had been quite a competition for potential sites to secure the final decision. In 1908 it was reported that a short list of 11 sites had been drawn up from all parts of the county, including four sites in the Bradford area. The council bought the land at the edge of the moors just to the north of Bingley, which welcomed the decision as the arrival of hundreds of students would boost the local economy. The building was designed in the Edwardian style (the architect was called Edwards) to include the main college building, five halls of residence and a services block.

Not everything went smoothly on the day the foundation stone was laid in 1909. The President of the Board of Education, doing the honours, was interrupted at least three times by heckling suffragettes – *'If you will allow the women to teach, why won't you give them the vote?'* In some exasperation he retorted: *'I hope the young lady will realise that we are met to found an institution for the education of women.'* (*Leeds Mercury,* 25 May)

Today's opening ceremony did not go well either as bad weather delayed it until 21 October. The newly appointed Principal, Helen Wodehouse, gave a short speech, welcoming the location: *'Mental fresh air and mental sunshine would be developed in the students through their association with green woods and purple moors and the sight of a valley full of stars at night.'*

Source: *Bingley: A Living History,* Alan Cattell (2016)

3 Oct 2018   Family firm Seabrook's Crisps goes Japanese.

Successful family-owned businesses are always likely to be bought out by corporate giants. Today that happened to one of Bradford's iconic food products. It was a shock to hear that the leading Japanese snacks producer had bought Seabrook – supplier of traditional Yorkshire crisps. The buyer was Calbee UK, subsidiary of Japan-based $2.3bn, Calbee Inc.

Widely known over Yorkshire for years, and even longer in Bradford, the Seabrook name had an unusual origin. Just before World War Two, Charles Brook from Bradford collected some photos. He noticed that the shopkeeper had accidentally labelled them 'Seabrook' instead of 'C Brook'. When he opened his first fish and chip shop, Charles decided to call it Seabrook.

Just after the war, Charles' son returned from the Navy. Together they discovered that with their fryer they could diversify their use of the potato. The result was Seabrook Crisps. Father and son moved into their first factory, a one-up one-down terrace house in Bradford. Seabrook began delivering crisps door-to-door and launched what were believed to be the first crinkle-cut crisps.

In 1956 the Brooks converted the old Allerton Liberal Club into their new factory. The World Crisp Eating Competition took place in Bradford, sponsored by Seabrook. They coined the slogan *'Lovingly Made in Yorkshire'*. Twenty-two years later, they purchased a site off Thornton Road and in 1980 opened its Princeville Factory to operate alongside its Allerton base. Seabrook launched its first prawn cocktail crinkle-cut crisps.

Seabrook were the first to use sunflower oil to cook their crisps. They went on to remove monosodium glutamate (artificial flavouring), e-numbers and other artificial ingredients. In 2013 Seabrook crisps were certified by Coeliac UK and now carried its gluten-free cross-grain logo. All crisps are also confirmed vegetarian-friendly.

In 2015 they made their first move away from a family-owned business backed by a private equity investor. Today they completed the transfer to the corporate world by going Japanese. The size of the company was approximately £28m turnover and 160 employees.

Such a move is only made because the parent company has ambitious plans to develop the market for the product. This always has risks in losing the distinctive brand that brought it success, as the Harry Ramsden Fish n' Chips story indicates. Only time will tell what happens to the prawn cocktail flavour.

Source: *Yorkshire Post* (3 October 2018)

4 Oct 1859 Charles Darwin travels unexpectedly to Ilkley to take the waters.

The first thing that Charles Darwin (1809-1882) did in 1859 after checking the final proofs of his ground-breaking and controversial *The Origin of Species* was to set off from his Kent home to Ilkley. Today he arrived, followed two weeks later by his wife and children.

He was exhausted and suffering from a mystery illness that had afflicted him for over 20 years ever since his epic five-year voyage to the Pacific on the *Beagle*. He had reason to believe that Ilkley might provide the cure; even at that time many would have been dubious that such treatment would work.

The illness was intermittent, but he was never completely healthy. The symptoms were palpitation, vomiting and abdominal pain. The cause unknown, Darwin convinced himself the water cure would help.

Darwin came to Ilkley for the water therapy at Wells House, a well-known spa on the edge of Ilkley Moor. This comprised the application of ice cold water in baths and showers, plenty of drinking of pure, cold water and many bracing walks in the fresh air.

Within two weeks he wrote: *'The house is at the foot of a rocky, turfy, rather steep half-mountain. It would be nice with fine weather; but now looks dismal. There are nice excursions and fine walks for those that can walk. The Water Cure has done me much good'.*

Charles Darwin stayed in Ilkley for nine weeks during which time *The Origin of Species* was published and early impressions and reviews were filtering back to him. Since then his stay has been commemorated twice locally.

First, in the 1990s after much debate Ilkley Parish Council supported as a millennium project the concept of Darwin Gardens above the original Ilkley Wells House Hydropathic Establishment (now converted into flats). The Darwin Gardens were opened in July 2000.

Second, in commemoration of his bicentenary, and, 150 years later of the publication, a giant sand sculpture of Charles Darwin was displayed in August 2009 in City Park in Bradford. It was designed by Jamie Wardley, who happened to be from Bradford (there are only around 500 sand-sculptors in the world). It was accompanied by live poetry readings by Shipley-born poet Andrew Mitchell from a specially commissioned 14 poem sequence about Darwin's stay in Ilkley and following his round-the-world voyage on the *Beagle*.

Source: *Telegraph & Argus* (4 December 2000)

5 Oct 1908   Ernest Busby opens his first shop.

There were two significant dates in the development of Busby's, one of Bradford's two famous shopping names that dominated the first half of 20th century Bradford (Brown Muff the other). Today Ernest Busby opened his first new shop on Kirkgate with a staff of 23. On this first day of trading, a police officer had to stand on guard as the queues were so long.

After the Kirkgate store was closed, the second opening on 26 April 1930 was the much larger, magnificent Gothic department store on Manningham Lane. This time Busby's was opened by Ernest's wife Amy. It was very well situated as shoppers got off trams right outside the store from the wealthier suburbs of Manningham, Heaton, Saltaire and off buses from further afield.

Promoted as *'The Store with the Friendly Welcome',* it had the reputation of being a very friendly family store, run by the family – three sons and a daughter who all had a role. It had a distinctive red and black logo, showing four marching and helmeted Coldstream guards, one in front, three behind (father and three sons).

It made the claim that it sold everything that any customer could need. Many departments were distinctive. Its dress department showed expensive gowns and had a facility for dressmaking. A furrier by background, Busby also created a furs department where furs were manufactured and cleaned on site. It had a restaurant, café, library, hairdresser, beauty salon, laundry and record counter. Pre-war, it even had its own petrol station. Post-war, it added an ice-cream factory and nearby Fountain Hall for functions. Busby's came into its own at Christmas with a Saturday Christmas Parade from the city centre and a Christmas grotto, a 'must-see' experience for children.

Children also marvelled at the pneumatic cashier system. Cash or cheque would be screwed into a pneumatic cylinder, then pushed into a hole in the wall to hurtle across the ceiling to a central cashier out of sight. A few minutes later it hurtled back with a receipt and change.

Branches were also opened in Ilkley and Harrogate. At its height by the 1950s it had over 800 employees. Just seven years later Busby died and Debenhams took over; it was the end of an era.

Source: *Busbys' - A Shop Full of Memories*, Michael Callaghan & Colin Neville (2008)

6 Oct 1981   The new Social Democratic Party holds its first annual conference at St. George's Hall.

Bradford has only ever twice hosted an annual conference for a mainstream political party. Both were events of hope, celebrating the official start of a new party. The first occurred in 1893 when the Independent Labour Party was formed, then later mainly subsumed within the Labour Party. The second occurred today when in St. George's Hall the new Social Democratic Party (SDP) convened – a party that later merged with the Liberal Party to become the Liberal Democratic Party (Lib Dems) in 1989.

The first movement in the 1890s had been a clean break towards a socialist future from a country and a city generally committed to the liberal tradition. In Bradford it came to be represented in the figure of Fred Jowett, a working man with minimal education, fervent socialist and proud of his roots.

The second movement in the 1980s was a swing against a socialist future back to more middle-of-the-road social democratic and liberal values, with the Tories also deeply unpopular. The new SDP was led by national figures, the 'Gang of Four' (Roy Jenkins, David Owen, Bill Rodgers and Shirley Williams). Locally, it was symbolised by Edward Lyons, Labour MP for Bradford West.

From Leeds, Lyons was a highly respected 'constituency' MP elected in 1966, well-educated lawyer and moderate Labour man who could not stomach the left-wing excesses from the likes of hard-left Militant Tendency. He was exactly the type of traditional Labour MP to be targeted by the left in a campaign for deselection, but he saw off the threat.

In January 1981 the Limehouse Declaration by the 'Gang of Four' led to the SDP being formed in March. At this point Lyons joined the new party, along with eleven other Labour MPs. Another 16 joined by the end of the year.

The SDP's first annual conference was to be different, being split over three venues. Lyons had influence and Bradford was chosen between Perth (first) and London (third). The event was full of optimism with more Labour MPs joining. Shirley Williams (not then an MP) agreed to take on Crosby (later winning it, famously overcoming a 19,000 Tory majority).

Nationally, the Falklands War broke out, the Tories overcame deep unpopularity and most SDP MPs lost their seats, including Lyons. The bubble was burst and the middle ground was squeezed until Tony Blair in the late 1990s.

Source: Edward Lyons obituary, *The Guardian* (10 June 2010)

7 Oct 1890   Lord Masham opens the new Children's Hospital.

Today as its largest benefactor Lord Masham (formerly Samuel Lister) opened the new Bradford Children's Hospital in St. Mary's Road, a few minutes' walk from his Lister's Mill. It was the culmination of nearly 30 years of help for sick children.

It began in a small way in 1862 when some women of the All Saints' Sisterhood, an Anglican order, visited the poor in St. Jude's Parish in Lumb Lane and ventured into Black Abbey, one of Bradford's most squalid areas. They found many ailing children who needed care in a cleaner environment, where they could be properly fed and nursed. In 1863 they converted two houses in Hanover Square into a small 12-bedded hospital and did all the nursing themselves, with the help of donations from friends.

The task grew and more help was needed. In 1884 the Mayor held a meeting to agree steps for a bigger facility. The appointed committee acquired three years later a large house in nearby Springfield Place, which doubled the number of beds. When that filled up straightaway, they looked again for something much bigger and came across a site on St. Mary's Road. They needed £12,000 to build a new hospital. Lord Masham donated £5,000.

The design had an unusual feature – two large two-storey circular wards, fashionable at the time, each ward containing 25 cots arranged in a circle around the room. The committee decided to phase the construction so that only the first such ward was built – the Samuel Cunliffe Lister Wing. The second wing was never built. At tonight's celebratory dinner Lord Masham expressed himself *'perfectly satisfied'* with how his gift had been used.

The hospital survived for nearly 100 years before its work was absorbed into St. Luke's Hospital. It became a nursing home. Now it has been converted into the Anjuman-e-Haideria Shia Mosque.

Source: *Telegraph & Argus* (2 December 2006)

7 Oct 2017   Bradford Bulls complete the cup and league double in first Women's Super League.

Today, at the end of the first season in the Women's Super League, Bradford Bulls became the champions, beating Featherstone Rovers 36-6 at the Manchester Regional Arena. After a close first half, they ran up another 20 points in the second half without any further concession. As they had already beaten the same team 50-16 in the Women's Challenge Cup, they had now won the cup and league double.

Source: www.rugby-league.com/article/51181/bradford-bulls-become-first-ever-womens-super-league-champions

8 Oct 1866   Bradford closes down for business to support a huge Reform League demonstration.

Today was no ordinary Monday morning in Bradford. Most factories were silent, most shops closed and most streets empty.

The people of Bradford were on their way to Woodhouse Moor in Leeds where the Reform League had organised a major West Riding demonstration.

Electoral reform had been the main driver of Chartism which had died away after the 1848 riots. Bradford had been a hotbed for the movement, but the issue of suffrage had not disappeared. There were campaigns in support of failed attempts by the House of Commons in 1859 and 1866 to introduce reform.

The new league was set up in 1866 to press for universal suffrage (more accurately, manhood suffrage). It represented both working and middle classes. Bradford had a strong branch led by Robert Kell, JP, prominent citizen and businessman.

The demonstration had been carefully planned. It represented all the West Riding. On high ground, one mile out of Leeds city centre, Woodhouse Moor was an ideal venue. However, the railway companies intervened by refusing to run trains from Bradford, Keighley and Halifax. This only meant that the demonstrators found other transport or just walked. Working men, indeed, had sacrificed one day's pay for attending; most of them walked there and back from Bradford some nine or ten miles away.

The Bradford part of the procession was acknowledged to be the most effective. According to the *Manchester Examiner*, '*No town in England can claim to be in more healthy political condition than this most rising and most thriving centre of the great Yorkshire (worsted) trade*'. The *Bradford Observer* praised the discipline and organisation. It described in detail the various contingents that marched in clear groups with their banners and flags from their towns and villages. Speeches by Robert Kell and Bradford MP, WE Forster, were cheered and all resolutions noisily supported. The paper estimated in all up to 200,000 protestors.

Another such demonstration to the same venue was needed in April 1867 before the argument was won.

The Reform Act of 1867 enfranchised part of the urban male working class. After the 1832 Reform Act one million out of seven could vote; now the new act immediately doubled that number. It would not be for nearly another 50 years (1918) before all males (and 60% females) could vote and another ten for all females (1928).

Source: *Bradford Observer* (11 March 1966)

9 Oct 1856 — Chief Constable claims that *'beerhouses without brothels are in a poverty-stricken state'.*

The creation of Bradford Corporation in 1847 led to the appointment of the town's first Chief Constable, William Leveratt. As a result reliable statistics about crime in Bradford started to become available.

In 1858 for the first time the Home Office requested that local police forces should submit an annual return about crimes in their area – the first of many steps in the gradual centralisation of police services over 150 years.

The headline from the figures was that drunkenness and prostitution were rife. This recalled the Chief Constable's comments two years before in today's *Bradford Observer* that *'beerhouses without brothels are in a poverty-stricken state'.* He quoted a stark example in this year's report about two beerhouse keepers in Southgate who had no fewer than nine brothels attached to their houses, with no fewer than 30 prostitutes resident. *'The street was a complete nuisance to the whole borough, being infested with thieves, prostitutes, and other drunken and disorderly characters.'* After applying under some ancient statute going back to King Edward III, the police managed to get the beerhouses closed. Thereafter, *'Good order at once prevailed, and since that period there has not been a single report of a robbery or disorderly conduct in the street'.*

Overall, at the corresponding period in 1857 the borough had 63 known brothels and 164 known prostitutes. Now, brothels were reduced to 40 and prostitutes to 92. Similarly last year there were eight beerhouses with brothels attached; now there are only two such houses. Last year, there were also eight beerhouses where prostitutes lodged, but now there were none where either prostitutes lodged or frequented.

Across all crimes 817 people were taken into custody, of whom 565 were English, 243 Irish, five Scottish and five foreigners. Given that the Irish population in Bradford might at that time have reached 10-15%, the percentage of Irish convicted is very high, reflecting perhaps high levels of drunkenness or prejudice by the police and others against the Irish.

By modern standards, the Chief Constable's report passed without any press comment in the *Bradford Observer* either in its comment columns or correspondence with its readers. In the early days of police forces crime cannot have been a very important topic of political debate.

Source: *The Establishment of Municipal Government in Bradford 1837-1857*, PhD thesis Adrian Elliott (1976)

10 Oct 1662   Bradford Grammar School receives royal charter from King Charles II.

As all its earliest records are lost, the date when Bradford Grammar School started is unknown, but the best estimate is about 1548 around which time a number of other ancient grammar schools in Yorkshire were founded. The first known reference to a headmaster is a Robert Hall, mentioned in the will of a Vicar of Bradford in 1563. The link between church and school was indeed close. The vicar had rights over the school, the boys of the school were choristers and the first school building was close by, as was its 17th century replacement, School House being underneath the steps of the Church Bank entrance to St. Peter's Church.

The first firm date that remains is today when the school was granted a royal charter. After the end of the Civil War when Bradford was sacked by Royalists, a group of citizens, presumed Puritans, came together to rebuild the township. Part of this was to restore the Grammar School that had lost key legal documents. They petitioned Parliament for restoration of rights, but Oliver Cromwell, Lord Protector, died, and it was not until King Charles II came back to the throne that the matter could be resolved (*Hoc Age,* Tony Moxon, 1999).

The new charter stipulated, inter alia, that:

- *'There shall be a grammar school to be called the Free Grammar School of King Charles the Second at Bradford for teaching, instructing and better bringing up children and youth in grammar, and other good learning and literature.*

- *There shall be thirteen men, of the most discreet, honest and religious persons in the neighbourhood, whereof the vicar of Bradford shall always be one who shall be governors and be a body corporate.*

- *Power is given to the governors ... to constitute a discreet and fit person who hath taken the degree of A.M. (now, Master of Arts) to be schoolmaster ... to continue so long as he shall be found by the governors to be diligent and faithful in his office, and fit for the same both by his religion, knowledge and conversation, and no longer.*

- *The governors may, upon one quarter's warning, displace the headmaster and elect another.'*

These governance arrangements remained in place until 1871 when the school was completely re-organised following the 1869 Endowed Schools Act.

Source: *The History and Topography of Bradford,* John James (1866)

11 Oct 1859   Town Clerk presents paper to prestigious conference on state of Bradford's public health.

Today was the start of the third annual conference of the National Association for the Promotion of Social Science. Founded in 1857, the Association was a progressive liberal reformist policy-making body, a kind of think-tank of its day until its demise in 1886. Participants included three Liberal Prime Ministers, other senior politicians (eg Bradford's most influential MP, WE Forster) and civil servants, thinkers and experts. Its remit for social science was broader than the term might imply now, covering jurisprudence, punishment and reformation, social economy, public health and education. Its work revolved around an annual conference that travelled around the country. Bradford had been proud to host the event after Birmingham and Liverpool. For example, this week's *Bradford Observer* devoted three of its nine pages to a full coverage of the first two days and another two pages the next week for the final two days. Some 1,000 delegates attended St. George's Hall.

The topic that was perhaps closest to Bradford was a paper presented in the afternoon by the Town Clerk on the town's public health.

Using figures from the previous ten years, he presented a rather optimistic picture of Bradford as a 'moderately healthy town' based on a mortality rate of 24.2 deaths/thousand in the 1850s, compared with 27.3 over the 1840s (ie a 13% improvement). Compare this with a UK mortality rate of 8.8 deaths/thousand in 2011!

Manufacturing towns were inherently unhealthier than agricultural areas and immigration had caused difficulties. *'In spite of a rapid increase in the population, partly contributed to by an immigration of labourers and their families from a distance, the majority of whom were from an inferior class, and on the verge of pauperism in their native homes, and had to come to a different and, in many instances, a more rigorous climate and more crowded district, the borough has actually become healthier as inhabitants have crowded on its previously vacant spaces.'*

The Town Clerk was able to point to a number of improvements such as the decline of manual woolcombing in homes, the removal of cellar dwellings and the extension of water services into houses. The major outstanding problems were smoke pollution and infant mortality.

Reinforced by complements made from the conference floor, the overall impression created was a town in control of its health improvements.

Source: *Bradford Observer* (13 October 1859)

12 Oct 1852   Isaac Holden writes to old tutor in Scotland about his commitment to self-improvement.

Growth in textile manufacture in 19th century Bradford was rapid and there were many 'rags-to-riches' stories. However, if we look at the four men considered to be the wealthiest, only one can be so described. Samuel Lister was born into landed gentry and considerable wealth, a start from which he became exceedingly rich. The fathers of Titus Salt (worsteds) and Henry Ripley (dyeworks) built up substantial businesses, which they passed on to their sons who continued their good work. Only Isaac Holden (1807-1897) can claim that he started life in poverty. His commitment to hard work and self-improvement took him far.

Born into a large family in a village near Paisley, Holden had a chequered education, often disrupted. After some time at a grammar school, he worked in a cotton mill, became a pupil teacher and Wesleyan Minister. Moving south he became a teacher in West Yorkshire and Reading.

In 1828 he returned to Scotland before accepting a bookkeeping position at a worsted manufacturing firm in Cullingworth. Here he worked 16 years, achieving semi-managerial status and developing through his own efforts an expertise in mechanical engineering. He became obsessed with finding a way of mechanising woolcombing, a problem which hitherto remained intractable.

All the while he kept in touch with a former tutor in Scotland. Here in today's letter he summarised his motivation.

'I am still aiming at something better, aspiring to advancement. There is no harm in doing so, I hope. To be enterprising, whether a defect or an excellence, is a natural quality of my spirit.

As to my studies, I direct my attention most exclusively to those branches and works which tend to make me completely master of my own business, such as the science and art of mechanics ... I study much to find out the defects of the machinery and general plans about our works and go cautiously to the work of reformation and improvement... It is my ambition not to be behind any man in this country in my knowledge and management of the worsted trade and manufacture if diligence can effect it.'

This philosophy was fully put to the test, and his life changed for ever, when he met Samuel Cunliffe Lister, one of Bradford's most prominent wool men. Their collaboration was to transform the business.

Source: *Poverty and Progress: Social Conditions in early and mid-19th century Bradford*, Gary Firth (1979)

13 Oct 1905   Sir Henry Irving, most famous actor of his day, dies after performing at Bradford's Theatre Royal.

Tonight witnessed the most famous death in Bradford's history – somebody who had no strong connection to the city, except when he died. It is also sadly the one event still associated with the Theatre Royal on Manningham Lane where he had just made his final appearance.

Sir Henry Irving, the most famous actor-manager of his generation, the first knight of British theatre and the Sir Laurence Olivier of his day, died just before midnight within minutes of collapsing in the foyer of the Midland Hotel.

Billed as his Farewell Tour, his week had started so well. On Tuesday he had been feted by the Mayor at a civic lunch in his honour. On stage he had given a series of strong performances, as reported by the *Bradford Daily Telegraph*:

'Sir Henry certainly gave a powerful performance of his old favourite role. His dressing for the part was remarkable, and calculated to excite the utmost repulsion in the beholder, cunning, vindictiveness, the passion for revenge were all developed, and at the fall of the curtain Sir Henry had achieved an artistic triumph.' (Monday as Shylock, to be repeated Saturday)

'Tennyson's fine drama "Becket" appears twice in Sir Henry Irving's programme this week. It is a favourite role of the actor's. Last night's was a satisfying performance. The Becket in the play is a commanding character, and the actor gives a subtle and illuminating interpretation. A word and a gesture convey the working of his mind.' (Tuesday, repeated Friday)

'This week's programme ... seeks both to show Sir Henry's versatility and yet provide him with subtle studies of human character. "Louis Xl" is a fitting addition to Shylock and Becket... Sir Henry Irving portrays this extraordinarily bad old man with every power.' (Wednesday)

'After last night's performance there certainly remains consolation in the fact that the famous actor is saying farewell to the stage whilst yet in the complete possession of his wonderful dramatic instinct and power.' (Friday - his final performance)

During Friday's performance he seemed unwell but managed to get through. His business manager, Bram Stoker (also author of *Dracula*) left him taking the taxi a short distance to the Midland Hotel. Stoker was summoned to the hotel to be told that Irving had just died from a heart attack.

On Saturday evening his body was conveyed to the Great Northern station past silent respectful crowds.

14 Oct 2010   Naila Zafar is the first Pakistani woman to be made a Dame.

Today, a Bradford headteacher became the first British woman of Pakistani origin to receive a damehood – the Most Excellent Order of the British Empire Dame Commander (DBE). It was awarded for her services to local and national education.

A teacher for over 30 years, Dame Naila Zafar was headteacher of Copthorne primary school, Horton Park, in one of Bradford's most deprived areas and largest concentrations of Pakistani immigrants.

Born in Kenya in 1955, she returned, aged eight, to Lahore in Pakistan, her parents' country of origin, where she lived until aged 12. Then, her father decided to come to Bradford. She was immediately put into the bottom set at secondary school, learning first-hand about barriers to succeed at school from teachers making assumptions about Pakistani children. Her mother challenged the school to justify this, asked for her to be given a test, after which she moved to the top set.

Like all her four siblings, Dame Naila gained a degree, but her father had to face criticism from their community for sending his daughter to a teacher training college away from home. She married after her first year, her father making her father-in-law promise that she could continue her studies.

After college, she had two daughters, and with her mother's support obtained her first teaching job. She did postgraduate work at Bradford College, teaching PGCE students. Missing contact with children, she went to Feversham School as a deputy head before becoming head at Copthorne in 1992. Her school became an 'outstanding' school, with inspectors praising its *strong team spirit where everyone's contribution is valued*.

She played her part as a teacher beyond school. She became a founder member of the General Teaching Council for England in 2000, spending five years as a Council member. An Ofsted inspector, she was active in teacher training, race equality and raising standards across Bradford. She also became executive headteacher at a second school, Lapage Primary School, Barkerend Road, near where she grew up.

Her delight at being recognised with such an honour was mixed with gratitude for the communities she served, the colleagues she worked with and her family that supported her.

Source: www.tes.com/news/

14 Oct 2020   Harry Gration steps down from BBC *Look North*.

Today, the Bradford-born presenter, aged nearly 70, announced his retirement after over 38 years as the voice of Yorkshire fronting the evening news.

Source: *Yorkshire Post* (14 October 2020)

15 Oct 2005   Brian Noble becomes first Rugby League coach to win three Super League Grand Finals.

Today in front of a 65,000 crowd at Old Trafford Brian Noble led Bradford Bulls to their third Grand Final. The 15-6 win over Leeds Rhinos was no classic. Their fourth such triumph since the Grand Final was introduced in 1998 (their third under Noble), and their sixth Grand Final appearance in eight years, this brought to a close a golden period of success.

Despite this ultimate achievement, it had been a tough season. In fact, it looked as if it would be their worst Super League system after they lost nine of their first 20 matches, including a 66-4 humiliation by rivals St Helens at Odsal. They won their last eight league matches to secure third place and home advantage in the first two rounds of the play-offs. They won those two rounds easily, but had the toughest of games at St Helens in the semi-final winning 23-18. This made it all the more creditable to beat the Rhinos who had played only one game under the play-off rules as a Top Two qualifier. Bulls became the first to win the Grand Final after not being in the Top Two.

Becoming the first coach to win three Grand Finals, in 2006 Noble went on to win the World Club Challenge between the best two teams in the Northern and Southern hemispheres, exactly as the team he coached did in 2002 and 2004 after the Grand Final victories against Wigan in 2003 and 2005.

From Manningham, Noble played more than 400 times for Bradford Northern as a hooker over 15 seasons, managing at the same time to hold a job as a policeman. The team did not win much, except one Yorkshire Cup Final. However, he gained international recognition, captaining the Lions for seven tests in the 1984 tour of Australasia. For six years after retirement he worked in the backroom staff, before being appointed coach in 2000.

Bradford-born and bred, Noble enjoyed a distinguished playing career and an even more distinguished coaching career for his home-town club. He was deservedly made freeman of the city in September 2006 – the first sporting hero to be given this honour – to round off the golden era of rugby league in Bradford, the most sustained period of success in team sport in Bradford's history.

Source: *The Guardian* (17 October 2005)

16 Oct 1847   Charlotte Brontë's *Jane Eyre*, an English classic, is published.

'There was no possibility of taking a walk that day.' These are the famous opening words of one of the great classic novels in the English language, published today. Written by Charlotte Brontë (1816-1855), born in Thornton and brought up in Haworth, *Jane Eyre* recounts the struggles of an orphan girl who grows up to become a governess and meets Mr. Rochester ...

The story captivated its first readers as recounted by Elizabeth Gaskell, Charlotte's first biographer: *'When the manuscript of Jane Eyre had been received by the future publishers of that remarkable novel* (Smith, Elder & Co), *it fell to the share of a gentleman connected with the firm to read it first. He was so powerfully struck by the character of the tale, that he reported his impression in very strong terms to Mr Smith who appears to have been much amused by the admiration excited...*

But when a second reader, in the person of a clear-headed Scotchman, not given to enthusiasm had taken the manuscript home in the evening, and became so deeply interested in it, as to sit up half the night to finish it, Mr Smith's curiosity was sufficiently excited to prompt him to read it for himself; and great as were the praise that had been bestowed upon it, he found that they had not exceeded the truth.'

The impact of *Jane Eyre* was immediate. It caught on like wildfire. Although some of the reviews in Gaskell's opinion were *'more tardy and more cautious'* than the popular reaction, one very positive response pleased Charlotte above all - William Makepeace Thackeray, a leading literary figure of the day whom Charlotte strongly admired.

What added to the story was the mysterious Currer Bell, the author. Nobody had heard of him. The publisher only found out the truth when Charlotte travelled down from Yorkshire to meet him, and introduced herself as the real author. Gradually, others in London literary circles found out, but the wider public who bought and read the novel knew very little.

The popular reaction to *Jane Eyre* was such that the publisher's rival, Thomas Newby, decided to bring forward the release of Emily Brontë's unpublished manuscript that he had been sitting on since the summer. Two months later, Victorian readers had the opportunity of reading a new novel called *Wuthering Heights* by Ellis Bell.

Source: *The Life of Charlotte Brontë*, Elizabeth Gaskell (1857)

17 Oct 1931   Yeadon Aerodrome opens for flights.

Surrounded by hills, and with little level ground, Bradford is not geographically suitable for aviation.

It may be a surprise to learn that Bradford's first aerodrome was built in 1910 on a reasonably level site at Rawdon Meadows, Apperley Bridge. This did not last. Bradford had to settle for a shared airport at Yeadon, three miles away inside the Leeds boundary but managed equally by the two cities.

After they bought jointly the site in 1930, the Leeds and Bradford Municipal Aerodrome opened today. Known more popularly as Yeadon Aerodrome, it was used for general aviation and training purposes. Sixty acres of grassland on a windswept plateau, alongside the old Bradford to Harrogate road, seems an unlikely site – at 681 feet above sea-level, Leeds-Bradford Airport is now the UK's highest commercial airport.

In April 1935 the first scheduled flights connected London (Heston), Yeadon and Newcastle, later extending to Edinburgh. In June, a service was launched to the Isle of Man. To accommodate passenger traffic, work started on the first terminal, but only the first wing was completed before war broke out.

The RAF requisitioned the aerodrome – it became RAF Yeadon. The British aircraft manufacturer Avro built a shadow factory. This was camouflaged, its roof disguised as a field with dummy cattle and agricultural buildings so that from the air it resembled the surrounding fields. At the time it was believed to be the largest free-standing structure in Europe. Large numbers of houses were constructed nearby for the workforce. The factory produced nearly 700 Lancaster bombers, as well as almost 4,500 Avro Ansons before it closed in December 1946

Civil flights restarted in 1947. The 1950s and 1960s brought routes to Belfast, Düsseldorf and Dublin and a daily service to London. In 1965, a new runway was built, and a new terminal building was opened three years later.

Tourism led to major expansion in the 1970s. By 1978 regional airport status was granted on condition that runways were extended. This work was completed in 1985 with a tunnel taking the A658 underneath the runway. Transatlantic flights to Canada ran from 1984 and the first chartered Concorde landed in 1986.

From unpromising beginnings Bradford now shares a major transport asset on an equal basis with its neighbour in stark contrast with its canal, rail and road communications, which all developed years later than Leeds.

Source: *Yorkshire Post* (18 October 2011)

18 Oct 1966   The University of Bradford receives its Royal Charter.

Despite being one of Britain's largest cities, Bradford had to wait to have a university for many years after almost all other similar Victorian cities had theirs. Today, it became the 40th British university.

It may have been that Bradford's success as a wool city prevented its broader educational development. The city needed technical education to make its wool industry more competitive and that led to the foundation of Bradford Technical College in 1882. After many years of campaigning for university status, the higher education side became in 1957 a College of Advanced Technology (Bradford Institute of Technology - BIT), while the further education side became what is now Bradford College.

The Charter itself reflects an interesting development of a university. Clause 2 contains standard wording for university charters: '*The object of the University shall be the advancement of learning and knowledge*'. Ted Edwards, Principal of the BIT and then the first Vice-Chancellor of the University, decided that this was not enough. He added an extra clause, '*and the application of knowledge to human welfare*'. He believed that the university should help solve the problems facing society: Thanks to this extra Charter commitment, the university created innovative facilities such as its School of Peace Studies.

A fortnight after the Charter, Harold Wilson, PM, was installed as the new Chancellor in St. George's Hall with a strong message about the importance of applied science and technology. The university's first honorary degrees were awarded to politician Barbara Castle and academic Alan Bullock, both Bradford-educated.

Bradford, finally, had its university.

Source   https://100objectsbradford.wordpress.com

18 Oct 1975   JB Priestley opens library in his name at the University of Bradford.

The rapid expansion of Bradford's university increased demand for library services. By the time a new library was opened, it had over 200,000 volumes and 53 professional and support staff. It was entirely appropriate that Britain's man of letters should give his name to it in his home city. After a small dinner party in the university attended amongst others by Harold Wilson, PM and the University's first Chancellor, Priestley unveiled a plaque today, then the party toured the new building and had a buffet lunch before a car took Priestley and his wife back home to Stratford-upon-Avon.

The library now houses a number of special collections of famous people connected with Bradford, starting with Priestley's own archive.

Source: www.bradford.ac.uk/library

19 Oct 1848 Samuel Lister secures an important patent for woolcombing with the help of Isaac Holden.

It was said of Samuel Cunliffe Lister that he obtained more patents for his inventions than anyone else in England. The one he secured today probably gave him more grief than all the others put together.

Lister devoted much of his long career to invention, taking out over 150 patents. His first patent in 1844 was a method for fringing shawls. He then turned his attention to mechanical woolcombing, the aim being to separate long fibres from the short, the long making worsted cloth, the short being used for woollens. Woolcombing was the last major wool process to be mechanised.

In 1842 Lister bought a woolcombing machine, which proved unsatisfactory. Unable to resell it, he aimed to improve it. By 1845 it evolved into a machine which produced the first pound of wool combed by machine. Further improvements led in 1848 to the square-motion comb. By this time Holden had been working with Lister and almost certainly had an input to this latest development.

Their subsequent partnership was very profitable, but in 1858 they fell out over ownership of the patent. The argument became public and lasted for the rest of their lives. In particular, a book by James Burnley (*History of Wool and Woolcombing*), financed by Holden, took Holden's side and fuelled the flames.

The whole dispute was not resolved until 7 November 1904 when Burnley withdrew his comments in a letter to Lister (now Lord Masham): *'In regard to the origination of the principle of the square motion woolcombing machine, and having perused the specification of your Patent No 11.469 of 1846 I find that such patent contains the first patented embodiment of the square motion invention ... the statement in my book that the "first patent in which the square motion principle was brought forward was dated 19th of October 1848" is necessarily incorrect, as it is now clear that the first patent dealing with the square motion principle is yours of 1846 ... and it therefore follows that any claim by Sir Isaac Holden to be entitled to the paternity of the idea is also incorrect.*

This retraction came 15 years after the incorrect statements were published, 56 years after the patent in question had been secured and, most frustratingly perhaps for Lister, seven years after Holden's death.

Source: Samuel Cunliffe Lister (*Oxford Dictionary of National Biography*)

20 Oct 1937   The King and Queen drive across Bradford.

Today was the second visit by a reigning monarch to Bradford, 19 years after the first. The new king's parents (George V and Mary) had visited Bradford in 1918. The context was the fourth year of a punishing war and the purpose was to raise morale by visiting people at work in factories. Within one day there had been no time for processions. Transport was by train and six factories were visited. It was a business-like visit.

This second visit recognised the new King and Queen (George VI and Elizabeth) who had come to the throne the year before in the most difficult and unexpected circumstances of the abdication. The context was a three-day midweek royal tour of Yorkshire. They spent Tuesday in Hull and York, staying over at Harewood House. It was a celebration, but still far from leisurely.

Unlike in 1918, only half a day was allocated for Bradford on Wednesday, but travel was by car, making possible a street procession. The schedule was tight, barely an hour for Saltaire and another hour for a ride across Bradford.

At Saltaire they just about had time to visit the main parts of Salt's Mill. They also met 21 employees who had completed 50 years at the mill, including one incredibly with 72 years' service. The party then set off past cheering crowds to Lister Park, closed off to the general public so that it could be filled by 18,000 schoolchildren. From the park, the royal car went slowly (six miles an hour) along Manningham Lane, down Cheapside and into Market Street for a 15 minute stop at the City Hall before leaving up Manchester Road. From here it travelled at normal speed to Odsal before slowing down again along Halifax Road. They were scheduled to arrive in Shelf at the Halifax boundary by 12.30pm for their onward journey.

There was little time for, and we have no record of, the new Head of the Church of England meeting his local representative, Bishop Blunt, who inadvertently triggered the abdication crisis that so dramatically changed the new king's life. Perhaps he might have taken a rueful look towards Bradford Cathedral as he turned into Market Street.

Source: *Yorkshire Post* (20 and 21 October 1937)

20 Oct 2015   Bradford wins Curry Capital of Britain yet again.

For a record-breaking six years in a row (2011-2016) Bradford won this award today.

21 Oct 1887 — Samuel Lister criticises the impact of free trade.

By 1887, aged 71, Samuel Cunliffe Lister was very wealthy and experienced. He had large investments here and overseas. He had recovered from the devastating fire at the old Manningham Mill in 1871, replacing it with the new, far grander mill. He had sold at a much-discounted price his Manningham estate to the Corporation to be turned into a public park (Lister Park) and bought a large estate at Masham in North Yorkshire. His was not a voice to ignore.

Today at the Jubilee exhibition in Manchester, Lister presented a paper on the problems with free trade (*'England's folly'*). It was a sweeping condemnation of the policies that were devastating industry ever since being implemented over forty years ago. In particular, they were wreaking havoc in the silk industry. Lister quoted examples of countries such as the USA that were embracing protectionism, and now prospering.

He could not understand why the working classes who suffered the impact had accepted free trade, asserting: *'Future historians must, indeed, marvel at the blindness of the working classes in not only permitting, but actually supporting a system so ruinous to their interests and the general prosperity of the country. It is not very creditable to their intelligence that they alone amongst all the workmen of the civilised world support a system that takes the very bread out of their mouths, however cheap it may be'.*

Three years later he spoke at the opening of the Children's Hospital which he had funded. He made further comments about workers: *'They were all less thrifty than the class above them. The working classes were most improvident, and some of their misery was caused by their want of thrift.'* At the same time he preached to his fellow capitalists: *'If employers approached their workmen without being overbearing and treated them respectfully, they would avoid strikes and irritation, than which nothing caused more friction between class and class.'*

Within two months these words sounded hollow as all these things came to a head. Lister's silk exports to the USA were badly damaged by new 49.5% tariffs imposed by President McKinley. He responded by imposing 25% pay reductions on 1,100 workers. They in turn went on strike. He complained about their *'utter want of thrift'.*

There was no meeting of minds in the 1891 Manningham Mills strike.

Source: *Bradford Daily Telegraph* (22 October 1887, 8 October 1890)

22 Oct 1816   After 46 years the Leeds/Liverpool Canal is finally completed.

Today was a momentous event in the life of one of the biggest infrastructure projects in late 18th / early 19th century England that had a major impact on its economic life. The 127-mile long Leeds / Liverpool Canal was finally complete. The first Leeds & Liverpool Canal Act had been passed in 1770 and, four years later the first stretch opened from Thackley to Skipton (Leeds to Thackley in 1777). The rest of the project had been a struggle, requiring three more Acts as the canal company sought to agree the precise route across the Pennines and into Lancashire.

The last stage from Blackburn to Liverpool had just been completed. On Saturday 19 October two large barges decorated with flags and streamers set off from Leeds. One barge had a flag inscribed with the name of John Hustler, the Bradfordian who was the one man to turn the canal into a reality. A third barge called the *Joseph Priestley* intended to accompany them, but a mishap prevented its arrival. The name belonged to the father and son, canal engineers from Bradford who had been key figures in the canal's construction. These Bradford names symbolised the canal's importance to the town's prosperity.

The barge procession reached Blackburn by the end of Monday. Today, the *Leeds Mercury* picked up the story: '*On Tuesday morning at eight o'clock, all the arrangements being completed, the proprietors' barge, attended by the Union Company and a number of other vessels decorated with flags, streamers etc and crowded by persons of the greatest respectability, entered the new part of the canal amidst the discharge of cannon and the heartfelt cheering of an immense number of spectators.*'

The excitement at the opening of the first stage in 1774 had perhaps been greater. In particular the opening of the Bingley Five Rise Locks, Britain's steepest lock staircase, led to these scenes reported in *the Leeds Intelligencer: 'This joyful and much wished for event was welcomed with the ringing of Bingley bells, a band of music, the firing of guns by the neighbouring militia, the shouts of the spectators, and all the marks of satisfaction that so important an acquisition merits; and ... it gives a pleasing prospect, not only of the practicability, but certainty, of the whole of this grand and most useful undertaking, being completed in a few years.*'

Well, more than a few years....

Source: www.bradford.gov.uk/media/2419/leeds_liverpool_2_historic_development.pdf

23 Oct 1712   Dr Richard Richardson is the first Bradfordian to be elected fellow of the Royal Society.

Scholar, botanist, physician, lord of the manor – there can have been few, if any, men like Dr Richard Richardson (1663-1741) in late 17th /early 18th century Bradford.

Four generations of the Richardson family (all boys called Richard or William) had lived at Bierley Hall before Richard Richardson was born on 6 September 1663. He attended Bradford Grammar School before studying at Oxford University and the University of Leyden in Holland. According to Bradford historian William Cudworth, this was *the highest university for medicine* at the time.

Although, having acquired a doctor's degree, he practised medicine on his return to Bradford, Richardson was wealthy enough not to have to make a living from it. His consuming interest became botany, stimulated no doubt by living as a lodger for three years with an eminent Dutch professor of botany. He travelled widely in Great Britain, in search of rare botanical specimens. He specialised in mosses and lichens.

He also built up an impressive network of like-minded collectors reflected in many volumes of correspondence. One important contact was Sir Hans Sloane, founder of Chelsea Gardens and the British Museum, also giving his name to Sloane Square. With a reputation of being the best collector in the North of England, Richardson was today elected to the Royal Society. His friend Hans Sloane was by now its president.

At Bierley Hall he built the second hothouse in England. His garden was full of exotic plants, For example, he introduced cedars from Lebanon, maybe the first in the country. In 1812 the largest was measured to have a circumference of 12 feet 8 inches.

Bierley Hall, its garden and its cedars are sadly long gone. One incongruous reminder of the family that remains is a boarded-up pub called Richardsons Arms, on Bradford Road, Oakenshaw. This was once a main road into the city but for many years deprived of passing trade by the M606 motorway that runs in parallel nearby. Near the pub stands also Richardson Street.

Source: *Round About Bradford*, William Cudworth (1876)

24 Oct 1988   Harry Ramsdens celebrate 60 years of fish 'n' chips.

The banner outside Harry Ramsdens at White Cross, Guiseley proudly announced the Diamond Jubilee Festival with a whole week of entertainment starting today. It celebrated 60 years of trading as the country's most famous fish and chips restaurant. A marquee named 'Harry Ramsden's Festival Theatre' was erected in the car park to accommodate performers and their audiences.

In 1928 Harry Ramsden (1888-1963) opened in a wooden hut, which he bought for £150, and created a special batter mix – a closely guarded secret and still used to the current day. Three years later and close to the old hut, he moved into new premises, the grandest seen for a fish and chips outlet, complete with fitted carpets, oak-panelled walls, and chandeliers. It once held the Guinness World Record for the largest fish and chips shop in the world, seating 275 people, serving nearly a million customers a year.

Ramsden worked tirelessly to build the business, not taking a holiday for ten years. He knew how to promote his name. His popularity grew during World War Two, because fish and chips were amongst a handful of items that were not rationed.

After the war the name became synonymous with the perfect location at Guiseley where the main road from the Dales splits to Leeds (through Horsforth) and Bradford (through Shipley). This also happened to be the terminus for buses from the two cities. Like many successful businesses, customers associated the product with the need to queue. On summer weekends day-trippers from Wharfedale would make Harry Ramsdens the final stop on the day out. Traffic slowed to a crawl well before the famous restaurant on the left, just before the road split, with queues of people snaking around the block.

When he celebrated 25 years of trading, one day he sold fish and chips at 1928 prices and set a world record, selling 10,000 portions that day. Large queues built up, but he laid on performers to entertain those waiting. These included his nephew Harry Corbett, who was a musician, but would soon become famous with his puppet Sooty.

After 1988 it all changed when Harry Ramsdens became a franchise operation and a classic case study of how expansion can so easily destroy the brand that has been nurtured so carefully. Eventually in 2011 the premises were sold to be reopened the next year as a Wetherby Whaler.

Source: https://www.aireboroughhistoricalsociety.co.uk/guiseley/harry-ramsdens-1988.aspx

25 Oct 1988   Councillor Eric Pickles leads the Bradford Revolution.

Today was momentous for Bradford City Council. With the tightest of margins the Conservatives gained control of the council by breaking the convention that the Lord Mayor, a Conservative, should remain neutral when voting for proposals. On this occasion he was allowed to vote for the 10-page document that the 36-year-old Leader called the Bradford Revolution.

With some 3,000 demonstrators in the streets and television camera crews everywhere, the council now voted for a controversial Thatcherite package of £50m cuts, privatisation and reorganisation and, with it, a one-third reduction of the council's workforce.

The Leader was Councillor Eric Pickles. Keighley-born (1952) and bred, he was elected as councillor in 1979 and then as Tory Group leader in February 1987. *'It should be the test of our party to remove Labour from the last vestiges of power in the North. If we can do it in Bradford, the birthplace of the Independent Labour Party, we can do it anywhere'*, he claimed.

After winning a few by-elections, the Conservatives were now in control. Pickles started to implement the proposals, but in May 1990 the Conservatives were voted out. The moment was lost.

Pickles himself moved down south and was elected an MP in Essex. In 2010 he came back to haunt Bradfordians with further rounds of austerity, this time as Minister of Communities and Local Government until 2015.

Source: *It's a Mean Old Scene*, Jim Greenhalf (2003)

25 Oct 1917   Bradford businessman loses money from Russian Revolution.

Sir James Roberts (1848-1935) owned Saltaire after Sir Titus Salt's family. As a businessman he visited Russia many times before World War One, learnt the language and made substantial investments there. However, today he lost his money after the outbreak of the Bolshevik Revolution. He tried unsuccessfully to recover the money via the Colonial and Foreign Department of Lloyds Bank where his contact was TS Eliot who worked there. In Eliot's *The Waste Land* (1922), the poet mocks the habits of Bradford businessmen who wore top hats to attend auctions at the Bradford Wool Exchange. Sir James Roberts is generally believed to be the subject of these lines:

He, the young man carbuncular, arrives,
A small house agent's clerk, with one bold stare,
One of the low on whom assurance sits
As a silk hat on a Bradford millionaire.

26 Oct 1958   BBC broadcasts documentary about JB Priestley's *Lost City*.

'Pity poor Bradford! Not only has it been lost by one of its most distinguished sons, Mr J.B. Priestley, but it remains lost.

Even the might of BBC-TV with its cameramen, technicians and producers, even the power of British Railways with its special trains, even the aid of a host of Bradfordians – all have failed to help him find it again.

Mr Priestley's verdict on the place after a sentimental journey to put the clock back more than forty years and so rediscover the days of its youth is that while it may not be mean and shabby it is not as good as it once promised to be.

It's not good enough for the real Bradfordian.'

So started the TV review in the *Telegraph & Argus* from last night's BBC-TV documentary and just one contribution to the local furore that accompanied the programme. This had even started on the basis of what the *Radio Times* said about it in advance, especially its title. On such slender evidence hostile letters were published in the local press before the programme was shown.

Over-sensitive Bradfordians thought that it was a film denigrating Bradford and that those who did not know the city would gain the wrong impression. Priestley was not entitled to comment about a city he had left long ago.

The reality is that it was a nostalgic and highly personal view from perhaps its most famous son that the city he remembered had disappeared. The film starts with Priestley, now 64 years old, being greeted off the train at Forster Square by a journalist who then takes him on a tour of the places he remembered – Saltburn Place where he lived from a boy, Swan Arcade where he worked as an office clerk, the markets he used to frequent, Lister Park where he heard outdoor concerts, the Theatre Royal which he visited, the Bradford Arts Club where he had had been member and the Civic Playhouse where he had been president He tried to call up old contacts from the past, but they had either died or gone away – Priestley lamented the loss of much of his generation from World War One.

Until his last few years Priestley had an uneasy relationship with the City that he had left. This was a very good example of the tensions.

Source: *The Rebel Tyke: Bradford and JB Priestley*, Peter Holdsworth (1994)

27 Oct 1899   Councillor Fred Jowett wins a difficult victory in securing a slum clearance plan.

Before he rose to be a significant force in the upper echelons of the Independent Labour Party (ILP), Fred Jowett cut his political teeth as a councillor for Bradford City Council. Elected in 1892 as its first-ever ILP councillor in the Manningham Ward, he was involved in several local issues over the next fifteen years.

One of the earliest he tackled was slum clearance. The 1890 Housing of the Working Classes Act empowered local authorities to condemn slum housing, purchase the land and finance new housing. At the end of the 19th century housing was a black blot on the city. Rows of soot-covered back-to-back housing separated only by brick yards and privy middens were extremely unhealthy places to live. Over one in five of all children born died before they were one year old, twice as many as those born in better housed parts of Bradford.

In 1894 Councillor Jowett started to speak at Council meetings about such slums. His motion that the Sanitary Committee on which he sat should take action under the new act received just five votes (at the time there were only three ILP councillors). His interest led him to become the committee vice-chairman and then in 1899 the chairman. He started a campaign to clear the slums.

The Conservative Leader of the day tried delaying tactics. For example, he passed a resolution that no privy midden should be replaced with a water-closet until the Committee had inspected it, which just led Jowett to issue large numbers of summons for inspections.

In 1898 Jowett persuaded the Medical Officer to declare officially that one of the worst slums, Longlands, containing over 900 people from large, wretched Irish families, was insanitary. Under the 1890 Act the Council was compelled to propose an improvement scheme. One scheme was rejected, but today after a powerful speech a revised scheme was agreed by one vote.

Victory was short-lived. Elections the next month changed the political composition against the scheme. Three months later an amendment from Jowett was again defeated. However, finally in August after a further amendment the improvement scheme was passed.

It was not the first or the last time when Jowett's tenacity won the day. His next cause was to become the first municipal service in the country for school meals.

Source: *Socialism Over Sixty Years: The life of Jowett of Bradford (1864-1944)*, Fenner Brockway (1946)

28 Oct 1907 — The first-ever school meals service in the UK is launched at Green Lane School.

Although Manchester provided some dinners for destitute and poorly nourished children from 1879, Bradford was the first local authority to organise school meals for all pupils. Today the first school meal was served at Green Lane Board School in Manningham – *'a meal of barley broth and fruit tart, with bread and a mug of water for each child'*.

The introduction of school meals is one of several examples of Bradford innovation in social welfare. From its earliest days as a booming wool town through the Victorian Age, the fast-growing city had seen great poverty among its industrial workers and their families. It became a centre of radical ideas and practice in alleviating these conditions, often strongly influenced by nonconformism, a strong sense of social obligation and the value of education.

The champions of this innovation were Fred Jowett, the city's first Socialist MP, and Margaret McMillan, social reformer, who had become very influential as a member of the Bradford School Board. Jowett was a pioneer of 'municipal socialism' to improve the lives of working people. McMillan saw from medical inspections that children were under-nourished and this was the most serious health concern in the city. It led to listlessness and disease, and meant children could not benefit from their education. However, until now schools were powerless to help.

After many years of campaigning, the Provision of Meals Act was passed in 1906 in Parliament and Bradford became the first council to offer this service. A school meals depot was set up at Green Lane School in 1907, supplying food to several schools in the poorest parts of the city. The headmaster was one Jonathan Priestley, father of Bradford's great writer, JB Priestley. The son was then aged 13 and recalled in his 1946 preface to Fenner Brockway's biography of Fred Jowett the great local and national press interest in the story.

It is fitting for Jonathan Priestley to be linked with this major innovation in welfare. From a poor family himself, he was a nonconformist, socialist and passionate believer in the value of education. His son remembered him as *'unselfish, brave, honourable, public-spirited. He was the man socialists have in mind when they write about socialism'*.

Source: (University of Bradford)
http://out.easycounter.com/external/100objectsbradford.wordpress.com
Object 81

29 Oct 1887   Closure of Saltaire exhibition provides boost to Shipley Glen.

In 1854 the *Bradford Observer* printed a letter from 'An Operative':

'I am a poor man. I live in a back street, where ground is measured out by inches. Dark, ill-looking dwellings, the hotbeds of disease, are my only prospect. What wonder, being so cooped up, that I often pine for pure air and unbounded prospect; that I long for the wide-spreading moor or the deep solitary glen where, untrammelled by the kerbstone of the street or the stinted footpath of the fields, I may roam unmolested.'

Life in cramped unhealthy conditions for workers in the mid-19th century led to such pleas for open space, fresh air and exercise that public amenities became popular. Laws controlling working hours were gradually loosened.

From the 1850s Shipley Glen became a popular local beauty spot attracting workers from nearby Saltaire village and, with the help of the new railway, from Bradford itself. Although it was technically in Baildon and at least a mile away from the nearest part of Shipley, the name stuck. It comprised a walk through woodland up to the edge of the moor on a grassy plateau shown on the map as Bracken Hall Green with some millstone grit crags over a steep valley to Loadstone Beck.

It attracted walkers, families, couples, Sunday School outings and sometimes mass meetings of protest beyond the jurisdiction of local towns. There were a few cafes, tea rooms and places for accommodation such as the British Temperance House. Bank holidays (four new paid days off work from 1871 after the Bank Holidays Act) and summer weekends became crowded with visitors.

The Royal Yorkshire Jubilee Exhibition in 1887 was conceived by Titus Salt Junior celebrating a new School of Art and Science in Saltaire and the Queen's Golden Jubilee. Opening on 6 May, it was a great success, attracting over 800,000 visitors by the time it closed today.

Much of the success lay in a series of adventurous features which re-appeared the next year on Shipley Glen, making this an even more popular destination. These included the giant Camera Obscura, the Toboggan Slide and the Ocean Wave Switchback. Thereafter, Shipley Glen became known not just as a local beauty spot, but as a fairground with exciting rides.

Eight years later it also became the home of the famous Shipley Glen Tramway.

Source: *Shipley Glen: The History and Development of a Victorian Playground*, Alan Cattell (2018)

30 Oct 1963 The longest strike in the textile industry starts – to end in ignominy.

When one considers the general state of industrial unrest in 19th century Bradford, it is a surprise to discover that the longest strike in the British textile industry started many years later in 1963. It is also a surprise that it started in a small mill on the rural outskirts of Baildon rather than in a large inner-city mill.

Today 250 workers walked out of the dyeworks at William Denby & Sons Ltd, because a foreman operated a machine during a work break. The next morning they each received a letter from the managing director, saying that they were sacked but could have their jobs back under certain conditions.

For 22 years the production side of the works had been a closed shop operated by the National Union of Dyers, Bleachers and Textile Workers. Now the letter stated that those who returned should agree to co-operate with the management instead of blindly following shop stewards. Employees could belong to a union, but the managing director, not the union, would choose who would work for him. In other words, he was not going to take back 'troublemakers', nor have a closed shop.

Around 100 employees found other jobs; 40 returned to Denby's, leaving 115 on strike (of whom 14 were women). Denby's took on more workers, mainly non-unionists and often untrained.

The end came on 24 February 1965. The press reported that *the union had decided no useful purpose would be served by continuing in its present form the dispute at William Denby & Sons but headquarters said it meant the firm should remain "black"*. The strike had lasted 481 days, believed to be the longest-running strike in the history of British textiles.

In its review of the dispute, three weeks later, the *Daily Mirror* reported the management's view that its actions had been justified. Productivity and profits were up despite the strike. Previous restrictive practices (eg complete ban on overtime) had disappeared. The union were equally adamant that they had been right. Management had only carried out the most profitable work during the strike. *'They were doing the easiest work because the blacklegs were not skilled enough to do the rest.'*

The *Daily Mirror*, newspaper for the workers, believed that it was a complete victory for management.

This was a classic dispute of its time. Since 1990 closed shops have been illegal.

Source: *Daily Mirror* (18 March 1965)

31 Oct 1986   His widow unveils statue to JB Priestley.

Very few statues have been erected to celebrate Bradford's famous. There can be little argument that JB Priestley's achievements deserve a statue, even if the city only recognised this posthumously. The statue was unveiled by Priestley's third wife, Jacquetta Hawkes. She and others had only the previous evening celebrated a major refurbishment of the Alhambra Theatre just across the road from the statue. Had he lived, her husband surely would have been a guest of honour at such a celebration of theatre in Bradford.

Standing above a square plinth, just in front of the National Science and Media Museum, the statue is, as befitted his personality, larger than life, coat blowing in the wind, looking out over the city centre towards the northern moors, barely visible even on a bright day (see photograph at end of December). On each side of the plinth are respectively the words 'JB Priestley', 'Author', '1894-1984' and 'Dramatist'. Underneath 'Author' is an engraved quotation from one of his most famous novels, and by all accounts his favourite, *Bright Day* (1946). This is a thinly disguised description of his native city:

'Lost in its smoky valley among the Pennine hills, bristling with tall mill chimneys, with its face of blackened stone, Bruddersford is generally held to be an ugly city; and so I suppose it is, but it always seemed to me to have the kind of ugliness that could not only be tolerated but often enjoyed; it was grim but not mean. And the moors were always there and the horizon never without its promise. No Bruddersford man could be exiled from the upland and blue air, he always had one foot on the heather; he had only to pay his tuppence on the tram and then climb for half an hour to hear the larks and curlews, to feel the old rocks warming in the sun, to see the harebells trembling in the shade.'

NOVEMBER

1 Nov 1987   Jonathan Silver opens the new 1853 gallery at Salts Mill dedicated to Hockney's art.

It was typical of Jonathan Silver's energy that, having bought the huge derelict Salts Mill just three months ago, he was now ready to open it as a major art gallery to exhibit the works of his old friend, Bradford's David Hockney.

Today he threw a champagne reception for hundreds of guests, including Hockney's mother. The old spinning room, 10,000 sq ft, was hanging 53 Hockney paintings, mostly from the old steam pipes that used to heat the room. The paintings were accompanied by large flower displays in exotic vases and by the sound of classical music. The next day it was open to the public, free of charge as it remains to the current day.

The 1853 Gallery, named after the year that the mill was first open, also had books and postcards for sale, and operas played in the background. Over the next ten years it exhibited what became the largest single collection of Hockney's work in the world from paintings that Silver bought (over 100) and borrowed. It also put on special exhibitions of his work (eg his opera set designs).

He held unique events such as the occasion on 10 November 1989 when Silver persuaded his friend to fax a painting from Los Angeles to Salts Mill. Forever an experimenter, Hockney faxed *Tennis*, made up of 144 sheets, taking 45 minutes to arrive over two machines. Guests at the evening event watched the painting being assembled on the wall, amid a blaze of media publicity.

In the old weaving sheds Silver put on opera and theatre productions, beginning with Opera North's community performance of *West Side Story* in 1988 and including the National Theatre production of *The Trackers of Oxyrhynchus* (1990) by his friend Tony Harrison. Silver also commissioned Harrison's *Poetry or Bust* (1993), the story of the Victorian poet John Nicholson, an employee of Sir Titus Salt.

In 1994 Salts Mill won the Arts Council's 'centres for arts' award. The development of Salts Mill generated jobs for over 1,000 people, and inspired other companies and organisations to undertake restoration projects.

Other external recognition of Silver's success was in the pipeline, but it turned out he was living on borrowed time.

Source: Jonathan Silver (*Oxford Dictionary of National Biography*)

2 Nov 1963   The Cathedral completes its celebration of the new East extension.

Bradford was made a diocese in 1919. The parish church of St. Peter's became overnight a cathedral. It took 44 years and four bishops of Bradford before building extensions were completed to create the feel of a cathedral. They comprised the new Sanctuary, the Lady Chapel and the Chapel of the Holy Spirit. Seen from the western side of the church, the extensions seemed almost to double the length of the building. The focal point of the Sanctuary was an altar, 11 feet long, built in oak.

Today (Saturday) saw the final day of three days of celebrations with a special 3pm choral evensong of thanksgiving for 700 lay representatives of parishes in the diocese, unable to attend the consecration.

Two days before, the Archbishop of York, Dr Donald Coggan, who had also been the third Bishop of Bradford from 1956 to 1961, consecrated the new extension. He said that *'(it) combined the beauty of the old and the new in wonderful harmony'*. A congregation of 1,000 included three Roman Catholic priests from the city, almost certainly the first time priests appeared officially in the building since the Reformation in the 16th century.

The extensions also included the refitting of the East Window, containing valuable stained glass windows designed by William Morris 100 years earlier. Originally one window, it was now refitted as three separate windows, a feat involving 30,000 pieces of glass.

The architect also had strong Bradford connections. Born in Ilkley, Sir Edward Maufe, whose father Henry Muff was a draper at Brown Muff & Co, married a niece of Sir Titus Salt. After changing his name by deed poll from Muff to Maufe, he became an architect with a national reputation, responsible for the design of Guildford Cathedral. He was present at this week's consecration.

Source: *Telegraph & Argus* (1 November 1963)

2 Nov 1982   Richard Whiteley launches Channel 4 with *Countdown.*

Today British television saw the arrival of Channel 4. At 4.45pm its first programme the quiz *Countdown* was launched. The first person on the new channel was Richard Whiteley. Born in Bradford and brought up in Baildon, he was educated at Giggleswick School and Cambridge University. He was to introduce *Countdown* for the next 23 years. After he finished, he was thought to have been seen on screen longer than any other, except for the girl who appeared on the old test card.

3 Nov 1973   Thirty-three are arrested after last-ditch protest against closure of Kirkgate Market.

Today, late on Saturday afternoon, 33 people had been arrested after demonstrations against the closure of Bradford's century-old Kirkgate Market. Police reinforcements were required before demonstrators were led out and bundled into waiting vans with crowds jeering at the police officers near the market entrance. The market was coming to a close, with most traders already having closed their stalls. They had not taken part in the protest.

It seemed a significant moment for those interested in retaining Bradford's Victorian heritage, similar to the closure of Swan Arcade some ten years earlier. Both were opened in the late 1870s, both representing a new type of retail experience for the time and now both would be gone.

Kirkgate Market was designed by Lockwood and Mawson, Bradford's leading Victorian architects. It seemed another nail in the coffin for the past and another undeserved victory for modern replacements, largely unloved. It had an impressive façade that dominated the whole of Kirkgate's top side. It was constructed around an iron cast frame, painted green and gold bronze, with two domes each 60 feet high, enclosing an area of 5,520 square yards. The outside was decorated in an Italianate style, with large figures of Pomona and Flora over the arched entrance.

At the corner with Darley Street stood in the early days the famous Leuchters Restaurant, a major social hub of the day. The name LEUCHTERS was engraved in stone at the top of the building, long after the restaurant ceased to exist.

Bradford had held a market here for centuries. Back in 1251, King Henry III gave Edmund de Lacy Lord of the Manor permission to hold a market every Thursday. The market place was where Ivegate joined Westgate, at one end of today's Kirkgate. In 1951 there was a celebration of the 700th anniversary that included a mayoral procession by horse and carriage, and a dinner and speeches inside the market.

The market moved its site many times over the passing years, until it settled on a site surrounding the old Manor House, which had been abandoned as a private residence.

It is impossible to imagine anyone protesting about the threat of closure of the Arndale Shopping Centre, a functional concrete block that replaced the old Kirkgate Market, or the current Kirkgate Shopping Centre that it later developed into.

Source: *Telegraph & Argus* (5 November 1973)

4 Nov 2010   Sir Ken Morrison receives the Freedom of the City for his contribution to UK retailing.

There can be no argument about Sir Ken Morrison (1931-2017), a proud Bradfordian, deserving the Freedom of the City today. The supermarket, Morrisons, had been a household name for many years, even though the man behind it was much less well-known outside West Yorkshire. It was one of the UK's top four with 375 stores, serving over nine million customers a week, by the time of his retirement in 2008. He was one of the richest men in the UK and also the longest-serving chairman of a top FTSE 100 public company.

Educated at Bradford Grammar School, he took over his father's small grocery business on return from National Service in 1952. His father had started selling eggs and butter from a single market stall. Morrison remembered school holidays spent checking eggs for defects. By the time he took over, there were three stalls in Rawson Market and a double shop unit in nearby James Street with a combined turnover of £121,000.

In 1961 he opened his first supermarket in a converted cinema in Girlington, spotting self-service as a new trend. Over the next 40 years he gradually acquired branches over Yorkshire, then up into the North-East and down into the Midlands. He made his money by small profit margins and volume selling. He had a reputation for meticulate attention to detail and regular unannounced checking of his shops for quality and freshness.

His rise was gradual and seemingly unstoppable. However, curiously, well after most would have thought of retirement, he embarked on a project which almost derailed the whole company. In 2004 Morrisons acquired Safeway. This felt strange at the time, because Morrisons had not grown through major acquisitions and mergers and Safeway did not seem a natural partner. Morrisons had a strong cost-conscious northern working class focus, whereas Safeway attracted the middle classes in the South and Midlands where the focus was on value. For some time Morrisons attracted bad headlines and profit warnings. It took two or three years before the integration finally seemed to work. Shortly after, he retired.

Morrison's success stood out because times in Bradford during his working life were hard for business with high unemployment and general economic decline. He died leaving a personal fortune of £235m and the UK's fourth-biggest supermarket with more than 500 stores bearing his name.

Source: Obituary, *The Guardian* (1 February 2017)

5 Nov 2015   At last the 'Wastefield' hole becomes the new Westfield shopping complex.

It was a long time coming. A large empty space had dominated the city centre for most of ten years. Where for a century Forster Square had dominated the same space, a bustling area with shoppers, office workers and others passing through, there had been a building site, most of the time boarded up with no sign of construction taking place. It was called 'Wastefield', or 'the Bradford hole' and many other names, a constant source of embarrassment to anyone with an attachment for the city or a memory of better days.

Now the hole was filled to everyone's relief. The construction over the past two years had come to fruition and a new shopping complex was today open for business. There was, however, no sense of the local pride that existed in the 19th century as Bradford pulled itself away from a town of squalor with fine new buildings such as St. George's Hall and the Wool Exchange. The new complex was hardly innovative or special to Bradford, being a Westfield development that had been seen in several other cities in the previous twenty years. The shops were bulk standard chains, without much character, though at least new and a better quality than generally found elsewhere in the city centre. It was called The Broadway with a nod to the city's past, but there was no return to the Forster Square of the past. The view across to the Cathedral and the old General Post Office (now the Kala Sangam arts centre) was now completely cut off. The statue to WE Forster, no longer in prime position by the railway station, was largely hidden from view at the back entrance to The Broadway.

Context is everything. This was a major investment in a city that had struggled for a long time with a negative image of a collapsing economy, lack of job opportunities for the young, poor transport connections and inner-city racial tensions, as ever being compared with neighbouring Leeds that over the past 20 years had been booming. Then came the credit crunch (which had triggered years of delay with the Westfield project) and public austerity (one third of the City Council's budget cut in five years).   .

It was a long time coming, but it is here and surely a step in the right direction.

Source: *The Guardian* (2 November 2015)

6 Nov 1914   The *Bradford Weekly Telegraph* prints roll call of first battalion of Bradford Pals.

On 4 August 1914 the United Kingdom declared war on Germany. The next day Lord Kitchener was appointed Secretary of State for War. On 7 August he initiated a volunteer recruitment drive which saw 100,000 men enlist in two weeks.

On 3 September the Lord Mayor of Bradford called for a new Bradford Battalion to fight the war. Today, two months later, the *Bradford Weekly Telegraph* printed a full list of all who had enrolled in the first Bradford Pals Battalion. In early 1915 a second Battalion was enlisted.

The roll call started with this preamble:

'When the history of our time comes to be written, the local historians will have abundant information as to how the citizens of Bradford rallied to serve their country. Perhaps the most notable chapter of that history will be the story of the formation of the Bradford Battalion of the Prince of Wales' Own West Yorkshire Regiment – a Battalion 1,064 strong with twenty-five officers, and one which we are hoping will win such fame in the future as to reflect the greatest credit upon a great city.

It is only about two months since the idea of forming a Bradford Battalion was first suggested, but in an amazing short space of time the full strength of the Battalion was achieved and a waiting list established. Throughout the city, amongst all classes, from mill-workers to professional men a wave of enthusiasm rolled at the country's call to service. They threw themselves into the preparatory drilling with a zeal and thoroughness that displayed a keen desire to be doing their country's fighting, and it was soon evident that Bradford's contribution to the Regiment would be a brave and efficient Battalion.

We are able to give a complete record of the full strength of the Battalion, and this, we venture to think, will prove an interesting document for many years to come. It shows at a glance where the real patriotic feeling lies, and should be an incentive to young men who may not have yet responded to their country's call.'

There follows lists of 25 officers, (for each, up to seven lines of background information) and 1,064 men (for each, just the civilian profession, trade, or job).

Fine words indeed!

By 1918 only three out of 20 of those listed returned home.

Source: *Bradford Weekly Telegraph* (6 November 1914)

7 Nov 1973   Little Germany is declared a conservation area.

Today marked an important point in the development of the city centre for all those who had watched with horror the destruction of fine Victorian buildings in the late 1950s and through the 1960s. The area known since the 19th century as Little Germany was now designated a conservation area.

Bounded by the triangle between current day Church Bank/ Barkerend Road, Leeds Road and Shipley Airedale Road, the area was developed from the 1850s as German merchants emigrated to Bradford. As their expertise lay more in exporting than manufacturing, they built warehouses for the storage and sale of their goods for export. Previously, textiles would be displayed at places like Piece Hall (closed 1853), but, as the wool industry grew, the new warehouses enabled merchants to display goods on their own premises.

The warehouses were tall imposing sandstone buildings in narrow streets, some of the finest in the UK. In the conservation area are 85 buildings constructed between 1855 and 1890, of which 55 are listed. The architecture is predominantly neoclassical in style with an Italian influence. Some merchants and workers lived in homes in the area.

They are now predominantly used for offices, such as Bradford's Chamber of Commerce which can be found here. Some have a very interesting history of change of use. For example, what was built as Temperance Hall turned into the home of the Independent Labour Party founded in 1893. It then became one of Bradford's early cinemas, was closed and re-opened as a theatre called Jowett Hall (after Bradford's first Labour MP). It was burnt down in 1935 and rebuilt as the Civic Playhouse, where it also showed films again. After changes of management it is now the Bradford Playhouse.

A unique conservation area, Little Germany has often been used for period productions on film and TV such as *Downton Abbey, Gentleman Jack, Peaky Blinders*.

Source: *Little Germany: A History of Bradford's Germans,* Susan Duxbury-Neumann (2015)

8 Nov 1816   Lesbian Anne Lister writes in diary using secret code about early lover.

Today's extract from Anne Lister's diary about an early lover, Anne Belcombe, is only accessible to the modern reader because of a Bradford schoolmaster.

'Anne & I lay awake last night till 4 in the morning. I let her into my penchant for the ladies. .... Told her that she ought not to deceive herself as to the nature of my sentiments & the strictness of my intentions towards her. I asked Anne if she liked me the less for my candour. She said no, kissed me & proved by her manner that she did not.'

Anne Lister (1791-1840) owned Shibden Hall, near Halifax. From her early teens until her death she kept a comprehensive diary. John Lister, a distant relative of Anne's, eventually inherited the manor house after her death. He found the diary hidden behind wood panelling. It describes the life and loves of a lesbian – the most personal parts being in code. It comprises 26 volumes – around five million words, one-sixth in code.

John asked his friend Arthur Burrell to help crack the code. Burrell taught classics at Bradford Grammar School from 1882 to 1900. Early one morning in the 1890s they cracked the code. Shortly before his death, Burrell wrote a letter in 1936 to reveal the code to the librarian at Halifax, now the custodian of the diaries.

'Up to that time we knew nothing of the cipher alphabet. I distinctly remember .... telling Mr Lister that I was certain of two letters, 'h' and 'e'; and I asked him if there was any likelihood that a further clue could be found. We then examined one of the boxes behind the panels and ... we found on a scrap of paper these words "In God is my....". We at once saw that the word must be "hope" and the 'h' and 'e' corresponded with my guess. The word 'hope' was in cipher. With these four letters almost certain we began very late at night to find the remaining clues. We finished at 2 am....The part written in cipher turned out after examination to be entirely unpublishable. Mr Lister was distressed but he refused to take my advice, which was that he should burn all 26 volumes. He was, as you know an antiquarian, and my suggestion seemed sacrilege, which perhaps it was'.

Source: *The Secret Diaries of Miss Anne Lister*, editor Helena Whitbread (2010)

9 Nov 1910   Jacob Moser is elected Lord Mayor.

One of a number of prominent Jews who emigrated from Germany in the middle of the 19th century, Jacob Moser (1839-1922) today became the second to be elected Lord Mayor. Like Charles Semon, his predecessor over 40 years earlier, he was a successful businessman, respected politician and generous philanthropist who contributed much to Bradford's civic life.

Remarkably he managed to maintain throughout his life the strongest links with his home town in Germany, his spiritual home in Palestine and his adopted city of Bradford.

Born in Holstein (then under Danish, later German rule), he worked in Hamburg and Paris before coming to Bradford in his mid-20s where he entered a partnership (Edelstein, Moser and Co) dealing in a wide range of finished textile products. It became very prosperous, enabling him to travel widely and play a full part in public affairs.

He was a leading figure in the city's small Jewish community, being the person behind the founding of the Reform Synagogue in 1881. He developed strong links in Palestine, becoming a member of the Zionist Central Council, the Anglo-Palestinian Corporation and the Jewish National Fund. For example, he made a major contribution to the establishment of the first Hebrew High School in Jaffa.

In Bradford Moser helped to found the Bradford Charity Organisation Society, the City Guild of Help and the Bradford Technical School that opened in 1882. He served on the board of the Infirmary from 1883 and helped fund the new hospital. In 1898 he was involved in setting up a benevolent fund for the old and infirm of the city. He supported the local Children's Hospital and gave 12,000 books to Bradford Central Library.

He entered local politics in 1896 as an Independent member for Manningham, then later served Heaton from 1901-04 and Little Horton from 1909. Honoured as Lord Mayor of Bradford, he also received the freedom of his home town of Kappeln in Germany.

Source: *How A City Grows*, Horace Hird (1966)

9 Nov 1899   Bradford is extended to include Eccleshill, Idle, North Bierley, Thornton and Tong.

Source: *How A City Grows*, Horace Hird (1966)

10 Nov 1980 Denis Healey fails by just 10 votes to become leader of the Labour Party.

Denis Healey (1917-2015) came the closest that anyone educated in Bradford has ever reached the office of Prime Minister. Today was the most critical date in his political career. Having led left-winger Michael Foot in the first ballot by a margin of 29 votes, the more moderate Healey was defeated by 139 votes to 129 in the second. The margin of 10 votes meant that he just fell short of becoming the Leader of the Labour Party.

In one of the key 'What if?' moments of the 20th century, Healey lost the opportunity to challenge Margaret Thatcher at the next election. For many commentators he was the 'best Prime Minister we never had', an opinion based partly on Thatcher's apparent view that he was the only Labour politician capable of beating her. Instead, Foot lost heavily in the 1983 election, Thatcher ruled for another nine years and the Social Democratic Party (SDP) was created.

Healey did, however, come out on top ten months later. After a difficult decade in the 1970s the Labour Party was fast moving left. Foot had won and now another left-winger Tony Benn challenged Healey for the Deputy Leadership. Another very close margin (just 0.8%) gave Healey victory. The effect for many was to save the Labour Party from being completely wiped out; it eventually led to Tony Blair's victory in 1997.

Born in Kent, five-year-old Healey moved to Keighley after his father was appointed head of Keighley Technical College. Healey was educated at Bradford Grammar School from the age of eight. He won an exhibition in classics to Balliol College, Oxford where he gained a double first.

After commendable active service in the war, winning a military MBE, Healey tried unsuccessfully for Parliament. He became Labour Party's international secretary, an influential role giving him invaluable experience and contacts. He won a by-election in 1952. In opposition until 1964 his outstanding ability and war record made him an ideal Defence Secretary where he had to oversee an unpopular series of budget cuts (1964-1970).

When Labour returned in 1974, he became Chancellor of the Exchequer in the most difficult circumstances, a sterling crisis forcing him to secure a loan from the International Monetary Fund.

Outside politics Healey developed a wide range of intellectual and artistic interests - his 'hinterland' that made him a more effective politician.

Source: Denis Healey (*Oxford Dictionary of National Biography*)

11 Nov 1342   On this day John Northrop's heirs will give three horn blasts at Bradford market-place.

In medieval times wild boars roamed. They were dangerous, capable of killing people. One such inhabited Cliffe Wood, north of the parish church. The lord of the manor offered a reward for its capture. One day, John Northrop of Manningham, walking through the wood, saw the boar drinking from a well. He was armed and speared the boar which died straightaway. Being on an errand, he could not claim his reward directly, but as evidence he cut the tongue from the dead boar and put it in his pouch.

Another man passed by, saw the dead boar and realised his opportunity. He cut off its head which he presented for his claim. As he was about to be rewarded, John Northrop appeared and produced the tongue, proving that he should be rewarded as the boar's killer. The reward was said to be a piece of land in Great Horton called Hunt Yard, which Northrop received in 1342. Hence forward, on St Martin's day (11 November) Northrop and his heirs should go with a hunting dog to the market-place (where Kirkgate crossed Westgate and Ivegate) and blow his horn three times in memory.

The tradition died out, but there is a record of it taking place as late as 1789.

When Bradford was granted a Charter of Incorporation in 1847, its coat of arms included the head of a tongueless boar, a well and three bugle horns, the whole topped by a sprig from Cliffe Wood.

Source: *Some Bits of Bradford History,* Janet Senior (2018)

11 Nov 1918   The Armistice is celebrated.

Overjoyed and orderly crowds

'When the glad tidings reached Bradford, flags were unfurled on the masts of public buildings and from business and private houses, and every conceivable kind of vehicle, from the pram, and to the tram, carried Union Jacks. At mid-day the mill whistles screeched for a long time, and almost with accord the workpeople ceased their labours. In the afternoon the whole city was on holiday, all ways led to the central streets, which were thronged with masses of happy people. At first the glad feelings were subdued after the restraint of four years of trial, but gradually as the younger spirits became more joyful, marching through the city singing patriotic airs, everybody appeared overjoyed.'

Source: *Yorkshire Post* (12 November 1911)

12 Nov 1921   John William Gott is arrested for sale of blasphemous leaflets.

'At 7.30pm (today) *the appellant was seen at Stratford Broadway* (London)*, assisted by another man, and surrounded by a large crowd, selling two papers, one entitled "The Rib-Tickler" and the other entitled "The Liberator"....The appellant and his assistant were also holding placards in front of them. There was no shouting to attract the crowd. The price of the papers was 2d, and a considerable number of persons bought them. One man said "You ought to be ashamed of yourself" and one woman exclaimed "Disgusting! Disgusting!" Nothing further occurred. The appellant was then arrested by an inspector of police.'*

The appellant was John William Gott (1866-1922), a self-employed tailor from Bradford, the speaker was a QC for the defence and the venue was the Court of Appeal which on 17 January 1922 was listening to an appeal by Gott for a conviction of nine months' hard labour for blasphemy arising from today's arrest.

The defence claimed that *'the test was whether the effect of the pamphlets, not on a person of strong religious feelings, but on the man in the street, would be such as to render likely a breach of the peace. The evidence was to the contrary. Moreover, people knew what they were buying and had to pay to read it, because on the cover of "The Rib-Tickler" appeared the words "JW Gott, prosecuted for blasphemy".'*

The Lord Chief Justice, giving the judgement, said that *'the documents were most offensively blasphemous and calculatedly offensive to anyone in sympathy with the Christian religion, whether he were a strong Christian or a lukewarm Christian.... It did not require a strongly religious Christian to be outraged by a description of "Jesus Christ entering Jerusalem like a circus clown on two donkeys".... There was no mis-direction, or non-direction in the summing up, and the Court would not interfere with the conviction'.*

So Gott became the subject of the last successful public prosecution in England for blasphemy.

He had previous. Three times he had been prosecuted for blasphemy. In Bradford, he was prominent in the National Secular Society, then he managed the *Truth Seeker*, a local penny monthly free-thought periodical. He was involved in numerous similar ventures, including speaking in anti-Christian lecture tours.

By modern standards, his offence was trivial, his punishment excessive. He died of cancer shortly after leaving prison.

Source: John William Gott (*Oxford Dictionary of National Biography*)

13 Nov 1956   Miriam Lord delivers a Margaret McMillan Memorial Lecture in the House of Commons.

As with most people she came into contact with, Margaret McMillan made a strong impression on Miriam Lord (1885-1968). Twenty-five years her junior, Miriam had devoted her working life to Margaret McMillan's ideals and now today she had the ideal opportunity to say so in public in the best possible way.

Born in Bradford into a socialist family (her father was a founder member of the Independent Labour Party), Miriam started working life as an untrained teacher at Belle Vue Girls' Secondary School, Manningham before attending a teacher training course at Saffron Waldron Teacher Training College. Qualified in 1908, she returned to teach at Belle Vue. Unusually for the time she took a further course in nursery school education at Manchester University. In 1920 she was appointed headmistress of a school in Cambridge before returning a year later as Superintendent of Lilycroft Open-air Nursery School.

The Nursery School Movement was in its infancy and Miriam's school on Lilycroft Road was identified as a showpiece of best practice, attracting many visitors from around the world to view it and hear her talks. Not far away, the Miriam Lord Primary School in Bavaria Place, Manningham still welcomes children in her memory.

American-born Margaret McMillan had only worked in Bradford from 1893 to 1902, but was instrumental in many educational and social reforms for children that became deeply embedded in Bradford and the country at large. They were built on the premise that children needed healthy lives to benefit fully from education. Nursery school education, including the open-air nursery school movement, was one such example.

In today's talk Miriam explained in detail how she had been inspired by Margaret McMillan's leadership that had made her own career possible. Margaret herself had experienced an idyllic early childhood in New York State that contrasted greatly with the dull, rigid early education that she witnessed in Bradford and elsewhere.

Miriam recalled the incredible power and passion in speeches that Margaret had given on Sunday nights at St. George's Hall. She claimed: *'This was no ephemeral, emotional experience. Those who had "seen" thereafter led changed lives. They discovered hidden depths within themselves. In service and sacrifice they found hidden joy in the release of new powers.'*

Source: *Margaret McMillan in Bradford*, Miriam Lord (1956)

14 Nov 1938   Record-breaking Civic Playhouse production of *When We Are Married* is first performed.

Today was the start of probably the most successful production of a play ever performed on a Bradford stage. The Civic Playhouse was one of the best amateur theatres in the country during the middle of the 20th century. Its president was JB Priestley and one of his classic comedies opened at the Civic – a landmark event for the local theatre.

All the local press reviews came to the same conclusion: *When We Are Married* was a resounding success. The *Telegraph & Argus* was in no doubt: '(The play) *had a hearty send-off last night at Bradford Civic Playhouse where every one of 15 players is admirably cast. It is a rollicking, unpretentious comedy about three Cleckleywyke couples who, about to celebrate their silver wedding anniversaries, were suddenly told that they weren't married. What with the husbands being leading lights in the township and at the Lane End Chapel, the fat was properly in the fire.'*

The Civic production of this classic-to-be is an admirable example of teamwork in which each part dovetails into the next with a finish that never fails to please. There is no forcing of character or dialogue, and while each player gives a distinctive performance that lingers on the memory, the final picture we take away is of the comedy as a whole, done with polish and relish, and rare Yorkshire wit'.

It was a sellout every night of its two-week run and a third week was added immediately. It was revived two years later for two weeks (1940) and again for two more weeks two years on (1942). In 1944 it was revived for an outdoor production over eight August nights in five of Bradford's biggest parks.

After the end of the war the revivals continued. Another two weeks' run was performed in 1952 and, finally, there was a fifth revival for one week in 1958, 20 years after the first production. In all, there were 66 performances. Only three members of the original cast from 1938 played in the final revival of 1958.

Over the years the press reviews stressed the consistently high performances of all the cast and hardly ever singled out any actor, such was the teamwork of the production.

Finally, in celebration of its 40th anniversary in 1969 the Playhouse returned with a completely new production of the Priestley classic.

Source: *Percy Monkman: An Extraordinary Bradfordian*, Martin Greenwood, (2018)

15 Nov 2018   Hockney painting sells for $90m, a record for a living artist.

The final price was agreed today only after an intense 10-minute battle between two bidders via telephone. The painting sold for $90 million (£70m), an auction record for a work by a living artist. The venue was the packed New York salesroom of Christie's. Those inside broke into applause when the hammer fell.

The painting was David Hockney's *Portrait of an Artist (Pool with Two Figures)*. Before its sale, it had been exhibited in London, Los Angeles, and Hong Kong and had been forecast to fetch approximately $80 million. Painted in 1972, it was one of the artist's most recognisable works. It had been the cover image of Tate Britain's Hockney retrospective in 2017.

The composition of the two figures began as two separate photographs on the artist's studio floor; one was of a figure swimming underwater and therefore quite distorted... the other was a boy gazing at something on the ground. Hockney would later recall. *'The idea of painting two figures in different styles appealed so much that I began the painting immediately.'*

The swimming pool was a regular setting for many of his paintings in the 1960s and 1970s. On arriving in California from Bradford, he realised that it was not a luxury to possess one. In Los Angeles he saw brilliant blue pools everywhere. In particular, they provided the gay Hockney with a space in which he was free to explore the male figure in pictorial terms.

Only six months earlier, he had broken his previous auction record with $28.5million (£21.1m) when he sold *Pacific Coast Highway and Santa Monica*, a large-scale oil painting dating from 1990 to a private Asian collector at Sotheby's. It depicts the Californian hills in bright, bold colours, and was described by Sotheby's as 'a *highly personal and whimsical landscape brimming with joie de vivre'.* The painting is a homage to the route that Hockney would take from his house in the Hollywood Hills to his studio on Santa Monica Boulevard while listening to opera, which he dubbed his Wagner drive.

Hockney moved to California precisely because its vibrant colours from the consistently warm climate were such a contrast from the grey, dour landscapes of his home city and they played to the strengths of his talent. Both these paintings are excellent and different examples of the best of his work.

Source: www.bbc.co.uk/news/entertainment-arts-46232870

16 Nov 1936   Elizabeth Denby is the first woman to address the Royal Institute of British Architects.

'I think that if ever there was justification for breaking a long tradition and inviting a lady to address one of our meetings, it has been in the address which Miss Denby has given to us tonight. I cannot imagine any mere man having the courage to stand up here and tell us that all the work of our architects and social reformers is in the wrong direction .'

With these words, the President of RIBA thanked Elizabeth Denby for her talk today. She had just delivered her paper *'Rehousing from the Slum Dwellers Point of View'*. It was the culmination of a major piece of research into social housing in six European countries funded by a Leverhulme Research Fellowship. The work also led to a substantial book, *Europe Rehoused*, published in 1938.

Her research concluded that *'of the vast quantity of new small buildings that had been erected since the (first world) war few can compare for quality with the output of any other European nation'*. Her critique was devastating and her conclusions controversial, challenging conventional thinking. Her research was full of practical insights (eg absence of lifts, need for private balconies, unimaginative use of land around flats). Giving her talk a vote of thanks, the Chief Architect at the Ministry of Health immediately disagreed with almost everything she said!

Yet the book was generally received positively. Founder of the Bauhaus movement, Walter Gropius commented that the book *'carried the weight of perfect expertness'*.

Born into a Bradford middle-class family (her father a doctor and mother a nurse), Elizabeth was educated at Bradford Girls' Grammar School and studied social science at the London School of Economics. She was one of many educated women in the inter-war years who developed an interest in social housing when major slum clearance in most cities was being undertaken.

Before her European research, Elizabeth had worked as a civil servant and then for Kensington Council of Social Service, learning about social work, welfare and inner-city housing. For example, she organised three 'New Homes for Old' exhibitions in London.

After the war her ideas fell out of favour for a while as Labour's Welfare State assumed direct control over social housing. Elizabeth also suffered from long-term ill-health. With a recent second edition, however, *Europe Rehoused* is now a standard work for students of housing and architecture.

Source: *Europe Rehoused*, (2nd edition), Elizabeth Denby (2015)

17 Nov 1856 — William Jackson is appointed the first conductor of the Bradford Festival Choral Society.

For the first time ever in the 1850s Bradford was starting to be recognised as a place that cherished fine music. This was a legacy of two people. The first was Samuel Smith who as mayor was the driving force behind the 1853 opening of St. George's Hall, Bradford's first concert venue, and later the founder of the Bradford Festival Choral Society. The second was William Jackson (1815-1866), who today became the first conductor of the newly formed society.

Although strongly associated with Bradford, he only came here in his thirties and, although he established a powerful reputation as a musician, music was only a hobby until he came to Bradford.

Born in Masham, North Yorkshire into a miller's family, he showed an aptitude for music from an early age, learning to play a fife (similar to a piccolo). At school he learnt to read music and sing. From finding out how to repair an organ, he learnt how to build one and he practised some cathedral music on one, all the while working full-time as a miller.

He started to compose anthems which a friend showed the York Minster organist who was highly impressed and supportive. In 1832 Jackson became organist at Masham Parish Church when it acquired a new organ. From 1839 he went into business as a tallow chandler while developing his musical interest. His reputation spread when he composed music for the Huddersfield Choral Society (1841) and had an oratorio performed in Leeds (1847).

In 1852 Jackson was encouraged to move to Bradford with his wife and five children. He entered into partnership as a music-seller and established himself enough as a musician to be the choral master at the opening festival held in 1853 at St. George's Hall. He became organist at Horton Lane Congregationalist Chapel where many of the most influential Bradfordians worshipped.

After today's appointment, Jackson built the reputation of the new choir to the extent that they were invited to perform before Queen Victoria at Buckingham Place on 28 June 1858. He led the choral music at the second and third triennial festival concerts (1856 and 1859) and also at early Subscription Concerts.

Suddenly, the 51-year-old, well-loved conductor, *'a man of spotless integrity'* (and now father of nine) died in 1866, the news *'spreading like an electric shock'* (*Bradford Observer*).

Source: www.undercliffecemetery.co.uk/about/history/william-jackson/

18 Nov 1837   The Chartist *Northern Star* newspaper appears for the first time.

One of the major influences behind the Bradford Chartist uprisings of 1840, 1842 and 1848 was the *Northern Star* newspaper.

Today its first edition was published. The owner was Feargus O'Connor, an Irishman who was the national leader of Chartism. He came to Leeds in the 1830s where he established the *Northern Star* in co-operation with the publisher Josiah Hobson, a veteran of the radical press.

They combined reports of local news, often sent in by contributors or culled from other newspapers, with leading articles that addressed more general political issues. These reports were mixed with accounts of meetings and other political activities usually sent in by secretaries of local associations. The descriptions of meetings were lengthy, detailed accounts that contained the contents of speeches and the reactions of the audience.

From its start, the *Northern Star* was a lively and innovative newspaper. Unusually for a provincial paper, each issue was published in up to eight editions tailored to different regions of the country.

The *Northern Star* became the main national communication for the Chartist movement and by July 1839 its circulation reached 50,000 copies, the second largest circulation in the UK. It was often read aloud in meeting places such as pubs and coffee houses. It claimed a readership of seven people for each copy bought. It had a strong connection with Bradford, a hotbed of Chartism. For its Bradford readers it often contained articles and news by prominent local leaders such as Peter Bussey.

As Chartism fizzled out after the 1848 uprising, O'Connor sold the newspaper. It then changed its title in May 1852 to *Star of Freedom,* but six months later ceased publication.

Source: *The Chartist Risings in Bradford,* DG Wright (1987)

18 Nov 2008   Bradford becomes a City of Sanctuary.

Today Bradford was only the third UK city to be formally recognized as a City of Sanctuary. This is a national movement to build a culture of hospitality for people seeking sanctuary in the UK. Bradford's vision is that:

'We celebrate the huge contribution that asylum seekers and refugees bring to the city and want to see this more broadly recognized. We aim to challenge some of the misinformation and negative stereotypes already in the public domain. We hope to stimulate opportunities for those seeking sanctuary to participate fully in the life of this city.'

19 Nov 1873   Lister's Pride overlooking Bradford is celebrated with a champagne luncheon.

Wherever you view Bradford from afar, whether from Baildon Moor to the north or coming off the motorway from the south, the skyline is dominated by the tall chimney of Lister's Mill. On pictures and photographs of the city it stands out as the focal point.

Today it was formally opened as part of the rebuilding of the old Lilycroft Mill on the corner of Heaton Road and Lilycroft Road in Manningham. That mill was destroyed by fire in 1871. Over two years later, a much grander new mill had now been built, its crowning glory being the new chimney, 225 feet high built in the style of an Italian campanile.

The *Bradford Observer* gave a full report of the opening of the new Manningham Mills (later generally described as Lister's Mill):

'The event is of considerable local interest, inasmuch as the chimney is perhaps the finest erection of its kind in the kingdom, and the ceremony of yesterday also betokened the approaching completion of this vast manufacturing establishment which owes its promotion to the enterprise of Mr. S.C. Lister. These works, when completed, will be the largest silk mills in Europe, and will give room for 13,000 to 14,000 silk and velvet looms, producing articles scarcely made elsewhere in England.

The handsome chimney stalk, which forms so prominent a feature of this vast establishment, is in every way in keeping with the extensive premises with which it is connected ... it presents architectural features altogether superior to any other, and from the commanding position on which the Manningham Mills stand, the chimney will in future be a landmark to be seen for many miles around ... It is especially satisfactory to record that this vast mass (including blocks weighing from four to five tons) has been prepared and the chimney reared without the slightest accident.'

A small group comprising the architect, builder, directors and Lister himself climbed to the top. The opening was celebrated with what was described as a champagne luncheon, although the paper commented that: *'The baptismal rite was performed by Mr. Lister breaking a bottle of wine.'* Champagne was better kept back for the numerous toasts!

The proud owner named the chimney as *'Lister's Pride'* – with some justification.

Source: *Bradford Observer*, (19 November 1873)

20 Nov 1837   Thousands of anti-Poor Law rioters protest in the centre of Bradford.

Today there was a violent attack at the Bradford Court House at a meeting of the newly elected Poor Law Guardians. The meeting started at 10am. Around noon a crowd of thousands milled around the Court House, finally bursting in and hurling stones. One of the Guardians was detained before being rescued. An earlier similar disturbance had taken place on 30 October when an Anti-Poor Law Commissioner from London was injured.

As a result of today's disturbance, the magistrates of Bradford wrote immediately to Lord Harewood, Lord-Lieutenant of the County:

'The lower orders in this neighbourhood are very much opposed to the introduction of the new Poor Law, and when Mr Alfred Power, one of the commissioners attended at the last meeting of the Board of Guardians, he was violently assaulted. Another meeting of the Board of Guardians was fixed for this day and further disturbance was anticipated. A Troop of the 15th Hussars was ordered here, by the Home Secretary, from Leeds. The Guardians met at 10am and the people assembled in formidable numbers in front of the Court House. The Police were able to keep out the people until 12 noon when the people began to throw stones and break the Court House windows. At 20 minutes before one the military arrived on the ground and in 10 minutes afterwards the riot act was read. The people then forced their way into the Court House and some of the soldiers had to dismount and drive them out by main force.'

This anger was prompted by changes in poor relief. The new 1834 Poor Law Amendment Act replaced the old 1601 Poor Law Act that required reform, but, administered locally, had at least been responsive to local needs. Centralisation that now imposed unwanted workhouses was resented.

The 1838 York Spring Assizes imprisoned for one month five Bradfordians who had already spent the winter in gaol awaiting trial. The riots also led to two outcomes. First, Bradford Moor Barracks was built in 1844 in order to deal with such disturbances – the first permanent home in Bradford for the military. Second, the resentment created amongst poor people was a major influence on the Chartist riots of the 1840s and on Bradford developing into a hotbed of unrest.

Source: *The Battle of Bradford: Riots against the New Poor Law,* Paul Carter (2006) in *The Antiquary*

21 Nov 1996   The Bradford Commission publishes the
lessons from the June 1995 Manningham riots.

Today, nearly 18 months after three days of rioting in the Manningham area on the weekend
of 9 to 11 June 1995, the Bradford Commission published its report into those events.

This organisation comprising public and voluntary agencies in the city was set up in
September 1995 to carry out this investigation. It appointed a three-person team, comprising
a Bradford University professor, an ex-local authority chief executive with knowledge of the
city and a local trade union representative.

The riots were sparked off by a complaint to the police about boys playing football in the
street. This minor incident escalated as parents became involved, leading to the arrival of
riot police. On the second night violent incidents intensified, but by the third and final day
calm started to prevail. At its height some 300 people were active on the streets with some
incidences of property damage estimated £0.5m, but no serious injuries were recorded.
Sixteen people were convicted of charges including four sent to prison. There was no
evidence of political agitation.

The main themes identified by the report from those consulted were listed as:

- *'ethnic conflicts and misunderstandings in Bradford*
- *the lack of employment opportunities, and most particularly the extent and unfairness of
  racial discrimination in the labour market*
- *street culture and criminal behaviour by boys and young men*
- *the problems of appropriate policing*
- *the poor educational level of some schools and the consequences for the educational
  attainment of many young people*
- *the ineffectiveness of local political processes.'*

The report warned that these issues *'cannot sensibly be ignored'* and *'the cost of not clearly
selecting and pursuing priorities will, if the present trends are left to gather momentum, be very
high'.*

The report was heavy on analysis (203 pages) and light on action (3 pages), a point which led
to one dissenting team member (the trade union representative) who criticised the lack of
firm recommendations for action. This also led Max Madden, the Labour MP for Bradford
West, to mention this in an 'Early day motion' in the House of Commons.

Five years later Bradford suffered much more serious riots that broke out on 7 July 2001.

Source: *The Bradford Commission Report: The report of an enquiry into the wider implications of public disorders in Bradford on
9, 10 and 11 June 1995* (1996).

22 Nov 1967   Alan Bullock gives the annual Raleigh history lecture to the British Academy.

Alan Bullock (1914 -2004) can claim to be the most distinguished academic to have gone to school in Bradford. An international expert in his field, he ended his career as the first elected Vice-Chancellor of Oxford University, also becoming a life peer as Lord Bullock of Leafield (Oxfordshire). En route, he established and then ran the only new Oxford college (St. Catherine's) for both undergraduates and graduates, built in the 20th century.

His impressive career had very modest beginnings. Born in Wiltshire, his father was a gardener and his mother a maid. When he was a child, his parents moved to Bradford where his father became a Unitarian minister. Bullock won a place at Bradford Grammar School. Another pupil at the school was Denis Healey who later said that, of all his school contemporaries, he most admired Alan Bullock: *'Alan had a range of knowledge and interests unique in our school; he seemed equally familiar with Wagner's letters and Joyce's Ulysses.'*

With first-class degrees in both classical greats and modern history from Wadham College, Oxford, he became a fellow, and then Dean, at New College, Oxford. In 1952, he made his name with *Hitler: A Study in Tyranny* – the first major biography. This remains a standard work.

Today, 15 years after this book was published, in a prestigious lecture Bullock updated his thinking about Hitler. Later biographers suggested that the weaknesses of the great powers in the 1930s had led to Hitler's rise, whereas he had placed the principal blame on Hitler. Now he believed that what he called the fanatic and the opportunistic sides to Hitler were both key factors.

'Not only did he create the threat of war and exploit it, but, when it came to the point, he was prepared to take the risk and go to war. For this reason despite all that we have learned since of the irresolution, shabbiness and chicanery of other governments' policies, Hitler and the nation which followed him still bear, not the sole, but the primary responsibility for the war.'

Source: *Hitler and the Origins of the Second World War*, Raleigh Lecture on History by Alan Bullock (1967).
Reproduced by permission © The British Academy 1968.

23 Nov 1967   The Mangla Dam project in North-East Pakistan is complete.

Today saw the finish of a mega-project in Pakistan that was to have a major impact on everyday life in Bradford.

After five years of construction, one of the largest dams in the world was ready. The President of Pakistan, Muhammad Ayub Khan, unveiled a large plaque to celebrate the event. The project was designed primarily to improve the irrigation from the flow of the River Jhelum and, secondly, to generate electrical power from this.

It was funded by an international consortium, comprising the World Bank and several countries in the developed world, including Canada, West Germany, the UK and USA. Despite many protests by local people, some 110,000 had to leave their homes as a result of the dam submerging over 280 villages and the towns of Mirpur and Dadyal in the area of Aza-Kashmir.

The lifeline for many of those affected was the provision of work permits for Britain. About 70% of the British Pakistani community come from Dadyal-Mirpur. In northern cities like Bradford some 75% of Pakistanis come from this area, such as cricketer Adil Rashid's family. At the time many took up work in the textile mills, owing to the acute shortage of workers locally.

Immigration from Pakistan and other parts of South Asia started in the late 1950s. The early immigrants may have not intended a permanent move, but gradually they brought their families. Naturally they tended to settle in areas where compatriots had settled in earlier years. Soon parts of the city, especially the cheaper inner-city areas, became dominated by the new immigrants. By the 2011 Census 27% of the city's population came from Asian ethnic groups compared with 67% classified as white. Electoral districts like Manningham and Toller had 90% concentration of Asian groups that understandably also shared the same religion (Islam).

As most came from the same area of Pakistani Kashmir (eg Mirpur), the new communities were close-knit. The example of the founder of the Bradford Grand Mosque in Little Horton illustrates the connection.

In planning a permanent move back to the UK in 1978 the Islamic scholar Shayk Mohammad Habib-Ur-Rehman Mahboobi had a choice of English destinations where he had been an imam. From Mirpur he chose Bradford because of his family's contacts in the city. That decision led to Bradford Grand Mosque and the impressive community of Suffa-Tul Islam.

Source: https://ejatlas.org/conflict/6-decades-of-resistance-against-the-mangla-dam-in-azad-kashmir-pakistan

24 Nov 1865   The first Bradford Subscription Concert is performed.

Although the new St. George's Hall had seen several first-class concerts in the 12 years that it had been open, they had not been profitable. Ventures such as the Bradford Triennial Festival (1853, 1856 and 1859) crowded good concerts into a three day period; some said it would be much better to spread them out over several months. From this emerged the idea of a subscription series. Subscribers could guarantee income over, say, six months. The idea crystallised amongst a number of prominent music-lovers. One such was Jacob Behrens who became the secretary of such a group under the chairmanship of Samuel Smith, the driving force behind St. George's Hall.

The subscription concerts starting today put Bradford on the map musically and lasted until the 1926/27 season. There were three factors behind their success. First came the venue itself which opened in 1853 to much acclaim. Built for the purpose, it quickly became a focal point in Bradford's cultural life, being the first public building for its citizens to enjoy in their spare time. It was designed to support grand social occasions. Significantly, it supported the social hierarchy by having separate entrances to the stalls for wealthy patrons in their full evening dress and to the galleries for the rest. From the outset the concerts were described as *'Bradford Subscription Full Dress Grand Concerts'*.

Second, the concerts included orchestral music. The presence of a strong German community encouraged for the first time in Bradford interest in orchestral music. This was developed as a result of friendship between the Behrens family and Charles Halle, founder of the Halle Orchestra whose home was in Manchester. The Halle became firmly associated over the years with Bradford as well.

Finally, the concerts featured choral music. The Bradford Festival Choral Society had been founded as a direct result of the opening of St. George's Hall. It comprised a massed choir of over 200 singers with William Jackson, Bradford's celebrated first conductor until he suddenly died in 1866.

The sale of the venue to New Century Pictures in 1926 changed everything. It became a cinema. The Concerts Committee accepted an alternative offer to use Eastbrook Hall. Although supporting the numbers, it never felt the same, being built as a Methodist Mission.

In the 1950s subscription concerts returned to St. George's Hall.

Source: *Bradford Subscription Concerts: Origins and Organisation*, Anne Wilkinson (2008) in *The Antiquary*

25 Nov 1919   The Diocese of Bradford is created.

Historically, Bradford was in the Diocese of Ripon. Its rapid growth in the 19th century made this increasingly inappropriate, given that at the start of the 20th century Ripon, 30 miles to the north of Bradford, was still a small rural market town, in contrast with Bradford, now a large industrial city.

At today's Privy Council, King George V, who had visited Bradford for the first time only the year before, ordered that a Bishopric for Bradford be founded. Eight years ago the previous Bishop of Ripon had raised the issue, believing that the Diocese of Ripon was too large to be conscientiously dealt with from Ripon and should be divided. The new diocese stretched through the Yorkshire Dales up to Sedbergh.

Before a new Bishopric could be founded, appropriate funds had been secured. Dividing Ripon Diocese like this still left it one of the largest in the country, and plans were intended to form a new Diocese of Leeds. On 8 January 1920 the first Bishop of Bradford was appointed.

The parish church of St. Peter would now become Bradford Cathedral, although it would be another 44 years before all the necessary extensions would be complete to give it the feel of a cathedral.

Ninety-five years after the Privy Council decision, Bradford Cathedral rang with the songs of hundreds of worshippers and guests as the Bradford Diocese celebrated its final anniversary. Bradford Diocese was about to be dissolved in a few days' time on Easter Sunday and merged with Leeds and Wakefield to become the Diocese of West Yorkshire and the Dales, centred on Leeds. The total population for the new diocese would be 2.6 million and include 656 churches, making it the largest diocese in the country.

This means that the Cathedral is now formally the parish church of the city centre, being the only Anglican church within the city's inner ring road.

Source: *Leeds Mercury* (26 November 1919)

26 Nov 1910   Suffragettes fail to disrupt Winston Churchill's rousing speech at St. George's Hall.

'There have been fiercer struggles, more turbulent contentions in the annals of British Parliamentary Government than that upon which we are now engaged, but nevertheless when in future years the history of the last 12 months comes to be written it will fill a vivid page in the story of British democracy. One great question awaits your solution at the current time ...

A voice, that of a man in the stalls: "And that is woman suffrage". Loud cries of "Order" during which the interrupter was ejected.'

In the years up to World War One, there were two major constitutional issues. One articulated here by Winston Churchill in full flow to a packed and excited audience in St. George's Hall was reform of the House of Lords. The other was women's suffrage, expressed unusually by a male heckler, who for his trouble fractured his knee as he was hauled out of the building.

In December 1910 a fiercely divided country went to the polls over the reform of the largely Tory House of Lords that was blocking Liberal legislation, eg the introduction of old age pensions. Originally a Tory, Churchill had converted to being a Liberal. Now 36 year-old already reputed to be one of the best orators, he had come to speak in Bradford. The audience, of course, would have been nearly all male.

Such meetings were a clear target for the women's suffrage movement then at its height. Some prominent suffragettes lived in Bradford and many had visited, including the Pankhursts. The least-known Pankhurst daughter, Adela, was the West Yorkshire organiser of the suffragette organisation, Women's Social and Political Union (WSPU). Adela had often spoken locally and disrupted public meetings. The organisers today would have had good cause to be concerned.

The night before, two suffragettes had broken into St. George's Hall and hidden under the platform all night. They waited until the hall filled up and Churchill walked on stage, then launched into their protest before being swiftly thrown out. Playing it down, the local paper reported that the only sign of a suffragette was a *'frantically agitated "Votes for Women" banner waved over the heads of the crowd'.*

Undeterred, Churchill was cheered off by a large crowd at nearby Exchange station straight after his speech.

Women's suffrage was finally resolved in 1928; controversy over House of Lords reform continues.

Source: *Bradford Daily Telegraph* (28 November 2010)

27 Nov 1852   Charles Dickens writes an article about Titus Salt, alpaca and Saltaire.

The invention that made Sir Titus Salt's fortune was the use of alpaca hair. On a trip in 1836 to Liverpool Docks, he came across a pile of 300 unwanted bales of hair from Peru. He took a sample back to Bradford where he discovered how to spin the hair into an even thread.

Sixteen years later, Charles Dickens recounted this story today in his weekly journal *Household Words* with a piece called *The Great Yorkshire Llama*:

'A huge pile of dirty looking sacks, filled with some fibrous material, which bore a strong resemblance to superannuated horse hair, or frowsy, elongated wool, or anything unpleasant or unattractive, was landed in Liverpool... it was agreed by all hands that the three hundred and odd sacks of nondescript hair wool were a perfect nuisance.

One day, a plain, business-looking, young man with an intelligent face and quiet, reserved manner, was walking along through these same warehouses in Liverpool, when his eye fell upon some of the superannuated horse hair projecting from one of the ugly dirty bales ... Our friend took it up, looked at it, felt at it, rubbed it, pulled it about; in fact, he did all but taste it, and he would have done that if it had suited his purpose – for he was "Yorkshire". Having held it up to the light, and held it away from the light, and held it in all sorts of positions, and done all sorts of cruelties to it, as though it had been his deadliest enemy and he was feeling quite vindictive, he placed a handful or two in his pocket and walked calmly away...

... The sequel was that the same, quiet business-looking , young man was seen to enter the office of C.W. & F. Foozle & Co. and asked for the head of the firm. When he asked for that portion of the house, if he would accept eightpence per pound for the entire contents of the three hundred and odd frowsy, dirty bags of nondescript wool, the authority interrogated felt so confounded that he could not have told if he were the head or tail of the firm... but eventually it ended in his making it over in consideration of the price offered.'

Titus Salt found a way of combining alpaca with cotton or silk to make a new mixed fabric.

Source: *Household Words*, Charles Dickens (1852)

28 Nov 1839   Rejection of hated church rate is reported from historic poll.

For the Rate	*938*
Against it	*3,103*
Majority against the Rate	**2,204**

'In the dullest and the darkest times, what glorious events occasionally burst upon us to cheer and re-animate their splendour! Who could have surmised, a few short days ago, that we're on the eve of circumstances that would constitute an era in the history of our town and parish ... Many noble deeds illustrate the history of Bradford, from the severe siege (Siege of Bradford, 1642), *sustained in the sacred cause of liberty and law, to the lead taken in the efforts to impart these blessings to the negro* (Anti-Slavery Campaign,1829-1833). *But none sheds more imperishable lustre on the name than this, which will referred to for many a year throughout the land, the Bradford Church Rate poll.'*

Today's *Bradford Observer* reports a triumphant victory on one of the big issues of the day.

Since the 1832 Reform Act the church rate had become the battleground between Anglicans and Nonconformists, especially in towns like Bradford with a growing and increasingly militant majority (eg Baptists, Congregationalists). An area of contention was the power of the established church to oblige everyone to fund its upkeep (eg payment of clergy, building repairs). Levied locally on ratepayers, the church rate was compulsory. Elected churchwardens had the power to raise it. Those with the vote who had lived in the parish for a year could approve the rate to be levied by churchwardens. When it was approved, non-payment on religious grounds (eg 'I am a nonconformist') was not allowed. Those who refused became liable for legal action, seizure of property or even imprisonment.

The issue became contentious during the 1830s. In 1834 an attempt to make the tax national failed. In 1835, then again in 1836 and 1837, it was agreed locally that no church rate needed to be raised. In 1837 another unsuccessful attempt was made to impose it nationally. In 1838 locally the Anglicans made a determined attempt to levy the rate, which almost succeeded.

After the death of the Vicar of Bradford at the end of 1838, the new Vicar, the Reverend William Scoresby, had a very different and more confrontational approach that led to this vote in late 1839. Although he lost the poll this time, he did not give up. The *Bradford Observer* made the case for giving him some more time.

Source: *Bradford Observer* (28 November 1839)

29 Nov 1954   The iconic Swan Arcade is reported as sold to the Arndale Property Trust.

When people complain about the 1960s' destruction of Bradford's city centre, the example they most often quote is Swan Arcade. This icon of Victorian Bradford with a frontage on Market Street, opposite the Wool Exchange, and two other frontages on adjacent streets was demolished in 1962.

The key moment, however, was the sale of Swan Arcade by public auction several years earlier. Today's brief news item in the *Telegraph & Argus* almost certainly caused no alarm, although with hindsight the name of Arndale Property should have sent the strongest of warning signals. This was the company associated with much of the worst in city regeneration in the 1960s across the north of England.

Back in the late 1870s when the new Swan Arcade was being built by Mayor Angus Holden, there was great expectation about the new concept of an arcade for shopping and offices. It was built on the ground where the once-famous White Swan Inn stood, recently demolished.

Covered by an ornamental glass roof, the arcade was to have four large archways with iron gates at its entrance. Swans were also part of the decoration. The arcade was planned to include 44 shops, 46 offices, 65 market rooms and several warehouses. Only London and a few major towns had such a facility. Weeks before it opened, the *Bradford Observer* (22 August 1878) declared it to be *'probably the most complete building of its kind in Yorkshire, if not in England'.*

Having worked as a teenager in one of Swan Arcade's offices, JB Priestley became one of the most trenchant critics of its demolition, saying *'It was no ordinary roofed-over huddle of gift shops; it was on the grand scale … Among English arcades it was a giant, five storeys high. The skylights were so far above my head that I hardly gave them a glance. I seem to remember up there an airy clutter and complication of galleries, windows, straight and curved metal supports and struts.'* (*Rebel Tyke,* Peter Holdsworth).

Generally, however, the opposition at the time was muted. Many later came to regret it more strongly, perhaps when they saw its replacement, Arndale House; in 1963 it was built on the site, all concrete and glass, and hailed by its architects as *'structurally the most advanced building to be constructed in the United Kingdom'.*

Source: *Stories of the Century, Telegraph & Argus* (1999)

30 Nov 1294   Henry de Lacy obtains a charter for starting a five-day fair in Bradford.

'The fair held on the day of St Andrew the Apostle still continues to be held on the same day – allowing for differences of styles, and that the fair began two days before the feast day.

To the great annual fairs that were held, merchants, pedlars and in short the whole host of traders, resorted with their wares and commodities for sale, and the surrounding people attended to lay in a stock of those articles which could not be procured at or near home. This accounts for the large sum raised by the toll of the fair here on the Feast of St. Andrew, amounting to about £40 of our money. The number of persons resorting to the fair, and of articles exhibited for sale, must, in order to account for this sum, have been very great. I have not met with any authority to prove that the fair held on the Feast of St Andrew was granted by charter, nor when it began. It must, however, have been a chartered fair; or ... else pains and penalties would have been incurred in holding it.'

In medieval times fairs were important opportunities for local people, being places where buyers and sellers of goods could meet and do business. The right to hold them could only be granted by the monarch who received a toll.

Today was almost certainly Bradford's first fair, the venue Westgate. We know from a reliable source, John James, Bradford's first historian, writing around 1840 that in 1294 King Edward 1 granted to Henry de Lacy, Earl of Lincoln, the right to hold an annual fair. He was a baron descended from supporters of William the Conqueror and owned much land in Yorkshire.

We might assume that today was the date when this right was granted. However we know from the same source that 31 July was the date. The fair was moved to St. Andrew's Day on 30 November. Why were the darker days of November preferred to the high summer? We do not know but there might have been a clash with nearby fairs.

Whatever the reason, St. Andrew's Day became a fixed date in Bradford's calendar as for over 500 years until around 1800 it celebrated an annual fair, which might have lasted five days.

Source: *The History and Topography of Bradford*, John James (1866)

DECEMBER

1 Dec 1936 The Bishop of Bradford makes a speech that prompts the abdication crisis.

'The benefit of the King's Coronation depends under God upon two elements: Firstly on the faith, prayer and self-dedication of the King himself; and on that it would be improper for me to say anything except to commend him, and ask you to commend him to God's grace, which he will so abundantly need, as we all need it – for the King is a man like ourselves - if he is to do his duty faithfully. We hope that he is aware of his need. Some of us wish that he gave more positive signs of such awareness.'

Spoken today by Bishop Blunt of Bradford, these words inadvertently triggered the abdication crisis. They suggested that King Edward VIII who had taken over back in January on King George V's death became detached from grace – the spiritual bond uniting God, the monarch and the people. Without this a king could not undergo the rites of coronation.

The day before, the king gave Prime Minister Stanley Baldwin an ultimatum – either Mrs Simpson became his queen or he would abdicate. The king's relationship with Mrs Simpson, an American divorcee (twice) had been the subject of rumour for months. He was the head of the Church of England, which did not then allow divorced people to remarry in church if their ex-spouses were still alive. Mrs Simpson would be an unsuitable queen.

The bishop's words may have gone unheeded, had not two *Telegraph & Argus* reporters been covering this Bradford Diocesan Conference. Their report quoted the words verbatim. The reporters agreed that the media might be interested and sent it to the Press Association. The story broke in the national press, which was widely disapproving of the king.

On 10 December the king abdicated to be replaced by his younger brother who became George V1. The day after, he broadcast to the nation about his abdication.

Source: *Stories of the Century, Telegraph & Argus* (1999)

1 Dec 1990 Bradford's most famous pork pie shop closes.

Today was a sad final day for Philip Smith's pork pie shop in Ivegate (*'Yorkshire's Oldest Pork Shop'*, it claimed). It had been selling pork pies for over 200 years. At this time of year it became a tradition to order a stand pie for Boxing Day. Even when you ordered it, you still had to queue round the block and into Sunbridge Road to pick it up.

2 Dec 1987   BBC *Chronicle* programme commemorates archaeologist Sir Mortimer Wheeler.

It was entirely appropriate that, today, in the second of two programmes about him, the BBC *Chronicle* programme should remember Sir Mortimer Wheeler (1890 -1976). He had made his reputation, first as an archaeologist, then from the 1950s as the first major TV populariser of archaeology. From 1966 to 1991 the *Chronicle* series was a long-running series, set up by Sir David Attenborough in his BBC days, to present archaeology to a mass audience for the first time. From time to time Wheeler also presented the programme in his later years.

Born in Glasgow, when he was a young boy, his family moved to Saltaire, then Shipley. Wheeler attended Bradford Grammar School for five years until his family moved to London. In his youth he acquired a love of the visual arts, literature, and outdoor pursuits. He read classics at University College, London before being awarded a studentship to do archaeological research.

After serving with distinction in World War One, culminating in a Military Cross, he resumed his career in archaeology at the National Museum of Wales, and then revitalised a run-down London Museum. With his wife, also an archaeologist, he founded the Institute of Archaeology in 1937.

Further work was halted by World War Two, when Wheeler again played an active role, ending as brigadier in the 1943 invasion of Italy. As director-general of the archaeological survey of India, he spent the immediate post-war years in India. On his return he continued research and writing, before as its secretary transforming a sleepy British Academy into the major grant-giving body for research in the humanities.

From the early 1950s his energetic efforts to popularise archaeology moved into television. He was a regular panellist in the successful quiz *Animal, Vegetable, Mineral?* in which experts had to identify an object from a museum. It ran from 1952 to 1959. On 24 October 1954, Wheeler was voted the first TV Personality of the Year by the Guild of Television Producers and Directors.

Wheeler was knighted in 1952. He received the Companion of Honour in 1967, and in 1968, a fellowship of the Royal Society. Eleven years after his death the two *Chronicle* programmes covered his impressive achievements as archaeologist, soldier and popular television personality. He was passionate about past civilisations and the importance of bringing them to life for a wide audience.

Source: genome.ch.bbc.co.uk/search/0/20?q=Mortimer+Wheeler#search

3 Dec 1835   Jonathan Glyde is called to the ministry at Horton Lane Chapel.

There is a strong case for making Jonathan Glyde Bradford's most influential religious leader in the 19th century. It was a nonconformist town and Congregationalists were the dominant faith.

Today was the start of what would be later seen as Bradford's golden age for Congregationalism. From Exeter, Glyde became Pastor at Horton Lane Chapel after a successful short trial. He had been recommended by a Bradford Parliamentary candidate who by chance had heard Glyde preach in Exeter and been impressed.

Horton Lane soon became the place of worship for the most powerful men in Bradford, who were overwhelmingly Congregationalists. Their principles of faith were that all church members had a right and duty to participate in the church's government and welfare and that no other body from outside a specific church could revise its decisions. The church belonged to its congregation and was independent of external control.

Dating from 1784, Horton Lane Chapel was the first Congregational chapel in Bradford and retained its pre-eminent position as new chapels were added to cope with the rising population in the early 19th century. When Glyde became minister, a pew plan for the chapel already showed its importance in the community. Titus Salt (second mayor) and his father had their own pews, as did his friends Robert Milligan (first mayor) and Henry Forbes (third mayor). Alongside them were William Byles, the editor of the liberal *Bradford Observer* for over 40 years, Samuel Smith (fifth mayor), James Garnett (grandson of one of Bradford's first woolmen in the 18th century), Henry Ripley, owner of the town's monopoly dyeworks, later MP, and Henry Brown (director of Brown Muff and also seventh mayor). Five of the first seven mayors worshipped here, and, with the exception of Ripley, they were all Liberals, rather than Conservatives. A pew was also allocated to Joseph Hinchcliffe, head of Horton Lane Academy, a school for pupils who were to become prominent Bradfordians (now, Glyde House).

Glyde was a firm believer in education and in improving people's lives. He founded the Academy, helped set up the Bradford Town Mission, strongly supported woolcombers in their claims for better conditions and was an advocate for the public park movement.

Doubtless he would have achieved more, but in the prime of his life, aged 47, he died leaving a strong record of devotion to public service.

Source: *Balgarnie's Salt*, Robert Balgarnie (2003)

4 Dec 2018   Investment by German émigré in City life ends in complete failure.

In the late 19th century a small but influential middle-class German immigrant community helped to make Bradford a more prosperous and civilised place. Only the outbreak of World War One put an end to their contribution.

When in 2016 the owners of Bradford City announced a sale of the football club to two German owners, supporters had grounds for optimism about its future. The club had always struggled for funds, except for the Geoffrey Richmond era (1994 to 2002), which ended in financial disaster. It then took the club ten years to recover gradually to a position of stability. Now was the time for some investment. Foreign owners in English football usually meant shady characters making wild promises, but here the German influence felt different.

Edin Rahic, the front man, had thoroughly researched English football and identified Bradford as a club with a strong fan base rooted in the local community. His partner was wealthy and happy to take a back seat. Rahic had management qualifications, a football background and spoke convincingly about his plans. Like his 19th century forebears he was prepared to uproot his family from Germany and commit to Bradford. What could go wrong?

One early warning after just one meeting with the new owners was the abrupt departure of Phil Parkinson, one of City's most respected managers. However, on the advice of the previous owners, they appointed club legend Stuart McCall as manager. In 2016/17 he took the team to a play-off final losing with four minutes to go.

Rahic let key players go. A new but less talented team emerged for 2017/18. Despite growing tensions, McCall kept the team near the top until a run of six defeats led to his sacking, to the dismay of most fans. Everything went downhill from that point.

McCall's replacement declined to continue for the 2018/19 season. Rahic took six weeks to replace him, but not before he bought a completely new squad. He then appointed an under-18s coach in the club who had not even applied and lasted just six weeks. The team dropped to the foot of the league, despite the efforts of two further new managers.

Today Rahic left the club, having lost all credibility. His arrogance, overbearing manner and micro-management led to his fall-out with everyone involved in the club.

The club was relegated to League Two. Who knows how quickly it will recover?

5 Dec 2015   Bust of poet Humbert Wolfe is presented to the City of Bradford.

Today, sculptor Anthony Padgett made a gift to the City Library. He donated a bronze bust of his great-great-uncle, one of five in different materials, each representing different facets of his life. This one represented his relative's Bradford upbringing.

Humbert Wolfe (1885 -1940) had an unusual life.

He was born in Milan, Italy into a Jewish family with a German father and Italian mother. Early in his life his father was made partner in a Bradford wool business. The family emigrated to Yorkshire. Wolfe was educated at Bradford Grammar School, winning a scholarship to Oxford University, where he gained a first in classics.

Wolfe joined the Civil Service, starting in the Board of Trade working for William (later Lord) Beveridge. When war broke out, ill-health prevented him from fighting. However, he became responsible for the organisation of labour in the newly formed Ministry of Munitions. In 1918 his contribution merited a CBE.

After the war Wolfe joined the new Ministry of Labour. His services included editing the Ministry's National Service Handbook and drawing up a list of the writers, archaeologists and artists who could help the war effort.

Alongside his life as a civil servant, Wolfe developed a parallel life in poetry, translation and literary criticism. He was prolific. He was a best-selling poet in the 1920s and 1930s, publishing over 40 books of his own poetry and prose, 10 books of literary criticism, and numerous anthologies and literary translations. Much of his poetry was about World War One.

In 1931 Wolfe became a Fellow of Royal Society of Literature and might have been Poet Laureate, but for strong competition (eg Rudyard Kipling, Edith Sitwell, WB Yeats). His 1916 poem, *Requiem: The Soldier,* is read at Remembrance Sunday services each year (first two verses below):

Down some cold field in a world outspoken
the young men are walking together, slim and tall,
and though they laugh to one another, silence is not broken;
there is no sound however clear they call.

They are speaking together of what they loved in vain here,
but the air is too thin to carry the things they say.
They were young and golden, but they came on pain here,
and their youth is age now, their gold is grey.

Source: *The Five Heads of Humbert Wolfe: Poet, Wit and Civil Servant,* A. D Padgett (2014)

6 Dec 1983   Set and filmed in Bradford, *The Dresser* opens to acclaim.

Many films have been located in Bradford, but few, like *The Dresser*, explicitly set here. As a struggling theatre company in wartime Britain embarks on a provincial tour, the Alhambra is the place where the company is about to stage *King Lear* and the film's action occurs. Returning to the city where he made his name on film in *Billy Liar*, Tom Courtenay stars as Norman, personal assistant to the company's actor-manager (known as 'Sir') played by Albert Finney. Temperamental, difficult and in declining health, Sir dominates and bullies the rest of the cast. Only Norman can manage him; even Sir's wife takes back stage. In their different ways both men are passionate about the theatre and Shakespeare.

Despite playing Lear for the 227th time, Sir has to be coaxed throughout the day. Taken as an emergency into hospital, he escapes the doctor's clutches, returns to the theatre and lets Norman deal with the rebellious company who in hope all expect the performance to be cancelled. The show must go on. It does, with the best and worst of outcomes.

The Dresser received five Oscar nominations including Best Picture, Best Director (both Peter Yates), Best Actor (Courtenay and Finney) and Best Adapted Screenplay (Ronald Harwood). It also received five similar Golden Globe Awards, from which Courtney won Best Actor. Finally, it received seven BAFTA nominations. In short, it was extremely well nominated without winning the final awards.

The film and location were perfectly matched. All the members of the theatre company were coming to the end of their careers and the theatre itself was badly in need of refurbishment, especially back-stage where most of the action takes place. Both cast and theatre had seen better days.

A major refurbishment was planned, but before it started, *The Dresser* was about to be filmed. Today, *The Dresser* went on first release in the USA to be followed by the start of the final pantomime at the old Alhambra.

The film presents a unique record of what the old Alhambra looked and felt like in the auditorium and on and off stage, as a famous play was being performed. It made a very good film and fine piece of theatre history. It could not be improved.

Source: *Domes of Delight: The History of the Bradford Alhambra*, Peter Holdsworth (1989)

7 Dec 1843   The *Bradford Observer* makes a powerful case
for elected municipal government.

Today, the *Bradford Observer* illustrated its reputation as a campaigning and radical
newspaper.

*'If, according to a Government Commissioner, Bradford is the dirtiest and worst regulated
town in the county of York, it is surely high time that the besom of reform were applied to it. But,
if the dirt and irregularity which give it a 'bad eminence' among the Yorkshire towns, are the
result of a social necessity, if they exist solely because there does not exist in Bradford constituted
powers competent to cope with them, it is high time that such powers were conferred upon some
parties.*

*But the following facts demonstrate that the town is not efficiently governed. A few weeks ago
a clever thief contrived to filch from a counting-house in broad daylight, and to make a clear
escape. A few months ago some daring burglars succeeded in blowing up with gunpowder the
safe of one of our merchants, in one of our most public watched streets and, about the same time,
the counting-house of Messrs. Ellis and Priestman, situated in the very centre of the town,
although barricaded like a castle, was forcibly entered by burglars — yet in neither case has a
trace of the perpetrators been discovered; and not a week elapses in which we have not to record
several acts of petty larceny committed in our busiest streets.*

*We have said that the Commissioners are under a moral obligation to make an effort, at least,
to remove the nuisances which disgrace the town. They are our existing 'government', and are
bound to the utmost of their power to see that the proper work of government be not neglected.*

*But, while we thus speak of them as the de facto government of Bradford, we must be understood
as giving no countenance to the principle by which they exist. They are self-elected and
irresponsible.... It is dangerous to prophesy, but we hesitate not to predict, that Bradford will
have a corporation. This is affirming nothing more than that it will be governed in accordance
with the constitutional principle that its inhabitants will have the power of governing themselves
... To the man who should meet us with the incredulous sneer or the mocking laugh, we should say:
"Which do you prefer, the constitutional government of England, or the despotic government
of Russia?".'*

Three years later this prediction came true.

Source: *Bradford Observer* (7 December 1843)

8 Dec 1999   Alan Titchmarsh and team design a special millennium garden for Nelson Mandela.

Today, BBC's *Ground Force* team started building a special garden to celebrate the millennium for just about the world's most famous person, Nelson Mandela, Nobel Peace Prize Winner and recently retired President of South Africa.

For Alan Titchmarsh it was the unlikeliest of meetings in the unlikeliest of circumstances. Born in Ilkley in 1949, he had started work as an apprentice gardener with Ilkley Council, before leaving as an 18-year-old for Shipley Art and Technology Institute where he studied for a City and Guilds in horticulture.

Titchmarsh then moved down south and developed his career as a horticulturalist at Kew Gardens. He first came into prominence as the BBC TV presenter for the *Chelsea Flower Show* for 30 years from 1983, complementing that role with presenting *Pebble Mill at One*, *Gardeners' World* and then *Ground Force*. In this programme the team performed makeovers on a range of gardens.

Born in Eastern Cape, South Africa in 1918, Mandela studied law, joined the African National Congress and became an anti-apartheid activist. After 19 years of campaigning he was arrested and imprisoned for 27 years before his release in 1990. After the ground-breaking 1994 General Election when everyone irrespective of colour voted, Mandela became President. He was universally hailed for uniting the nation.

In his island prison on Robben Island Mandela came to enjoy gardening. He later wrote:

'A garden was one of the few things in prison one could control. To plant a seed, watch it grow, to tend it and then harvest it offered a simple but enduring satisfaction.'

It was appropriate, then, that *Ground Force* should design a garden to celebrate the millennium for such a man universally respected across the world. Built as a complete surprise over three days when Mandela was visiting the USA, the garden had to cope with an unusual climate of long hot dry seasons with bursts of heavy rain, It featured a pergola under which he might gaze at his garden, two long ponds crossed by a bridge and the focal point of an old millstone on which his mother used to grind corn.

This special edition was broadcast on 2 January 2000.

Mandela told the *Ground Force* team that he saw gardening as a metaphor for leadership. He promised Titchmarsh that, as long as he had time to be at his home, he would tend the new garden.

Source: www.theguardian.com/media/1999/dec/15/broadcasting.mondaymediasection

9 Dec 1858   The 'Humbug Billy' case comes to court.

Hodgson, Goddard and Neal, had all been arrested for manslaughter. Today, the headline-grabbing 'Humbug Billy' case came to court in York.

It started on 30 October. William Hardaker (known as 'Humbug Billy') always liked to sample the sweets that he sold from his market stall where the old Rawson Market stood. Having earlier that Saturday afternoon bought ten batches of lozenges, he opened one for sale and tried a sample. By half past five he was so ill that he had to be taken home. Luckily he recovered.

Many people, however, had already bought a bag of these sweets and were not so lucky. By the end of Sunday, at least four children had died and many others reported vomiting. Three days later, numbers had increased to 17 deaths and 198 people falling ill. The final death toll came to 20.

Quick action by the police soon traced what had happened. Hardaker had bought his sweets from a local wholesaler, James Neal. On Monday 18 October Neal had asked a lodger on his way back from a visit to pick up a quantity of 'daft' from Charles Hodgson's, a druggist in Shipley.

The most expensive ingredient in sweet-making was sugar. Confectioners commonly diluted it with a white calcium compound known as 'daft'. On this day Hodgson was unwell and the shop was attended by a young assistant William Goddard. He had been told by Hodgson that the 'daft' was in a cask in the attic. What he picked up turned out to be a different package with 12 pounds of arsenic (also white), despite being warned by Hodgson to avoid it. The only labels of their contents were underneath the casks.

One of Neal's sweet-makers was James Appleton who made the sweets to Neal's instructions. Although both noticed that the sweet mixture looked a little different from normal, they ignored this. Both tested the mixture and later felt unwell, but did not link it to what they had eaten.

In today's case, Goddard and Neal were immediately acquitted as they could not have known about the arsenic. Two weeks later Hodgson was also acquitted, as he was judged to have given correct instructions.

In August 1860 the Government passed the Adulteration of Food or Drink Act, Sadly, neither of Bradford's two MPs spoke in the debates (one being Sir Titus Salt).

Source: *The Bradford Poisoning of 1858*, George Sheeran (1992)

10 Dec 1947   Sir Edward Appleton receives the Nobel Prize for physics.

Today, Sir Edward Appleton (1892 -1965) became the only Bradfordian to win a Nobel Prize. His background was ordinary. Born in Bradford Moor, his father a warehouseman, he attended Hanson Grammar School from where he gained a scholarship for St. Johns College, Cambridge. Here he achieved a double first in natural sciences in 1914.

Returning from active service in World War One, he started research into radio waves at the Cavendish Laboratory in Cambridge. In 1924 he was appointed Professor of Physics at London University where he stayed 12 years, returning to Cambridge to take the Chair of Natural Philosophy. His area of research was the ionosphere, the region that forms a border between the earth and the universe. He discovered a new layer that enabled the reflection of short wave radio around the world, the 'Appleton' layer'.

At the start of World War Two he was appointed Secretary of the Department of Scientific and Industrial research, the most senior government post for physical science. Here, his task was to turn the focus of the department from peacetime to wartime activities, eg development of radar.

In 1949 Appleton returned to academic work as Principal and Vice-Chancellor of the University of Edinburgh where he stayed until his death.

Nine years after the Nobel Prize, Appleton achieved another prestigious first for a Bradfordian – being invited to give the annual series of six BBC Reith lectures. His subject was *Science and the Nation.*

Source: Edward Appleton (*Oxford Dictionary of National Biography*)

10 Dec 2016   Innovative underground complex opens its doors.

Opened today, Sunbridge Wells is a secret tunnel system beneath the city centre, transformed into Bradford's first underground market. It incorporates Victorian and contemporary shop units, together with streets, barrows, restaurants and bars in a setting that reflects Bradford's history and ambience.

The highly respected writer about cities, Simon Jenkins, approved: '*I recently visited perhaps the most desperate city centre in Britain, the virtually empty Victorian downtown of Bradford. Two years ago saw the arrival, glowing in its centre, of Sunbridge Wells, a subterranean warren of craft beer hangouts, gin bars and studios, buried in hillside tunnels and surrounded by boarded-up shops and warehouses..... Always respect the old fabric of a city, be it Notre Dame or a tumbledown Bradford cellar. The past is the one sure investment in the future.*'

Source: *The Guardian* (20 April 2019)

11 Dec 1975   The man-hunt for the Black Panther ends.

The High Court Judge stated in June 2008: *'This case... justifies a whole life order. The manner in which the young girl was killed demonstrates that it involved a substantial degree of premeditation or planning. It also involved the abduction of the young girl. The location and manner of Lesley Whittle's death indicates that she must have been subjected by the applicant to a dreadful and horrific ordeal.'* He rejected the appellant's claim that the life term, handed out in 1976, should now revert to 30 years.

The appellant was Bradfordian Donald Neilson (1936-2011), known as the Black Panther. Although he had already in 1974 murdered three sub-postmasters in Accrington, Harrogate and Oldbury, the case that everyone remembers was the kidnapping and murder of 17-year-old Lesley Whittle in Shropshire in January 1975.

It was a calculated crime committed over 130 miles from his home in Thornbury, Bradford. Lesley Whittle had a large inheritance from her recently deceased father. She was snatched from her bed at the family home with her mother asleep in the house. Soon after Lesley's brother received a ransom demand for £50,000. He arranged a meeting with the caller but was late in turning up. The police thought it might be a hoax.

Lesley Whittle's body was found on 7 March, hanging from a wire 50 feet below ground at the bottom of a drain shaft. The man-hunt intensified for the Black Panther, so called by a reporter noting that the wife of one of those killed in 1974 said of the killer who was dressed in black that he was *'so quick, he was like a panther'*.

Today, eleven months later, two police officers spotted a man seen acting suspiciously in Mansfield. When they challenged him, he threatened them with a shotgun, but they finally overpowered him.

Born Donald Nappey in Bradford, Neilson had an unhappy childhood, losing his mother when he was ten. Then, married at 18 and with a child, he changed his name to Neilson because he had been bullied with his birth name. As his business did not work out, he turned to crime and became a professional burglar, committing hundreds of crimes. He started to raid post-offices and killed three postmasters who tried to stop him. He then read about the young heiress, Lesley Whittle.

Three years after his High Court appeal Neilson died of motor-neurone disease.

12 Dec 1976   Photographer Sir Don McCullin provides major Bradford feature in colour supplement.

'I wish I had been born in Bradford, and had its beautiful dialect, and its warm, relaxed attitude. Bradford's full of energy and enthusiasm – an exciting giant visual city.

It's not the most attractive city in England, but it's certainly the most interesting. It's a city that I have quite clearly in my heart'.

Today *The Sunday Times* published its main colour supplement feature about Bradford – *Save Our Cities,* one of several assignments Don McCullin has completed in Bradford in between visits to war zones. For example, his retrospective at Tate Britain in 2019 had several sections, each devoted to a theme in his life – The East End childhood, wars in Congo, Biafra (Nigeria), Vietnam, Cambodia and Northern Ireland, and finally Bradford and the North.

'When he returned home from conflict assignments, he often turned his attention to the tough lives of people in Britain. He photographed communities living in northern cities like Bradford and Liverpool, focusing on areas that had been neglected and left impoverished by policies of deindustrialisation. McCullin saw similarities between their lives and his own childhood. Although he was indeed 'reporting' on poverty and social crisis, he also identified deeply with his subjects; picturing the lives of others as a means of learning more about himself.'

Tate Britain (5 February to 6 May 2019)

For a Londoner, Don McCullin, the country's most famous photo-journalist, is certainly a firm friend of Bradford. Born in 1935, brought up in the East End in poverty and now long-term resident in Somerset, he only had purely professional connections with Bradford, but his extensive travels across the world and in the UK make him well-qualified to judge the city like this.

After making his name documenting foreign wars in the 1960s, he started coming to Bradford, taking stunning pictures of working-class inner-city life. For example, he came in the 1980s to make his first film for the BBC, an Arena special called *Home Front.* He has had exhibitions featuring photographs of Bradford at what is now the National Science and Media Museum in 2009 and again in 2018.

His are some of the best photographs ever taken in Bradford.

13 Dec 1849   The *Bradford Observer* investigates the living conditions of the working class.

Today, Bradford's newspaper published a 4,000 word feature by a special correspondent from the London-based *Morning Chronicle*. It focuses on how the working classes live their daily lives.

Setting the scene, the writer described Bradford:

'With the exception of a few of the main thoroughfares, which are bustling, and characterised by good shops... Bradford may be described as an accumulation of main streets, steep lanes, and huge mills — intersected here and there by those odious patches of black, muddy, waste ground, rooted up by pigs, and strewed with oyster-shells, cabbage stalks, and such garbage, which I have so often noticed is commonly existing in manufacturing towns.

He visited one quarter containing *'some of the low Irish haunts. As usual, the great majority of the adults are hawkers... (Their) average earnings are stated as from 1s. to 1s.6d. a day. Their houses almost always consisted of a single room—generally a cellar — a low, dark, foul-smelling place, with rough stools and a broken table or so lying about; coarse crockery, either unwashed or full of dirty water; knives without handles, and forks with broken prongs; bits of loaves smeared over by dirty hands; bundles of rags, buckets of slops, and unmade beds huddled on the stone or earthen floor in corners.'*

Many families had moved to Bradford from rural poverty. He featured two cases where on the husband's death the parish had bribed the widow to come to Bradford. One with a large family was tempted by a gift of 21 shillings, but the children had been too ill to work in the town and are supported by parish relief. The writer visited the house of another, from Ireland, with three young children ... *'I had never witnessed a more striking instance of cleanliness taking away all the squalor of poverty.'* Again she relied on the parish. *'Well, sir, the parish are very good to me, and give me 3s. each a week — 2s. for the rent and 1s. for coals — and we live and clothe ourselves on the other 8s. We live chiefly on bread. I get a stone and a half of flour every week, and I bake it on Sundays. Then we have a little tea or coffee, and sometimes we have a little offal meat, because it's cheap.'*

Source: *Bradford Observer* (13 December 1849)

14 Dec 1893   Bradford's first female high-flyer becomes the first woman to present to the Royal Society.

Born in Hull, Marion Greenwood (1862-1932) grew up from the age of seven in Oxenhope where her father managed a mill. From that point at every stage of her education she broke through barriers as a female high-flyer studying in the male preserve of science.

As one of its first pupils, she attended the new Bradford Girls' Grammar School when it opened in1875. (Her obituary-writer said that *'she spoke often of the school with love and pride'*.) When just 17, she won a scholarship to Girton College, Cambridge's first college for women, founded in 1869. By 1879 Girton had just 33 students in her year, of whom four took science. Here she was the first from her college to take a double first in the natural sciences tripos, newly available to women – Part One in 1882 in botany, physiology, and zoology and Part Two in 1883 in physiology.

In 1884 Newnham College, Cambridge's second college for women, founded in 1871, appointed her demonstrator and lecturer in physiology and botany at the newly opened Balfour Laboratory. This supported practical work for women students in the sciences, the main university laboratories being closed to women.

From 1890 to 1899 she was head of this laboratory, supported by only an untrained boy as general laboratory attendant. Despite a heavy teaching load, she regularly published research on the digestive system. For example, today she became the first woman to present a paper at the Royal Society, but a man had to read it! Only Fellows could read papers and, as women were not admitted as Fellows until 1945, it was a male Fellow who read her paper on this auspicious occasion.

Ironically, her academic research came to an end in 1899 when she married George Bidder, a distinguished marine biologist of independent means. They had two daughters who both became Cambridge scientists, one at Girton and the other at Newnham. As Marion Bidder, staunchly liberal, she became president of the Cambridge Women's Liberal Association and a committed suffragist, (rather than the more militant suffragettes), campaigning locally for women's rights and promoting women's election in local councils. She was heavily involved in the management of both Girton and Newnham Colleges and developed a number of roles in the local community (eg teachers' training, mental health).

Source: Marion Bidder, nee Greenwood (*Oxford Dictionary of National Biography*)

15 Dec 1926   After a merger, the new *Bradford Telegraph & Argus* publishes its first edition.

The city's two daily newspapers finally buried the hatchet today. They merged to become the new *Bradford Telegraph & Argus*.

Ever since the *Argus* had appeared on the streets of Bradford in 1892, they had been bitter rivals, spurring each other on. The story was told that in the early 1920s to be the first with the Derby winner, the *Telegraph* employed a man on the top of its Piccadilly building to signal the result by flag to a group down the hill in the city centre who were ready to hand-stamp the winner in the 'Late news' column. Much earlier in 1897, the *Argus* had gambled successfully on a major scoop by Richard Appleton, pioneering cinematographer, showing same day newsreel from the Queen's Jubilee in London to excited Bradford crowds in the evening.

The early 1920s had seen important changes. In 1923 the *Bradford Daily Argus* became the *Yorkshire Evening Argus*. In 1925 the *Telegraph* moved from Piccadilly to Hall Ings down in the city centre. In fact, curiously this took it back to its original home. The Hall Ings offices started off in an impressive warehouse belonging to Milligan, Forbes & Co, Stuff Merchants, part of which then became occupied by the *Bradford Observer*, much later the *Yorkshire Observer*. This title, bought by the same owners as the *Telegraph* in 1909, co-existed with it. Now the *Telegraph*'s new home brought together under the same roof, not just the *Yorkshire Observer*, but the *Keighley News* and the *Yorkshire Sports* (a sporting spin-off from the *Telegraph*).

The merger had started earlier in 1926 when the Westminster Press acquired the *Telegraph* before making the move for the *Argus*. The *Bradford Telegraph & Argus* ('Bradford' was dropped in 1947) announced: *'It will not be a party political paper. It will be an impartial newspaper. It will give a complete news service, with special emphasis on the woollen and allied industries, which are, and must remain, the lifeblood of the city and district.'*

Since 1926 the '*T & A*' has retained the same owners (Westminster Press, now a home for many provincial newspapers) and still operates from Hall Ings, although the printing has been outsourced to Teesside. It has become a strong part of Bradford's identity, despite facing the challenges of the digital age.

Source: *Read All About It: The story of Bradford's Telegraph & Argus* 1868 -1981(1981)

16 Dec 2001   UNESCO inscribes Saltaire with World Heritage status.

'Overview

Saltaire is an exceptionally complete and well preserved industrial village of the second half of the 19th century, located on the river Aire. Its textile mills, public buildings, and workers' housing are built in a harmonious style of high architectural quality and the urban plan survives intact, giving a vivid impression of the philanthropic approach to industrial management.

Integrity

The integrity of Saltaire as a model industrial village is almost total. The boundary of the property coincides with the extent of Titus Salt's original development: the model village and its associated buildings, the majority of the mill complex and the Park. Some buildings (representing only 1% of the original buildings) were demolished in the past but those existing at the time of inscription and the layout of the complex are still intact. Mill machinery was removed after industrial activities ceased in the mid-1980s. There are limited opportunities for new development within the site. Beyond the site's boundaries, development has surrounded the property to the east, south and west for the last century, with the remnant Aire river landscape to the north.

Authenticity

An intensive programme of sensitive rehabilitation and conservation of the entire complex has meant that its attributes - form and design, materials and substance, and function (in terms of a living community) - continue to thrive and express its Outstanding Universal Value. The original rural river valley setting has gradually disappeared over the last one hundred years but significant views remain. Given that part of Salt's original intention was to locate Saltaire in a healthy environment, the buffer zone is important in this respect.'

Today, when UNESCO formally inscribed it in its world-wide list, Saltaire became the 24th UNESCO World Heritage Site in the UK. These three paragraphs are extracts from the full text.

The inscription reflects the vision of two people. The one was Sir Titus Salt, the original owner in1853, and the other was Jonathan Silver, the new owner in 1987 who bought it from the company who bought it from the Salt family.

Salt had the vision of a workers' village where all who worked at the mill could live well in adjacent housing as part of a community which met their needs. Silver had the vision to regenerate the mill in a sustainable way – were it to remain empty and unused, that community would gradually die.

Source: http://whc.unesco.org/en/list/1028

17 Dec 1788   The new Bowling Ironworks enters into its first contract.

Today Bowling Ironworks signed its first contract for the minerals under the estate of Jeremiah Rawson and other landowners.

The operation included mining coal and iron ore, smelting, refining, casting and forging to create finished products. Initially small items such as grates and fire-irons were made, but soon they led to bigger things. Cast-iron guns from Bowling were used at Trafalgar and Waterloo.

Bowling Ironworks exhibited the worst excesses of the Industrial Revolution. William Cudworth dramatically described the scene that it shaped 100 years after the mining started:

'... a sort of deep horseshoe valley, the banks which surround it consisting chiefly of shale and cinders, the accumulations of a century's workings. The whole area, enclosed by a high stone wall, is somewhat more than a mile and a half round. Looking from the counting-house at the entrance, on the right is a large waste space, with the steaming lake and cinder hills behind. At night, when live scoria and ashes glow from the sides of the latter, and the lake is lighted up by vivid and fitful gleams emitted from the blast furnaces, the scene is strange and weird-like ... one might almost fancy himself in immediate proximity to an active volcano. Puffs of white vapour rise incessantly from the sides and summit of the cinder hill, over which hangs a dense canopy of smoke.'

Between them, the two main ironworks, Low Moor (the larger) and neighbouring Bowling, mining the same seams, almost vied with each other for their ability to pollute: 'The condition of Bradford is dreadful. Low Moor iron-forges most extensively spread their suffocating exhalations on the one side ... On the other side, Bowling Iron Hell (for it is one truly) casts a still denser atmosphere and sulphurous stench.' (AB Granville,1841). The official line seemed to be that jobs mattered more than smoke prevention notices; many industrialists were also local councillors.

Not only did the mine leave a deep scar on the landscape, the working conditions were appalling. Child labour was rife. Boys were hired to drag heavy carriages along tracks to the miners and then drag them back, fully loaded, to the pit shafts. Sometimes they were below the legal age of ten!

Unloved, the Bowling Iron Company went into liquidation first in 1898, was rescued and then finally collapsed in 1921.

Source: *History of Bowling,* William Cudworth (1891)

18 Dec 1642   The Parliamentarians win the first Siege of Bradford.

Bradford's first contact with the Civil War was in December 1642. The township was Puritan and sympathetic to Oliver Cromwell, and his idea that Parliament, not the King alone, should have the final say in all matters of law. Surrounding areas, however, were generally Royalist.

The Fairfaxes were the leading military commanders for the Parliament in the north – Fernando Lord Fairfax of Denton Park, Otley and his son Sir Thomas Fairfax. Neither side had overall control in the north. The Royalists needed to subdue troublesome towns like Bradford.

In late October Royalists had come to Bradford after establishing a base in Leeds, but were beaten off by the townspeople of Bradford. This led to a new Royalist leader – the Earl of Newcastle in charge of a force of 9,000 men. He turned his attention to Bradford. As the town had no regular Parliamentarian soldiers, he assigned a small force of 900 under Sir William Savile to take control of the town.

He positioned his men a few hundred yards on high ground to the north of the centre at Undercliffe, overlooking the parish church of St. Peter, occupied by a few men with muskets. Savile called upon the inhabitants to surrender, but the defending force of around 300 irregulars tenaciously refused. The next day, with defeat likely for the Parliamentarians, the weather intervened with a blizzard and one of the big Royalist cannons exploded, killing several of their soldiers.

The Royalists retreated, but, as they were likely to return, the Parliamentarians reinforced their defences the next day, a Saturday. The plan was to turn the parish church into a fortress. If that worked, Bradford might be saved. They hung large sheets of wool over the steeple and placed the best dozen shots or so around it.

Today, Sunday morning, the Royalists attacked again, expecting the opposition to be at prayer. After an inconclusive exchange of fire, midday reinforcements from Bingley and Halifax gave the Parliamentarians the upper hand and the Royalists were brutally routed in what became known as the Battle of the Steeple.

The first Siege of Bradford was over, but within six months the second Siege of Bradford would start with a very different outcome.

Source: *The Story of Bradford*, Alan Hall (2013)

19 Dec 1942   Bradford's 'Clown Prince of Football' scores twice as Park Avenue thrash Bradford City.

Football fans who remembered him claimed that Len Shackleton (1922-2000) was the finest-ever player born in Bradford, the Paul Gascoigne of his era. Sir Stanley Matthews said: *'He was unpredictable, brilliantly inconsistent, flamboyant, radical and mischievous, which he undoubtedly was. But such a character would not go down well with the blazer brigade who ran English football.'*

Yet he only won five international caps and never played in a side that won the Football League or the FA Cup, the two major national competitions of the day. However, his career was blighted by World War Two, which broke out when he was a highly promising youngster.

Shackleton signed as amateur schoolboy for Bradford Park Avenue but was snapped up by Arsenal as a 15-year-old apprentice. This time spent away in London did not work out and he was told he was too small to be successful. Returning to Bradford, he signed as a professional for Park Avenue in 1940.

In wartime football he scored 171 goals in 209 league and cup appearances for Avenue. The most notable match was today's 10-nil thrashing of local rivals at Valley Parade, Shackleton scoring twice. City never suffered a worse defeat before or since. However, wartime matches are excluded from official records and so this defeat usually disappears from view.

The war over, he continued for just seven games with Avenue. Despite scoring four times, he tired of being barracked by local fans who disliked his individualist style. He had many 'mickey-taking' tricks to irritate the opposition, like taking the ball to the corner flag and sitting on it (the ball).

Shackleton was sold to Second Division Newcastle United where he scored six goals in his first game, a 13-nil victory over Newport County. However, after several disputes with the club, he was transferred in 1948 to neighbours Sunderland for a British transfer record of £20,050.

Here he spent the rest of his career. During this time he played five times in six years for England. The highlight was a 3-1 victory in 1954 over world champions, West Germany, when he scored *'my most memorable scoring effort in a lifetime of soccer'*.

How might such a talent have coped with the 21st century high profile footballer life of the Premier League, TV analysis and scrutiny and social media exposure?

Source: *Clown Prince of Soccer: The Len Shackleton Story*, Colin Malam (2004)

20 Dec 1990 Promising playwright Andrea Dunbar dies prematurely in Buttershaw local.

Andrea Dunbar's life (1961-1990) was short, chaotic, depressing and uplifting. Today she died from a brain haemorrhage, drinking alone in her local pub aged 29. Playwright Shelagh Delaney called her *'a genius straight from the slums'*.

Dunbar was brought up in Buttershaw, the most deprived estate in Bradford and certainly one of the worst in the country. She frequently played truant from school, was pregnant at fourteen, but miscarried after a car crash. She had three children by three fathers, but never married. She spent time in a woman's refuge. She smoked and drank too much. She suffered from and contributed to abusive relationships. Her generally sordid life was lit up with a talent for writing, recognised and supported by sympathetic teachers.

When she was just a 15-year-old schoolgirl, never having been to a theatre, Dunbar wrote her first play in green biro on pages torn from a school exercise book. *The Arbor*, based on Brafforton Arbor the road where she lived, depicted an abusive father and daughter relationship. Two years later she entered it into a national competition for young writers. Her work impressed the director of London's Royal Court Theatre, where she became the youngest writer to have a play performed.

This led to her being commissioned to write the best-known of her three plays *Rita, Sue and Bob too,* a comic drama in which two teenage schoolgirls living on a run-down Bradford council estate are seduced by an older married man for whom they babysit regularly. After being performed at the Royal Court, the play won for her an award for promising young playwright. Her writing showed a talent for dialogue, sharp wit and honesty.

In 1987 the play was turned into a film, which led to quite a furore. It had mixed reviews and brought criticism from the Buttershaw community and Bradford councillors who did not like the way that it portrayed life on the estate. Dunbar herself did not like the way that the film changed the ending from her play.

After Dunbar's death, her story continues to fascinate writers. In 2019 there were productions of two plays about her life, one in the theatre (first staged in a Bradford pub), *Black Teeth and a Brilliant Smile,* and one for Radio 4, *Rita, Sue and Andrea too.*

Source: Andrea Dunbar (*Oxford Dictionary of National Biography*)

21 Dec 2010   The Crossbow Cannibal is convicted of the Bradford murders of three sex workers.

The latest in a line of serial murderers associated with Bradford was today jailed for life in one of the most gruesome cases in British legal history.

Stephen Griffiths who lived in Thornton Road near the city centre admitted the murder of murdering Suzanne Blamires (aged 36, between 20 May and 25 May), after CCTV coverage of his attack on her at the block of flats where he lived had been spotted by the caretaker leading to his arrest on 25 May. He later admitted to the murder of Susan Rushworth (aged 43, between 22 June 2009 and 25 May 2010) and Shelley Armitage, (aged 31, between 25 April and 25 May). All three victims had worked as prostitutes in Bradford. Griffiths called himself in court the Crossbow Cannibal for reasons that became only too clear during the trial.

When arrested, he told West Yorkshire Police: *I've killed a lot more than Suzanne Blamires. I've killed loads'.*

The caretaker had seen footage of Griffiths and Ms Blamires chatting as they walk along the corridor. She enters his flat willingly. Minutes later, a terrified woman is shown running for her life along the corridor, chased by the killer, now wearing black gloves and with his teeth bared like a snarling animal. She was later dragged on the floor by her leg by Griffiths, who had something in his hand. She had been shot with a crossbow before Griffiths gestured by holding a finger up to the CCTV camera. The court was also told that Griffiths owned *'disturbing video recordings and images'.* Never before has such explicit footage of a murderer in action been revealed. A major search and recovery operation began after Ms Blamires' remains were recovered on 25 May from the River Aire.

The mother of Suzanne Blamires said: *I wake up and think about my bright, articulate and much-loved daughter every day and I am serving a life sentence as a result of what this man has done.'* Shelley Armitage's mother said: *'Her death will haunt us for the rest of our lives'* and Susan Rushworth's mother said: *'Our lives will never be the same without her'.*

Griffiths was a PhD student at the University of Bradford researching murders in Bradford as part of his thesis, *Homicide in an Industrial Society.* His flat contents indicated he had been heavily influenced by the Yorkshire Ripper.

Source: www.bbc.co.uk/news/uk-england-bradford-west-yorkshire-11541168

22 Dec 1847   Chief Constable is issued with instructions about responding to fires.

'In the event of a fire within the Borough, it is the duty of the Chief Constable immediately to repair to the place. Immediate notice of the fire must be given to the several fire officers. The keys of the Engine House are to be kept at the Borough Police Office and may be procured immediately...

In the event of a fire breaking out on his beat, the Constable is immediately to spring his rattle and cry Fire. His first duty is to alarm the inmates, if any, of the house on fire; and his next duty is, if possible, to put out the fire. If it is quite obvious that he can put out the fire instantly, he is to give no further alarm; but if he has doubt of being able to do so – and it is better to be wrong in giving the alarm than to be late – he is to send the first Officer who comes to his assistance, to the Police Establishment in Swaine Street, and the person so sent is to run all the way himself, and he is not to send another, but, as he goes along, he is to knock and tell every Constable who comes to him where the fire is, the name of the street and the nature of the property, and he is to do all this briefly and without stopping for a moment'.

Today at a special meeting of the Watch Committee the duties of a Chief Constable were laid down about responding to fires – in contemporary life, a strange task for a policeman, but a very early and necessary example of laying down firm operating procedures.

In April Bradford had obtained borough status. The newly elected Corporation took over responsibilities from the previous regime of self-appointed Commissioners. Inheriting a town of some 70,000 inhabitants with over 400 mills, warehouses and collieries plus thousands of dwelling-houses, it made the Chief Constable responsible for handling fires. The number and scale of properties was a considerable fire risk.

The only fire protection came from a voluntary Fire Brigade, which practised just once every two months and had no proper helmets or clothing. They had three horse-drawn fire engines from 1806 – one bought by the Commissioners, one donated by an insurance company and the third funded by four prominent mill-owners.

Source: *History of the Bradford Fire Brigade*, George Ellis (1952)

23 Dec 2014 — Right-to-die campaigner Debbie Purdy dies.

Today the sad news was announced that Debbie Purdy from Undercliffe, had died in a Bradford hospice.

Her bravery in the face of her painful terminal illness had featured regularly in the national media ever since she started to campaign for the right to die.

In 2009, she won a ruling to get clarification on whether her husband would be prosecuted if he helped her to end her life. Lord Falconer, the former Lord Chancellor, said Ms Purdy's role as a campaigner against the law on assisted suicide was *'absolutely key'* and she had transformed the debate. The House of Lords ordered the Director of Public Prosecutions to issue a policy setting out when those in her husband's position could expect to face prosecution, ruling that the current lack of clarity violated the right to a private and family life. However, it still remains an offence to encourage or assist a suicide, or suicide attempt, in England and Wales.

Diagnosed with primary progressive multiple sclerosis in March 1995, she could no longer walk and had gradually lost strength in her upper body. She had been a wheelchair user since 2001. She spent her final year in the city's Marie Curie Hospice, sometimes refusing food.

In her final interview with BBC TV she said about her illness: *'It's painful and it's uncomfortable and it's frightening and it's not how I want to live. If somebody could find a cure for MS, I would be the first person in line. It's not a matter of wanting to end my life, it's a matter of not wanting my life to be this.'*

Source: *The Guardian* (29 December 2014)

23 Dec 1902 — The Conditioning House moves into custom-built premises.

Today, the Conditioning House moved into a new four-storey building in Cape Street near the city centre.

This unique municipal institution was created by a special Act of Parliament in 1887. First it moved into a building adjacent to the Town Hall in 1891. Now it had grown to require much larger premises where some hundreds of people worked.

Wool changes in weight according to atmospheric moisture; this was a cause of frequent disputes between buyers and sellers of wool. Bradford merchants were at a disadvantage compared with their European competitors. The Chamber of Commerce lobbied the Corporation to set up an independent testing facility.

Source: *The Conditioning House*, Ian Mason (1992) in *The Antiquary*

24 Dec 1898   Inauspicious Bradford pantomime debut by local 'gaiety girl' leads to much higher things.

Gertie Millar (1879 -1952) was born in a back-to-back house in Bradford, a stone's throw from the Theatre Royal. She can scarcely have imagined that she would die a countess and a rich widow.

By the time she made her pantomime debut on a Bradford stage, the 18-year-old girl was already a seasoned professional. She had first performed as a ten-year-old in Saturday evening entertainments at the Mechanics' Institute before appearing two years later in a Manchester production of the pantomime *Babes in the Wood*. Further engagements followed before today's Christmas Eve debut as principal girl in *Dick Whittington* at Bradford's Prince's Theatre.

The opening review was generally favourable without being ecstatic. *'Whether ...(it)... be popular remains to be seen, when Dick and fellows settle into their places, develop their business, and eliminate much that at present is superfluous .... Viewing the pantomime as a whole its main defects are a lack of cohesive incident, an absence of anything rising above the commonplace'.* In the only reference to Gertie, her performance is *'mainly satisfying'.*

Not a ringing endorsement of the production or its rising star! Two weeks later the reviewer returned. This time, *'A prosperous run is now assured. Several acceptable changes have been made since the commencement ... Miss Gertie Millar... has also been securely in public favour, and for her dainty rendering of "Baby Sweetheart" is receiving nightly encores'.*

Two years later she returned to Bradford, this time at her very local Theatre Royal, when a 30-year-old and well-connected Lionel Monckton was struck by the local singer with a rising reputation, who sang a song he had composed. He persuaded his boss at the Gaiety Theatre to watch her. She was immediately placed in a West End musical. Overnight she became a superstar; Monckton fell in love with and married her.

They continued to prosper, he as a producer and song-writer and she as the 'gaiety girl'. Her most popular role was as a Yorkshire shop girl in *Our Miss Gibbs,* which ran for 636 performances. When 40, she retired. Sadly her husband died soon after.

Within a year she remarried as the new countess of the Earl of Dudley. Eight years later, she became a widow again. For the rest of her life she lived in comfort in Southern France, then Surrey... a true rags-to-riches story.

Source: *Bradford Daily Telegraph* (27 December 1898)

25 Dec 1863   On Christmas Day Walter Calver takes his marionettes to the workhouse.

Walter Calver was a very popular entertainer and showman. He travelled across the north of England with his troupe of up to 500 marionettes (from 14 inches to four feet tall) and a mobile theatre for an audience of up to 1,000 customers. Although he was born and brought up in Hull, he married and settled in Bradford.

Today Calver entertained children at the Bradford Workhouse based at what became St. Luke's Hospital. Advertisements that have been kept from 1863 show the range of his repertoire.

In January he performed a new pantomime called *Blue Beard* in the Market Place, Bradford before moving across to Manchester where he also produced the drama *The Miller and his Men*. A month later, still in Manchester he performed *Babes in the Wood*.

Then in May Calver performed at a fair in Sheffield where he was joint top of the bill with his marionettes, alongside Taylor's Theatre and Mickey Bent's sparring booth. In November he came back to the Sheffield Peoples Fair, where the main attractions were Mander's collection of wild beasts, and Calver's marionettes.

Source: www.undercliffecemetery.co.uk

25 Dec 2016   On Christmas Day a baby boy is born and sets a record.

Today baby Finley James Mellor was born to the Hanson family in Bradford. This made him the first person in the sixth generation of a family all alive at the same time. It was thought to be the first-ever such occasion for a family in Britain.

Baby Finley's great-great-great-grandmother was Hilda Hanson, aged 103, known affectionately as *'little gran'*. His arrival made him the 44th living member of the family.

Finley's great-grandmother Sue Godward, 62, commented: *'When Finley was born, my daughters Nikki and Melissa started researching big generation families and they could not find anybody else in Britain with six generations living. Nobody else has come forward with six generations.'* They did find one in Alberta, Canada, and the Guinness World Records entry for most living generations is seven, achieved in 1989 by a family in the USA.

She added: *'When Finley arrived, it was the perfect Christmas present, and Hilda, my grandmother, turned 103 a couple of weeks later. She met him on Christmas Day but as she has Alzheimer's she cannot remember meeting him.'*

Source: *Daily Mail* (21 January 2017)

26 Dec 2013   *'Bradford Synagogue Saved by city's Muslims'* says *Muslim Observer.*

Today's *Muslim Observer* carried a story considered unique in the world. Bradford's only remaining synagogue was rescued by local Muslims.

The Reform Synagogue in Bowland Street, just off Lumb Lane in Manningham, had always supported a small Jewish community. Since the 1960s the area had been heavily dominated by Pakistani Muslims.

About a year before, the synagogue's trustees faced the problem that they could no longer support the cost of its Moorish Grade II-listed building. The roof was leaking and the eastern wall was badly damaged, but the modest annual subscriptions by the 45 members just could not cover the cost of repair.

It seemed certain that the building would have to be sold and that the city's Jews would have to travel 12 miles to worship in Leeds. The situation was saved by three local Muslims – the secretary of a nearby mosque, the owner of a popular curry house and a local textile magnate. They led a local fund-raising effort which brought in six-figure lottery finance.

The local political climate in this Muslim-dominated area was not favourable to such collaboration. George Galloway, Respect Party MP, had won a highly controversial by-election in Bradford West (which includes Manningham). An open opponent of Israel, he had been praised by many of his Muslim voters for organising convoys to Gaza and after refusing to engage in a debate with an Israeli student at Oxford University earlier this year. In addition, David Ward, Liberal Democrat MP for Bradford East, had the whip withdrawn over disparaging remarks about Jews and Israel as an apartheid state, but was publicly supported by many of his Muslim constituents.

The small Jewish community had always kept themselves to themselves. After the 2001 race riots, for example, it had taken down the synagogue's plaque to avoid drawing attention to itself. Yet despite this climate of hostility, collaboration built up after the owner of a restaurant, a few doors away from the synagogue, asked the rabbi to help oppose a planning permission for yet another curry house in the area. He agreed and the application was blocked. This led to the rabbi becoming friendly with the secretary of the Bradford Council of Mosques, also on the board of the central Westgate mosque a few hundred yards up the road from the synagogue.

In such a way has some inter-faith tolerance been established.

Source: *Muslim Observer* (26 December 2013)

27 Dec 1954   The start of this season's pantomime at the Bradford Alhambra marks the end of an era.

For over 50 years Francis Laidler had attended first nights of his Christmas pantomimes. Tonight his absence was noticed but only his wife knew that he had just suffered a heart attack. Ten days later he died. It was certainly the end of an era.

Laidler was by far the most important person in variety theatre in Bradford in the first half of the 20th century. When he first got involved in 1902, he quickly realised that the key to long-term commercial success lay in successful pantomimes.

His record as a producer was phenomenal. Laidler managed over 250 productions not just in Bradford, but across the country in Bristol, Leeds, London, Manchester, Newcastle, Nottingham and Sheffield. No producer before or since has matched the record. His national reputation as the King of Pantomime was fully earned.

He put on 52 productions in Bradford. They comprised *Cinderella* (9 productions), *Aladdin* (8), *Red Riding Hood* (7), *Cinderella* (6), *Mother Goose* (5), *Babes in the Wood* (4), *Jack and the Beanstalk* (4), *Humpty Dumpty* (3), *Robinson Crusoe* (3), *Ali Baba and the Forty Thieves* (2) and *Robin Hood* (1). He was 35 years old for his first production and 87 years old for his last one. The first 29 took place at the Prince's Theatre before they were transferred to the Alhambra just across the road for the next 23 productions – he owned both venues! His second wife Gwladys took over the role for the next three years after his death, before her life took a different direction.

One innovation which made his pantomimes special and different was the tradition of the Sunbeams – dancing troupes of young girls, recruited and auditioned locally who often joined in the comic routines of each production. Started in 1917, they were an immediate success, bringing a ray of sunshine to the dark war years.

Laidler managed their welfare impeccably. They were carefully chosen, had to be at least 12 years old, no taller than 4ft 3in, slim, in perfect health and attend school regularly. He provided food and, if necessary, accommodation in a large rented house, managed by a house-mother. He also provided an attractive uniform, pocket money and money paid into each girl's bank book, which was handed over to the parents at the end of the season.

Source: *Domes of Delight: The History of the Bradford Alhambra*, Peter Holdsworth (1989)

28 Dec 1882   The massive chimney at Newlands Mill collapses, killing 54 people.

Christmas in 1882 left many families feeling a bitter loss as loved ones perished in Bradford's worst-ever civil disaster (until the 1985 Bradford City fire). Just the day before, people had returned to work after the Christmas break. Early today the chimney at Newlands Mill in West Bowling collapsed in high winds, killing 54 people, including 32 children and 16 women working at the mill on the first shift. Some further 70 people were injured and pulled out of the debris. It took several days to recover all the bodies.

It soon turned out that it may not have been just a case of a bad weather accident. Before the day was out, the *Bradford Daily Telegraph* was hinting at complications. There was a history of problems.

The mill owner, Sir Henry Ripley, who died seven weeks before the disaster, had commissioned the chimney in 1862. He was a powerful man in the city and insisted on it being built his way. For example, he wanted to make the chimney more ornate. Unfortunately, the extra work weakened the chimney and a definite tilt became obvious, with a bulge in the brickwork at one side and a corresponding hollow on the other. Local people had been concerned for years about the chimney's safety, even up to days before the tragedy.

The inquest by jury started on 8 January and took over three weeks to report. The court heard that Ripley had acted almost as his own architect. In the end, however, the verdict stated: *'That the owners did all that unpractical men could be expected to do under the circumstances and therefore we do not attach any blame to them or find them guilty of negligence and we give as our verdict accidental death. We are of the opinion that the foundation was good, and the fall of the chimney was partly due to the cutting, aided by the strong wind on the morning of the accident. We regret that the works were not stopped during the repairs.'*

The verdict was greeted with much disquiet. The local paper printed adverse comments from several prominent newspapers that had been taking an interest. After listing all the reported defects, the *Manchester Evening News* considered the verdict *'an unduly mild expression of opinion'.*

By any current standard the tragedy was a scandal from start to end.

Source: www.on-magazine.co.uk/yorkshire/history/collapse-newland-mill-chimney-bradford/

29 Dec 1888   Analyst Felix Marsh Rimmington is called in to investigate brutal child murder.

For nearly 180 years hundreds of people every day have walked past FM Rimmington's Pharmacy on Bridge Street opposite City Hall. How many notice its sign *'Bradford's heritage pharmacy since 1842'*? How many are aware of the contribution to crime forensics made by its founder?

In his mid-twenties Felix Marsh Rimmington (1818-97) opened this chemist's shop, originally in Ivegate, and became knowledgeable about the chemical composition of substances. He played a critical role in two cases, in particular, that quickly attracted national attention.

First, his knowledge was very useful in 1858 in the case of the mass poisoning from buying sweets from 'Humbug Billy'. As the scale of the poisoning became known on the weekend of 30 October, the doctor investigating the early reports of people feeling very unwell asked Rimmington for help. He confirmed that the sweets contained arsenic and this led to the police being involved. At the magistrates' hearing on Friday that week his testimony was compelling. He was able to prove that each losenge contained an average of 14 grains. Three men were then charged of manslaughter. Although the men were later acquitted, the case indicated a glaring loophole in the law. Rimmington gave advice in the Adulteration of Food or Drink Act, which was then passed in 1860.

He was frequently asked to advise police, courts and coroners. His experience in forensic work led him to being formally appointed in 1874 as borough analyst by Bradford Corporation.

The second national case in which he became involved occurred right at the end of 1888. On 27 December an eight-year-old boy was reported missing after failing to return to his Manningham home from collecting some milk. Today, his body was discovered in a stable just a stone's throw away from his home, *'mutilated with a savagery almost indescribable'.* The police immediately called for Rimmington's help.

At that time Jack the Ripper's crimes in the East End had caught the national headlines. Could this be a copycat killing? Some even thought the Ripper had moved north. There was, however, an obvious suspect – the local milkman who had been seen giving the boy a lift. He was arrested on circumstantial evidence.

Rimmington's meticulous analysis showed that a knife and clothing found in the suspect's home did not in fact have any traces of blood. The man was released. Sadly, the murder was never solved.

Source: www.leedstrinity.ac.uk/blogs/leeds-centre-for-victorian-studies/the-bradford-murder-mystery-jack-the-ripper-up-north

30 Dec 2009 104-year-old Ivy Bean tweets before her last New Year's Eve.

In her 105th year Ivy Bean was known for being the oldest person in the world on both Facebook and Twitter.

Born Ivy Asquith in Bradford on 8 September 1905, she went to school in Thornton, leaving at 14 to work at Prospect Mill. She later married Harold Bean, a soldier. After Harold left the army, they went to work in service in Northamptonshire. Here they had their only daughter.

Several years later they returned to Bradford. After working at Crossland's Mill, she finally retired aged 73. Soon after, Harold died. Ivy remained on her own until she was 92, when she moved into a residential home. She stayed here ten years, until the home closed, and then moved into another, just before her 102nd birthday.

In 2007 she first used the internet via a computer given by social services to her care home. Then, still 102, Ivy joined Facebook, making her one of its oldest members. She quickly became more widely known. She discussed her life in a care home, her favourite meal, and TV programmes she had seen.

The highlight of 2010 was a visit to 10 Downing Street where, travelling down in a special chauffeur-driven Bentley, she met Prime Minister Gordon Brown and his wife, and also the actor Richard Wilson. She tweeted several times about her experience – the Prime Minister was very nice to her, Richard Wilson was a '*right laugh*', she had seen Big Ben and had used the PM's toilet.

On 28 July 2010 she died after a short illness. She had 4,962 Facebook friends and more than 56,000 Twitter followers.

Ivy Bean @IvyBean104 • 30 Dec 2009
Hi everyone how are you all today

Ivy Bean @IvyBean104 • 30 Dec 2009
What are your plans for new years eve

Ivy Bean @IvyBean104 • 31 Dec 2009
Good afternoon everyone just a quick tweet to say hello before i have my dinner

Ivy Bean @IvyBean104 • 31 Dec 2009
Beth Cunningham hello happy new year

Ivy Bean @IvyBean104 • 31 Dec 2009
@pearsonlaurauk thank you so much for my card and my scarf. It was lovely of you to send them. the scarf will keep me nice and warm

Ivy Bean @IvyBean104 • 31 Dec 2009
id just like to wish all my friends a happy new year. i hope you have a wonderful 2010. tweet you next year

31 Dec 1976 Actress Billie Whitelaw gives an interview to *The Times* about her career.

Today, Sheridan Morley, theatre critic of *The Times,* spoke with 43-year-old Billie Whitelaw, one of the UK's most prominent actresses of the 20th century.

Born in Coventry, she was one of two daughters of an electrician, whose firm moved him to Bradford at the outbreak of the war. While she was aged nine, he died and her mother remarried. Her stepfather was a buyer at Busby's department store. She grew up around the shop and the Bradford Civic Playhouse where her mother sent her as a child, hoping that some theatrical training might cure a chronic stutter.

"And it did, except that the stutter comes back if ever I get really tired or nervous. Someone from BBC Radio in Manchester saw me acting at the Civic and thought I might be useful for Children's Hour. So from 11 to 16 I used to work there playing countless little boys in drama series. The Civic, too, was a wonderful training ground: Bill Gaskill was there in my time, and Bernard Hepton.

Whitelaw trained at RADA and made her stage debut in 1950 at age 18 in London. Her career certainly never stuttered from there and she played a stream of roles in theatre, film and TV throughout her career.

She made her film debut in 1954 and became a regular in British films. Highlights include starring with Albert Finney in *Charlie Bubbles* (1967), which won her a BAFTA award as Best Actress in a Supporting Role. She gained international acclaim for her chilling role as Mrs. Baylock, the evil guardian of the demon child, Damien, in *The Omen* (1976), her performance winning her the Evening Standard British Film Award for Best Actress. She played the fiercely domineering and protective mother of psychopathic twin murderers in *The Krays* (1990), which earned her a BAFTA nomination.

In the theatre, the story was the same – many different roles, never typecast, in a wide range of plays. She was Variety Club Actress of 1960 and she worked at the National Theatre from 1964 to 1966. Her main achievement, however, was the professional relationship that she developed over 25 years' working with the playwright Samuel Beckett. She came to be the best interpreter of his work and he came to write plays for her, describing her as *'the perfect actress'.*

Source: *The Times* (31 December 1976)

BELOW: The statue of JB Priestley looks proudly out over the city of his birth (story on 31 Oct).
Credit: Richard Wilson Photography

ABOVE: Bradford's celebrity hotel was the scene of the sudden death of Sir Henry Irving, then Britain's greatest actor (story on 15 Oct).
Credit: Richard Wilson Photography

BELOW: 19th century German merchants built their warehouses in Little Germany, now a valued conservation area (story on 7 Nov).
Credit: Richard Wilson Photography

ABOVE: It took over 40 years for the Cathedral to celebrate the extensions planned since Bradford became a diocese (story on 2 Nov).
Credit: Richard Wilson Photography

BELOW: Lister's Pride dominates the city's skyline from every direction (story on 19 Nov).
Credit: Richard Wilson Photography

ABOVE: JB Priestley's *When We are Married* performed at the Civic Playhouse was probably the most successful production of a play ever performed on a Bradford stage (story on 14 Nov).
Courtesy: Bradford Civic Playhouse

BELOW: Felix Marsh Rimmington, chemist, helped to solve the 1858 Humbug Billy case and his shop on Bridge Street is still open for business (story on 29 Dec).
Credit: Richard Wilson Photography

ABOVE: Sunbridge Wells is an innovative underground complex designed to attract visitors (story on 10 Dec).
Credit: Richard Wilson Photography

APPENDIX **STORIES BY THEME**

ACADEMIA
HUMANITIES
13 Jun 1887	Joseph Wright is approached to compile the first *English Dialect Dictionary*.
22 Nov 1967	Alan Bullock gives the annual Raleigh history lecture to the British Academy.
18 Sep 1978	*The Times* commends Asa Briggs' appointment as Chancellor of the Open University.
12 Feb 1991	Sir Robert Jennings is appointed presiding judge of the International Court of Justice.
1 Aug 2000	On Yorkshire Day, Dr Arthur Raistrick is commemorated as *'Dalesman of the Millennium'*.

SCIENCE
9 Mar 1694	Edmund Halley urges mathematician Abraham Sharp to apply for prestigious job.
23 Oct 1712	Dr Richard Richardson is the first Bradfordian to be elected fellow of the Royal Society.
25 Aug 1888	Bradford's great mathematician George Adolphus Schott wins important chess game.
14 Dec 1893	Bradford's first female high-flyer becomes the first woman to present to the Royal Society.
5 Feb 1924	Sir Frank Dyson introduces the Greenwich 'pips'.
10 Dec 1947	Sir Edward Appleton receives the Nobel Prize for physics.
28 Mar 1949	Sir Fred Hoyle coins the term 'Big Bang' in a radio talk.

ADVENTURE
17 Sep 1864	Emma Sharp sets off to be the first woman to walk 1,000 miles in 1,000 hours.
21 May 1933	Adventurer Maurice Wilson sets off on bizarre solo attempt on Mount Everest.
16 Aug 1964	Barry Watson becomes the fastest person to swim the Channel.
30 May 1970	Baildon climber Ian Clough is killed in the Himalayas.
23 Jan 2000	Ann Daniels is a member of the first all-women team to reach the South Pole.

BUILDINGS
21 Mar 1851	Lockwood and Mawson secure their big break in becoming Bradford's premier architects.
29 Aug 1853	St. George's Hall opens with a three-day music festival.
28 Aug 1854	After consecration of half of Undercliffe Cemetery, a message of thanks is sent.
21 Apr 1864	John Ruskin's talk criticises designs for proposed Wool Exchange.
21 Jun 1869	Titus Salt Junior commissions a new country mansion at Milner Field.
9 Sep 1873	Bradford's new Town Hall is opened.
19 Nov 1873	Lister's Pride overlooking Bradford is celebrated with a champagne luncheon.
11 Mar 1893	William Gay of Undercliffe is laid to rest in the cemetery he designed.
13 Apr 1904	Lord Masham opens the Cartwright Memorial Hall in Lister Park.
16 Nov 1936	Elizabeth Denby is the first woman to address the Royal Institute of British Architects.
4 Sep 1952	Bolling Hall is designated a Group 1 listed building.
29 Nov 1954	The iconic Swan Arcade is reported as sold to the Arndale Property Trust.
11 Apr 1962	1960s Bradford is now described as *'a new city, designed for a multi-level style of living'*.
3 Jul 1963	The City Council votes to demolish Horton Hall.
3 Nov 1973	Thirty-three are arrested after last-ditch protest against closure of Kirkgate Market.
7 Nov 1973	Little Germany is declared a conservation area.

BUSINESS
COMMERCE
23 Mar 1827	Businessmen in Bradford meet to discuss a new bank for the town.
9 Aug 1864	Lord Palmerston lays foundation stone for Wool Exchange.

25 Jul 1877	The public funeral takes place for philanthropist Charles Semon.
4 Feb 1889	The Chamber of Commerce presents Sir Jacob Behrens with a portrait of himself.
20 May 1895	Photographer Lund partners with bookseller Humphries to form publisher Lund Humphries.
22 Apr 1898	Bradford Corporation belatedly honours Sir Henry Mitchell as its first freeman.
9 Nov 1910	Jacob Moser is elected Lord Mayor.
29 Sep 2008	We say goodbye to Mr Bradford and Mr Bingley.

INDUSTRY

13 Mar 1714	Sir Walter Calverley of Esholt purchases Dixon Mill at Shipley, the first of five fulling mills.
6 Jul 1768	Entrepreneur Joseph Dawson is ordained.
17 Dec 1788	The new Bowling Ironworks enters into its first contract.
16 Aug 1791	The first casting takes place at Low Moor Ironworks.
17 Apr 1822	Luddites destroy new machinery at Shipley mill.
28 Sep 1830	Factory-owner John Wood persuades Richard Oastler to campaign against child labour.
7 Apr 1847	Isaac Holden loses first wife to tuberculosis at critical stage of his working life.
8 Feb 1848	Family will illustrates how Keighley's Butterfield dynasty prospered.
19 Oct 1848	Samuel Lister secures an important patent for woolcombing with the help of Isaac Holden.
23 Aug 1849	Titus Salt creates the tradition of the works outing.
12 Oct 1852	Isaac Holden writes to old tutor in Scotland about his commitment to self-improvement.
27 Nov 1852	Charles Dickens writes an article about Titus Salt, alpaca and Saltaire.
20 Sep 1853	On his 50th birthday Titus Salt's new mill at Saltaire opens.
20 Sep 1856	On his 70th birthday Titus Salt has his best-ever celebration.
22 Mar 1866	Henry Ripley issues the first tender for construction of Ripleyville.
8 Aug 1866	Another Illingworth marries another Holden.
15 May 1875	A statue of Samuel Cunliffe Lister is unveiled in Lister Park.
5 Jan 1877	The death of Sir Titus Salt attracts record funeral procession across Bradford.
13 Mar 1886	*Bradford Weekly Telegraph* runs a feature about the Polish Saltaire.
21 Oct 1887	Samuel Lister criticises the impact of free trade.
23 Dec 1902	The Conditioning House moves into custom-built premises.
25 Jun 1904	Samuel Lister has the last word in his long-standing argument with Sir Isaac Holden.
25 Oct 1917	Bradford businessman loses money from the Russian Revolution.
15 Mar 1935	Inventor Percy Shaw starts making 'catseyes'.
27 Apr 1987	Consultants advise council to redevelop Salts Mill as new industrial and leisure complex.
31 Jul 2006	Professor David Rhodes announces his retirement as Filtronic's chief executive.
28 Jan 2008	Car designer Afzal Kahn pays record price for prestigious F1 number plate.
4 Jan 2016	From start-up to cash-cow, Saltaire-based Pace plc is bought out by American giant.

RETAIL

19 May 1212	King John II grants Bingley a market.
30 Nov 1294	Henry de Lacy obtains a charter for starting a five-day fair in Bradford.
2 Aug 1773	The new Piece Hall opens for business.
5 Oct 1908	Ernest Busby opens his first shop.
28 Jun 1910	The Fattorini family creates one mail order company, and unintentionally another.
20 Apr 1964	Brown Muff & Co celebrates 150 years of trading.
4 Nov 2010	Sir Ken Morrison receives the Freedom of the City for his contribution to UK retailing.
5 Nov 2015	At last the 'Wastefield' hole becomes the new Westfield shopping complex.
10 Dec 2016	Innovative underground complex opens its doors.

APPENDIX

TRADE UNIONISM

20 Jun 1825	The strikers in the Great Bradford Strike strike back.
19 Feb 1880	Striking Bradford dyers are vindicated for their militancy.
19 Apr 1891	Strikers win a propaganda victory to no avail over management at Manningham Mills.
27 Sep 1921	Julia Varley (with another) becomes first woman elected to the TUC General Council.
30 Oct 1963	The longest strike in the textile industry starts – to end in ignominy.
26 Feb 1969	Vic Feather is elected General Secretary of the Trades Union Congress.

CRIME

12 Jun 1605	The notorious murders by Walter Calverley, lord of the manor, become public knowledge.
9 Dec 1858	The 'Humbug Billy' case comes to court.
31 Mar 1884	State executioner James Berry carries out his first hangings.
29 Dec 1888	Analyst Felix Marsh Rimmington is called in to investigate brutal child murder.
23 Feb 1956	Albert Pierrepoint resigns as last state executioner.
11 Dec 1975	The man-hunt for the Black Panther ends.
2 Jan 1981	The Yorkshire Ripper is arrested to everyone's relief.
19 Jan 1982	The Home Secretary makes a statement to the House about the Yorkshire Ripper case.
9 Jan 2006	John Humble of Sunderland is charged with hoaxing the police over the Yorkshire Ripper.
8 May 2009	Prime Minister Gordon Brown unveils a memorial to PC Sharon Beshenivski.
21 Dec 2010	The Crossbow Cannibal is convicted of the Bradford murders of three sex workers.

CULTURE
ART

24 Sep 1848	Branwell Brontë leaves as his legacy the only portrait of the Brontë sisters.
26 May 1888	John Sowden paints a cripple as part of his series of street characters of Bradford.
13 May 1920	William Rothenstein is offered the post of Principal of the Royal College of Arts.
15 Feb 1941	Richard Eurich is appointed an official war artist to the Admiralty.
1 Nov 1987	Jonathan Silver opens the new 1853 gallery at Salts Mills dedicated to Hockney's art.
1 Jan 2012	David Hockney becomes the second Bradfordian to be awarded the Order of Merit.
9 Jul 2017	The city gives David Hockney an 80th birthday present at the Cartwright Hall.
15 Nov 2018	Hockney painting sells for $90m, a record for a living artist.

LITERATURE

8 Nov 1816	Lesbian Anne Lister writes in diary using secret code about early lover.
24 Aug 1847	Emily and Anne Brontë have Charlotte to thank for getting their first novels published.
16 Oct 1847	Charlotte Brontë's *Jane Eyre*, an English classic, is published.
28 May 1849	Anne Brontë dies aged 29 within sight of a favorite sea-view.
7 Feb 1857	Elizabeth Gaskell completes a controversial biography of her friend Charlotte Brontë.
26 Sep 1912	Willie Riley moves easily from one career to another with first-time best seller.
2 May 1924	Newspaper reports Bardic Chair for Bradford poet at Eisteddfod.
4 Aug 1928	Local boy made good opens the Brontë Parsonage Museum.
29 Jul 1929	JB Priestley publishes *The Good Companions*, an instant success.
18 Oct 1975	JB Priestley opens library in his name at the University of Bradford.
31 Oct 1986	His widow unveils statue to JB Priestley.
5 Dec 2015	Bust of poet Humbert Wolfe is presented to the City of Bradford.
17 Jun 2017	AA Dhand launches his first Asian detective thriller set in Bradford.

THEATRE

13 Oct 1905	Sir Henry Irving, most famous actor of his day, dies after performing at the Theatre Royal.
14 Nov 1938	Record-breaking Civic Playhouse production of *When We Are Married* is first performed.
1 Jun 1972	*The Times* obituary for theatre director Esme Church omits her important Bradford years.
31 Dec 1976	Actress Billie Whitelaw gives an interview to *The Times* about her career.
17 Aug 1982	Actor Bernard Hepton achieves a life-long ambition.
20 Dec 1990	Promising playwright, Andrea Dunbar, dies prematurely in Buttershaw local.
5 Sep 1993	Play about the Airedale Poet has its 'world premiere' at Salts Mills.

MUSIC

15 Sep 1855	The Black Dyke Mills Band is formed.
17 Nov 1856	William Jackson is appointed the first conductor of the Bradford Festival Choral Society.
24 Nov 1865	The first Bradford Subscription Concert is performed.
22 Sep 1930	Future Wurtlitzer organist, Arnold Loxam, watches the opening night at the New Victoria.
29 Jan 1962	Bradford starts the celebrations for centenary of birth of Frederick Delius.

PHOTOGRAPHY

7 Jan 1863	The failure of Thomas Appleton's first photographic venture is soon forgotten.
12 Feb 1895	The Royal Photographic Society makes Henry Snowden Ward one of its first fellows.
12 Dec 1976	Photographer Sir Don McCullin provides major Bradford feature in colour supplement.

FILM

6 Apr 1896	The Riley Brothers put on the first provincial cinema performance at the People's Palace.
22 Jun 1897	Richard Appleton shows country's first-ever same-day newsreel for a Bradford audience.
22 Sep 1930	The New Victoria cinema becomes the largest cinema outside London.
28 Jul 1954	Bradford's man of film, Steve Abbott, is born.
22 Jan 1959	The BAFTA-winning film of John Braine's *Room at the Top* is released.
21 Sep 1962	Tony Richardson's film *The Loneliness of the Long-Distance Runner* is released.
16 Sep 1963	Filmed mainly in Bradford, *Billy Liar* opens on general release.
16 Jun 1983	The National Museum of Photography, Film and Television opens.
6 Dec 1983	Set and filmed in Bradford, *The Dresser* opens to acclaim.
16 Jun 1999	The NMPFT receives a major refit.
22 Feb 2009	Screenwriter Simon Beaufoy wins an Oscar for *Slumdog Millionaire*.
8 Jun 2009	Bradford becomes the first UNESCO City of Film.

CURIOSITY

11 Nov 1342	On this day John Northrop's heirs will give three horn blasts at Bradford market-place.
1 May 1884	A commemorative key is presented to the man who broke the bank at Monte Carlo.
11 Jun 1906	Woman balloonist dies in tragic accident at Haworth gala.
19 Aug 1920	Two young girls hoax the world with photos of the Cottingley fairies.
22 May 1936	The Hindenburg makes mysterious flight over Keighley.
21 Jan 1963	A man's body is dug out of the snow in the Big Freeze.
30 Dec 2009	104-year-old Ivy Bean tweets before her last New Year's Eve.
25 Dec 2016	On Christmas Day a baby boy is born and sets a record.

EDUCATION
PRIMARY

17 Feb 1870	WE Forster introduces his new Elementary Education Bill.

14 Sep 1870	James Hanson places advertisement for private evening classes.
3 Jun 1930	Margaret McMillan is awarded the Companion of Honour.
13 Nov 1956	Miriam Lord delivers a Margaret McMillan Memorial Lecture in the House of Commons.
14 Oct 2010	Naila Zafar is the first Pakistani woman to be made a Dame.

SECONDARY

10 Oct 1662	Bradford Grammar School receives royal charter from King Charles II.
15 Feb 1870	An inspector calls - Bradford Grammar School is failing its pupils.
17 Jan 1872	Rev DH Keeling starts 44 years as headmaster of a reformed Bradford Grammar School.
6 Aug 1875	Queen Victoria approves the endowment of the new Bradford Girls' Grammar School.
24 Jul 1937	The foundation stone is laid for the new Bradford Grammar School building in Frizinghall.

TERTIARY

23 Jun 1882	Bradford's first-ever official royal visitors open the Bradford Technical School.
2 Oct 1911	The new Bingley Teacher Training College for Women receives its first students.
18 Oct 1966	The University of Bradford receives its Royal Charter.

ADULT

14 Feb 1832	After a false start the Bradford Mechanics' Institute is formed.
12 Apr 1839	A Bradford Philosophical Society finally gets off the ground.
6 Sep 1851	German-born Fanny Hertz marries a yarn merchant from Bradford.
15 Jun 1872	Bradford's first public library opens its doors.
14 Mar 1908	A marble bust of its benefactor is unveiled at the first-ever Carnegie library.

EMERGENCY

25 Feb 1871	Lilycroft Mill is destroyed by fire.
28 Dec 1882	The massive chimney at Newlands Mill collapses, killing 54 people.
15 Aug 1907	The inquest cannot explain a mysterious, tragic death in Thackley Tunnel.
21 Aug 1916	Forty people are killed by explosion at Low Moor munitions factory.
8 Apr 1968	Brave air stewardess Barbara Harrison dies in runway drama of burning plane.
2 Jul 1968	The city centre floods yet again, this time with an inch of rain in half an hour.
30 Aug 1979	Busby's famous department store burns down.
11 May 1985	Fifty-six fans die at Bradford City fire disaster.
16 May 1985	Roger Suddards completes the terms of reference for the Bradford City Disaster Appeal.
15 Apr 2015	Thirty years on, victim of Bradford City fire raises legitimate concerns.

HEALTH
PUBLIC HEALTH

10 Feb 1837	The Bradford Poor Law Union is formed.
19 Jul 1845	Living in Bradford turns German visitor, Georg Weerth, into a Communist.
10 May 1848	A 31-year-old woolcomber dies of starvation.
14 Jun 1848	The *Bradford Observer* reports another outbreak of cholera.
13 Dec 1849	The *Bradford Observer* investigates the living conditions of the working class.
7 Mar 1850	A council committee reports on the moral condition of Bradford.
4 Apr 1850	The government inspector is shocked by sanitation at Haworth.
11 Oct 1859	Town Clerk presents paper to prestigious conference on state of Bradford's public health.
2 Sep 1868	William Stansfield of Esholt Hall complains about excess sewage in the River Aire.
6 Jan 1895	Three days after rabies clampdown, rabid dog with damaged muzzle has to be destroyed.

22 Aug 1918	Government finally accepts Friedrich Eurich's recommendations for preventing anthrax.
20 Feb 1919	German prisoners of war (POWs) are hit by Spanish 'flu.
7 Sep 1936	On his birthday Sir Anthony Gadie completes topping-out for Scar House Reservoir.
5 Jul 1956	The Clean Air Act offers a major breakthrough in reducing air pollution.
11 Jan 1962	Outbreak of smallpox is confirmed after death of patient in St Luke's Hospital.
30 Apr 2020	Centenarian Captain Tom brightens the coronavirus gloom.

HEALTH CARE

18 Apr 1825	The Bradford Dispensary is officially opened.
21 Feb 1850	Finally, a design is selected for the new Bradford Union Workhouse Infirmary.
4 Oct 1859	Charles Darwin travels unexpectedly to Ilkley to take the waters.
7 Oct 1890	Lord Masham opens the new Children's Hospital.
5 Mar 1920	Workhouse inmate Mary Brannan dies aged 106.
23 May 1959	BMJ reports new treatment for breast cancer by Bradford's two cancer specialists.
17 May 2001	Bradford-educated optometry professor receives Asian Women of Achievement Award.
18 Feb 2003	One-time 'lunatic asylum' closes at Menston.
20 Jul 2011	Bradford City fire hero is honoured with doctorate by the University of Bradford.
23 Dec 2014	Right-to-die campaigner Debbie Purdy dies.
19 Mar 2018	Lord Patel is appointed Chair of Social Work England.

LEISURE
AMENITIES

13 Aug 1850	A public meeting agrees the idea of a public park to commemorate Sir Robert Peel.
18 Jan 1887	Opening of Manchester Road Baths at last marks a turning point.
18 May 1895	The Shipley Glen Tramway starts to operate.
19 Jun 1915	The Lord Mayor opens open-air swimming pool in Lister Park.
10 Jun 1987	Jonathan Silver buys Salts Mill.
16 Dec 2001	UNESCO inscribes Saltaire with World Heritage status.
24 Mar 2012	City Park becomes the new focal point of the city centre.

ENTERTAINMENT

3 Feb 1825	Bradford celebrates the festival for Bishop Blaise for the last time.
25 Dec 1863	On Christmas Day Walter Calver takes his marionettes to the workhouse.
23 Aug 1875	The Star Music Hall opens as first stage of new entertainment complex.
29 Oct 1887	Closure of Saltaire exhibition provides boost to Shipley Glen.
24 Dec 1898	Inauspicious Bradford pantomime debut by local 'gaiety girl' leads to much higher things.
8 Sep 1902	Francis Laidler steps into theatre management at the Prince's Theatre.
4 May 1904	The Prince and Princess of Wales open the Bradford Exhibition in Lister Park.
18 Mar 1914	The impresario's wife, Mrs Annie Laidler, opens the Alhambra Theatre.
21 Jul 1914	*Yorkshire Post* promotes tomorrow's opening of Great Yorkshire Show at Bradford Moor.
13 Jul 1931	Bradford holds a Historical Pageant in Peel Park.
30 Mar 1936	The boy Ernie Wise makes his first stage appearance.
23 Sep 1940	Bradford's celebrity hotel marks the visit of George Formby.
27 Dec 1954	The start of this season's pantomime at the Bradford Alhambra marks the end of an era.
12 Mar 1956	The *Yorkshire Observer* reports a surprise visitor to Bradford.
2 Feb 1963	Bradford is the first place outside Liverpool to experience Beatlemania.
9 Aug 1965	Harry Corbett and Sooty appear on *Desert Island Discs*.
7 Aug 1976	Kiki Dee and Elton John complete six weeks with a No 1 single.

3 Mar 1996	Jonathan Silver organises cancer charity event as a 'thank-you' (but finally succumbs).
9 Feb 2002	Gareth Gates makes his name as runner-up on ITV's *Pop Idol*.
30 Jan 2013	Magician Dynamo wins Best Entertainment Programme of the Year.
9 Jun 2013	The BBC commissions Bollywood-style spectacular of *Carmen* in City Park.
25 Mar 2015	Wishing to become a 'normal 22 year old', megastar Zayn Malik quits *One Direction*.

FOOD AND DRINK
27 Feb 1838	England's first Temperance Hall is consecrated in Bradford.
11 Aug 1869	Magistrates tighten up the licensing of beerhouses.
28 Oct 1907	The first-ever school meals service in the UK is launched at Green Lane School.
17 Jul 1919	After 12 years in Bradford, Swiss baker opens the first Bettys in Harrogate.
24 Oct 1988	Harry Ramsdens celebrate 60 years of fish 'n' chips.
1 Dec 1990	Bradford's most famous pork pie shop closes.
12 Aug 2014	Timothy Taylor's Boltmaker wins the annual Champion Beer of Britain award.
20 Oct 2015	Bradford wins Curry Capital of Britain yet again.
3 Oct 2018	Family firm Seabrook's Crisps goes Japanese.

TELEVISION
26 Oct 1958	BBC broadcasts documentary about JB Priestley's *Lost City*.
2 Nov 1982	Richard Whiteley launches Channel 4 with *Countdown*.
2 Dec 1987	BBC Chronicle programme commemorates archaeologist Sir Mortimer Wheeler.
16 Feb 1998	Soap *Emmerdale* is about to be transferred from its old Esholt to its new Esholt location.
8 Dec 1999	Alan Titchmarsh and team design a special millennium garden for Nelson Mandela.
5 Mar 2009	*Red Riding* three-parter starts tonight on TV, inspired by the saga of the Yorkshire Ripper.
14 Oct 2020	Harry Gration steps down from BBC Look North.

NEWS
6 Feb 1834	Bradford's first significant newspaper appears on the streets.
18 Nov 1837	The Chartist *Northern Star* newspaper appears for the first time.
16 Jul 1868	Bradford's first daily newspaper rolls off the presses.
20 Mar 1906	Antiquarian William Cudworth dies, leaving a valued legacy about Bradford.
6 May 1908	Bitter rivalry between Bradford's two main newspapers breaks out in fisticuffs.
31 Jan 1913	An 18 year-old JB Priestley appears in print for the first time.
15 Dec 1926	After a merger, the new *Bradford Telegraph & Argus* publishes its first edition.
2 May 1981	The pink *Yorkshire Sports* prints its final edition.
20 Jan 2006	After nearly 50 years Michael Wharton writes his last Peter Simple column.
12 Jan 2011	Alastair Campbell gives evidence to the Iraq Enquiry.

PUBLIC AFFAIRS
GOVERNANCE
10 Mar 1801	The first national census provides Bradford's population baseline.
10 Jan 1803	Prominent Bradfordians meet to propose an Improvement Commission.
3 Apr 1822	The Bradford Gas Light Company is empowered by an Act of Parliament.
7 Jun 1832	Bradford is to be represented in Parliament at last.
7 Dec 1843	The *Bradford Observer* makes a powerful case for elected municipal government.
24 Apr 1847	The Privy Council grants a charter for Bradford to become a municipal borough.
1 Oct 1847	Bradford Corporation hosts its first mayoral dinner.
22 Dec 1847	Chief Constable is issued with instructions about responding to fires.

APPENDIX

9 Oct 1856	Chief Constable claims that *'beerhouses without brothels are in poverty-stricken state'*.
1 May 1882	Bradford is extended to include Allerton, Bolton, Heaton, Thornbury and Tyersal.
10 Jul 1897	Bradford is granted City status.
9 Nov 1899	Bradford is extended to include Eccleshill, Idle, North Bierley, Thornton and Tong.
1 Apr 1930	Clayton merges with the County Borough of Bradford.
20 Oct 1937	The King and Queen drive across Bradford.
1 Apr 1974	Bradford Corporation expands into the City of Bradford Metropolitan District Council.
29 Jun 2010	First Cabinet meeting of new Coalition Government takes place at Odsal Stadium.

POLITICS

20 Nov 1837	Thousands of anti-Poor Law rioters protest in the centre of Bradford.
27 Jan 1840	Robert Peddie fails in starting a Chartist revolution.
14 Apr 1841	Future Bradford MP Edward Miall launches *The Nonconformist*.
14 Aug 1842	A Chartist camp meeting at Bradford Moor triggers four days of riots across Bradford.
16 Mar 1848	The *Bradford Observer* reports a mass workers' meeting at Peep Green.
10 Apr 1848	Local Chartist meetings give strong support to National Convention in London.
29 May 1848	The military put an end to the Chartist uprising in Bradford.
11 Feb 1861	WE Forster wins the first of a record six elections as Bradford MP.
8 Oct 1866	Bradford closes down for business to support a huge Reform League demonstration.
15 May 1869	A statue of Richard Oastler, the 'Factory King', is unveiled.
16 Jan 1893	Local paper casts doubt on inaugural meeting of Independent Labour Party.
27 Oct 1899	Councillor Fred Jowett wins a difficult victory in securing a slum clearance plan.
13 Jan 1906	Fred Jowett is elected the first Independent Labour MP in Bradford.
14 Feb 1907	Lillian Armitage is arrested for trying to break into the Houses of Parliament.
27 Aug 1908	Emmeline Pankhurst reports on a mass rally of suffragettes on Shipley Glen.
26 Nov 1910	Suffragettes fail to disrupt Winston Churchill's speech at St.George's Hall.
27 Jun 1936	Campaigner Florence White speaks at Great Spinsters' Rally in London.
10 Nov 1980	Denis Healey fails by just 10 votes to become leader of the Labour Party.
6 Oct 1981	The new Social Democratic Party holds its first annual conference at St.George's Hall.
25 Oct 1988	Councillor Eric Pickles leads the Bradford Revolution.
6 Jun 1997	Barbara Castle becomes the only 'freewoman' of the City.
7 May 2015	After years of poverty, abuse and family turmoil, Naseem Shah is elected Bradford MP.

IMMIGRATION

22 Jul 1844	Those convicted of manslaughter in the Irish riot case return to court for sentencing.
13 Sep 1845	Irish newspaper announces the arrival of potato blight.
3 Aug 1914	Thirty young German Bradfordians leave Bradford to fight for Germany.
23 Nov 1967	The Mangla Dam project in North-East Pakistan is complete.
11 Jul 1981	The police find two crates of petrol bombs left by the Bradford 12.
16 Apr 1985	The House of Commons debates the Honeyford affair.
21 Nov 1996	The Bradford Commission publishes the lessons from the June 1995 Manningham riots.
7 Jul 2001	Riots break out across the city.
12 Jul 2001	The Ouseley Report on race relations in Bradford is published.

APPENDIX

RELIGION
ANGLICAN
23 Apr 1702	On St. George's Day Bradford's Archbishop of York preaches at the Queen's coronation.
28 Nov 1839	Rejection of hated church rate is reported from historic poll.
14 May 1841	Rev William Scoresby wins a hollow victory on church rates.
25 Nov 1919	The Diocese of Bradford is created.
1 Dec 1936	The Bishop of Bradford makes a speech that prompts the abdication crisis.
2 Nov 1963	The Cathedral completes its celebration of the new East extension.
1 Mar 2018	Anne Dyer is consecrated as the first woman bishop of the Scottish Episcopal Church.

ROMAN CATHOLIC
17 Mar 1852	On St.Patrick's Day, the bishop lays the foundation stone for new Roman Catholic church.

NONCONFORMIST
27 Jul 1776	Rev John Wesley writes about the new Octagon Chapel in Horton Lane.
29 Feb 1824	The Prophet John Wroe attempts to walk on water.
30 May 1830	Rev Benjamin Godwin is invited to make a book of his successful anti-slavery lectures.
3 Dec 1835	Jonathan Glyde is called to the ministry at Horton Lane Chapel.
30 Mar 1851	New census finds Bradford the most militant non-conformist town in England.
8 Jun 1853	The UK spiritualist movement starts in Keighley.
20 Sep 1876	Saltaire Congregational Church is completed.
21 Mar 1904	Eastbrook Hall opens.

JEWISH
29 Mar 1881	Bradford's Reform Synagogue is consecrated.
26 Jan 2005	The President of Poland presents honour to Bradfordian Rabbi.

MUSLIM
14 Jan 1989	1,000 Muslims celebrate the burning of Salman Rushdie's novel *The Satanic Verses*.
3 Sep 1999	Council leader gives total support for the plans to build new Bradford Grand Mosque.
26 Dec 2013	*Bradford Synagogue Saved by city's Muslims'* says *Muslim Observer*.

GENERAL
25 Jan 1850	Christian leaders agree cross-denominational approach for new Bradford Town Mission.
12 Nov 1921	John William Gott is arrested for sale of blasphemous leaflets.

SPORT
RUGBY UNION
5 Apr 1884	Bradford FC win the prestigious rugby union Yorkshire Challenge Cup for the only time.
28 Apr 1884	Manningham FC agrees a new claret and amber strip for the new 1884/85 season.
25 Sep 1886	Valley Parade sees its first sporting action with rugby union.
9 Apr 1890	The Barbarians Rugby Club is conceived in Leuchters' Restaurant.

RUGBY LEAGUE
25 Apr 1896	Manningham FC are the first champions of the breakaway Northern Rugby Union (NRU).
15 Apr 1907	The 'great betrayal' splits Bradford FC.
5 May 1954	World record crowd attends Rugby League Challenge Cup Final replay at Odsal Stadium.
2 Jun 1978	17-year-old Ellery Hanley signs for Bradford Northern to become Great Britain's greatest.

10 Aug 1997	The new Bradford Bulls take the Super League in its second season with 18 straight wins.
15 Oct 2005	Brian Noble becomes first Rugby League coach to win three Super League Grand Finals.
7 Oct 2017	Bradford Bulls complete the cup and league double in first Women's Super League.
1 Sep 2019	Bradford Bulls play their last game at Odsal Stadium (or do they?).

FOOTBALL

1 Sep 1903	Bradford City play their first professional match in the Football League.
27 May 1907	Bradford City members meet to resolve a proposed merger with Bradford Park Avenue.
13 Feb 1909	Park Avenue's redeveloped football ground attracts Bradford's only England international.
26 Apr 1911	Bradford City beat Newcastle United in a replay to win the FA Cup for the only time.
6 Mar 1929	Albert Whitehouse scores a record seven goals in one match for Bradford City.
19 Dec 1942	Bradford's 'Clown Prince of Football' scores twice in 10-1 wartime defeat of Bradford City.
25 Apr 1964	Jim Fryatt of Park Avenue scores fastest-ever goal in English professional football.
3 May 1974	Bradford Park Avenue goes into liquidation.
9 May 1999	Club legend Stuart McCall leads Bradford City into the Premier League.
10 Aug 2002	The Geoffrey Richmond rollercoaster ends in resignation.
24 Feb 2013	Bradford City reach a Wembley cup final for the first time.
24 Jan 2015	Bradford City knock champions Chelsea out of the FA Cup at Stamford Bridge.
12 Sep 2015	An Open Day is held at the unique archaeological site of Park Avenue football ground.
4 Dec 2018	Investment by German emigre in City life ends in complete failure.

CRICKET

25 May 1920	Emmott Robinson snatches victory from the jaws of defeat in Park Avenue Roses match.
26 Aug 1946	Captain Brian Sellers leads Yorkshire CCC to sixth county cricket championship.
11 Sep 1948	Sir Learie Constantine plays his final match in the Bradford League.
26 Jul 1949	Brian Close becomes the youngest ever cricketer to bat for England.
31 May 1950	Jim Laker takes 8 wickets for 2 runs at Park Avenue.
27 Aug 2009	Adil Rashid becomes first English international cricketer from Pakistani family.
3 Jan 2016	Jonny Bairstow dedicates his maiden Test century to his father David.
8 Jan 2019	Asian girls balance cricket dream with home life in TV documentary.
14 Jul 2019	Two Bradfordians help England win its first Cricket World Cup in sensational finish.

OTHER SPORTS

2 Jun 1952	For the only time in its long history the Bradford Walk ends in a dead heat.
15 Aug 1971	Harvey Smith gives a V sign to show-jumping judges.
24 May 1976	Richard Dunn fights Muhammad Ali for the heavyweight championship of the world.
2 Apr 1983	Boris Rankov makes his record-breaking sixth win in the Boat Race.
5 May 1986	150-1 outsider Joe Johnson beats favorite to become world snooker champion.
19 Sep 1988	Adrian Moorhouse wins the 100m breaststroke at the Seoul Olympics.
23 May 1993	Richard Nerurkar wins his first Marathon.
17 Jun 1995	Yvonne McGregor breaks the classic cycling world record.
18 Aug 2016	The Brownlee brothers win gold and silver in the Rio Olympics triathlon.

TRANSPORT
CANAL

19 May 1770	The first Leeds and Liverpool Canal Act is passed.
15 Jan 1771	John Hustler's influence secures the funds for the Bradford Canal.
29 Apr 1771	An Act of Parliament approves the Bradford Link from the Leeds/Liverpool Canal.

| 22 Oct 1816 | After 46 years the Leeds/Liverpool Canal is finally completed. |
| 15 Jul 1922 | The Bradford Canal sees its final barge after years of neglect. |

TRAIN

4 Jul 1844	The Leeds & Bradford Railway Act finally gives Bradford its train link.
30 Jun 1846	The Leeds & Bradford Railway is officially opened.
5 Aug 1873	The Halifax, Thornton & Keighley Railway Act is passed.
1 Jun 1874	The first Pullman train in Britain leaves Bradford Midland station for London.
4 Mar 1890	The Prince of Wales rewards Bradfordian at opening of Forth Railway Bridge.
14 Jul 1904	The Lord Mayor cuts the first sod on the country's only municipal railway.
30 Sep 1920	The Bradford Through Lines Act reaches the end of the line.
27 Mar 1963	The 'Beeching axe' proposes closure of 13 railway stations around Bradford.
29 Jun 1968	On the day of a national rail strike the Keighley & Worth Valley Railway reopens as heritage line.

TRAM

30 Jul 1898	New electric trams start to replace horse and steam trams.
5 Sep 1899	Christopher Spencer submits his patent for the Spencer (slipper) track brake.
1 Feb 1918	Yet another tram accident, this one bucks the trend.
8 Apr 1919	The tram girls step down.

TROLLEY-BUS

| 24 Jun 1911 | Bradford leads the way with Leeds in using trolley-buses. |
| 26 Mar 1972 | Bradford's last trolley-bus completes its journey. |

ROAD

18 Jun 1753	Mob runs riot in destroying turnpikes around Bradford.
23 Jul 1914	Alfred Angas Scott writes in *Motor Cycle* magazine about benefits of a two-stroke bike.
12 May 1922	The formation of a Jowett Owners' car club is advertised.
8 Jul 1973	The M606, Bradford's motorway, opens.

PLANE

| 17 Oct 1931 | Yeadon Aerodrome opens for flights. |

GENERAL

| 27 Mar 1977 | Integrated public transport at last becomes a reality at Bradford Interchange. |

WAR AND PEACE
WAR

18 Dec 1642	The Parliamentarians win the first Siege of Bradford.
30 Jun 1643	The Royalists defeat the Parliamentarians at Adwalton Moor in Bradford's only battle.
28 Feb 1645	The House of Commons confirms new officers for Sir Thomas Fairfax's New Model Army.
18 Jun 1815	War hero Christopher Ingham from Keighley wins his medal at the Battle of Waterloo.
26 Jun 1857	Bradford-born private is one of first to receive the new Victoria Cross in Crimean War.
2 Mar 1900	The *Bradford Daily Telegraph* has a big news day from the Relief of Ladysmith.
6 Nov 1914	The *Bradford Weekly Telegraph* prints roll call of first battalion of the Bradford Pals.
1 Jul 1916	1,000 Bradford Pals die fighting at the Battle of the Somme.
5 Jul 1916	Bradford footballer Donald Bell wins a posthumous Victoria Cross at the Somme.
4 Jun 1917	Thomas Maufe's bravery in action earns him a Victoria Cross.

20 Aug 1917	Jimmy Speirs, Bradford City's FA Cup hero, is killed at Passchendaele.
29 May 1918	The first-ever reigning monarch visits Bradford.
18 Jul 1919	A soldier writes to the *Bradford Weekly Telegraph* the day before Peace Day.
5 Jun 1940	JB Priestley gives the first of his famous *Voice of Britain* radio talks about the Blitz.
31 Aug 1940	The Luftwaffe carries out its most serious night of bombing the city in World War Two.

PEACE

9 Sep 1917	3,000 women in the Bradford Women's Humanity League hold an anti-war protest.
11 Nov 1918	The Armistice is celebrated.
17 Feb 1958	JB Priestley is involved in formation of Campaign for Nuclear Disarmament (CND).
8 Mar 1973	Adam Curle is appointed world's first Professor of Peace Studies at Bradford's university.
10 Sep 1992	Conference paves the way for Bradford's unique Peace Museum.
18 Nov 2008	Bradford becomes a City of Sanctuary.

INDEX

- Names of people are only included if they have a strong connection to Bradford, unless being a national figure they are the topic of the story.

- Names of places (eg buildings, streets, parks) are only included if they are in Bradford and district. Street names are assumed to be in Bradford itself unless qualified by another place (eg Keighley).

- The categories of stories used in the Appendix are generally excluded (eg industry, art, football).

- No items from the Preface, Appendix and Further Information are included.

- Page numbers shown in bold indicate that the entry is the key topic of a story, or referenced in one of the photographs.

- All items shown in italics refer to titles (eg books, plays, films).

FURTHER INFORMATION

General books on Bradford's history (in sequence of year of publication by author)

John James
1866   *The History and Topography of Bradford*

William Cudworth
1876   *Round About Bradford*
1877   *Condition of the Industrial Classes*
1881   *Historical Notes on the Bradford Corporation*
1888   *Worstedopolis - A Sketch History of the Town & Trade of Bradford*
1891   *History of Bowling*

William Scruton
1889   *Pen and Pencil Pictures of Old Bradford*
1897   *Bradford Fifty Years Ago: A Jubilee Memorial of the Bradford Corporation*

Horace Hird
1966   *How a City Grows: Historical Notes on Bradford and its Corporation*
1968   *Bradford in History: Twenty-Four Essays on Life By the Broad Ford from the Celtic Age to the Present Day*
1972   *Bradford Remembrancer*

Joseph Fieldhouse
1972   *Bradford*

Gary Firth
1979   *Poverty and Progress: Social Conditions in early and mid-19th century Bradford*
1990   *Bradford and the Industrial Revolution: An Economic History, 1760-1840*
1993   *Street Characters of a Victorian City: John Sowden's Bradford*
1997   *A History of Bradford*
2006   *JB Priestley's Bradford*

George Sheeran
1984   *Village to Mill Town: Shipley and Its Society 1600-1870*
1990   *The Victorian Houses of Bradford*
1997   *The Bradford Poisoning of 1858*
2017   *Bradford in 50 Buildings*

Jim Greenhalf
1998   *Salt & Silver: A Story of Hope*
2003   *It's a Mean Old Scene*

Telegraph & Argus
1981   *Read All About It: The story of Bradford's Telegraph & Argus 1868-1981*
1999   *Stories of the Century*

Derek AJ Lister
2004   *Bradford's Own*

Alan Hall
2013   *The Story of Bradford*

Paul Chrystal
2018   *Bradford at Work: People and Industries Through the Years*

Useful websites

The Antiquary (many, but not all, research articles available online)
www.bradfordhistorical.org.uk/antiquary.html

British Newspaper Archives (most, but not all, local newspapers available online)
www.britishnewspaperarchive.co.uk

Oxford Dictionary of National Biography
www.oxforddnb.com

150 years of the *Telegraph & Argus*, 1868-2018
www.thetelegraphandargus.co.uk/tahistory/tanda150/

Undercliffe Cemetery
www.undercliffecemetery.co.uk

100 Objects from Special Collections at the University of Bradford
https://100objectsbradford.wordpress.com

Specific books on Bradford's people, events and issues
(in sequence of author surname)

As well as general histories about Bradford, there are many books about specific people, events and issues associated with the city. Those used to document specific stories as their main source are listed here.

Rosemary Ashton
1989   *Little Germany: German Refugees in Victorian Britain*

Jonny Bairstow & Duncan Hamilton
2018   *A Clear Blue Sky*

Robert Balgarnie
2003   *Balgarnie's Salt*

Patrick Beaver
1981   *A Pedlar's Legacy*

Harry Behrens
1925   *Sir Jacob Behrens 1806-1889*

Rachel Bellerby
2019   *Struggle and Suffrage in Bradford*

James Berry
1892   *My Experiences as an Executioner*

Bradford Commission
1996   *The Bradford Commission Report: The report of an enquiry into the wider implications of public disorders in Bradford on 9, 10 and 11 June 1995*

Bradford Corporation
1912   *Esholt Sewage Disposal Scheme*

Fenner Brockway
1946   *Socialism Over Sixty Years: The life of Jowett of Bradford (1864-1944),*

Brown Muff
1964   *The Bromuff Story*

Alistair & Jonathan Brownlee
2013   *Swim, Bike, Run*

Sir Lawrence Byford
1981   *The Yorkshire Ripper Case - Review of Police Investigation*

Michael Callaghan & Colin Neville
2008   *Busbys' - A Shop Full of Memories*

Alan Cattell
2011   *Bingley and Surrounds: Forgotten Moments from History*
2016   *Bingley: A Living History*
2018   *Shipley Glen: The History and Development of a Victorian Playground*

Colin Clark & Reuben Davison
2004   *In Loving Memory – The Story of Undercliffe Cemetery*

Joe Cooper
1998   *The Case of the Cottingley Fairies*

DJ Croft
1982   *A Century of Public Transport in Bradford, 1882-1982*

Mark Davis
2013   *West Riding Pauper Lunatic Asylum Through Time*

Elizabeth Denby
2015   *Europe Rehoused*, (2nd edition), (2015)

John Dewhirst
2014   *A History of Bradford AFC in Objects*
2016   *Room at the Top*
2018   *Life at the Top*

Charles Dickens
1852   *Household Words*

Susan Duxbury-Neumann
2015   *Little Germany: A History of Bradford's Germans*

John Earnshaw
1902   *The Records and Reminiscences of St. Patrick's Church*

Adrian Elliott
1976   *The Establishment of Municipal Government in Bradford 1837-1857*, PhD thesis

George Ellis
1952   *History of the Bradford Fire Brigade*

C. Federer
1906   *The Bradford Mechanics Institute*

Paul Firth
2005   *Four Minutes to Hell: The Story of the Bradford City Fire*

Anne Fletcher
2018   *From the Mill to Monte Carlo*

Martin Fletcher
2015   *The Story of the Bradford Fire*

Terry Frost
1988   *Bradford City: A Complete Record, 1903-1988*

Neville Gabie & Jason Wood
2051   *Breaking Ground: Art, Archaeology and Mythology*

Elizabeth Gaskell
1857   *The Life of Charlotte Brontë*

Rev. Benjamin Godwin
1855   *An Autobiography of the Reverend Benjamin Godwin*

Martin Greenwood
2018   *Percy Monkman: An Extraordinary Bradfordian*

Duncan Hamilton
2019   *The Great Romantic: Cricket and the Golden Age of Neville Cardus*

Bill Hampshire
2000   *The Water Mills of Shipley*

Astrid Hansen
2000   *Sharp to Blunt: the story of Horton Hall, Bradford*

Tony Harrison
1993   *Poetry or Bust*

Tony Holden
2015   *Holden's Ghosts*

Peter Holdsworth
1989   *Domes of Delight: The History of the Bradford Alhambra*

Gerald Howat
1975   *Learie Constantine*

Dr. Kathryn Hughes
2015   *Bradford: Remembering 1914-18*

Paul Jennings
1995   *The Public House in Bradford, 1770 -1970*

Jewish Communities and Records
1975   *Provincial Jewry in Victorian Britain*

Rev. WH Keeling
1912   *Bradford Grammar School 1662 to 1912*

Miriam Lord
1956   *Margaret McMillan in Bradford*

Colin Malam
2004   *Clown Prince of Soccer: The Len Shackleton Story*, (2004)

Albert Mansbridge
1932   *Margaret McMillan: Prophet and Pioneer*

David Markham
2010   *Bradford City Miscellany*

Lord Masham
1904   *Sir Isaac Holden and the Square Motion*

GJ Mellor
1997   *Movie Makers And Picture Palaces: A Century of Cinema in Bradford 1896-1996*

Tony Moxon
1999   *Hoc Age - Bradford Grammar School 1818-1996*

AFH Newell
1972   *Bradford City Libraries 1872-1972*

Charlotte Jane Newman
2010   *The Place of the Pauper*, PhD, University of York

Sir Herman Ouseley
2001   *Community Pride, not Prejudice: Making Diversity Work in Bradford*

A. D Padgett
2014   *The Five Heads of Humbert Wolfe: Poet, Wit and Civil Servant*

David Pendleton
2010   *Glorious 1911*

Albert Pierrepoint
1997   *Executioner Pierrepoint: An Autobiography*

Geoff Powter
2016   *Strange and Dangerous Dreams*

Jack Reynolds
1983   *The Great Paternalist: Titus Salt and the Growth of 19th Century Bradford*

Mark Rowe
2017   *Brian Sellers: Cricket Tyrant*

Janet Senior
2018   *Some Bits of Bradford History*

Eric Silver
1973   *Victor Feather*

Colin & Fleur Speakman
2006   *The Yorkshire Dales Society: 1981-2006: The Story So Far: A Personal Account*

UNITE
2015   *Julia Varley – Trade union organiser and fighter for women's rights* (booklet)

Stephen Wade
2008   *Heroes, Villains and Victims of Bradford*

RL (Bob) Walker
2008   *When was Ripleyville built?*

DG Wright
1987   *The Chartist Risings in Bradford*

DG Wright & JA Jowitt (editors)
1981   *Victorian Bradford: Twelve Essays*

Mrs EM Wright
1932   *The Life of Joseph Wright*

Yorkshire Race Walking Club
2003   *The Bradford Walk*